PIERS PLOWMAN

WILLIAM LANGLAND was born in the Malvern region of Worcestershire, probably around 1330, the son of Stacy de Rokayle, a gentleman of Shipton-under-Wychwood in Oxfordshire. Little is known of his life, which he seems to have spent mainly in London, where he earned his living as a psalter-clerk. He was married and had one child, a daughter. The three versions of his poem *Piers Plowman* were written between *c.*1370 and *c.*1386. He is spoken of as dead before 1387.

A. V. C. SCHMIDT is Fellow and Tutor of Balliol College, Oxford, and Lecturer in English at Oxford University. He was an editor of *Medium Aevum* from 1981 to 1989. His books and articles on medieval literature include *The Vision of Piers Plowman: A Critical Edition of the B-Text* and *The Clerkly Maker: Langland's Poetic Art*. He is editing a parallel-text edition of all versions of *Piers Plowman*.

OXFORD WORLD'S CLASSICS

*For almost 100 years Oxford World's Classics have brought
readers closer to the world's great literature. Now with over 700
titles—from the 4,000-year-old myths of Mesopotamia to the
twentieth century's greatest novels—the series makes available
lesser-known as well as celebrated writing.*

*The pocket-sized hardbacks of the early years contained
introductions by Virginia Woolf, T. S. Eliot, Graham Greene,
and other literary figures which enriched the experience of reading.
Today the series is recognized for its fine scholarship and
reliability in texts that span world literature, drama and poetry,
religion, philosophy and politics. Each edition includes perceptive
commentary and essential background information to meet the
changing needs of readers.*

OXFORD WORLD'S CLASSICS

WILLIAM LANGLAND

Piers Plowman
A New Translation of the B-Text

Translated with an Introduction and Notes by
A. V. C. SCHMIDT

OXFORD
UNIVERSITY PRESS

OXFORD

UNIVERSITY PRESS

Great Clarendon Street, Oxford OX2 6DP

Oxford University Press is a department of the University of Oxford.
It furthers the University's objective of excellence in research, scholarship,
and education by publishing worldwide in

Oxford New York

Athens Auckland Bangkok Bogotá Buenos Aires Calcutta
Cape Town Chennai Dar es Salaam Delhi Florence Hong Kong Istanbul
Karachi Kuala Lumpur Madrid Melbourne Mexico City Mumbai
Nairobi Paris São Paulo Shanghai Singapore Taipei Tokyo Toronto Warsaw

with associated companies in Berlin Ibadan

Oxford is a registered trade mark of Oxford University Press
in the UK and in certain other countries

Published in the United States
by Oxford University Press Inc., New York

© A. V. C. Schmidt 1992

The moral rights of the author have been asserted

Database right Oxford University Press (maker)

First published as a World's Classics paperback 1992
Reissued as an Oxford World's Classics paperback 2000
Reissued 2009

British Library Cataloguing in Publication Data

Data available

Library of Congress Cataloging in Publication Data

Langland, William, 1330?–1400?
[Piers the Plowman]
Piers Plowman: a new translation of the B-text/William Langland;
translated with an introduction and notes by A. V. C. Schmidt.
p. cm.—(Oxford world's classics)
Includes bibliographical references (p.) and index.
1. Christian poetry, English (Middle)—Modernized versions.
I. Schmidt, A. V. C. (Aubrey Vincent Carlyle). II. Title.
III. Series.
PR2013.S3 1992 821'.1—dc20 91–8906

ISBN 978–0–19–955526–0

15

Printed and bound in Great Britain by Clays Ltd, Elcograf S.p.A.

For
Renée and Frank
as promised
with all my love

ACKNOWLEDGEMENTS

Although I have not consulted other translations of *Piers Plowman* in the course of preparing this one, I have been conscious throughout of my indebtedness to the editors of the poem in its various versions and to the compilers of English dictionaries old and new, those wondrous necessary men and women without whose painstaking scholarship any attempt at an accurate rendering would be doomed to failure. I have been particularly grateful for the notes in the edition of the C-text by Derek Pearsall and that of the B-text Prologue and Passus I–VII by the late J. A. W. Bennett; both have helped to shorten my labours in writing the notes to this book.

The translation has been carried out in the intervals left over from my work on the forthcoming parallel-text edition of *Piers Plowman*. I am deeply grateful for much practical help in increasing the time available to my wife Judith, who has also been a tireless hearer and heartener of the work. Other support has come from colleagues in the English Faculty at Oxford who helped in a reading of the translation before publication, in Michaelmas Term 1990, and from the Langland Society at Malvern, who were the first to hear portions of the text read in the fourteenth-century hall of Little Malvern Priory Court. I should like to thank the Librarian of Balliol College for kindly allowing me to keep the Middle English Dictionary and an indefinite number of other volumes connected with Langland on virtually indefinite loan. I am grateful to Mrs Shirley Enoch for typing the manuscript.

My final thanks are to the dedicatees of this translation, my sister and brother-in-law, for innumerable nameless unremembered acts of kindness and of love, of which I single out only one that has contributed distantly but directly to the present work, the gift of a squat little Douai Bible for my tenth birthday. With them, I should like to couple the name of my Latin teacher, Mr R. L. Roberts, who taught me, amongst other things, that one translates ideas, not words. I

hope that they, in particular, will find a few hours of
enjoyment in this book.

A.V.C.S.

Oxford – Suffolk
1988–90

CONTENTS

PIERS PLOWMAN

INTRODUCTION

I. *PIERS PLOWMAN*: THE POEM, THE AUTHOR, AND THE AGE

> We already and first of all discern him
> making this thing other.
>
> (David Jones, *Anathemata*)

Piers Plowman is now widely recognized as a masterpiece of medieval English literature, worthy to stand beside Chaucer's *Canterbury Tales* as representative of the culture of its age. Readers have long admired its truthful picture of the life of the common people in the fourteenth century, now humorous, now harsh and grim, its passion for religious sincerity and social justice, and its passages of sublime poetry that make it comparable to *Paradise Lost* in a later age. More recently, its intellectual depth and complexity have been progressively revealed, and the last decade has seen its verse and language appreciated for their pioneering originality. The text of *Piers Plowman* has been re-edited several times in this century,[1] and a great deal has been learned about its structure, background, and art since the first complete prose translation was published some thirty years ago.[2] The time seems ripe for a new, fully annotated rendering into contemporary English which will take these developments into account, and make the work accessible to a new generation of non-specialist students and general readers.

Piers Plowman exists in three successive versions which are generally acknowledged as the work of one man, William Langland. They are the A-text of *c.*1370 (unfinished), the B-text of 1378–9 (the present text; completed), and the C-text of *c.*1386 (final revision not completed). In addition, the 'Z'

---

[1] For a list of editions see the select Bibliography. Early translations were all based on Skeat's edition of 1886.

[2] By J. F. Goodridge (Harmondsworth, 1959); often reprinted.

text (before 1370) has been claimed to be a draft version earlier still than A, but is not yet universally accepted as authentic.[3] The poem in its B-version is usually thought to be the best as poetry, and it is also the version which made a historical impact in its own time and at the Reformation. In 1381 John Ball, a leader of the Peasants' Revolt, urged the men of Essex in a letter to 'stand together in God's name, and bid Piers Ploughman go to his work . . . And do well and better, and flee sin', alluding to the poem's titular hero and one of its key ideas ('Do-well').[4] Two centuries later, after Edward VI's first Act of Uniformity (1549), the poem was published by the Protestant Robert Crowley (1550), and reprinted twice in the same year, becoming known to the major Elizabethan poets and critics such as Spenser, Marlowe, and Puttenham. To some medieval readers it seemed to assert the claims of the common people against an oppressive nobility and clergy; it was offered to the Tudor public as a cry for reformation of the Church, and especially as prophesying the dissolution of the monasteries (accomplished under Henry VIII between 1536 and 1540).

Both views are misunderstandings, and they probably go back to the author's own lifetime. Yet *Piers Plowman*, despite its boldness in making a ploughman, rather than a knight or saint, its hero, and in criticizing the abuses amongst the clergy from the pope downwards, does not advocate radical changes in the doctrine and government of the Church or in the structure of the social order. The reform it calls for is a return to the true spirit of Christian life and the traditional bonds and duties of an organic, hierarchically arranged society. But it does this through a long and impassioned examination, in the form of a series of allegorical dream-visions, of the fundamental issue of the purpose of man's life.

The poem begins with Will asking Holy Church how he is to save his soul. Her answer—'by living a life of spiritual integrity (*treuthe*)'—leads to his learning that collective but personal repentance and conversion from sin is necessary if

[3] Edited by A. G. Rigg and Charlotte Brewer; see Bibliography.
[4] For the full text see K. Sisam (ed.). *Fourteenth Century Verse and Prose* (Oxford, 1962), 160–1.

justice is to be effectively established in society at large. For living out a life of 'truth', Piers Plowman receives a pardon from Truth (God); although its validity is questioned by a priest (the first sign of a major clash between a spiritual and a formal understanding of religion), Will, the Dreamer, accepts the promise of the pardon that those who *do well* will go to heaven and those who *do evil* will be condemned to hell.

Will now embarks on a prolonged quest to discover *how* to do well through the use of his intellect. It fails, and he becomes disillusioned with learning, the church, and religion. He is rescued from his crisis by learning the virtue of patience, acquired through suffering in humility. By a series of painful stages he comes to see that 'doing well' is a discipline of the heart rather than the mind, and depends on openness to grace. He recognizes his solidarity with the most abandoned of sinners, and is given a glimpse of a God who has shown himself through Christ as merciful love, or charity. Will is privileged to witness the crucifixion of Christ and his ensuing triumph over death and hell, the establishment of the Christian Church by the Holy Spirit, and the subsequent trial and testing of true believers under fierce attacks from the powers of sin, powers which number among their weapons corrupt and worldly members of the clergy. Spiritual purification of these groups thus becomes a paramount need if the transformation of society into a community of justice and love is to become possible. The work ends with the poet making us aware that, as things stand in the world, that day is a long way off; in the present, spiritually disordered Church, the place of a conscientious Christian is a problematic one.

This sketch, which is filled out in much greater detail in Section III of this Introduction, indicates only the seriousness of the poem's argument; it says nothing about the colour, drama, narrative skill, and brilliant description that make it a great literary work. And it was as a work with a message that its earlier readers received it. Somewhat surprisingly, however, little information survives about the author of the message apart from that contained in the text itself. An early inscription in the Trinity College, Dublin, manuscript of the C-text tells us that the author's name was William Langland

and that his father was a gentleman, Stacy de Rokayle, a tenant of Lord Despenser living at Shipton-under-Wychwood in Oxfordshire.[5] A punning anagram in the B-text, which reads in the original 'I have lyved in *londe* . . . my name is *Longe* Wille' (B. xv. 152), tallies with the name; but no other source attests that the poet was a legitimate or illegitimate son of de Rokayle. Other passages in both A and B confirm the name, and passages in C argue against illegitimacy.[6]

The 'life' of Will Langland has to be deduced from the text, on the assumption that a first-person dream-vision poem gives an accurate picture of the author, qualified by local elements of irony and exaggeration (examples are his womanizing and the sexual demands of his wife (pp. 111, 248). He was born in the Malvern region of Worcestershire (this is confirmed by the poem's dialect) but lived most of the time in London. He was educated by his family and destined for a career in the Church, perhaps proceeding from a monastic school to study the arts course at a university and at least begin theology. He received minor orders but was never ordained a priest, possibly because of his marriage, and lacking a benefice earned his living as a psalter-clerk, saying prayers for the souls of the dead in return for payments in money or kind from their relatives. He lived with his wife Kit and daughter Calote at their cottage on Cornhill in the City of London, but sometimes also *opelond*, 'in the country'. Langland eked out his income by copying legal and other documents. He lived close to the poor, and either lacked or scorned the means of advancement.

From internal evidence we may infer (without great certainty) that Langland was born about 1330 and died c.1386; he is spoken of as dead by John But, who himself died in 1387. He must have spent the thirty or so years of his mature life on writing and revising *Piers Plowman*. We do not know whether he had patrons or supporters, and he neither refers to nor is mentioned in the writings of his better-documented contemporaries, Chaucer and Gower. This suggests that he moved in a different milieu; and the fact that

---

[5] For the passage in full see Schmidt (ed.), *Vision of Piers Plowman*, xiii.
[6] See A. xi. 118, B. xi. 8, C. iii. 366, V. 63–5.

manuscripts of the poem were owned by clerics in the first instance and, secondarily, by pious laymen, indicates that he moved mainly in clerical circles. The protagonist, Will, is represented in emphatic terms as a clerk, and the poem is saturated in the values of the 'clerkly' culture of his day. Though he evidently sensed some tension between his vocation as a psalter-clerk and his calling as a poet, he defended himself with subtlety and vigour (see pp. 114, 126) against charges of failing in his proper duties. He thought seriously about his art and about his moral responsibility as what I have called elsewhere a 'clerkly maker'.[7] But Langland never tells us why he abandoned the A-text or why he revised B, which he published, and we have to rely on guesswork.

One possibility is that Langland was filled with horror and alarm at the misinterpretation of his work as a call to overthrow the social and religious order by violent means. The murder of Archbishop Simon Sudbury by the rebels in 1381 was an act for which he might have felt some share of responsibility, and looking at the ruins of the palace of John of Gaunt in the Strand he might have wondered, like Yeats: 'Could my spoken words have checked | That whereby a house lay wrecked?'[8] One reason for removing Piers's tearing of the pardon and toning down his quarrel with the priest could have been that he wished, like T. S. Eliot, to 'let these words answer | For what is done, not to be done again'.[9] It seems probable that the audience he had in mind when turning the B-text into the version we call C was that which had first read B, and had perhaps expressed disquiet and misgivings to the poet. Whatever the case, he was forthright in criticizing Richard II's tolerance of corruption (C. III. 207–9) and, far from abandoning his poetic role, devised for himself a subtle defence of his interpretation of his calling. Against Conscience's accusation of idleness, he says: 'in my *conscience* I know what it is Christ would like me to do.' This is 'prayer

---

[7] See Schmidt, *The Clerkly Maker: Langland's Poetic Art*, chap. I.
[8] From 'The Man and the Echo', in W. B. Yeats, *Collected Poems* (London, 1958), 393.
[9] From 'Ash-Wednesday', in *Collected Poems and Plays of T. S. Eliot* (London, 1969), 90.

and penance'—just what Imaginative prescribed in the B-text—and he does not defend 'making' as he did there. He *concedes* Conscience's objection that his life leaves much to be desired; but although his subsequent defence refers ostensibly to a future life of greater devotion, the text *can* be read as covertly alluding to what was truly his 'life's work', the poem (something he is, of course, engaged in while composing this very critique by Reason and Conscience):

> What you say is true: I freely admit that I've wasted my time, used it badly. But still I carry on hoping, like someone who's embarked on one venture after another and lost his money every single time, until at last he gets one good chance which makes his fortune for ever. When that comes, he doesn't care a jot for his previous losses—such is the profit he makes through *some lucky words*. ... That's how I hope to lay my hands on some tiny little morsel of God's grace, and set off on a period that'll make every moment I've lived a source of ultimate profit and success. (C. V. 92–101)[10]

The italicized phrase ('words of grace' in the original) refers presumably to receiving divine guidance through the Scriptures; but it may also be read as his persisting hope for inspiration to write so as to hit the target of truth right in the centre. His stance is more modest than Dante's or Milton's; Langland doubtless found pride odious because he detected it in himself. But the attitude, if not arrogant, is confident, the tone like Chaucer's when asked if he is looking for fame:

> Sufficeth me, as I were ded,
> That no wight have my name in honde.
> *I wot myself best how y stonde.*
> (*House of Fame*, 1876–8; italics added)

Lacking, perhaps, the Renaissance poet's motive (and terminology) for making more grandiose claims for the status of poetry, Langland seems to leave it to his readers to work out what a 'clerkly maker's' true responsibility might be in a time of such social and spiritual upheaval. What is original about this view of his clerkly vocation is to see it as that of a serious

---

[10] For the original see the edition of the C-text by Derek Pearsall.

religious writer, waiting in hope for 'words of grace' that would make his (spiritual *and* artistic) 'fortune' for ever.

II. THE INTELLECTUAL AND RELIGIOUS BACKGROUND

because there is no end
To the vanity of our calling, make intercession
For the treason of all clerks.

(W. H. Auden)

The chief difficulty in translating Langland lies not in his language, which is easier than that of the *Pearl*-poet, say, but in his thought-world or '*mentalité*', what I shall call here his 'culture'. The Middle Ages possessed a common civilization that fused Christianity with the customs, institutions, and languages of the peoples who embraced it during the millennium after the fall of the Western Empire (fifth century AD). The moral and spiritual unity of what came to be called 'Christendom' derived from the understanding of individual and social life developed by the Church. This medieval *culture*, communicated to the masses through sculpture, stained glass, and vernacular preaching, had a common core shared by all from the pope to the simplest peasant. But as a spiritual *religion*, Christianity ran the risk of becoming submerged in everyday material concerns. The Church, when not actively growing as a 'spiritual organism', ran the risk of losing its religious identity, even while expanding as a 'material organization'.[11] Even after the formal conversion of Europe, its missionary impulse had continually to be renewed by outstanding individuals, the communities they founded, and the ways of life they developed or reformed.

At the beginning of the period the genius of St Augustine gave Western Europe its basic understanding of the meaning of Christian life in the world. His ideas survived the fall of Rome through being preserved by generations of monks living according to the Rule of St Benedict (sixth century AD). At the

---

[11] I take the phrases from T. S. Eliot, *Notes Towards the Definition of Culture* (London, 1948), 119.

height of the Middle Ages, in the twelfth century, St Bernard developed a lofty conception of individual holiness which revived the monastic movement and could still inspire the men of Langland's age. But the most recent wave of Christian renewal was that of the thirteenth century, when St Francis and St Dominic pioneered their dynamic orders of friars to spread the Gospel to the urban masses affected by ignorance, indifference, and heresy. It was the friars who gave the most powerful impulse to the study of theology in the new institutions of higher learning, the universities. At major centres like Paris and Oxford the understanding of faith in the light of reason was extended, clarified, and systematized by great thinkers such as St Thomas Aquinas, who stands to the end of the period as Augustine did to its beginning. His *Summa Theologiae* covers every aspect of theology with incomparable fullness and precision.

The fruits of all this theological and devotional effort were scattered throughout society especially through sermons preached in the vernacular, the Franciscans in particular making effective use of poems and songs. Preaching, like study in the schools (universities) or spiritual meditation in the cloister (the monasteries) was based on Scripture. Knowledge of the Bible was made available in various ways, including the readings of the Church's liturgical cycle and the various art forms that supplemented them, notably the new vernacular miracle plays. But only to those trained to read Latin, the tongue into which St Jerome had translated the Bible, was scripture in the full sense 'an open book'. These were the clerks; and until the half-century after Langland's death, the higher medieval culture was the preserve of those who had received a clerical education.

Acquaintance with *some* aspects of 'clerkly' culture was not, of course, confined exclusively to tonsured clerks destined for the service of the Church. A 'living' was not to be had even for all of these, while many who had learned Latin did not seek a career in the 'cleric's garb' Langland speaks of (C. v. 41). It is not known if the *Pearl*-poet was in orders (he could have been a married clerk like Langland), but both Chaucer and Gower were laymen, secular moralists, but also 'men of the world' and not, like Langland, 'men of holy church'. Chaucer observes the whole social scene, including the ecclesiastical, and his *General Prologue* owes much to Langland's. But like Gower and the *Gawain*-poet (who is also the author of *Pearl*), his chief interest before the *Canterbury Tales* lay in the life of the nobility and the *courtly* culture. In this, not religion but chivalry, love, and the beautiful things of this world are the chief concern. Conflict between a 'courtly' and 'religious' perspective is, admittedly, evident in his *Troilus*; but the shockingly abrupt rejection of the values of 'this litel spot of erthe' in the poem's epilogue indicates how marginal religious priorities are in the body of the work. *Pearl* also explores the tension between heavenly and earthly love, though here more directly and pervasively. It *is* a religious poem, but the plight of the father learning to love the soul of his dead daughter with a disinterested spiritual love is the plight of a 'man of the world', not a 'clerk of holy church'.

In *Piers Plowman*, then, the conflict between a particular human love and love of God, as a conflict between St Augustine's 'cupidity' and 'charity',[12] never becomes a key focus of debate. And while the poets of the 'courtly culture' show knowledge of the 'clerkly culture' (and outside England Dante even tried to bridge them), Langland has little interest in the former. His 'courtly' personage, Lady Meed, is thoroughly corrupt, and though Langland shares his view of Christ as the source of all true 'nobility', he makes no particular effort to *reconcile* courtly and religious values as does the *Gawain*-poet by means of his hero's heraldic device (the pentangle) that emblematizes the ideal unity of both systems and stands for 'integrity' (*trawthe*). Chaucer's authorial persona in the Prologue to *The Legend of Good Women* encounters the God of Love (Cupid) and the pagan heroine Alcestis; Langland's argues with Reason or with Scripture. Even *Pearl* is set in a garden that recalls the love-gardens of the French courtly tradition; Langland's poem opens in a wilder-

---

[12] Respectively 'love of the world' and 'love of God'. For an acute discussion see A. Nygren (tr. P. Watson), *Agape and Eros* (New York, 1969), 482–503.

ness where the points of orientation are those familiar from Christian instruction—heaven and hell, with middle earth as the locale where man must choose which of the others he will go to after death. However, it is not the religious content or homiletic purpose as such which make Langland a 'clerkly' poet; both are found in *Purity* and *Patience*, two other works ascribed to the author of *Pearl*. Langland's clerkliness resides in his manifest identification with the perspective on life of the ordained members of the Christian community. He may be an imperfect or a failed cleric; but it is the outlook and predicament, the anguish and the responsibility of the churchman that he shares. Even his 'anti-clericalism' does not contradict this; the most vehement criticism of the Church came not from laymen but from clerks, as Wyclif's case vividly illustrates.

The encounter with the allegorical figure Honest Fidelity (*Lewte*) in Passus XI *seems* to suggest that this character sees Will as a layman:

'It is legitimate for ordinary laymen to affirm what's true if they wish it: that's their right in both Canon and Civil Law. But this doesn't hold for parish priests or for the higher clergy, of course. They're the ones who should avoid making public statements—even ones which are factually accurate—if the subject that's involved is somebody's sin.' (p. 114)

The subtle distinction drawn here can be misunderstood; but Will is not being *equated* with laymen (as one who is neither priest nor prelate), he is being *associated* with them in the matter of 'testifying' about sin (as one who, while a clerk, is unconstrained by the secrecy of the confessional or the discretion of a high office like a bishop's or an abbot's). His 'amphibian' status as a married clerk in minor orders allows him to be 'in the world' while not 'of it', and to draw close both to the most centrally 'secular' of his characters, Piers and Haukin, and to 'marginal' characters like the pilgrim-hermit Patience. From the fourth vision onwards, his sympathies lie increasingly with the figure of Conscience, who fits into the action of this and the last two visions as the upright religious knight that he began as in the first vision. The close bond he

envisages between Conscience and Piers *could* be interpreted
as an argument for basing the Christian community on its
pious lay elements alone, and bypassing or abolishing the
Church establishment. But this reading, which was possibly
that of some of his audience, founders on the fact of the
identification of Piers in the later passus first with Christ and
then with the apostle Peter. The notion that Langland could
have wished the *Church* to be governed by ploughmen and
knights cannot be sustained. In the fifth vision, the argument
of Anima (the Dreamer's soul) is that what the Church needs
is holy priests and heroic bishops; one of his exemplars of the
latter is Thomas Becket, a symbol of resistance to oppression
of the Church by the secular power of his day.

None the less, a crucial turning-point occurs in Will's *view*
of the Church in his own quest for the true Christian life of
Do-well, Do-better, and Do-best. It is a literal parting of the
ways, when Conscience and Patience leave Clergy (the Church
in its pastoral and formative function) and the Doctor of
Divinity (the Church as theological authority) to set out on
pilgrimage in search of charity. Significantly, Will does not
stay with the clerks but accompanies the laymen, who now
encounter in Haukin a distorted mirror-image of the common
humanity shared by clergy and laity alike, but especially an
emblem of the *uneducated* layman. This turning-point,
however, is really a *point de repère*. For Haukin exemplifies
what the laity can be reduced to when they ignore the
Church's teaching and sacraments. What Anima goes on to
show in the next vision is that the evil *example* of clerks has
much to answer for in the vicious life of 'lewed' (or lay,
uneducated) people. But his attack encompasses the learning
which we know to have benefited so little the clerkly
characters in the poem, from the Doctor of Divinity down to
Will himself; and 'learning' is the life-blood of a clerk, as Will
had been assuming until Vision Four:

If you eat too much honey, it cloys your stomach, doesn't it? Now
supposing you open your ears to twice as much virtuous doctrine as
the next man—what then? Unless you *live* twice as well, the doctrine
just does you double the amount of harm! (p. 168)

Those who feed too heavily on the honey of clerkly culture and fail to turn it into the spiritual energy of charity end more ill than those who never taste it.

The fundamental point Langland makes through Anima is that the clergy, far from being dispensable, are the root cause of the good as well as the evil in the whole community. Their holiness makes it holy, their viciousness makes it vicious, because lay-people understand their teaching *through* their example. The reform of the clergy must lead, therefore, to the transformation of society into something nearer that of the early Christian period. Modern historians link the poor condition of the clergy with the plague, which reduced the number of priests by half and led to unqualified men being ordained to replace them. While Langland does not state this explicitly, he is aware that one reason why priests were preoccupied with money was the poverty of parishes whose populations had been decimated. However, *he* sees the decline as resulting from a *spiritual* malaise, and even interprets natural disasters as punishments for the people's sin, something he traces to the clergy's evil example. A particular cause of moral decline he finds in the giving of easy absolution by confessors, especially the friars, who fail to insist on rigorous observance of the Church's penitential laws. At the end, he sees this as the chief reason for the fall of Unity Holy Church: the crisis foreseen in the Prologue, if the friars are not properly controlled, results in Conscience going out from Unity, to wander in quest of charity outside its breached walls.

That Langland attacks the friars as exemplifying the worst corruption of the best ideal does not mean he spares the rest of the clergy. And his seeing their venality as occasioned by their need for material support does not constitute an *economic* explanation for spiritual phenomena. For while he wishes the friars endowed with means that would obviate the need to beg, he finds the deeper reason for their state in a betrayal of their original ideal through the sins of envy and pride; and while the envy may be due to lack of money, the pride is not. Langland sees the friars' concentration on higher learning as having led them to lose the motivation of their founders— desire to imitate the apostolic life and pursue study so as to further growth in holiness. His disillusionment is at bottom not just with the orders, or the clergy, but with *theology*, the heart of the clerkly culture. This underlies his looking to Piers and Conscience as model figures uncorrupted by the irreligion of such as Haukin, at one end of the scale, and the complacency of the doctor or the priest who rebukes Piers, at the other.

The great constructive thinkers of the thirteenth century had found their poetic equivalent in Dante. *The Divine Comedy* is a work in which the clergy (including popes) are criticized; but it reveals a confidence in the union of reason and faith which made the idea of 'Unity Holy Church' seem a realizable possibility. That confidence had been undermined in the first half of the fourteenth century by developments connected with William of Ockham and his followers, the *Moderni*.[13] These thinkers called in question the system of thought based on deducing doctrine from premises founded on scripture and the writings of the Fathers. Most fundamentally, they raised doubts as to whether God's will *could* be known with certainty through the Church, and whether the ordinary means to holiness, the sacraments, could be relied on as an adequate channel of grace. Many of them were members of the orders of friars.

The *Moderni* found opponents such as the formidable Archbishop Bradwardine, who reasserted what he called 'God's case against the Pelagians' (Pelagius had argued for reliance upon man's own efforts to gain salvation, a view that seemed to follow from calling into question the 'ordinary' means of grace—the Church's teaching and sacraments). In the later fourteenth century, in Langland's day, Wyclif drew the 'logical' conclusion that if the ministration of an evidently corrupted Church was not sufficient for salvation, it was probably not necessary either. The result was to identify the 'true' believers with those who led lives in accord with the Gospel, and to undermine the rationale of the clerical order by removing the means of grace from its exclusive control. Wyclif's teaching was condemned and his followers firmly

[13] For a clear account see G. Leff, *Medieval Thought: St Augustine to Ockham* (Harmondsworth, 1958), 279–302; cf. also J. Coleman, *'Piers Plowman' and the Moderni* (Rome, 1981).

suppressed; but the dissatisfaction they aroused led to widespread anticlericalism in the following decades. It was reinforced not only by the unedifying lives of many priests and religious but by scandal at the highest level of the Church. In 1378 the Great Schism produced two rival popes who asserted their claims to supreme *spiritual* authority by force of arms and, in doing so, divided not only the clergy but Europe as a whole. The Roman pope was supported by England, the Avignonese antipope by France; theology became embroiled in the power-struggles of the two leading nations of Christendom. The first seeds of the Reformation had been sown.

As well as heresy, the crisis in scholastic theology drew another kind of reaction, the growth of affective devotional and mystical movements, both in monastic circles and among the laity (an early example, and an influential one, was Ockham's contemporary, the hermit Richard Rolle). Writers such as Julian of Norwich developed a life of prayer based upon the individual soul's direct approach to God, and, while faithful to the Church, they say little about the sacraments. Langland was neither a polemicist like Wyclif nor a mystic like Julian, though like the one he was deeply critical of the clergy, and like the other he stresses the centrality of the Passion of Christ for the individual believer. Unlike Wyclif, however, he believes in the religious authority of a sacramental priesthood. He thus sees reform of the *clergy* as a matter of life and death, since it is they who hold 'the keys of Christ's treasury'—access to grace through baptism, penance, and the Eucharist. But, unlike the mystics, he is deeply engaged in the life of society. His interest in the soul is inseparable from a burning desire to see England a just and loving community; and since, for him, charity is quite literally nothing if not practical, economic and social (and therefore political) concerns become not marginal but absolutely central.

Langland's theological 'position' could be described as 'semi-Pelagian'[14]—attaching weight to both grace and good

[14] For a good, non-technical account see J. Simpson, *Piers Plowman: An Introduction*, 124–6.

works (or Do-well) in achieving salvation. But it is unwise to try and be too precise, since his work is a poem describing an adventure rather than articulating a thesis. It seems fairly clear that he did not suppose he could find an answer to every question man's mind can put to God; systematic theology could not reconcile the antinomies of his real experience of individuals and institutions. But at the end of the poem, Conscience does not *reject* the Church when he leaves it, like a pilgrim, on a lonely quest to find, in Piers, a remedy for its ills. Langland's faith, the leading feature of his vision, is less 'belief that' than 'trust in'. It is that very *treuthe* that Holy Church affirms at the beginning: trust that God *is* love, and demands love from 'true' believers. The contradictions reason uncovers must have a 'reason' behind them (in this he is at one with Julian), but man's task is to imitate Christ in trusting God, and to realize that patience and suffering are not incidentals but indispensable prerequisites for the growth of charity. *Piers Plowman*, therefore, comes down firmly on the side of literal poverty and simplicity of life as the antidotes to envy, greed, and pride. It is among the patient poor that humility appears, and this is the soil where charity has the best chance of growing.

I have called Langland's poem an 'adventure', a word which implies risk, the danger of defeat. But, paradoxically perhaps, it is at the same time a *structure*—a planned expedition with a map and a sense of direction. Its meaning lies in what can be described as its 'twofold struggle'—to master the difficulties of its *material*, and to develop a *form* adequate to the poet's vision. The two are so closely connected that in the next section I shall examine them both together.

III. THE SHAPE AND SENSE OF THE POEM

And the end and the beginning were always there.
(T. S. Eliot)

Piers Plowman constitutes an artistic adventure not only for the author but also for the *reader*, who is required to

participate in its quest for wholeness of spiritual under-
standing, which is at the same time an effort to achieve
integrity of poetic form. For Langland, unlike Yeats, man is
not forced to choose between 'perfection of the life or of the
work'; for a 'clerkly maker', the two become inseparable.

The form of the poem has four distinctive features. Instead
of the usual single vision with waking prologue and (optional)
epilogue, it consists of eight main visions, each with a
prologue, and has no final epilogue. Two subsidiary visions
('inner dreams') are also inserted, one in the third vision
(occupying most of Passus XI) and one in the fifth (occupying
about half of Passus XVI). The abrupt ending of the whole is
a disturbing departure from the serene formal 'closure'
favoured in medieval poetry. Secondly, *Piers Plowman* is
divided into a prologue and twenty *passūs* which segment the
longer visions into shorter units providing pausing-places like
the chapters of a modern book. The last three visions,
however, fill a whole passus apiece, conveying a sense of
accelerating pace. Every vision begins at a new passus, but for
convenience all beginnings of major and inner visions, and the
endings of the latter, have been indicated in this edition.

A third set of divisions, perhaps authorial, perhaps the
work of a scribe who sought to make the poem's contents
clearer, is into two titled 'thematic sections'. The first two
dreams together are called 'the Vision of Piers Plowman',
the last six 'the Life of Do-well, Do-better, and Do-best'
(respectively the *Visio* and *Vita* for short). In many manu-
scripts, such as the one this translation is based on, the
Vita is further subdivided, 'Do-well' covering Visions Three
and Four, 'Do-better', Visions Five and Six, and 'Do-best',
Visions Seven and Eight. A fourth structural principle, this
one internal to the text, is what I call 'recapitulation', which
involves repeating at a higher, symbolic level an action which
occurs at an earlier point in the poem (for example, the
ploughing in Passus XIX which 'recapitulates' that in Passus
VI). This is as much a method of thematic organization as an
element of formal structure, and is indicated in the notes but
not in the text.

These four principles point to considerable planning in
the larger composition of *Piers Plowman* (a feature matched

in the original at the level of verse-structure). They testify that Langland, for all his interest in drama, conflict, and discovery, was concerned to give his audience a 'thing made', a product, and not just the process of 'making'. But his poem lacks the mathematical patterning of Dante and the *Pearl*-poet (who may have read Dante). This is perhaps because its subject is dynamic, not static—not the condition of the soul after death, but God's action in 'England and nowhere. Never and always'. Supremely interested in 'The point of intersection of the timeless | With time',[15] Langland understandably makes the dramatic climax of the poem Christ's crucifixion, when life conquers death, and eternity reconciles time with itself. Yet he never uses his dream-vision form to describe heaven, and his scene in hell is not a vision of the inferno of the damned, only a locale for Christ's speech vindicating God's action in history. The poem is about our world, and it is wedded to time and the contradictions of our earthly experience, the 'actual'.

Vision One (Prologue and Pass. I–IV)

Actuality is what Will encounters in the Prologue, where the field, though pitched between two supernatural extremes, is recognizably our Middle Earth. But in it he can meet a figure from the tower-world he will never enter, who provides the poem's programme and perspective. Holy Church identifies the enemies of Truth in Meed and her supporters, leaving Will to observe the conflict of venality and moral principle allegorically enacted in the domain of high politics. The vision ends hopefully, with Meed defeated and the King resolved to rule by reason and conscience. The 'shape' of the vision is that of *debate*, a form familiar to Langland's audience from poems like *Winner and Waster*.[16]

Vision Two (Pass. V–VII)

However, for society to function justly, there must be justice in the souls of the individuals who form it. This Langland

---

[15] For the two Eliot quotations see 'Little Gidding' and 'The Dry Salvages', in *Collected Poems and Plays*, 192, 189.

[16] This text is conveniently accessible (ed. T. Turville-Petre) in B. Ford (ed.), *Medieval Literature: Chaucer and the Alliterative Tradition*.

sees as necessitating true repentance for sin and the paying of one's debt to God. The 'shape' of Vision Two is that of a four-part *action*—sermon, confession, pilgrimage, and pardon[17]—linked to Vision One through Reason's sermon, preached before the King. Its long epilogue (which may have been the conclusion of the poem in its very earliest version, the 'Z'-text) asserts the value of dream-visions, warns the rich against an unspiritual view of salvation, and urges 'Do-well', recognized and embodied in Piers Plowman, as the surest way to salvation.

Vision Three (Pass. VIII–XII)

The *Visio* concluded, the *Vita* commences with a long waking prologue that links the third to the first two visions by being set in the Prologue's summer season. It reverts from action to debate-form, Will becoming the protagonist, not a spectator. The arguments take place within his mind, but also mirror the experience of formal clerkly education. Will is highly disputatious, both with the friars in the waking world and with the personifications met in the dream—which may be why Study gets angry with Wit for instructing him. Most readers find this vision hard going, but liveliness returns with Scripture's spirited attack on scoffers at religion. Clergy, personifying the Church's teaching authority, criticizes the actual clergy's ignorance and sloth, and foretells their reform at the hands of king and nobles. This provokes Will's waspish question, whether Do-well means worldly rule, Scripture's denial unleashing a keen dispute. The dispute in turn leads to Will's attack on learning and to his insisting that, since Do-well means *acting* rightly, the least educated may achieve it, while learning may even lead a man astray. He touches here on current disaffection with the clergy amongst the people. Though articulating a general clerkly dilemma, Will also voices personal chagrin at the failure of education to make him a better Christian, and attacks Clergy partly because of rage against himself. The rebuke he draws from Scripture arouses a violent surge of anger and mortification.

---

[17] See J. A. Burrow, 'The Action of Langland's Second Vision', repr. in *Essays on Medieval Literature* (Oxford, 1984), 79–101.

At this central point comes the bold innovation of a dream-within-a-dream,[18] into which Will's temper precipitates him (as it does the dreamer in *Pearl*). To indicate how extreme is his revolt against the Church, which becomes a rejection of religion, not a turning to Piers's simple faith, Will is shown given over to Fortune, a personification of the world's mutable pleasures. When he becomes poor, he finds the friars unwilling to help him. It is here, at the nadir of Will's 'clerkhood', that Honest Fidelity tells him to rebuke the abuses of the clergy, and Scripture lends support. But despite this encouragement to pursue his calling as a 'maker', Will remains anxious about his 'calling' as a Christian: *is* he chosen (predestined) for salvation? Remembering Holy Church here calls to mind the 'programme' she outlined in Vision One for a life of 'truth'. But Trajan's vehement intervention at this point challenges the unquestioned assumption that membership of the Church is *necessary* for a man to be saved. Langland's belief in 'learning' here meets its ultimate test; but he somehow manages to refrain from inferring that, since good deeds are necessary for salvation and baptism alone insufficient, good deeds may be sufficient and baptism unnecessary. The vestiges of his clerkly training save him from a potentially fatal error in logic, and make it possible for him to receive from Imaginative a resolution of the dilemma.

Spiritually exhausted, Will is summoned by Kind to be shown another vision; but what he sees now is not the field of folk (society) but the whole creation (*omnis mundi creatura*), human, non-human, vegetables and stars. One of the poem's rare moments of natural beauty follows; but even this is marred by the disorder of man's sin, which makes Will protest against Providence. Doubting the Church has led to doubting God's wisdom and so, inexorably, his very existence. The adventure that began with 'Thought' seems to have led to the imminent loss of faith. Reason's answer provides a bridge for Will across the chasm that seems to lie before him. Evil does exist; but God too has to put up with it, only, however, so that a greater good (unknown to us) can

[18] See Schmidt, 'The Inner Dreams in Piers Plowman', *Medium Aevum* 55 (1986), 24–40.

emerge. Man's part is to do as much, trusting God's goodness and power to defeat evil, since man cannot. Here is Will's first *intuition* that sin, in Julian of Norwich's phrase, is 'behovely' (necessary), something *explained* only in the great sixth vision. When Will wakes from the inner dream, he has grasped the place of suffering in life and (potentially) that of patience, the virtue that enables man to accept it. He is ready to learn from Imaginative, whose arrival Scripture had predicted would answer laymen's questioning of God's wisdom—precisely what the clerk Will has been doing in challenging Reason.

Imaginative's crucial discourse attempts to reconcile the contradictions encountered in the attempt to apply reason to the mysteries of life and faith. His approach is gentler in face of Will's new receptiveness, as is shown in his drawing on images as well as arguments, and in his concession to Will's case that the ignorant may be saved more easily than the learned. This, he says, '*is* true of certain people; but only in a certain way' (p. 131). To answer Will's rejoinder that the Church *insists* on knowledge of Christian teaching for salvation, he builds on Trajan's case (showing thereby that Langland had taken the *Moderni* seriously). He argues essentially that even the *ordinary* means of grace are not fully intelligible to man: the sacraments are mysteries, with a depth corresponding to the divine nature they are ordained to mediate, and there is more to 'baptism', say, than meets the eye of reason. Faith actually 'understands' more deeply, and it is to the faithful, the 'true' believers, that God who is Truth will give eternal life. Here he seems to echo a Wycliffite idea, but not with Wyclif's intention;[19] Will does not abandon orthodoxy but comes back to it, glimpsing 'Holy Church' through the lineaments of her imperfect embodiment in the actual institution.

Langland's achievement in these passūs is to create poetry of high emotional pressure from difficult material that could have proved cold and pedantic, and to do it through a novel and daring formal device. Vision Three is the heart of his 'clerkly' adventure, debating problems at once acutely

[19] See P. Gradon, 'Langland and the Ideology of Dissent', *Proceedings of the British Academy* 66 (1982), for a balanced account of his affinities with Wyclif.

personal and central to the age. Though tough and forbidding, it is of fundamental importance for understanding *Piers Plowman* as a whole, and has been dwelt on at such length here for that reason.

Vision Four (Pass. XIII–XIV)

Now we return to action, followed by dramatized description and discourse. The vision is in two parts, preceded by a prologue summarizing the third vision, from which it grows. The dinner at Conscience's house validates Will's point that the learning of *some* clerics does not make them better men but scandalizes and corrupts laymen (such as Haukin). In the person of the doctor of divinity, a friar, the whole notion that clerkly culture can engender Do-well is exposed as a sham. But Will now is learning to 'suffer' corruption in others, even while exercising his right to rebuke it. The important new character Patience embodies the virtue recommended by Reason in the inner dream, and Conscience's decision to leave with him is a crucial point in the poem (cf. p. xxi above). In the scene with Haukin, Will is more a seeing eye than an agent; and what he sees justifies Imaginative's (qualified) claim for Clergy; for Haukin is the very nadir of the uninstructed layman, his pride, greed, and hypocrisy a mirror-image of the learned doctor's. But 'learning' is coming to be increasingly understood in spiritual rather than intellectual terms.[20] This, tellingly, makes Haukin's sinfulness *less* of a barrier to conversion than the doctor's, when once he is brought to see it.

Haukin 'recapitulates' the folk of the field with whom the Dreamer was identified after Reason's sermon. Will can thus sympathize with the wretched wafer-seller, too, sharing his shame at failing to live up to the demands of his baptism. The failed clerk can see in the minstrel *manqué* something like his *alter ego*, and in this shared experience lies the beginning of Will's spiritual recovery from the exhausted collapse in Vision Three. Patience and Conscience combine in the vital task of Haukin's 'conversion'—his recognition that 'true' repentance

[20] See J. Simpson, 'From Reason to Affective Knowledge: Modes of Thought and Poetic Form in *Piers Plowman*', *Medium Aevum* 55 (1986), 1–23.

is based on sorrow for offending a loving God, not just on fear of punishment ('recapitulation' is not mere repetition, but involves advancing to a higher plane of understanding). Will's own crisis here reaches full resolution as he looks in the mirror of himself and sees Haukin's features there. He accepts his total dependence on grace, and is willing to wait to see more. Conscience is active in him, and patience is beginning to form.

Vision Five (Pass. XV–XVII)

This vision is at once a pausing-point, the scene of deepest self-communing, and the vision which, through its inner dream, effects a transition to the sustained series of linked actions that constitute the last three. What he has learnt drives Will into an inner domain; his outer life is described in the prologue as being like that of someone who has gone mad in ordinary worldly and social terms. Its mode is largely discursive, a 'debate' with only one speaker. Langland uses the figure of Anima to give voice to a stirring call for the renewal of Christendom from within. The core of this is that ordination and, supremely, consecration as a bishop, is not a form of earthly advancement but a summons to responsibility that may entail martyrdom. Giving one's life is the ultimate act of 'charity', the antithesis of 'cupidity' or love of one's own life and pleasure. Anima's diatribe on the decline of culture includes the famous passage about how clerks no longer know how to write poetry. But his chief theme is the *heroic* spiritual ideal. This serves to highlight our sense of the poem as an 'adventure' by adumbrating the image of Christ as a knight errant coming to 'venture all' for the sake of love.

When Will thanks Anima 'on Haukin's behalf' he shows how he has come to identify himself again with the common man, not with a privileged élite. Anima's mention of *Piers*'s name enables Langland to deploy for a second time, and even more powerfully, the device of an inner dream. What this does here is to 'realize', make tangibly present the 'suffering' (patient endurance of evil) urged on Will by Reason in the first inner dream. And suffering is what the 'passion' of Christ (seen as the first 'martyr' and 'bishop') literally denotes.

Debate now takes second place to action until the climactic debate between Christ and the Devil, although long discursive speeches such as the Samaritan's on the Trinity occur. The pace now becomes almost feverish, and once the poetry has flared into life, it does not flag till the last line.

As Kind in the first inner dream showed Will nature, Piers now reveals a glimpse of God's own nature (love). He also discloses more fully the union of human and divine accomplished by the Incarnation, a theme first broached in Holy Church's words on love as the plant of peace. This plant has become a tree, the tree of human nature in historical time, on which, through grace, the fruits of charity will appear. The whole vivid sequence shows the deep impress of the liturgical offices of Passiontide, and Will's 'return to the Church' is to be seen not as a 'notional' assent to academic arguments but a 'real' immersion in prayer and a rediscovery of faith through imaginative and affective means. He recovers his calling as a Christian through recovering his calling as a clerk, recognizing it for the first time as a *vindication* of the time he has spent on poetry. 'Making' renews the belief that 'thinking' had nearly destroyed. It becomes clear now that Imaginative's role was not just to furnish a good argument but, in fusing both 'memory' and 'imagination', and instructing the dreamer through images, to lead Will into his deep inner self (his Anima), the source of creativity as well as of life and thought. He is now enabled to repossess, with passionate excitement, the meanings contained in the poetic-theological pattern of the paschal liturgy. Through it he re-enters the reality of faith that had been obscured by the corrupt actuality of the English Church he knew.

Vision Six (Pass. XVIII)

Langland's recreation of the events that lie at the heart of Christian belief and worship, Christ's victory over evil through his own suffering and death, is amongst the highest achievements of medieval English poetry; it is certainly the fine flower of 'clerkly making'. The poetry bursts with energy and colloquial freshness, but the veining of Latin quotations and half-lines keeps constantly before us the sacred world of the transcendent that is mediated by the Church's liturgy. Langland's mastery of action and debate is at its peak, both structure and style seeming effortless and inevitable. Vision-form and passus-division coalesce, and this remains the pattern for the remaining visions. The Harrowing of Hell is a triumph of hope after the agony and uncertainty that preceded, and the debate of the Four Daughters of God which ends in a carol (a secular dance transformed to 'sacred mirth') brings to its end the process by which, in Eliot's phrase, 'past and future . . . are conquered, and reconciled'.[21]

Christ's speech to the Devil is the triumph of 'clerkly culture', a culture which is now redeemed and justified in its union of cunning and love. The jubilant Easter bells that waken Will to communion with God and his fellow Christians could, in principle, have brought *Piers Plowman* to a satis-fyingly 'medieval' end. The loving reality of God has been rediscovered through suffering, and God himself has em-barked on the adventure of human life with man. The convic-tion that evil is necessary for the highest good has been illuminated and underscored. Yet, it is not to be. Will has to wake from the 'real' into the 'actual', from consoling 'truth' to painful 'fact.'

Vision Seven (Pass. XIX)

Before Will can renew his commitment to the Church and its Easter sacrament of unity, he falls asleep and sees Piers, carrying a cross and bleeding. The 'actual' has, as it were, burst into the dream-world: Christ continues to bleed in *our* world in every just man suffering oppression for his 'truth'. The renewal of *individual* faith is not enough. Will now longs for the reconstitution of the actual Church as a religious reality by returning to its origin. For although Christ has reconciled time and eternity, the final end of history is not yet at hand. Hope must be hope for a future, and Langland's historical sense is accompanied by his 'patient' awareness that truth's triumph is slow, with many set-backs before it comes. Christ's personal 'conquest' must be embodied in a durable

---

[21] From 'The Dry Salvages', in *Complete Poems and Plays*, 190.

'empire', but in a *spiritual organism* whose birth is commemorated as the liturgical cycle advances from Easter to Whitsun. The purpose of 'Unity Holy Church' is to bring to maturity the seeds of virtue planted by Piers and tended by him and his successors under Grace. But just as 'wasters' had preyed on the literal ploughman, the vices under Pride now attack the Church, attempting to destroy Unity by undermining its sacramental heart and stronghold. Resistance is led by Conscience; but ominous notes are sounding as Will wakes to write down his dream.

Vision Eight (Pass. XX)

Transcendent 'reality' is now under dire stress from the 'actual', for the vision opens with Will's exposure to Need, which puts him in the predicament of all clerks who betray their calling because of material necessities. The poem's darkest moment is at hand, with the coming of age, disease, and the prospect of death. Langland's 'adventure' has reached the point common in romances when the hero, having won jousts, must now take part in war. Unity is under siege from the massed powers of sin, defended by Conscience's 'fools', who refuse to betray their vision and submit to evil. Yet, fierce as the battle is, it is through treachery not force that Conscience finds himself worsted. This time, the 'guile' of Antichrist (the Devil's agent) works through a corrupt friar-confessor, whose easy absolution prevents the wounded from recovering to fight again. The sacraments that should heal bring harm if received unworthily. When Conscience, emblem of faithful lay Christians, calls on Clergy for aid, he learns he has been bewitched by the friar's spell: the calamity foreseen in the Prologue has occurred. Through the friars, hypocrisy has entered souls, and Unity, betrayed by the clergy, is open to the enemy; the 'doctor of death' has poisoned the wells of life.

In the world of history, concord was already collapsing. The Church was in schism. England had renewed war with France. To finance the war, poll-taxes were levied, the second of these precipitating the rising of the common people in 1381. At every level, secular and religious, 'unity' was being lost. Conscience, who returned 'from abroad' in Vision One, now 'hunts the whole earth' to find someone in whom unity of profession and action, discourse and deed, 'truth' and 'love', are embodied—Piers Plowman. All that now remained for Langland was to give the poem to the world, and especially to the clergy, who seemed to need it most. *Piers Plowman* has no epilogue; there is nothing more to debate; the time now is for action.

IV. LANGLAND'S FIGURATIVE MODES

The unread vision in the higher dream.

(T. S. Eliot)

Although discourse and debate abound in *Piers Plowman*, it is often illustrated by parables and exempla, and the dominant mode of the first two and last four visions is broadly narrative. But it is *allegorical* narrative, a kind unfamiliar today and one little used by Langland's major contemporaries. Allegory is a means of talking about one thing in terms of another; it is a 'figurative mode'. In one variety, 'symbol-allegory', an object or action has a further, non-literal meaning: the tower on the hill *stands for* heaven, wandering in the wilderness for 'a state of perplexity', looking to the east for 'turning to God for illumination'. The most complex instance is that of the Tree of Charity. But this symbolic mode, favoured by Dante, is not Langland's main one. This is 'personification-allegory', which is predominant in all except Vision Six and the second inner dream. Here, abstract ideas are *personified* as agents: mental faculties like Reason, activities like Study, ethical and religious ideas like Holy Church or Patience. An action like Conscience's refusal to kiss Meed thus represents the irreconcilable opposition between the moral disposition and the principle of venality. In a third variety, 'figural allegory' (*figura*), a character or event *foreshadows* or is *recalled by* another. This mode is common in the miracle plays, where an Old Testament 'type', a character or event (Isaac; Noah's flood) 'figures' its 'anti-type' in the New (Christ; the Last Judgement). Langland daringly adapts *figura* when he makes his

Samaritan (and with him Piers Plowman) a 'type' of Christ. His handling of the structural device of 'recapitulation' (for example, the two 'pardons' Piers receives in Pass. VII and XIX) is also based upon this idea.

The poem offers rich and complex permutations of these modes, 'personified' or 'figural' characters interacting with symbolic ones (the Doctor; Haukin) and individuals with a representative dimension (pre-eminently Will himself). The rationale of the allegorical mode is belief that a metaphysical 'reality' exists beneath the 'actuality' of the empirical world of the senses. 'Human nature' or 'envy', therefore, are not just ideas in the mind; there is something called 'sin' which underlies every person's particular vicious acts. Thus, Haukin is not an exceptionally depraved individual but a symbol of the baptized soul fallen into sin, and he 'recapitulates' the Sins who confess in Vision Two. Allegory may function in a purely expository way (Anima in the Castle of *Caro*), or spring half-unconsciously to life, as in the Samaritan's 'horse called *Caro*, which [he] got from human nature' (p. 201), where humanity is a 'vehicle' for the Son of God, as a horse is that which 'carries' its rider. Langland's clerkly training would have acquainted him with all three: the figural allegory of the biblical readings in the liturgy and the patristic interpretations in the Glossed Bible, the personification-allegory of writers like Alan of Lille, and the symbolic significances of the Church's visual art (for example, the Tree of Jesse in a 'Jesse window'). But his *greatest* allegorical writing is produced by an intense pressure welling up from deep in his imagination; and the effect is not one of rational exposition but of visionary discovery or revelation.

The notion of allegory as a mode of 'discovery' is of a piece with our general sense of *Piers Plowman* as a spiritual and artistic 'adventure' into uncharted, and dangerous, terrain. Nowhere is this truer than with its most original creation, Piers himself. He is by stages literal, symbolic, and figural. He embodies (if he does not 'personify') charity, a quality which is never personified like Patience, say, but is 'recognized' in the Samaritan, who figures, in different ways, both Christ and Piers. It makes sense also of the Tree of

Charity, an image as strange as it is rich. The tree's 'fruits' include Abraham, who elsewhere symbolizes faith and is unable to help the wounded man (sinful humanity) as can the Samaritan, an 'embodiment' of the virtue charity. Here, though, we need to think of Abraham not as an exemplar but as an *object* of charity (God's love). Simultaneously, in the image of the *levels* of the tree's fruits, ripeness (which depends on closeness to the sun) symbolizes holiness, and the sun's warmth, grace. Piers and the Tree can be hard to interpret, by comparison with the personified ideas and their actions; but their imaginative power more than makes up for any obscurity at the rational plane, and they are deeply characteristic of Langland's way of thinking.

Under the most confusing dream-experiences there lies, for Langland, a sense of all things being connected by hidden links, and allegory is as much concerned to recover old, lost meanings as to discover or create new ones. A bold instance is a moment which stands out by its incongruity and violence from the calmly expository manner of the surrounding context, the elaborate 'hand' and 'torch' parallels for the Trinity. Thus, in speaking of Christ's passion as bringing healing through the sacraments that flow from it, the Samaritan uses cannibalistic images associated with Satanic rites of child-murder and diabolic baptism. Here, with extraordinary force, the evil that Christ's passion aims to vanquish itself provides a 'vehicle' for the doctrine of the real efficacy of baptism, penance, and the Eucharist, which forms the bedrock of the poet's entire faith.

To the Middle Ages, the sacraments were much more than 'images with meaning'; they were regarded as 'outward signs' of an 'inward grace'. But there is a wider sense of 'sacramental', that developed by David Jones in his essay 'Art and Sacrament', which is highly illuminating for *Piers Plowman*. Jones sees *all* art as a 'sign-making' (or 'sacramental') activity based on man's very nature as evidenced from earliest palaeolithic times. The general religious and the specific Christian sense of 'sacrament' are developments that presuppose this common, much older understanding.[22] Langland is a poet who not only

---

[22] In *Epoch and Artist* (London, 1959), 143–179, esp. 155, 161.

deals with the Christian Sacraments but thinks sacramentally about the most elemental objects and events we experience—water, fire, and light, tempest and drought, the animal and vegetable creation. Like Alan of Lille, he sees in *omnis mundi creatura*, 'every created thing in the universe', a *fidele signaculum* or 'trustworthy vehicle' of meaning applicable to all aspects of 'our life, death, condition and end'.[23] Without denying that 'everything is itself and not another thing', the view of common sense, this approach also finds in the material creation an uncreated reality to which 'things', properly interpreted, can guide us. Against such a background of thought, preserved in the clerkly culture from Augustine onwards, Langland can see in his tower, ditch, and field (all potential features of an actual English landscape) *meanings* such as heaven, hell, and earth, 'beatitude', 'sinfulness', and 'temporal existence'.

A striking illustration of the 'sacramental' idea is the tempest that, Reason says in his sermon, up-ended great trees *in tokenynge of drede*. This phrase is rendered 'as a fearful presage' in context, but the original has a richer and less explicit sense. For the storm is not merely a natural phenomenon sent by God to warn; its form and action signify his angry breath (the force which, elsewhere, is the Pentecostal Spirit's breath of life), and also his angry *word* (the 'Z'-text states, 'Word is but wind'). In the light of the Samaritan's statement that the Trinity 'hold the whole wide universe in themselves' (p. 203), everything can signify, nothing is meaningless. The disorder that is sin lies, in a sense, in the mis-assignation of *names*. This begins with Lucifer, who sees himself as the origin, not just the bearer, of light, and so falls from heaven 'into the dark depths of hell'; here his name becomes a lie, not the vehicle of 'true' meaning. For man, the storm that recalls the disruption of order through Lucifer's act of pride is a genuine *signaculum nostrae sortis*, a 'tokening' or sacramental sign: the trees' upturned roots reveal how man will lose his nourishment and die if he inverts spiritual values through his sins.

[23] Alan of Lille, *Omnis mundi creatura*, in F. J. E. Raby (ed.), *The Oxford Book of Medieval Latin Verse* (Oxford, 1959), no. 242.

For Langland, spiritual evil (sin) threatens to drain *meaning* from creation, producing a 'darkness' in which nothing can signify, because nothing can be distinguished. Sin is *unkynde*, 'against the nature of things', as is clear from images like the dirt on Haukin's coat, the vomit of Glutton that repels the starving dog, the poisonous 'medicine' of the Devil (the 'doctor of death', as Christ calls him). Langland sees the purpose of life as a movement towards the brightness and warmth that properly figure Truth and Love, his joint synonyms for God. The aim of both wisdom and art, therefore, is to affirm the *signacula* so that inner and outer correspond, face reveals heart, and existence is a showing-forth of essence. The special evil of hypocrisy is its betrayal of Truth, and this vice is worst of all in clerks, because they are the custodians of speech, the 'plant that springs from grace, God's minstrel, heaven's proper pastime' (p. 90).

Underlying Langland's clerkly culture, then, is a much more primitive apprehension of the elements of experience. Darkness, cold, blood, fire, wind are all 'natural signs' of non-material realities—evil, love and its cost, power, and grace. To enter Langland's world we need, even more than a knowledge of his reading, a capacity to 'read' the entire world as a 'book of signs'. The prime difficulty his art poses results from our having lost the sacramental vision. Thus, what came relatively easily to his original readers may seem to us laboured and obscure at times. But what has been lost *can* be rediscovered, as writers like David Jones and T. S. Eliot have shown in our own time. Langland's first audience had a familiarity with breviary, Bible, and liturgy which many modern readers may have to acquire for the first time through reading Langland's poem. But the full intensity of his sacramental vision would probably have come as a revelation to them as much as to us. They, too, would have been as startled as we are by that 'voice loud in a light' uttering 'breath' that bursts hell's bars asunder. The poet's 'word' may well be 'but wind'; but this Introduction and the translation that follows have been done in the belief that *Piers Plowman* still continues to blow strong and fresh.

TRANSLATOR'S NOTE

I have based this translation on the new revised text of my Everyman critical edition, *The Vision of Piers Plowman*, the text which will appear in future printings of that book and in the Parallel-Text edition of the poem to be published by Longman. No mention has usually been made in my notes of the many corrupt and uncertain readings in the B-text, but where I have tried to bring out both of two alternative readings I have drawn attention to the fact.

Translating Langland's vision into what Auden calls 'the vulgar lingo | Of armed cities'[1] has been a challenging task, not least because the Middle English original was itself a 'vulgar lingo' of extraordinary variety and resource, generously laced with Latin phrases and quotations. A longish example of Langland's verse at its most linguistically exuberant is given in the Appendix, an extract from the celebrated Harrowing of Hell scene. But a couple of short examples here may suffice to illustrate the virtual impossibility of doing justice to the original when the meaning depends on word-play in two languages at once. At the opening of Passus XIII, Langland describes how the gluttonous Doctor of Divinity and his man eat expensive foods provided by wrongdoers. This, he says, is something they will pay for by being punished in the next life:

> Ac hir sauce was over sour and unsavoury grounde
> In a morter, *Post mortem*, of many bitter peyne . . .

> (XIII. 42–3)

In my translation I have been able to keep the trans-linguistic word-play only by retaining the Latin phrase *post mortem*; this I could do because it is still current in English, though now largely in a specialized medical sense ('examination of a body

---

[1] From 'The Age of Anxiety', in *Collected Poems* (London, 1976), 373.

after death'). But a few lines further on there comes something altogether harder to render:

> And siththe he drough us drynke: '*Dia perseverans*—
> As longe', quod he, 'as lif and lycame may dure.'
>   (XIII. 49–50).

This I have translated (p. 138) as:

And then he poured us something to drink: 'This is a medicinal draught of perseverance; it will work', he ended, 'as long as life and limb hold up.'

What has been lost here is the pun on two Latin words, *dia* 'a drug' and *diu* 'long', and with it something of Langland's point that the effects of the virtue of patience upon the soul are like those of a 'long-lasting medicinal potion,' just as the two words are alike. I could not keep *dia* because it is no longer familiar in current English, as it apparently was in Middle English.

My approach has been a very simple one. Recognizing that alliterative poetry is a highly formal art, with a dense texture that cannot be reproduced with naturalness in contemporary prose, I have confined myself to translating *what* Langland says and have not felt obliged to retain the *way* in which he says it (although I have sometimes done so when I could find no other form of words). It is therefore a 'free' translation that I offer, true (I hope) to Langland's meaning, tone, and general stylistic register in the context, but often nearer to a paraphrase than a gloss. As such, it complements the Everyman edition's more literal footnote translations, and should be a stimulus to students interested in the problems of translating a text written in an earlier stage of our own language. The present translation will benefit from being read aloud, as I have tried to write for the ears as well as the eyes.

The notes are copious, and include not only explanations of facts and ideas likely to be unfamiliar to a modern reader, but also biblical sources and a good deal of cross-reference, making it possible to follow up a particular theme. They add up to something like a continuous commentary on the work and are designed, with the Introduction, to make the text as accessible as possible without misrepresenting its complexity and depth.

I am grateful to Messrs Weidenfeld and Nicolson and to Longman for generous permission to translate the B-text for the World's Classics. I hope this translation will encourage a wider audience to go on to read the original.

A CHRONOLOGY OF *PIERS PLOWMAN*

1381   Peasants' Revolt

1384   d. Wyclif

c.1385/6   *Piers Plowman* (C-text)

1386   Richard's ministers impeached

c.1386   Chaucer's *Troilus and Criseyde*; ? d. Langland

1387   Chaucer's *Canterbury Tales* begun

1388   Merciless Parliament; Scots defeat English at Otterburn

1389   Richard's resumption of rule; d. John of Gaunt

1390   Gower's *Confessio Amantis*; Wycliffite Bible; ? *Pearl*

1392   Julian's *Revelations*

1399   Deposition and murder of Richard II; Henry IV king

1400   d. Chaucer

SELECT BIBLIOGRAPHY

TEXTS

J. A. W. Bennett (ed.), *Piers Plowman: B-text, Prologue and Passus I–VII* (Oxford, 1972).

G. Kane (ed.) *Piers Plowman: the A-Version* (London and Los Angeles, 2nd edn., 1988).

G. Kane and E. T. Donaldson (eds.), *Piers Plowman: the B-Version* (London and Los Angeles, 2nd edn., 1988).

Derek Pearsall (ed.), *Piers Plowman: the C-text* (London, 1978).

A. G. Rigg and C. Brewer (eds.), *Piers Plowman: the Z Version* (Toronto, 1983).

A. V. C. Schmidt (ed.), *The Vision of Piers Plowman: the B-text* (London, 1978; rev. edn., 1987).

W. W. Skeat (ed.), *Piers Plowman: Parallel-text Edition* (Oxford, 1886).

TRANSLATION

J. F. Goodridge, *Piers the Ploughman* (Harmondsworth, 2nd edn., 1966).

CRITICISM

J. A. W. Bennett (ed. Gray), *Middle English Literature* (Oxford, 1986).

J. A. Burrow, *Ricardian Poetry* (London, 1971).

B. Ford (ed.), *Medieval Literature: Chaucer and the Alliterative Tradition* (Harmondsworth, 1982).

R. W. Frank, *Piers Plowman and the Scheme of Salvation* (New Haven, 1957).

M. Godden, *The Making of Piers Plowman* (London, 1990).

E. Salter, *Piers Plowman: an Introduction* (Oxford, 1962).

A. V. C. Schmidt, *The Clerkly Maker: Langland's Poetic Art* (Cambridge, 1987).

J. Simpson, *Piers Plowman: an Introduction to the B-text* (London, 1990).

A. C. Spearing, *Medieval Dream Poetry* (Cambridge, 1976).

M. Stokes, *Justice and Mercy in Piers Plowman* (London, 1984).

BACKGROUND AND REFERENCE

Holy Bible: Douay-Rheims Version (London, *CTS*, 1956).

A. Colunga and L. Turrado (eds.), *Biblia Vulgata* (Madrid, 1965).

M. Haren, *Medieval Thought: the Western Intellectual Tradition from Antiquity to the Thirteenth Century* (London, 1985).

M. Keen, *The Pelican History of Medieval Europe* (Harmondsworth, 1975).

G. Leff, *Medieval Thought: St Augustine to Ockham* (Harmondsworth, 1958).

F. Procter and C. Wordsworth (eds.), *Breviarium ad Usum Insignis Ecclesiae Sarum* (Cambridge, 1879–86).

Piers Plowman

VISION ONE

PROLOGUE

One summer time, when the sun was mild, I dressed myself in sheepskin clothing, the habit of a hermit of unholy life, and wandered abroad in this world, listening out for its strange and wonderful events. But one May morning, on Malvern Hills,* out of the unknown, a marvellous thing happened to me. I was tired out after wandering astray, and I turned aside to rest under a spacious bank beside a stream. And as I lay down and leaned back, and looked at the water, I grew drowsy and fell asleep, so sweet was the music that it made.

Then there came to me an extraordinary dream. It seemed I was in an empty desert place, with no notion of where it might be. But as I gazed eastward, up on high towards the sun, I saw upon a low hill an elegantly built tower. Beneath it was a huge hollow containing a dungeon, with deep, dark ditches that struck terror into the beholder. Between them I made out a beautiful field* full of all kinds of people, humble and rich, working and wandering about as life in this world demands.

Some set themselves to the plough, rarely relaxing. They laboured strenuously at planting and sowing, and earned what rapacious men destroy with their greed. Others gave themselves to pride, donning its raiment, and stepped out in a fine fashion of deceit. Many devoted themselves to prayer and penance and lived ascetic lives for love of our Lord, in the hope of winning beatitude in the Kingdom of Heaven. These were anchorites and hermits who remain within their cells and have no itch to go straying about the land to pleasure their flesh with a life of lechery.

And some chose trade; *they* did well—to judge, at any rate, by the way they seem to prosper. And some chose to be minstrels, and earn their money by music-making—a blameless pursuit, to my mind. But as for obscene jesters with dirty mouths—those sons of Judas* dream up disgusting displays and transform themselves into fools. And yet they have sufficient good sense to hold down a proper job, if they felt like it. I don't intend to spell out here what St Paul preaches about these people: 'the fellow who utters filthy words'* is Satan's slave.

Beggars hungry for handouts bustled about eagerly until their stomachs and their scrips were stuffed to bursting. They put on quite a front to procure their victuals, and then came to blows over their beer. Dear God, they go to bed with their guts gorged, and rise up randy, those thieving guttersnipes! Their constant companions are sleep and sheer idleness.

There were pilgrims there who made vows to go on pilgrimage to the shrines of St James or the saints at Rome.* These set out on their journey full of sage speeches, and thereby earned the right to lie about it for the rest of their lives. I saw some who declared they had gone looking for 'Holy Ones', but from what they said it seemed that their tongue was tuned to untruth, not the thing it was made for. A gaggle of hermits with crooked staves set out for Walsingham,* with their whores behind them. Great strapping layabouts, foes of a fair day's work, dressed up in copes to look different from the rest, and, hey presto! they've become hermits—gentlemen of leisure.

I found there all four orders of friars* preaching to the people for the benefit of their bellies. They interpreted the Gospel as it fitted their book, reading into it whatever meaning they fancied, in their greed for smart clothes. Many of these masters can afford to dress as they please because their costs and their earnings fit like hand in glove. Now, since Charity's turned trader and heads the queue for hearing noblemen's confessions, many untoward things have happened in the last few years. Unless the friars and the Church can improve their relations, a terrible calamity will soon hang over our heads.

There was a pardoner* preaching there, for all the world as if he were a priest. He produced an indulgence covered with episcopal authorizations, and said that he himself had the power to absolve all and sundry who had failed to observe their fasting-penances, or had broken solemn vows. The ignorant put their full trust in him (*they* liked what he said!) and came up to him on their knees to kiss his bull. He gave them a sharp tap with his mandate and made their eyes water; and with that roll of indented parchment he netted a haul of rings and brooches. This, good people, is how you lay out your cash—to support gluttonous skivers. You hand it to layabouts who toss it to their tarts. Now, if the bishop were a man of God (and if he had a decent pair of ears!), his seal would not be at the service of men who con ordinary people. But the *bishop* doesn't intend this—that charlatans should go about as preachers. No, it's the parish priest who splits the silver with the pardoner—money that would reach the poor of the parish, if it wasn't for the pair of them.

Rectors and vicars were there, complaining to their bishops that their parishes had been destitute since the time of the plague.* They asked for special permission to reside in London and sing mass there to a more profitable tune—the sweet sound of silver. Bishops were there too, and learned clergy—bachelors, masters, and doctors of divinity—men who hold a responsibility under Christ and are crowned with the tonsure as a symbol of their duties towards their people: hearing their confessions, preaching to them, praying for them, feeding the poor among them. In Lent* and at other seasons these, too, settle their haunches in the capital. Some become royal servants and keep account of the King's monies; some handle the crown's claims for payments overdue to the Exchequer or the Chancery, raking in the royal advantage from guardianship-cases, ward-meetings, bits of lost property, waifs and strays. Other clerics take service with the nobility and discharge the functions of stewards, passing judgements in the manorial courts. But their religious duties of saying mass, matins, and the canonical hours are carried out gracelessly, so that I fear that day when the final grand sessions* is held. What a heavy sentence Christ will pass upon the whole pack of them!

I had a glimpse of the power entrusted to St Peter—the power 'to bind and unbind',* in the phrase of Scripture. I saw how he bequeathed it, in a spirit of love, as Christ commanded, to the keeping of the four Cardinal Virtues,* which are so called because their 'virtue' is pre-eminent. They are gates that close and open the entrance-way to Christ's Kingdom, letting in those who possess them, and keeping out those who do not. But as for the cardinals at the papal court who have assumed that name, and presumed with it the power to make a pope possessor of St Peter's powers* . . . well, I shan't set about questioning them! Electing the Pope belongs (does it not?) to those endowed with love and learning; for which reason I can—I mean can't—say more about *courts*.

Next there came a king. Knighthood preceded him, the power of the Commons established him as ruler. And then Kind Wit* came, and he created the order of clerks, the men of learning, to act as royal counsellors and to protect the common interest. The King, together with knights and clerks, arranged it so that the common people would provide their living for them. The Commons, then, through the agency of Kind Wit, developed skills and crafts; for everyone's benefit they established ploughmen, whose task was to till the earth, labouring in a life according with the demands of truth and honesty. The three of them, King, Commons, and Kind Wit, brought into being law and justice—the principle of 'each to his own; to each his own'.*

At that point a mad fellow, a scrawny-looking creature, looked up, and said to the king, kneeling and speaking in clerkly phrase: 'May Christ watch over you and your realm, Sire! May he grant you the power to rule your land so that just men and Justice itself will smile on you. And may you receive your reward in Heaven for ruling justly!' Whereupon, from high up in the sky—from Heaven—an angel descended and spoke. What he said was in Latin, because the uneducated common people lacked the capacity to dispute and distinguish one argument from another in vindicating their claims. Theirs is to suffer, theirs is to serve! For which reason, the angel said:

'You say, "I am king, I am prince". That is a thing
Tomorrow may take away. You who hold sway

Over the law sublime of Christ the King,
The better to do what you must, be holy, be just!
Clothe naked statute with love's soft array:
Your harvest will abound where the grain's sound.
Strip justice bare, and God will judge you barely;
Sow goodness, and He'll pay your wages fairly.'*

Then one of those scurrilous clerkly buffoons, a goliard,* a vomiter of verbiage, grew hot under his collar and shouted up at the angel:

'The name *rex* comes from *regere*, a verb which means "to rule":
Who scorns the law lacks rule; call him not king but fool!'

Whereupon the Commons as a whole proceeded to chorus a verse of Latin before the King's Council (interpret it as you will):

Precepta Regis sunt nobis vincula legis![1]*

And in a trice a bevy of rats and small mice came running out,* more than a thousand of them: they were assembling to discuss a matter of concern to them all. There was a cat at court who used to come when he pleased and pounce on them, seize them at will, and play a deadly game, tossing them about with his paws.

'We are in such a panic', they said, 'that we hardly dare peep about in any direction! And if we utter a protest at his little games, he'll make us feel his displeasure. He'll scratch us, he'll claw us, he'll hold us tight in his clutches, so that by the time he drops us, we'll be past caring whether we're dead or alive. If only we could hit on some plan for resisting his little tyrannies, then life would be worth living again. It would feel as if we were all lords!'

A rat of some repute, with a persuasive tongue, proposed a perfect solution to their problem. This was his speech:

---

[1] 'The bidding of a king has the binding-force of law.'

'In the City of London', he said, 'I've seen people who wear
shining necklaces and cunningly fashioned collars around
their necks. They wander about without a leash over the
warrens and open spaces—wherever they like in the world, as
far as I can see. Dear Christ! It strikes me, that if bells were to
be attached to their necklaces, people could know which way
they were heading and show them a clean pair of heels! Now',
said the rat, 'that is exactly why common sense dictates *we*
buy a bell, made of brass or bright silver, fasten it to a
collar—we'll all stand to gain by it—and hang it around the
cat's neck! Then we'll be able to know whether he's going
riding, or at rest, or taking his pleasure out of doors. If it suits
his mood to be playing games, we can have a look, and show
up before him while he's minded to play; and if he's in a bad
temper, we can be on our guard and keep well out of his way.'

The whole crowd of rats were in favour of this line of
argument. But when the bell was procured and hung on the
necklace, there wasn't a rodent among them, if you had given
him the whole of France for it, or all England as a prize, who
had the courage to tie the bell around the cat's neck. They
realized they were not bold enough for the task, and their
stratagem was a miserable failure, all their effort and lengthy
deliberation so much labour lost.

A mouse, who seemed to me to have very good sense, went
up firmly before them with a frown, and delivered these
words:

'Even if we were to *kill* the cat, another one would appear
and scratch the lot of us, though we crept under the benches.
This is why my advice is, to leave the cat alone. Let's never
be so rash as to produce the bell before his eyes. As long as
he's busy catching rabbits or feeding on venison, he won't
want *our* carcasses. Let's never do anything that might offend
his dignity. A small nuisance is preferable to an injury with
long-term consequences. And even if we got rid of one
individual enemy, we'd still have a general worry remaining to
us. Look, I recall hearing my father tell me seven years ago,
"It's a pretty miserable kind of court where the cat is a
kitten." Scripture, if you care to read it, would support him
there: "Woe to the land where the king is a child!"* You see,

the rats would become so active by night that no one would get a wink; we mice, for our part, would consume all the malt, while you rats would chew up people's clothes—if it were not for the fear we have of that court cat making a sudden pounce. You rats, if you had the chance, would have no idea how to govern yourselves.

'As far as I'm concerned', said the mouse, 'I foresee such ill consequences that I'm resolved against provoking either the cat or the kitten. I'm opposed to all discussion of this collar, which *I* never contributed to buying (though if I had I wouldn't let it be known). I'd rather put up with what he wants, and do as he pleases. Let the pair of them go freely, with or without a leash, and hunt where they like. To every sensible man here present, my warning is: stick to your own business!'

What this dream means, good people, I'd rather leave to you to interpret. God knows, *I* don't dare to!

And so, up came a hundred senior barristers-at-law wearing silk coifs. They pleaded their cases for fees small and large, but wouldn't open their lips once for pure charity's sake. You'd have more chance of measuring the mist upon the Malvern Hills than of getting so much as 'Hmm—er . . .' out of them, without first putting cash down for it.

In that crowd I saw, as I'll tell you in a moment, noblemen, citizens, and serfs, too. There were bakers, brewers, and butchers a-plenty; weavers of wool and of linen; tailors, tinkers, and market-toll collectors; builders, miners, and various other skilled men. Every kind of labourer came bustling forth—navvies and ditch-diggers who do a bad job of work and spend the whole day singing 'God bless Mistress Emma!'* There were cooks and their serving-men who shouted, 'Hot pies, hot pies! Lovely geese! Juicy pork! Come and eat, come on!' The same tune was taken up by the publicans: 'White wine from Alsace! Wine from Gascony! Rhine wines!* Wine from La Rochelle!* Just right to help you digest your roast!'

All this I saw in my sleep, and much, much more.

I shall now explain to you clearly what all this means—the mountain, the dark valley, and the field filled with people. A lady with a beautiful face,* clothed in a linen dress, came down from the castle and called me in gracious tones: 'Son', she said, 'are you asleep? Do you see how busy these people are, wandering about in their maze of concerns? The majority of those who live out their lives on this earth desire nothing better than worldly success and esteem. The only heaven they can be bothered about is a heaven on earth!'

Beautiful as she was, the expression on her face cowed me; and so I said: 'Lady, forgive me, but what does all this signify?'

'The tower on the hill', she replied, 'is where Truth* lives. What he wants is for you to do as his word teaches. He is the Father of Faith, the one who created every hair upon your bodies and the features of every one of your faces. He provided you with five senses, to use in his honour throughout the days of your life. For that purpose he commanded the earth to sustain every one of you—with wool, with linen, and with enough of everything to enable you to live a decent human life. Out of his bounteous kindness, he willed that three things should be provided for all to share in common.* Apart from these three, nothing else is strictly necessary. I am going to go through them in order, and you can repeat to yourself what I shall say.

'The first thing is clothing, to protect you from the cold. Next, food for you to eat, to prevent you suffering from hunger. And then, drink when your throat is dry—but you mustn't indulge in it to excess, so that you end up unable to work when you have to! Think of what happened to Lot on one occasion because he was too fond of drink.* He did something with his daughters that brought much pleasure to the Devil. In taking the kind of pleasure in drink that Satan desired, Lot also took to lechery. He had sex with both his daughters, and he blamed that abomination on the wine, nothing but the wine! The Book of Genesis records what they said: "Let's get our father drunk on wine, sleep with him, and so get him to make us pregnant." Yes, Lot was brought low by wine and women, and in that sorry state he fathered offspring who turned out evil.

'So—go wary of the pleasures of drink, and you'll live a much better life if you do so. Though what you long for is another, and another, it's drinking just enough that will prove the real remedy.* Not everything that your belly craves is good for your spiritual part; nor are things that satisfy the soul necessarily beneficial to your bodily nature. But don't believe what your body tells you! Isn't its own teacher totally untrustworthy? I mean that wretch the world, whose desire is to undo you. Bringing up the rear is the Devil, hand in glove with your own fleshly nature.* Your soul takes cognizance of this, and whispers a message to you in your heart.* I am giving you the soundest advice there is. And why? In order to put you on your guard.'

'And I'm deeply in your debt for it, my lady', I answered. 'What you have been saying falls on my ears like music. But now, tell me. This worldly wealth that people hang on to so tight—who in reality does it all belong to?'

'Go to the Gospel', she said. 'Turn up what God himself said on the subject, when some people brought a penny and questioned him in the Temple. They were asking him whether they might use it to pay divine honour to the emperor. But God put a question to them in return. Who did the inscription on the coin refer to,* and whose likeness was to be seen there? "Why, Caesar", they declared, "that's clear enough to us all." "Then give Caesar", God replied, "What belongs to Caesar, and give to God whatever belongs to God. Do anything else, and what you do will be wrong."

'Don't you see, what should properly govern your life is Reason? And Kind Wit, your natural understanding, should act as the custodian and supervisor of the wealth that is yours. Let him be the one who gives it to you as you need it. Thrift, after all, is Kind Wit's closest comrade.'

Then, invoking the name of her Creator, I courteously put to her another question. 'That dungeon down in the valley', I said, 'which strikes terror in the beholder—what can it possibly mean, my lady? I beg you now, please tell me.'

'That is the Castle of Misery', she replied. 'Whoever enters
it may curse the day he came into existence as a creature with
a body and a soul. In it there dwells a being whose name is
Wrong.* He is the father of lies and it is he who built the
castle. It was he who incited Adam and Eve to do what was
evil, and he who put it into the mind of Cain to take his
brother's life. He it was who undid Judas by means of money
paid by the Jews—he, too, who finished him off by hanging
him on an elder tree.* It is he who stands as a stumbling-
block in love's way, and he who utters falsehood in people's
ears. And it is those who place their trust in his reward that
are the first to feel his treachery!'

At this I began to wonder within myself: who could this
woman be, that she knew how to expound Scripture so
wisely? So I adjured her in the name of Almighty God, to tell
me truly, before she left me: who was it that gave me such
valuable counsel?

'I am Holy Church', she answered. 'Surely you recognize
me? It was I who received you from earliest days and
instructed you in the faith. And you for your part gave me an
undertaking to carry out my bidding, and to love me loyally
all the days of your life.'

At this, I fell to my knees and begged her forgiveness. In a
reverent tone I entreated her to pray for my sins, and to teach
me the true path of Christian faith, so that I might do the will
of the one who had made me what I was, a living human
being. 'Do not show me the way that leads to treasure!' I
exclaimed, 'but tell me one thing only. You are called
"Holy"; tell me how to save my soul.'

'When every treasure has been put to the test,' she
answered, 'the best one will prove to be Truth. I base my
assertion on what the Bible itself declares: *God is Love.** And
Truth is of no less a price than God Himself, whose love-gift
it is. A man who possesses a truthful tongue—who speaks the
truth and who lives the truth, intending evil to no one—such
a man, the Gospel assures us, is no less than a god in the sight
of men and angels. According to St Luke, he is the image of
our Lord. The learned, who are aware of this, should make it
known to the world, for everyone—Christians and non-
Christians alike—lays claim to possession of "truth".

'Kings and knights, without question, should act to protect truth—by riding abroad and suppressing wrongdoing throughout their domains. They should arrest lawbreakers and imprison them securely, until truth has passed final judgement on their offence. King David, in his day, set up an order of knights, making them swear on their swords to serve truth at all times. And that, plainly, is the special responsibility of a knight, not to fast on Friday for a century-long stint, but to support every man and woman who stands up for truth and honesty, and never to abandon them for love or for money. Any knight who falls foul of either is guilty of an act of apostasy against the very order of knighthood.*

'Christ, however, who is the King of kings, created ten orders of knights. These were the Cherubim, the Seraphim, and another eight more like them. It pleased his sovereign majesty to entrust authority to them, making them archangels over his other hosts of lower rank. Through the working of the Trinity, these were instructed to know truth and obey his bidding; nothing else at all were they commanded. Lucifer, along with the legions under him, acquired knowledge of the truth in Heaven; and he stood second to our Lord alone in beauty—until he broke his vow of obedience. Then he forfeited his condition of blessedness, and took on the likeness of a devilish being, and fell from the heavenly company into the dark depths of Hell, to abide there for all eternity. With him were flung out countless myriads more, transformed into hideous shapes for putting their trust in Lucifer's lying words:

> I shall set my foot in the region of the North,
> And as the peer of God shall I march forth!*

No heaven was able to hold angels whose hopes lay with this claim. But they fell in the likeness of devils, for the space of nine whole days. Then at the last God saw fit to shut the gates of Heaven, put an end to the tumult, and make everything tranquil once again.

'But those evil creatures who had been cast out carried on falling in the strangest way—some through the airy regions, others down to the earth, and some into the deep recess of Hell. But lower than all the rest of them lies Lucifer; and

because of the pride that puffed him up, his punishment will
have no end. Everyone, likewise, who spends his life in
wrongdoing, will go when he dies and harbour with the Evil
One. But those who act rightly, as the Scripture says, those
who end their days in truth (which, as I said before, is the
best of all things), may be certain that their souls will go to
Heaven. And there Truth, in the person of the Blessed
Trinity, will set up each one of them on a throne of glory.
That is why I say again what I said before, when I referred to
this text: when *every* treasure has been assayed, Truth will
emerge supreme. Teach this doctrine to the ignorant, for the
educated already know it: Truth is the rarest treasure on all
the earth!'

'But I have no real inward understanding of all this', I
replied. 'You will have to instruct me further. Through which
of my bodily faculties does truth arise? And where?'

'Idiot!' she exclaimed. 'Fool! What a dullard you are! You
didn't absorb much Latin when you were a lad, did you?

> Too little I sought truth
> While yet I had my youth.*

Truth is a kind of instinctive understanding located in the
very depths of your heart. It teaches you to love the Lord
your God more than your very self, and never to commit a
mortal sin, even at the cost of your own life. This, I believe, is
truth. If anyone else can teach you better, make sure you let
him have his say, and take the lesson to heart. That is how
God's word bears witness to the truth; your part is to act in
accordance with it.

'You see, Truth tells us that love is a heavenly salve: no sin
is visible in one who relies on that rare condiment. Truth
performed every act of his through love, as was his will. He
taught Moses that love was the most precious thing there was,
and the most heavenly—the plant of peace, most valuable of
all virtues.* Heaven could not hold love in, it had grown so
heavy, until at last it ate its fill of the earth. And when it had
assumed an earthly body of flesh and blood, no leaf on a lime
tree could have been lighter, no needle more delicately poised

and penetrating—so that nothing at all could bar its way, neither coat of armour nor lofty walls.

'This is why Love is the leader of God's heavenly people; and Love is a mediator, too, like a mayor between the king and the common people. Yes, in this way, Love is a leader and determines the working of the law, imposing penalties on human beings when they act wrongfully. You want a direct understanding of what it is? It originates, then, through the action of God's power, and its ultimate source, its deepest springing-place, is within the human heart. In that instinctive understanding hidden within the heart, a power stirs into life. This is the special province of God the Father; he created us all, looked lovingly upon us, and allowed his own Son to die in humble submission for our sins, in order to reconcile us all. He, the Son, for his part, harboured no ill-will against his torturers; no, instead he humbly opened his lips, beseeching God to be merciful and take pity on those who tortured him to death.

'Here, in him, you can see for yourself an example without any parallel. He was at once all-powerful and utterly humble, proffering mercy to those who hung him high upon the cross and pierced him through the heart. That is why I counsel those of you who are rich, to have pity upon the poor. Though power and influence in the law-courts may be yours, always act with humility. For when you leave this earthly existence, you will be weighed by the same standard you used here*—whether it was just or unjust. You may be someone who speaks the truth and turns an honest penny; you may be as chaste as a baby that cries in church; but unless you really love, and give to the poor a goodly share of the goods that God sends you, you derive no more credit from attending mass and saying the Offices than Ugly Anna from keeping her virginity, when nobody wants to take it!

'Good St James has laid it down in his letter:* without actions religion is worth absolutely nothing. It's as dead as a doornail without deeds to drive it home! "Faith without works is dead". Chastity, likewise, without charity, will end up shackled in Hell; it's utterly useless, like a lamp in which there's no light.

'Many priests are chaste enough, and yet totally lacking in love. In fact, when they get on in the world, there's *no-one* tighter-fisted than the clergy! They can be thoroughly unkind to their own relations, as well as to Christian people in general. They gobble up their "charity", then fight and squabble for more. Their kind of loveless chastity is sure to end up fettered fast in Hell! Any number of parish priests keep themselves chaste—physically. Yet they lie firmly under the thumb of greed; lust for possession has grasped them in so tight a grip it has left not a chink through which they can poke their heads. That's not the faith that comes to us from the Trinity; it's the falsity whose proper place is Hell! And the lesson such behaviour teaches the laity is this: don't you be in any great hurry to give! But just consider what words are written in the Gospel: *"Give"*, says God, *"and it shall be given to you*; for I am the giver of all. Giving is the key to the lock upon love's door, through which my grace finds passage, bringing consolation to anxious souls who are burdened down by their sins."

'Yes, Love is the physician who brings life. It stands closer than any other to God Himself. It is the one direct straight road to heaven. And so I say what I said to you before; look at the text exactly as it stands:

> When every treasure undergoes the test,
> Truth and Truth alone remains the best.

'Well, I have now told you what truth is: that *no* treasure in the world is better than Truth. Now I cannot stay with you any longer. May God be with you now as your protector!'

I remained on bended knees, and begged a favour of her.
'Please, my lady', I said, 'for the love of Mary in Heaven,
mother of that blessed Child who redeemed us on the Cross:
teach me some way by which I can recognize what is false.'

'Look on your left hand',* she said, 'and there they stand:
Falsity, and with him Deceit, and their whole gang of
cronies!'

I looked towards my left, as the lady had told me to; and
what I saw there was a woman. She was dressed in a
magnificent robe* trimmed with the choicest fur you could
find, and on her head she was wearing a diadem as splendid as
the King's. The fingers of this lady were elegantly circled with
delicate gold rings; these were inset with rubies as red as
glowing coals, with diamonds of the first water, with oriental
sapphires and sapphires coloured like sea-water, gems that
possess the power to vanquish poisons. Her dress was made of
rich, deeply tinctured scarlet cloth, adorned with ribbon-
ornaments of burnished gold, and costly jewels. The sight of
her raiment took my breath away; never had I set eyes upon
such opulence. Marvelling who she might be, I asked myself,
whose wife have we here?

'This woman wearing such splendid array', I exclaimed,
'who is it?'

'That', replied the lady, 'is Mademoiselle Meed;* and she is
someone who has done me a great deal of harm! She has
spoken scandal about my lover Fidelity and told lies about
him to powerful noblemen who are responsible for
administering the laws. In the Pope's palace she moves about
as freely as I do myself; yet if the truth were known, this
would not happen. Why, she's a bastard! Her father is
Falsity,* whose treacherous tongue has never uttered a true
word since the day he arrived on this earth. Meed, as you
would expect, takes after him: "Like father, like child"; "it
takes a good tree to bring forth good fruit".*

'By rights, I ought to take precedence over her, since I
come of better stock. *My* father is Almighty God Himself, the

source of every grace, the eternal and uncreated lord of all. I
am his gracious daughter, and he has given me Mercy as my
spouse.* *Everyone* who shows mercy, and loves me faithfully,
will be my husband, and I shall be his beloved in Heaven
above. As for anyone who accepts Meed, I wager my life that
he will forfeit *Caritas*,* if he gives his love over to her. What
is it that King David says about the fates of different kinds of
men—those who manipulate Meed, and those who take their
stand by Truth? How does he say you are to be saved? Think
about the testimony of the Psalms: "Lord, who shall dwell in
your tents, or rest in your holy mountain?"*

'And now this Meed is about to marry a damnable villain
called False Fickle-tongue, the offspring of Satan himself.
Thanks to his winning rhetoric, Deceit has bewitched all and
sundry; and it's entirely through Liar's machinations that this
young woman is due to be given in such a union. If you want,
that's where you can find out who they all are—the lesser and
the greater rogues who make up her retinue. Get to know who
they are, if you possibly can; but keep careful guard against
the whole pack of them. Don't attempt to criticize them; hold
on till you see the seat of justice occupied by Loyalty, backed
by plenary authority to punish these people. Then will be
time enough to bring forward your case! Now', she ended, 'I
commend you to the keeping of Christ and his Virgin Mother.
May your conscience always remain unclouded by low desire
for Meed!'

And that is how the lady left me, lying fast asleep. After
which, I went on to dream about Meed's marriage; and I saw
all the splendid retinue of those who lord it with Falsity
invited to the wedding party—every kind of person, poor and
rich, from both sides of the match. Great numbers of people
turned up for this lady's nuptials:* there were knights,
clerics, and other, ordinary folk; jurymen, summoners,
sheriffs and their clerks, beadles, bailiffs, retailers, purveyors,
provisioners, and ecclesiastical lawyers. I cannot begin to
enumerate all the crowds who thronged about Meed; but her
closest companions, I perceived, were Simony* and Civil
Law. It fell to Deceit to lead her forth from her chamber; and

he, as the one responsible for the match, took her on his arm to be joined in marriage with False.

When Simony and Civil Law perceived what both of them desired, they consented to say just what was wanted—for a fee. Then Liar rushed up and declared: 'Look! Here is a charter that Guile* has granted the pair of them, with a good deal of swearing of solemn oaths.' Liar asked Civil Law to cast an eye over it, and Simony to read the document through. At which, that pair got to their feet, unfolded the deed of endowment, and bellowed out at the tops of their voices as follows:

'Be it known hereby to all present and to come, et cetera, et cetera . . . Let everyone living on earth take careful note of this: *Meed* is being taken in marriage more because of her property than any good qualities she possesses, like beauty or noble blood. Falseness is keen to have her because he knows her to be rich; and Deceit, with his insidious phrases, is endowing her with the title, "Princess of Pride". She is required to treat the poor with contempt, engage in malicious and boastful gossip, bear false witness, rail, scold, utter slander, follow unruly and headstrong ways, and defiantly break every one of the Ten Commandments. We grant to the pair of them the joint Earldom of Envy-and-Anger; the Castle of Quarrels, and Tatlers' Tower; the demesne of Greed with its adjacent territories, Usury* and Avarice, together with the messuages of Wheeling-and-Dealing, Middleman Heights, and Burglarsville for good measure. To which may be added the extensive properties of Lust-in-Action: these include deeds, words, provocative looks, clothes, desires, and erotic imaginings that have to suffice when the itch is on but you cannot manage to get the thing up.'

They gave them Gluttony, and blasphemous words—the chance to drink all day long in one tavern after another, the fitting place in which to talk filth and do down one's fellow Christians. They privileged them to break the fasting-day rules:* to start up at the very first opportunity, then sit and stuff till drowsiness overcame them. After which, they sink comfortably into bed and copulate like pigs, till their flesh feels smooth with the stroking of sloth and sleep. At length, when consciousness returns, a feeling of despair presses them down; all will to alter their way of life is gone, believing themselves to be lost as they now do. And that is the state they sink into at the end!

'Let them and their heirs', continued Simony and Civil Law, 'have and hold a dwelling-place with the Devil, and then be damned for ever and a day. Let them amass all the sufferings of Purgatory,* and then encounter the torments of Hell itself. In exchange for all this heritage, they are to yield up their souls to Satan at the close of a year, and then endure sorrow and punishment with him for as long as God holds sway in his Heaven.'

The first one to come and witness this charter was Wrong.* He was followed by Piers the pardoner, a member of the Pauline* persuasion; Bette, a beadle from Buckinghamshire; Reginald, a reeve from the Soke of Rutland; Munde the miller, and a number of others beside.

'In this sorry year of our liege Lord Satan', he said, 'I am sealing this deed in the presence of Master Simony, and with the full agreement of Civil Law!'

Theology,* when he heard these words, flew into a rage and exclaimed to Civil Law: 'May you be damned for setting up marriages like this, which are bound to bring down Truth's wrath! But before the business actually goes through, I hope you get what is coming to you. Meed, remember, was lawfully born: she's the offspring of Amends.* God's plan was that Meed should be given to Honesty, yet you have handed her to a lying trickster. God's curse upon you for it! Truth is aware this is not what the Scriptures say; for "The labourer is worthy of his reward".* Yet you have given that reward, Meed, to False. Shame on this law of yours! You make your living through a tissue of lies and lechery. You and Simony are undermining the Church, and along with your henchmen, the drawers-up of deeds, you've become a complete menace to the fabric of society. By God who made me, you'll both pay dearly for it!

'Why, you deceiving scoundrels, you're fully aware—only an idiot could fail to be—that False is utterly untrustworthy in everything he does; the fellow's a bastard scion of the

Devil's clan. You know, too, that Meed is legitimate, the offspring of a very good family; she is worthy to kiss the king as she might her own cousin, had she a mind to do so.

'The wise thing to do—and it's also the sensible thing—is to take her along to London, where legal cases are tried; there you can find if the law will decree they should sleep in one bed together. However, even if the court should find in favour of this marriage, you should avoid being party to the union. Truth is no fool; his bosom-counsellor is Conscience,* who is far from being a stranger to the pair of you. And should *he* find you wrongfully siding with False, things will go hard with your souls on Judgement Day!'

Civil Law was prepared to go along with this, but Simony held back until he had been paid for providing his seal and the notaries' official stamp. At this point, Deceit produced an ample supply of cash and gave instructions to Guile: 'Go and distribute gold in various places; be sure, in particular, that the notaries don't miss out! And give a big bag of florins* to False Witness, by way of a retainer; he's the one who knows how to put pressure on Meed and get her to do what I want.'

When this gold had been handed out, there were choruses of 'thank you' to False and Deceit for providing such splendid gifts. Folk came along to support False in his difficulties: 'Count on it, your honour', they declared, 'we'll never let up till Meed is your wedded wife. We'll all pool our wits to bring the matter about. We've used all our powers of cajolery to overcome her scruples, and now she's nice and willing to go up to London and see if the law will bless this happy and—we hope—long-lasting union of the two of you!'

Then False cheered up, and Deceit felt his spirits begin to revive. They started drumming up all kinds of people from the outlying districts. These they told, beggars and all, to get ready to make for Westminster to witness the business in hand. But the first requirement was horses to get them there; so Deceit procured a clutch of foals and mounted Meed on a newly shod sheriff. False got up on a juror, who trotted gently along, and Deceit set himself astride an elegantly attired flatterer. The notaries found themselves horseless, and were quite put out because Simony and Civil Law were going to

have to walk. But they said they'd be damned if they would;
let summoners be saddled to provide transport for the pair
of them! 'And let provisors* be made to act as mounts',
said Civil Law. 'Master Simony himself will sit on their
backs. Deans and sub-deans, get together! Archdeacons,*
church officers, registrars, here's cash at hand to pay for
your saddling, and then you can carry away our various
misdemeanours—divorce, adultery, and usury under the
counter. And you can pay the expenses of bishops as they ride
on their visitations. The Paulines will do for me: they're good
at handling sensitive cases in the consistory courts. Harness
the bishop's legate, let him pull our provision-cart; he can
extort supplies from the tribe of fornicators. Turn Liar into
a long vehicle to bring along all the rest, including the
confidence-tricksters and crooks who run about on their own
feet.'

This, then, is how False and Deceit set off on their journey,
with Meed in the midst of the company and the rest bringing
up their rear. But I haven't the leisure to linger over the
whole list of hangers-on, who were drawn from every level of
society; so I'll just note here that Guile rode on ahead, to
provide refreshments on the way and act as guide to them all.

Truthfulness* got a clear view of these people. He made
little comment but, spurring his horse, overtook their train
and came to court. Here he informed Conscience, who duly
reported the matter to his sovereign.

'Now, in Christ's name!' exclaimed the King,* 'if I succeed
in getting hold of False or Deceit, or any of these other
accursed malefactors, I'm going to get my revenge on the
whole gang! I'll have them hanged by the neck, and all who
abet them. No man alive will stand bail for the smallest fry
among them. No—let the great axe fall, thus, just as the law
will have it!'

With that, he issued orders to a constable, who appeared
promptly, and told him: 'Go and round up those little
Caesars. Whatever bribes or gifts they may offer', he
continued, 'my command is that Falseness be put in chains;
and as for Guile—chop off his head. Make sure he doesn't get
away! And whatever the whole gang may get up to, you are to

bring Meed here to me. If you get your hands on Liar, don't let him slip away, however loud his entreaties. Put him into the stocks! Those are my orders.'

Dread* was standing at the door, and heard this grim announcement—all the king's instructions to his constables and sergeants-at-arms to fasten False and his crew firmly in chains. Off he flew like the wind to give False warning, and urged him and his whole gang to fly, if they wanted to save their lives! Falseness took fright at this, and made a quick getaway to the friars, as did Guile, who was petrified at the prospect of death. But some merchants who met him got him to stay with them, shut up safe in their shops; to enable him to display their wares and serve their customers' needs, they dressed him up in the clothing of an apprentice.

Then Liar, too, took to his heels, furtively slinking through side-streets and alleys, jostled and pushed by the crowds. But because of his endless tale-telling, everyone gave him the cold shoulder; he was hounded out and unceremoniously ordered to pack up and go! Eventually, however, the pardoners took pity on him, and dragged the fellow into their lodging-house. They sponged him down and dried him off and gave him old jumble to wear. Then on Sundays they sent him to various churches, with seals of authorization. Here he would hand out pardons and accumulate piles of pennies that ran into several pounds.

The physicians took umbrage at this, and got in touch with him by letter, offering him a job with them as an inspector of urine-specimens. Vendors of spices had a word with Liar, too, and asked him to cast an eye over their wares; after all, he was well up in their trade, and knew all about the slimy substances they dealt with. On one occasion, some minstrels and bearers of messages came across him, and these kept him in their service for a good six months and more.

From here he was fetched by some smooth-talking friars, who fitted him up as one of their order to prevent him being recognized by visitors. For all that, he enjoys the freedom to roam about as he pleases; he is always sure of a warm welcome from them, and frequently finds his lodging in the friary.

So, the whole crowd took to their heels and disappeared from view into dark corners. With the sole exception of Mademoiselle Meed, not a single one of them dared to remain behind. And as for her, the fact is, she was quaking with apprehension; and when *she* was arrested, she wrung her hands together and burst into tears.

And now young Lady Meed, all by herself, was led into the King's presence by the beadles and bailiffs. The King summoned one of his bevy of clerks to take charge of her and see she was made comfortable. 'I intend to examine her myself', he said. 'I shall question her closely about who it is she particularly favours as her husband-to-be. If she behaves sensibly, and is happy to do what I want, I shall overlook this offence of hers, I swear to God!'

Then the King's clerk, at his master's bidding, politely offered his arm to Meed and conducted her into the royal presence-chamber. Musicians played for her delectation, and Westminster's lobbying denizens* did her honour. With smiling courtesy, some of the law-lords repaired to the room where the charming creature was lodging. With Clergy's permission, they proffered their warmest support, and said: 'No tears now, Meed! Don't be upset. We'll offer the King our advice and smooth the way for you, so you can marry whoever it is you fancy. Whatever Conscience intends to do, and whatever he thinks he can do, we'll work the matter, rest assured of it.'

At this, Meed humbly thanked them for their great kindness, and gave each of them bowls made of pure gold, silver cups, rings inset with rubies, and a variety of rich gifts. Even the most lowly of her supporters got a gold coin at least. And when these law-lords had taken their leave of Meed, learned churchmen came forward to offer her their support, too. They urged her to put on a smile, saying, 'We're on your side, Meed, your faithful followers all the days of your life!' And she for her part graciously promised she would do the same by them—love them faithfully, make lords of them all, and have them nominated to practise in the courts of the Church.

'No ignorance', she declared, 'will prevent anyone *I* favour from getting on,* since my name carries considerable weight in circles where even highly qualified clerics have to take second place.'

Then a confessor came forward, dressed in the habit of a friar.* He bowed deferentially to Meed and said to her *sotto voce*, as if they were in the confessional: 'If you had shared your bed with the simple and the subtle, or had employed Falsehood to bear up your train for the last fifty years, I wouldn't hesitate a moment in giving you absolution; provided you paid me a substantial sack-load of corn. I'd even say prayers for you, and convey your privy correspondence back and forth between clerics and knights, with the aim of getting in the way of Conscience!'

So Meed got down on her knees before this man to confess her sins, but without, I warrant you, the tiniest spark of compunction. She told him anything that came into her head, and handed him a gold noble* to act as her intercessor with God—and play the part of her pander on the side. Without delay, he gave her absolution, and after this remarked, 'We have a window being built, which is going to set us back a fairly steep sum. Now, if you were willing to provide the glass for this gable—and, of course, allow your name to be engraved on it—you could rest assured that your soul would reach heaven by that route!'*

'If I could be sure of that', answered the woman, 'there's nothing I wouldn't do for you by way of friendship, good brother. As long as *you* cast an indulgent eye on noblemen who are a little bit prone to lust,* and refrain from castigating ladies who are similarly disposed, *I'll* never let you down! After all, if you look at what the books say, lust is just a kind of physical weakness—a perfectly natural impulse, really— and we've all been created by Nature, have we not? As long as you don't end up getting a name for it, the harm itself is got over in a trice. Among the major vices, it's the one that can be most readily absolved. Look', she went on, 'you be sympathetic towards people who go in for it, and as far as I'm concerned . . . well, I'll have the roof of your friary-church repaired, the walls plastered, and the windows filled with glass; and, of course, have a stained-glass panel installed depicting the kind donor, so that all and sundry will notice I've become an honorary sister of your worthy Order!'*

(Yes; but what does *God* think of these things—inscriptions in glass that trumpet your benefactions?* God forbids all the truly virtuous to meddle with any such thing. And why? For fear pride should set up its home there, and with it, worldly minded complacency. Your inner intentions and deepest desires are as open to the eyes of God as the precise details of the cost, and the greedy self-regard that declares who financed the whole thing. So my advice to the nobility is—give up this practice of recording your benefactions in windows! Don't go touting for religious orders when you think of giving alms, in case you end up by having your reward here on earth, and with it all the heaven you'll ever get. 'Do not let your left hand know what your right hand is doing . . .'.* *That* is how the Gospel bids virtuous men to give alms.)

Accompanied by their mace-bearer, mayors now processed forth. Their office is to act as intermediaries between the king and the common people in the operation of the law. Their responsibility is to mete out the pillory and the punishment-stool to offending brewers, bakers, butchers, and cooks. These are the ones who do more harm to the poor than anyone else, since *they* have no choice but to buy their food by retail, in small amounts. Being prepared, often enough, to poison their customers, they make a fortune in retail trade* and buy themselves property from what poor people should have to fill their bellies with. For you can be certain, if the profit they made was a fair one, they would never be able to build themselves great mansions, or else get hold of tenements for renting out!

Lady Meed, however, entreated the mayor to accept cash-offerings from such traders, or, alternatively, gifts in kind, like silver vessels, rings, or other valuable items, as a consideration for supporting the retailers' cause. 'Love them all for my sake', said that lady, 'and let them have some leeway to sell their goods at inflated prices.'

Now, didn't Solomon, that prudent king, pen some instructions in former days for the guidance of mayors and those who administer the laws? This was his theme, if I may just cite the text here:

*Ignis devorabit tabernacula eorum qui libenter accipiunt munera.** This is what scholars interpret that Latin to mean: 'Fire will come down and burn to a cinder the dwelling-places of those who look for bribes, or other types of retainer, in payment for doing what is their simple duty.'

Now the King came forth from his council chamber, and asked to see Lady Meed. She was sent for immediately, and a large flock of barristers accompanied her into the royal presence with sprightly step and happy, expectant features. Then the King spoke up courteously, and this is what he said to Meed: 'Woman, you have more than once behaved unwisely; but never more so than in accepting False as a husband. However, I shall forgive this fault of yours, and grant you my royal pardon. But from this day forth, never do such a thing again, as long as you live! Now, I have a knight here with me, Conscience,* who has just come back from abroad. If he is willing to marry you, will you, on your side, be prepared to have him?'

'Oh yes, my liege', cried the lady, 'God forbid that I should refuse! If I am not one hundred per cent at your disposal, take me out and have me hanged at once!'

Thereupon, Conscience was summoned to appear before the King and his counsellors, spiritual and temporal.* Falling to his knees, he bowed before the King, and asked him what it was he wished him to do?

'Will you marry this woman', asked the King, 'if I am willing to give my assent? She, for her part, is happy to take you as her spouse.'

'In Christ's name, no!' cried Conscience to the King. 'May disaster befall me before I marry such a woman! She is quite incapable of remaining faithful; nothing she says can be trusted; and time and again she leads men into evil ways. She harms scores of people who rely on her for reward. She teaches the paths of promiscuity to wives and to widows, and gives lessons in lust to those who go for her gifts. She it was who brought about your father's fall through her hollow promises.* She has poisoned popes* and undermined Holy Church. I swear by the God who made me, you couldn't find a more accomplished bawd if you scoured the earth from end

to end. She's anyone's for the asking, the chattering little
minx! She's available as the open road to every kind of
unsavoury fellow—monks, minstrels, or lepers who lodge by
the hedgerows. Jurymen and summoners—that's the sort of
people who honour her; and county sheriffs would be
bankrupt men without her. She causes men to forfeit both
their lands and their lives. She often pays cash to get prisoners
freed, and hands over gold and silver groats* to unfetter False
from his chains and let him go scot-free. But how does she
treat an honest man, who never did anyone harm? She grabs
him hard by the hair of his head, binds him hand and foot,
and has him hanged—and all this out of sheer malice.

'She doesn't care a jot if she's condemned in the Consistory
Court. She simply produces a cope for the chief officer, and a
robe each for his clerical assistants. Absolution she can get as
and when she pleases. In the space of a single month she can
get four times as much done as can, my lord, your royal
commands sent out under your own privy seal.* She has, too,
direct access to the Pope—a fact well known to provisors
looking for livings; aren't their authorizations sealed by
Master Simony along with her good self? She's happy to
consecrate unlearned bishops, obtains advowsons for rectors,
and winks at priests who share their bed with a mistress—the
result of which is a crop of clerical bastards!

'Now, where Meed enjoys the favour of the king,* heaven
help the country! For *her* favourite is False, and the one who
gets injured is Honest Integrity. Jesus, Lord! The whole
operation of royal justice is brought to a standstill by her
precious stones. She simply tells lies to stop the law taking its
course, and Honesty's claims cannot glimpse the light of day
thanks to the rain-cloud of coins she pours upon it. Why, this
woman leads the law by the nose! Just consider her use of
settlement-days,* a device through which people lose what
would be theirs by law if the case ever came to court. But
doesn't law seem just a labyrinth to simple people, however
long they wander about within it? Law has such a stately
carriage it never reaches the far end of the driveway!
Certainly, the way bribes work, whether in money or in kind,
it brings satisfaction to very few indeed!

'Noblemen and citizens alike get into serious trouble thanks to Meed. So do the common people—at least those who care about living an honest life. The reason is that Meed has married the clergy to greed. And that is the kind of life this lady goes in for. May God's curse light upon her, and may every kind of ill come down on those who support the followers of Meed! Meed has got such a monopoly amongst the well-to-do that poor people *have* no way of protesting, even when they feel the pain in all its sharpness!'

After this, Meed burst into tears and protested to the King that she wanted a chance to speak and put the argument in favour of her case. The King proved willing enough to grant her leave. 'Defend yourself if you can', he said; 'there's no more *I* can say. Conscience's indictment amounts to a demand that you should be permanently banished!'

'Far from it, my liege!' exclaimed the lady; 'see whether you still believe him when you know for certain where the wrong truly lies. Meed has the power to assist people when great misfortunes befall them. You yourself, Conscience', she said, 'are well aware that I didn't come here to engage in a quarrel or make spiteful personal attacks on *you*. You are also perfectly aware, you cunning creature—now don't you try to deny it—that there were times enough in the old days when you took my side. Oh yes, you've let your fingers paddle in my pockets and handed out my largesse exactly where you pleased. It really quite amazes me why you should be in such a towering rage now. Yet, forgetting all that, it lies in my power—and I might well have the inclination—to do you proud with what's at my disposal. I could raise your expectations, my good sir, well beyond what you could reasonably imagine!

'But no; you have been slandering me infamously right in front of the King. Yet did *I* ever kill a king,* or give my voice to support his murder? I utterly deny everything you say I've done, and I appeal to his majesty to hear me out. It isn't my fault that he has had such trouble in Normandy;* on the contrary, it was you who brought dishonour on him, and not just once. Oh, how you went and skulked under the tent-flaps when your fingertips felt the frost! You fancied the

cold season was never going to end. You went in fear that
every storm-cloud would be the death of you. And then off
you scurried homewards when your stomach felt a wee bit
hollow. And yet, for all that, you thieving rogue, you were up
to preying on the poor, and carrying off their brass cooking-
pots on your back to exchange them for cash when you got to
Calais! I meanwhile remained with my royal master to keep
close guard on his life. I cheered up his soldiers and got them
out of the dumps. I slapped them on the back and put new
heart into them—in fact I had them fairly skipping with
expectation of enjoying me to the full! I swear to you by our
Lady, had I been commander of the King's army, I'd have
bet no less than my life on getting him complete control of the
last square foot of France. I'd have had him King of that
country, and given him such wealth to advance his kindred
that the most insignificant cadet of a fifteenth-cousin could
have been raised to the ranks of the peerage with it! What a
coward you were, Conscience, advising him to have done and
leave behind the domain that was his by right—the richest
soil that ever drank the rain! And for what? For a handful of
silver!

'I say that it's entirely right and proper for a King who has
a realm to govern to give rewards*—yes, "meed"—and gifts,
as signs of honour to everyone, foreigners included, who gives
him obedient service. Meed wins a king love, and it also
earns him the reputation of being a "splendid fellow". Look
at emperors, earls, and noblemen of every rank—don't they
all keep retainers? These are young men whose job is to go
about their business, on horse or on foot. The Pope, and all
the higher clergy, receive presents and disburse payments—
"meed"—to men whom they entrust with the administration
of their courts. It's simply a reality of life that serving-men
accept meed from their employers in return for their services,
on the basis of what has been agreed between them. Beggars
ask for meed in return for saying prayers, and minstrels
request meed for providing entertainment. The King himself
uses meed to pay his men for keeping peace in the land.
Those who teach pupils require fees from them—that's meed.
Priests who preach in order to edify their congregations—they

too appeal for meed, in the form of a penny at mass or an offering of foodstuffs. Craftsmen of every description insist on meed for the expense of training their apprentices. And there's no doubting that meed and commerce are totally inseparable. In fact, I don't suppose a single person in the world could get on with the business of living without recourse to meed!'

'By Christ!' the King exclaimed to Conscience, 'it looks to me as though Meed deserves to come out top in this argument between you.'

'By no means!' said Conscience to the King, kneeling on the ground. 'Sire, by your leave: what I say is, that there are two forms of "meed".* One of these comes from Our Blessed Lord as an act of divine favour, and it's granted to those who live virtuous lives during their time on earth. This is what the prophet David has in mind when he preaches to us in the Psalm *Domine, quis habitabit*—I mean where he asks this question:

Lord, who shall dwell in your house with your holy ones?
Who shall take up his rest in your holy mountain?

The Psalter-text shows him providing his own answer:

He who walks without blemish, and does the works of
    justice.*

This is the one who enters in robes of a single hue,* and in singleness of heart; the one who has acted in accordance with justice and right reason. It is the man who does not practise usury but assists the poor and pursues honesty and truth:

He who does not give out his money for usury
Or accept bribes against the innocent man.*

This means everyone who helps the innocent and takes the side of the just, benefits them, and helps the cause of truth without taking any "meed" or reward for himself. It is men of this sort, my liege, who at their moment of greatest need (I mean the hour of their death) will receive from God this first variety of "meed".

'There is also, however, another, disproportionate kind of "meed", which the powerful of this world set their hearts on. These people accept meed as a means of providing support for wrongdoers. The concluding passage of one of the psalms alludes to them: "In their hands rests iniquity, while their right hand is filled with gifts."* Dear God! I swear to you now—the man whose own palm closes upon their coin will pay a heavy price for it, if there's any truth in Scripture! Yes, priests who hanker after a life of ease and accept monetary reward for saying masses—these are getting their meed here in this life. What does St Matthew's Gospel teach us on this matter? "I say to you solemnly, they have received their reward."* Now, the money that ordinary uneducated working men get from their employers isn't "meed"—not meed of *any* kind. No, it's an appropriate *wage*. I will go further and affirm that "meed" plays no part in commercial transactions, either. What you have here, quite clearly, is an act of *exchange*:* goods worth so much are given for goods of another sort, but worth the same in value.

'Ah', he said, 'what a little twister you are, Meed! Have you ever read the Book of Kings—the story of King Saul?* Do you know why the wrath of God fell upon Saul and his family? God had sent word to Saul through the prophet Samuel; he told him that Agag, King of the Amalekites, together with his whole army, would have to perish on account of his ancestors' evil deeds. "And so"—went Samuel's message to Saul—"God Himself orders you to submit humbly and carry out His will. Advance against Amalek with your forces, and whatever you come across— kill. Burn to death men and beasts together! Widows, wives, children, goods and chattels—every single thing you find, burn it! Carry nothing away, whatever its worth in itself or if sold for money: make certain you destroy it. Put an end to it all, spare nothing and no one; then you will prosper indeed."

'But Saul was greedy to have the Amalekites' wealth. And so he spared their king and all his cattle, as the Bible records, in defiance of the prophet's warning. For this, God told Samuel that Saul must die: for committing that sin, he and his entire progeny would come to an ignominious end. Such was the disaster that "meed" brought down on King Saul, earning God's perpetual enmity against himself and all his line.

'There's no need for me to spell out every last implication of this specific example*—in case it gets me into hot water! Things have come to such a sorry state these days that anyone who utters unvarnished truths to people in authority is invariably the first to feel their displeasure!

'I am Conscience and I know this, because Kind Wit* informed me. But I tell you, the time is coming when Reason shall be ruler in this kingdom,* and certain people will experience Agag's fate! Samuel will slay him, and Saul will be held to blame. David will be crowned and put all things under his feet; and a single Christian king will rule over each and every man. Meed shall no longer hold sway as she now does; but love, humility, and loyalty together will be in charge, so that honesty and truth may be properly protected. And if anyone offends against Truth, he will feel the force of the law at the hands of Honest Fidelity,* and no one else. The day is approaching when no barrister will earn enough to afford a silken coif or a fur cloak for doing his job of pleading at the Bar!

'Meed has been turning criminals into rich men, taking it on herself to govern kingdoms against the governor's own laws. But one day Real Love* is going to arrive, in company with Conscience; and together they will reduce the legal profession to labouring with their hands. Such love, peace, and honesty of life will arise among the people that the Jews will be struck with wonder and rejoice, supposing that Moses or the Messiah has appeared on the earth,* because of the marvels of truthful and honest conduct to be observed among men.

'All who bear weapons of war—daggers, broadswords, lances, axes, or hatchets—will be condemned to death unless they have them hammered into sickles and scythes, or coulters, as Scripture says: "They shall turn their swords into ploughshares".* Every man will be actively engaged, with plough, pickaxe, or spade, or else spinning, or spreading manure on the fields. If he does nothing, let him come to nothing! Parish priests and rectors will hunt with the call "I shall please the Lord",* and do shooting-practice all day with but one target—the Book of Psalms, I mean. If they go in for actual hawking and hunting, that will be the end of the benefice they hold.

'No authority, whether king or knight, constable or mayor, shall overburden the ordinary people, or summon them to the courts, or empanel them as jurors, or put them on oath. Only one sentence will be passed—in exact proportion to the act in question; and whether mercy is granted or withheld shall be as Truth alone will determine. The King's Court, the Common Court, the Consistory Court and the Chapter Court* shall all be turned into one single court, with one single justice to preside there. And his name will be True-Tongue,* a virtuous man who has never caused me grievance. There will be no more battles; no one will carry arms. And if anyone pays a smith to forge them, he shall be smitten to death with his own blade! As Scripture says: "Nation shall not lift up sword against nation."*

'But before all this occurs, things are first going to take a turn for the worse.* The sign of this will be *six suns, a ship, and a quiverful of arrows*. The middle phase of the moon will bring about the conversion of the Jews, while the Muslims, seeing this, will burst out singing "Glory to God in the highest!" Both Mahomet and Meed will then be brought low, for "A good name", Scripture tells us, "is better than a store of wealth." '*

In a trice, Meed became as furious as a howling gale. 'So you think I don't understand Latin?' she cried. 'But the authorities will show you how things stand! Just see what Solomon says in the Wisdom books. He tells us those who give gifts win victory, and honour to go with it. As Holy Writ declares: *"Honorem adquiret qui dat munera."* '[1]*

'I'm not doubting, madame', came Conscience's reply, 'that the Latin you quote is accurate enough. But you remind me of a lady who was reading a passage of Scripture that went *"omnia probate"*, "try everything". Oh, that tickled her fancy well enough! The words, however, came just at the foot of the

---

[1] 'He who gives gifts wins honour.'

page. If she'd bothered to turn over and look at the second
half of the sentence, she'd have found a few more words, and
those severe ones: *"quod bonum est tenete"**—"Hold fast to
what is good." Now *that* text was the handiwork of Truth.
And so, good lady, you too have gone astray, it would appear.
You could find nothing more on this theme as you sat there
conning the Book of Proverbs by yourself? Yes, I can see
what you quoted would suit the nobility well enough, at any
rate. But what you lacked was a learned scholar who knew
that the page required to be turned! If you look at Proverbs,
you'll discover that there follows a rather uncomfortable text
for those who receive the gifts *you* offer: "Meed carries off the
souls of those who take it."* That, lady, is the sharp end of
the passage whose gentle opening words you put before us.
What it says is that, though we *might* win "victory" and
"honour" by means of meed, the soul of the man who gives it
or takes it ends up enmeshed in the tangles of that net!'

'Stop!' cried the King. 'I won't have any more of this from the pair of you! I insist that you make it up, and *both* of you can serve me. Kiss her, Conscience. And that is an order!'

'In the name of Christ, no!' exclaimed Conscience. 'I'd much rather you dismissed me outright! Unless Reason* were to counsel me to do so, death would be preferable.'

'Very well, then', replied the King to Conscience. 'Ride straight to Reason and bring him here. Command him to come and listen to what's in my mind. He is the one who is going to govern my kingdom and advise me properly what to do about Meed and the rest of them, and say who *is* to marry her. He'll do a strict audit of your affairs, Conscience, I swear by Christ!—and he'll throw light on what you've been putting across to my subjects, the clergy and the ordinary lay-people as well.'

'I'm quite content with these conditions', answered Conscience, and rode off directly to Reason. In confidential tones, he told him what the King had proposed, and then took his leave.

'Wait a few moments', said Reason, 'and I'll get ready to ride, too.' Then he called his servant Cato,* a well-spoken fellow he, and Tom True-Tongue,* who tells no tales or lies-for-a-laugh, since Reason has always abhorred such behaviour. 'Saddle my horse Endurance',* he said, 'who bides his time till the moment comes to act. Fasten him firmly with the girth-straps of shrewd advice, and hang a heavy bridle on him to keep his head well down, or he'll toss and neigh for all he's worth before we reach our destination.'

And so Conscience set out on horseback, with Reason riding beside him. In muffled tones they discussed the various ways in which Meed manipulates the affairs of everyday life. They were closely shadowed on their way by someone called Warren Wise and his partner, Clevercraft,* who had some business afoot in the courts of Exchequer and Chancery.* They wanted a legal action against them dropped, and the cause of their haste was the hope that Reason's expert advice—for which they'd pay him—would get them out of their embarrassing predicament.

Conscience, however, was fully aware that these people were caught in the clutches of greed, and he urged Reason to put on speed and ignore the pair of them. 'What they say is full of deceit, and they're hand-in-glove with Lady Meed herself. They pick up their earnings in places where violent rage and conflict flourish, but never grace with their presence the portals of love and loyal faith:

> Destruction and wretchedness lie in their path
> And the ways of peace they have not known.

As for God? They don't care a goose's feather for Him! "There is no fear of the Lord before their eyes."* Why, they'd do more for a dozen chickens than for the love of Christ or his holy saints in Heaven! So, Reason, let those solid citizens get where they want by themselves; I can tell you, neither Conscience nor Christ is prepared to acknowledge them.'

With that, Reason spurred along on the highway as Conscience directed, until they came to the King. He, courteously, came out to meet Reason, and gave him a seat on the royal bench between himself and his son the Prince,* where they had a deep discussion about various weighty affairs.

Then Peace* entered the Parliament Hall, and brought forward a formal bill of complaint. Wrong, he said, had raped his wife and abducted Rose, who was due to marry Reginald, and deflowered Margaret, however hard she had struggled.

'His gang of thugs', protested Peace, 'simply walk off with my geese and pigs, and I'm so scared of them I don't dare resist or complain. Wrong "borrowed" my horse, but he's never returned it or paid me a penny for it, however often I ask. He aids and abets his retainers, who murder my own workmen; he buys up goods before they are put on sale, to push up the prices, and at market-time he stirs up trouble. He smashes down the doors of my barns and carries off my corn. And what does he let me have in return? Nothing but a notch

on my tally-stick* as "payment" for ten quarter-sacks full of
oats! And that's not all. He roughs me up, too, and forces my
maidservants into his bed. The result is, I hardly dare to put
my face out of doors, I'm so scared of meeting him!'

The King knew that what Peace said was the truth, because
Conscience told him that Wrong* was a double-dyed villain,
who went about causing a great amount of mischief. Wrong,
on hearing this, became uneasy, and turned to Wise.* His
hope was to try and work out a monetary settlement, so he
said: 'As long as my liege-lord casts a kind eye on my doings,
I don't give a damn if Peace and his crowd go on complaining
till kingdom come!'

Then Wise, with Master Clevercraft, went up and gave
Wrong a prudently worded warning, since he'd been getting
up to such serious mischief. 'Anyone who acts in a violent
temper tends to arouse hostility against himself. Look, this is
my opinion, and I've no doubt whatever you'll find it turns
out as I say: unless Meed smooths things over, friend, your
troublemaking days are finished! Your property and your life
now depend on the mercy of the King.'

At this, Wrong started urging Wise anxiously to put things
right through a monetary settlement—by hook or by crook,
fair means or foul. So Wise and Clevercraft got down to work
and took Meed along with them to try and obtain the King's
mercy.

Peace now came on the scene, showing his bleeding head.
'Look,' he protested, 'God knows this injury's no fault of my
own!'

The true facts were well known to Conscience, and to the
people at large; but for all that, Wise and Clevercraft left no
stone unturned in their efforts to put pressure on the King
through the power of cash. But the King gave his solemn
word, swearing, by Christ and his crown, that Wrong was
going to suffer for his crimes. Ordering a constable to put him
in irons, he said: 'Don't let the scoundrel catch sight of his
feet for the next seven years!'

'God knows, my liege', interjected Wise, 'surely that isn't
at all the best thing to do! If Wrong is capable of making
compensation, why not let him be granted bail, and bear all

the costs of the whole case to boot? That way, he can put right what's amiss, and everyone will be permanently better off as a result.'

Clevercraft chimed in with this, adding: 'Surely it's preferable to put an end to a grievance by paying up, than to insist on punishing the perpetrator, without providing any redress for the injured party?'

At this juncture Meed, with a self-deprecatory smile, entreated the King's mercy, and offered Peace a present of the finest gold. 'Accept this from me, my friend', she said, 'as some small amends for all the harm you've suffered. Believe me, I'll guarantee that Wrong will never trouble you in this way again!'

At this Peace, in a conciliatory spirit, begged the King to show mercy to the man who had done him injury over and over again. 'The reason is', he declared, 'that he's paid up a substantial indemnity, as Wise recommended. And so, for my part, I'm more than happy to forgive him the harm he's done me. Provided my lord the King is agreeable, I have no better proposal I wish to make. Meed, you see, has arranged for compensation to be paid, so there remains no more for me to ask.'

'Not so!' declared the King, however. 'So help me God, Wrong is not going to wriggle out of this—not without my first finding out more about it. If he got off so easily, he'd have a good laugh over it, and henceforth feel free to go on outrageously persecuting my subjects. No! Unless Reason has pity on him, Wrong is set to remain in the stocks for the rest of my reign. I tell you, the only bail that is going to do *him* any good is humble repentance!'

At this, some of those present urged Reason to have pity on that scoundrel Wrong: let him advise the King and Conscience to allow Meed to stand as surety for the fellow.

'Don't tell me I should have pity', answered Reason,* 'till the day comes when the nobility—and I have both sexes in mind!—become devoted to decency and sworn foes to filth, refusing to listen to it or to utter it. Then the proudest woman will pack away her furs in the cupboard, and children, instead of being spoilt, will be sensibly punished with the help of a stout stick. The "virtuous" lives of the inwardly vicious will be valued as they deserve—at precisely nothing! The greed of the clergy will be greed only for the good, a covetousness for clothing and feeding the destitute. Errant members of the religious orders will keep to their cloisters and there chant "Lord, remember",* as their Rule requires, whether it be that of Benedict, Bernard, or Francis. What preachers preach sermons upon will be borne out by the example of their own lives. The advice given by the king's council will be given for the common good. Bishops, instead of buying fancy horses, will spend their cash on housing the homeless beggar, and sell off their hawks and hounds to provide for religious who are vowed to poverty. As for pilgrimages to St James's shrine*— these will depart in directions *I* shall determine; and if people do go to Galicia, let them go there once and for all, and never come back! No one who trudges the path to Rome* to line the pockets of foreign profiteers will be permitted to carry cash overseas: no coin of the realm bearing the impress of the King, nor, for that matter, *any* gold or silver, whether stamped or unstamped. Any such person arrested at Dover* will have the currency confiscated, with these exceptions only: merchants or their representatives, messengers carrying letters, clergy seeking ratification of their benefices, or persons performing a prescribed canonical penance.

'And that is not all,' resumed Reason. 'I swear by the cross of Christ, I shall have *no* pity at all so long as Lady Meed holds sway in this council chamber! Let me give you some more examples of what would be possible if *I* were king and the government in my control. *No* act of Wrong's that came to my knowledge would go unpunished if I had the final say, nor would Wrong ever obtain my support through his gifts. I swear this by my soul, so help me God! And no form of payment whatever would induce me to have mercy—only a payment of pure humility.* This is how it would be:

> *No-Evil* meets *Unpunished*, and he
> Demands, "Let *No-Good* forfeit his fee!"*

Get your confessor, Sire, to sort this verse out for you in good plain English. However, I'm prepared to bet my ears that if

you actually put this into practice, the legal profession would
shut up shop and all of them turn ploughmen;* they'd cart
manure to the fields, while your country was governed by
Love, in accordance with your every wish.'

At this, those clergy who were licensed to hear confessions
got together in pairs to try and interpret the saying. But their
true concern was the King's material advantage, not the good
of his soul or the benefit of his subjects. And did I not
glimpse Meed in the council chamber tipping the wink to the
lawyers, most of whom quit Reason and made off post-haste
to join Meed?

Warren Wise winked back at Meed in return. 'Madam', he
said, 'you can count on me, whatever noises my mouth may
actually make. Just let me lose my footing on some silver', he
concluded, 'and mum's the word—my lips are sealed for
ever.'

All the honest people present, however, gave it as their
opinion that Reason was speaking the truth. Kind Wit
agreed,* too, and commended what he had said. So did the
majority of the commoners, and a fair number of the high-
ranking folk. Humility was adjudged the palm, and Meed was
regarded as a damned deceiver. Love took a very low view of
Meed, and Honest Fidelity* a still lower, expressing it in such
resonant tones that no one in the hall could fail to hear it:
'Believe me, whoever wants to marry Meed for her money and
possessions can rest assured of a pair of cuckold's horns. If
I'm proved wrong, you're free to cut off my nose!'

At this, Meed started to cry, and looked utterly miserable,
for the roughest of the rabble there said 'She's a whore!'
However, there were a juryman and a summoner who still
stuck firmly to her side, and a sheriff's clerk flung abuse at
the whole assembly: 'Many's the time', he cried, 'that I've
helped you people when you came up before a magistrate; and
what did you give me for it? Not so much as a bloody brass
farthing!'

The King now summoned Conscience and, after him,
Reason, who he solemnly declared had given a just account of
how matters stood. With brows knitted menacingly, the King
turned his gaze upon Meed, and his rage swelled up against

the Law, whose workings Meed had more or less
undermined.

'Thanks to you', he declared, 'a number of estates that
should revert to the Crown are being lost through corrupt
practices. Meed simply holds the law in leading-strings, while
she blocks the progress of every honest claim. But I swear, if I
remain King for very much longer, Reason will settle
accounts with you and judge you each according to your
deserts. This you can be sure of, I swear! By Mary in Heaven,
Meed will never stand bail for you again! I'm going to have
justice prevail in the law—no, I won't listen to another word
of yours! And as for Wrong, let him be judged as the majority
here plainly consider he warrants.'

At this, Conscience said to the King: 'I think I must tell
you, Sire, that unless the Commons* agree to this, you will
have a hard time bringing it about. It won't be easy setting
your loyal subjects on a course as straight as this!'

'By the cross of Christ!' Reason rejoined to the King.
'Unless I *do* rule your land like this, Sire, tear out my bowels!
But you will have to order Obedience to take my side in the
matter.'

'Yes, by our Lady! And I'm on your side', said the King.
'Just wait till the lords, spiritual and temporal, next meet here
in Council! But you, Reason, I won't let you ride off and
leave me—not as long as I live!'

'For my part, Sire', said Reason, 'I am at your disposal, for
ever, if you need me. I should like nothing better, provided
Conscience here may be privy to all our close deliberations.'

'Yes, of course!' cried the King, 'God forbid we should lose
him! For the rest of our lives, let all of us keep together!'*

VISION TWO

PASSUS V

The King and his knights made their way to church to hear matins, followed by mass. And I now stirred from my slumbers;* but how miserable I felt not to have remained more deeply asleep, and so to have seen more! However, before I had walked two hundred paces, I suddenly began to feel drowsy; why, I felt I couldn't move another foot for lack of sleep! So I sat down quietly, and set about saying my Creed; and as I did so, the sound of my own voice murmuring the prayers made me drop off asleep.

And then I had a vision of much more than I've already described. I saw the field full of people which I mentioned before, and Reason getting ready to preach to the whole realm at large.* I saw how he took a cross and, standing before the King, proceeded to give a homily in the words that now follow. The recent plague,* he demonstrated, had been brought down on our heads solely on account of our sins; and the strong south-west wind* that raged on Saturday evening was clearly caused by our sins of pride and nothing else whatever. Pear trees and plum trees had been levelled by great gusts, as a sign, my friends, that you must amend your ways! Beeches and great oak trees were blown flat and turned their roots to the sky; that was a fearful presage that, before Doomsday itself approaches, the severity of their sins will be our people's undoing. This is a theme I could say much more on, but all I shall do, please God, is describe my vision of Reason preaching, and the blunt and forthright terms he used to the people.

He urged Waster* to go and do some work, as he well knew how to, and earn what he spent by plying some sort of trade. He appealed to Petronella,* the paragon of pride, to doff her furs and lock them away in her chest against a day of need.

He instructed Tom Stowe to get a good pair of canes and
fetch his wife Felicity home, before she ended up on the
ducking-stool* for shrews! He gave a warning to Walter that
his wife was getting into bad ways, wearing a hat worth
twenty times his own poor hood. And he ordered Bud to cut a
couple of branches and give his Betty a sound thrashing if she
wouldn't get down to work.

Next, he urged merchants to bring up their children
strictly: 'Don't let your growing prosperity lead you to spoil
them while they are little! Take care not to cosset them
beyond what's reasonable because of the anxiety for their
well-being which the terrible attacks of the plague have made
you feel. My father and mother both brought it home to me,
that the more you love a child, the more care you must take to
bring your child up well. And Solomon, author of the books
of Wisdom, concurred: "Spare the rod", he wrote, "and spoil
the child!"'*

After this, Reason addressed an appeal to both the higher
and the lower ranks of the clergy. 'You yourselves must put
into practice', he said, 'whatever you exhort your hearers to
do in your sermons. Make your teaching a reality in your own
lives, and the consequences for you will surely be happy. If
you lead lives such as you urge us to pursue, won't we take
your teaching all the more to heart?'* And then he
admonished members of religious orders to adhere firmly to
their Rule of Life. 'Otherwise', he warned, 'the King and his
Council are going to reduce your revenues drastically. They'll
come and take over the management of your endowments
until you manage to put your own houses in order.'*

Having said this, he advised the King to love the common
people. 'They', he said, 'are your real treasure, and your
sovereign remedy in time of supreme need—if only we were
sure no treason was lurking amongst them!'

He went on to implore the Pope to have pity on the state of
Holy Church, and to put his own affairs to rights before
granting favours and indulgences to others.

'And you', he went on, 'in whose hands lies the
administration of the law—don't hunger and thirst for golden

gifts, but the treasure of truth and right; that is the way to win the Almighty's favour. Remember what He himself says in the Gospel to those who act against truth: "I say to you solemnly, I do not know you."*

'You pilgrims', he said, 'who search for St James or the martyr-saints of Rome, go and look for St Truth:* he is the one with the power to save you all. In the name of the Father, and of the Son, and of the Holy Spirit: a blessing on all who follow what I preach!'

Those were Reason's final words. And at once Repentance* rushed forward, and went over again the substance of what he had said, bringing water-drops from Will's eyes. Petronella,* that proud-hearted dame, flung herself face down upon the ground and lay there for a long time, before crying out at last, 'Mercy, Lord, have mercy!' Thereupon she swore a vow to the Creator of us all: she said she would unpick her undergarment and put in its place a hair-shirt, to discipline her flesh, which was boldly bent upon sin. 'Swelling self-regard', she cried, 'will master me no more from now. Instead I shall humble myself, and meekly endure the harsh words of others—something I have never done in my life before. But now my wish is to abase myself, and to beg mercy for all that crabbed resentment I have long been harbouring deep within my heart!'

Then Lust* let out a lament, and cried to the Blessed Virgin to obtain God's mercy for the many evil acts he had performed. He vowed that every Saturday for a period of seven years he would taste only what ducks drink and eat only one meal that day.

Next Envy,* with heavily burdened spirit, asked to be confessed, and in anguished tones uttered his 'Mea culpa,* through my own fault I have sinned.' His features were as pale as a cannon-ball of stone, and he seemed to be shaking all over. I couldn't begin to describe what he was wearing: it was an under-jacket and coat of some coarse material, the front part of the sleeves like those the friars wear,* and by his side he carried a knife. With his hollow cheeks and hideous grimace he resembled a leek that has spent a long time lying out in the sun. His body was all swollen up with rage and resentment, and he kept on biting his lip. He walked along with clenched fists, always dreaming up ways of getting his own back, verbally or physically, if he should see a chance. Every word he uttered was like a viper spitting poison. He spent his whole life in quarrels and accusations, backbiting and slander, and bearing false witness. This was as far as his good-fellowship went, whenever the fellow appeared on the scene.

'I want to make my confession', the scoundrel said, 'if shame would let me do so! But, God help me, I'd be much happier if old Gib there suffered some setback or other than if someone offered *me* an enormous Essex cheese! I've got a neighbour nearby whom I've often got into trouble, what with telling lies about him to the powers-that-be, just to put him out of pocket. Thanks to this crooked tongue of mine, I've turned his own friends against him. But every success and bit of good luck he has make me curl up inside with misery!

'I often stir up conflict between one household and another; the things I say lead to loss of life and limb! At market-time, if I meet a man whom I've really got it in for, I greet him as warmly as an old friend; the real reason, though, is he's more than a match for me—so I haven't actually any choice in the matter. But oh, if I could just get the upper hand, God knows what I'd do, I can tell you!

'When I go to church and the time comes to kneel before the cross and say the bidding prayers as the priest directs— you know, for pilgrims, and for the whole community, too—I cry out, as I am kneeling there, "Christ curse the fellow who walked off with my bowl and that old tattered bed-sheet of mine!" Then, as I turn my eyes away from the altar, what should I notice but our friend Harry, who's gone and got himself a new coat. At once I wish it was mine—every last bit of thread in the blessed thing. Still, I can have a good gloat over his losses; that, now, really lights up the gloomiest day! But when he makes a profit, I end up down in the dumps. I'm always criticizing other people's faults—though my own, as it happens, are fifty times worse than theirs. And if anyone else criticizes *me* for that reason, he's my enemy number one from that moment on!

'What I'd really love is this: for everyone to have to do just what I want! You see, I become quite livid at anyone who's got more than myself. Well, that's the sort of loveless existence I lead—just like some vicious, good-for-nothing cur. The result is my whole body seems bloated with the bitter juices bubbling up inside me.* I've been finding it hard to eat properly for years now. And why? Because envy and malevolence are damnably hard to digest! Ah, isn't there any sugar or syrup that could bring about some relief from this swelling? Isn't there any sweet medicine to flush the stuff right out from deep inside me? Will no confession do the trick, no act of mortification? Nothing short of having my stomach-wall scraped?'

'Yes, yes, of course there is!' said Repentance, urging him to look on the brighter side. 'Sorrow for sin is what saves a man's soul.'

'Well, I'm always *sorry*!'* cried Envy. 'I'm seldom anything else. And that's just what makes me lose so much weight— the fact that I have no outlet for my desire for revenge. I've often moved in business circles, amongst the London merchant-traders, and I've employed Messrs Slander and Co. as my agents to bring my rivals' wares into disrepute. When they would bring off a sale, and I proved unsuccessful, I was quick off the mark with some lie or other and a knowing scowl at my colleague—anything that would serve to make his transactions look shady. But now, through the power of Almighty God, I want nothing except to put all this behind me—if only I can!'

After this Anger got up; the whites of his eyes were showing, his nose was running, and the skin of his neck hung down in a flap. 'I'm Anger', he growled. 'Time was, I was a friar, and worked in the friary garden, grafting shoots on trees. Ha! I used to graft lies on learned mendicants and lectors,* until they would put out leaves of lick-spittle language—the sort of stuff the nobility love to lap up. And next thing, they started to bud into private boudoir-confessions,* and you know the fruit that produces in the end: people now much prefer confessing to a friar rather than to their own local parish priest. But now that the parsons have grasped that the friars are eating into their portion,* they've started to preach sermons attacking the brethren! The friars, for their part, proceed to find fault with the parish clergy, as anyone can tell you; and what happens then? Well, when they deliver their public sermons in one place or another, your good friend Anger is right in there with them, lending them lessons straight out of my library. Oh, yes, they spend so much time going on about "spirituality" that either side soon ends up bitterly hostile to the other. Both end up out of pocket and have to live off *my* kind of "spirituality"; or else, one party corners the lot and can then afford a nice little horse to ride on. But I'm Anger and I never give up my pursuit of these unsavoury people; isn't that, after all, my special gift?

'Let me tell you about my aunt, who's a nun—an abbess, In fact. She'd rather faint dead away—no, more, she'd rather die—than endure a single moment's physical pain. I've worked as a cook in her kitchen,* and spent a number of months employed by her convent (I've been with monks, too, but more of that anon). Anyway, I used to make stews for the prioress and those other good ladies vowed to a life of poverty. What turbulent dishes I used to stir up for them! I said that Lady Joan was illegitimate, and Lady Clarissa . . . she, admittedly, *was* the daughter of a knight, but not of her "father" (he, poor chap, was a cuckold!) As for Lady Petronella . . . well, now, she was a priest's pretty little poppet—not quite the stuff that prioresses are made from! Didn't she have a baby come last June? The whole chapter* knew what was going on! What vile vegetables I used to boil up from these vicious asides of mine! It wasn't too long before it all came spewing out in one go—"You're a liar!" "No, *you're* a liar!"—and each one slapped the other across the mouth. Christ Almighty, if the creatures had been carrying knives, they'd have done each other in there and then! Don't you think St Gregory was a wise old pope? He had a pretty shrewd notion of what might easily happen, when he laid down his rule that a prioress must never be ordained a priest. Why, they'd have lost their claim to a good pastoral reputation from the very first confession they ever heard. Women can't keep a secret to save their lives!*

'Now, I could have settled down for the duration with our friends in the monasteries, but on the whole I've tended to give that lot a miss. A number of them keep a pretty strict watch on my cronies*—what with their prior, and their sub-prior, not to mention old Father Abbot himself. If I ever let my tongue wag amongst those people, they get in a huddle together, and the next thing I know I'm on bread and water every single Friday. In the chapter house I'm forced to own up, as if I was still a kid—yes, and I even get beaten on the bum, and without so much as a pair of pants in the way! That's why I don't care to hang about with those chappies. I get nothing to eat but some half-grown tiddly fish, and as for the beer—it's about as thick as water. There are occasions, though, when they bring wine round after dinner, and if I get the chance, ah, do I drink! My nose ends up running so badly my mouth tastes foul for a week. And every last bit of scandal I know about any of my precious brother-monks—well, I vomit it up in the cloister, and the whole lot of them step right in!'

'Now', rejoined Repentance, 'repent what you've done! And never again repeat anything private you know of—don't let it out by so much as a word or a look. And don't drink as if you were some sort of master of wines, or else some common boozer. It's the main thing that will lead you into your sin again—the road to wrath. Be sober, man, be sober, do you hear?' Saying this, he gave me absolution,* and urged me to aim at real contrition as the chief means of amending my evil ways.

And then Greed* came forward. I cannot begin to describe old Sir Harvey, his face looked so famished and caved-in. He had beetling brows, thick lips and a pair of inflamed eyes, and his cheeks flopped down like a leather purse, trembling with age and drooping below his chin. His beard was all covered with grease, like a workman's after eating his bacon. On his head there was a hood and on top of it a hat crawling with lice. He was wearing a tattered jacket that had seen a dozen years' use, but the Welsh flannel it was made of had grown so threadbare that a louse would have found no foothold there— unless it was a champion jumper!

'I have gone in for greed', muttered this wretched creature, 'I openly avow it to you here. For a time, I was apprenticed to Simon Stylegate, and contracted to look after my master's interests. I started off by learning a page or two of falsehood, my first lesson being on how to handle fraudulent weights. I used to go along to the fairs at Weyhill* and Winchester, with all kinds of goods, as my master instructed me. And by God, if the devil's own luck hadn't been with me, that stuff would have stayed unsold for seven whole years!

'Next, I got in with the cloth-merchants,* to qualify in my Rogues' Rule-book: the subject was stretching the selvage to make a piece of material appear larger. What a lot I learned there, sitting in the middle of those fancy striped fabrics! I would sew them with a pack-needle, then fold them over together and give them a real old racking in a clothes-press, until ten or twelve yards of cloth were stretched out to measure thirteen.

'My wife was a weaver whose business was making woollen cloth. She'd drop a word to the spinning-women to spin the wool out very fine. The pound-weight she used to value the wool actually registered four ounces more than my own steelyard, which I kept for weighing true. I used to buy her barley, too, which she'd brew up to be sold. She would dilute the good strong beer with some of the cheap penny-a-gallon tipple.* Now, the brew for the labourers and riff-raff used to stand in a place by itself; but the best ale was kept in my inner closet or else in our bedroom. Well, whoever got a taste of *that*, naturally bought it up, paying not less than four times the price per gallon, when it was brought out to them by the cup. This was my wife's little fiddle. Her name was Rose the retailer, and she's practised this line of hers for the last eleven years. But now I swear, so 'elp me Gawd a'mighty, I'll have done with that sin, and I'll keep off dishonest weighing and adulterating my wares. I'll go on pilgrimage to Walsingham, and so will that wife of mine, and we'll pray before the great Bromholm Cross to be released from our guilt!'*

'Have you ever repented?' asked Repentance, 'or ever made restitution?'

'Oh, yes!' he replied. 'On one occasion I was staying in the same inn as a party of merchants; and when they'd all gone to bed, I got up and rifled their bags.'

'You call that restitution?'* Repentance let out. 'That wasn't restitution, it was downright robbery! You deserve to be hanged just for that—more, in fact, than for any other sin you've mentioned.'

'But I thought rifling *was* restitution!' protested Greed. 'I've never learnt to read, and I assure you I don't know a word of French. Nobody does who comes from the far end of Norfolk!'*

'Have you ever in your life practised usury?'* went on Repentance.

'Oh, no!' he answered. 'Except when I was young. I picked up a thing or two when I was living among the Lombards and the Jews. I learnt how to work out the weights of silver pennies, and then take clippings off the heaviest ones. I also became quite devoted to the cross—I mean the one on coins that I took to lending. I also learned how property is pawned and forfeited. To prevent my victim absconding, though, I'd make sure to have the agreement in writing. Oh, I've acquired more real property by foreclosing on defaulters than from presents given to me by any grateful person I generously lent to in his time of need. I've also made loans in kind to members of the nobility,* male and female, and subsequently done duty as their agent, too, and bought back the very same goods myself! My stock-in-trade is wheeling and dealing, with a special line in currency-exchange. I lend to people whose aim seems to be to lose a shaving off every shekel they borrow. Equipped with bills of exchange from Lombard bankers, I've carried bullion to Rome.* This is how I've done it: I'd calculate the amount due by tally on this side, and give them another figure on arrival.'

'Have you ever made loans to the nobility just for the sake of enjoying their protection?'*

'Oh, yes—I've lent to such people; and precious little kindness they've shown me for it! I've turned more than one

knight into a kind of cloth-merchant without his having to
hand me a pair of gloves like a new apprentice.'

'Have you shown compassion towards the poor when they
are forced by sheer need to borrow?'

'Compassion? Yes, like a pedlar towards cats.* Don't they
care for their skins so much they kill 'em if they can catch
'em?'

'Are you generous with food and drink towards your
neighbours?'

'I'm no more welcome to them', he answered, 'than a cur in
a kitchen. That's about the sum of my standing amongst my
neighbours.'

'Now', said Repentance, 'unless you repent straight-away, I
hope God will *never* grant you the grace to make good use of
your money!* May your heirs after you get no joy from your
fortune! May your executors fail to make proper use of what
you bequeath them! And may the wealth that you dishonestly
acquired end up being spent by criminals and thieves! I tell
you, if I were a friar in a house where charity and good faith
were still to be found, I couldn't see my way to spending a
penny of your money—not on clothes, or on church-repairs,
or on little personal luxuries—God damn my soul if I'd do it!
Not for the richest book in the place, even if its leaves were of
burnished gold—if I knew for a fact you were what you say
you are.

> Seek fancy foods, another's slave you'll end;
> Eat simple bread, and you'll remain God's friend.*

'What an unnatural monster you are!' cried Repentance. 'I
can see no way to give you absolution until you make
restitution—pay back all that you owe wherever it's due. And
till Reason can honestly record in the ledger of Heaven that
you *have* made good, there is no way for me to absolve you:
"The guilt will cling until the goods go back."* And I give
you my solemn assurance: anyone who *possesses* any of your
property will also be required at the Last Judgement to help
you in your duty of restitution. Anyone who doesn't believe
what I say is true, I advise him to look at the gloss upon
Psalm 50, a text in which "truth"—honesty—is referred to:

"Have mercy on me, O God . . . for indeed you have loved the truth!"* No labourer on earth will prosper on the money you've acquired. *"Cum sancto sanctus eris"*:[1]* just find out what that means in English!'

At this, that villainous creature lost all hope, and tried to hang himself. But Repentance managed to bring him to his senses, before he could go through with it, and this is what he said:

'Keep the thought of *mercy* in your mind, and beg for it—mercy—with your mouth! Remember, *"Misericordia eius super omnia opera eius"** —God's mercy is a greater thing than every other one of his works. Every possible evil human beings could perform, or even imagine, can no more survive before the mercy of God than a glowing ember that falls into the ocean. And so, always keep *mercy* in your thoughts; and as for material wealth—I say, renounce it! Really, you have no genuine means to buy yourself a muffin for your breakfast*— not without begging, or working with your hands. The whole future you've built up for yourself is founded on a lie, and so, as long as you live, you'll go on falling still deeper into debt, always unable to pay back a single penny. Now, if you have no idea about who you should actually make restitution to,* or if you don't know where to go, take the money to the bishop, and humbly beg *him* to dispose of it, in some way that will do real good for your soul. If you do this, then he will bear the responsibility of answering for you at the final reckoning; he'll be the one who's called to account in your case—and also, doubtless, for many others as well. Put your faith completely in what he taught you during Lent; rely on that portion of *God's* great spiritual treasure, which the bishop lent to you to save you from sinning!'

And now Gluttony set out to make his confession, and took himself off to church to make a clean breast of it all. But Betty the brewer greeted him with 'Good morning!', and then asked him where he might be off to?

'To church', grunted Glutton, 'to hear mass. After which I intend to go to confession and give up sin for ever.'

---

[1] 'With the holy you will be holy.'

'I've got some good ale, Glutton my friend!' she answered.
'You wouldn't like to come and give it a try?'

'Have you got any hot spices?'* Glutton asked.

'I've got pepper and peony seeds', she replied, 'and a
pound of garlic, as well as a farthing's worth of fennel-seed—
good fare, all this, for fasting-days!'

So Glutton entered the tavern with a mighty oath. Cicely
Shoemaker was sitting there on the ale-bench, and with her
Walter the warren-keeper and his wife, Tim the tinker and a
couple of his lads, Hick the horse-hirer and Hugh the needle-
seller, Clarissa of Cock's Lane with the parish clerk, Sir Piers
Pridie the priest and Petronella the Fleming, Davy the
ditcher, and a dozen others. There was a fiddle-player, a
rat-catcher, a Cheapside scavenger, a rope-maker and an odd-
job man; Rose the dish-seller, Godfrey of Garlickhithe, and
Griffin the Welshman.* A gaggle of old-clothes dealers who
had got there early gave Glutton a cheery greeting and offered
to buy him a drink.

Before long, Clement the cobbler threw down his cloak,
offering it to all comers in a game of barter.* Hick the
horse-hirer flung down his hood in suit, asking Bud the
butcher to act as his second. Some small traders were selected
to put a value on the goods; they decided that whoever took
the hood would be paid the difference between its worth and
that of the cloak. They got up smartly and had a whispered
discussion, and then everyone involved privately valued the
goods put up for barter. A good deal of swearing went on,
because someone was bound to end up with the worse
bargain. They found it impossible, in all conscience, to reach
a basic agreement. Eventually, therefore, they begged Robin
the rope-maker to get up and be nominated as umpire, to stop
any disputes from arising. Hick the ostler got the cloak, on
condition that Clement bought drinks for everyone, took
Hick's hood, and considered himself satisfied. And anyone
who had second thoughts about the bargain would have to get
up and provide, *gratis*, a gallon of ale for Glutton.

There followed a good round of laughter and much pulling
of faces, with cries raised of 'Let the drinks go round!' A
great deal of bartering and imbibing of ale took place, and the

whole crowd sat there till the hour of evensong,* bursting into song from time to time, till Glutton had succeeded in putting away rather more than a gallon down his gullet. His guts now started to rumble like a pair of greedy sows, and he pissed four pints in the time it takes to say one Paternoster. Then he blew a resounding blast on his bum-bone; everyone hearing that horn play held their noses, and heartily wanted the thing waxed with a handful of prickly furze!

Glutton could not walk or stand up straight without the support of his stick. Then he began to move forward like a minstrel's trained dog—now to one side, now backwards, like a fowler laying down nets in lines to trap birds. When he got near the door, his vision became misty, he lost his footing on the threshold, and fell flat on the ground. Clement the cobbler caught him round the waist, managed to get him upright, then lowered him onto his knees. But Glutton, being a massive brute, was the very devil to lift, and succeeded in spewing a mess in Clement's lap. I don't think all Hertfordshire would yield a dog so near to death's door that it would ever have licked up those left-overs, so horrible did they smell!

A miserable time now followed for Glutton's wife and his serving-woman as they carted him home and got him into his bed. After this little bout of indulgence, he had a severe attack of sloth,* and slept through Saturday and Sunday right until dusk. Then, at long last, he stirred from his slumbers and rubbed his eyes. The first word to come from his lips was 'Where's the jug?'

His wife, and his own returning sense of sin, reproached him for the vicious life he was leading; and Repentance, too, at the same time rebuked him: 'Glutton, the life you've been living is an utter disgrace—your words are as wicked and worthless as your actions! Make your confession, now! Be ashamed of what you've done; and *show* you are, by acknowledging it openly.'

'I'm a glutton!' the fellow declared, 'I know I'm guilty. I've sinned with this tongue of mine time out of mind. I've sworn "By God's soul and sides!" and "So help me the Holy Relics!"—getting on for a thousand times,* without any call whatever. I've over-eaten so grossly at supper-time and at lunch that sometimes I've spewed the whole lot up before I'd gone a mile. Yes, that way I've wasted food that could have been saved and given to someone who had nothing to eat. There've been feast-days when I've eaten and drunk over the odds, and sometimes I've sat over my food so long that I think I've fallen asleep and carried on eating! I've stuffed myself in taverns just in order to spend longer drinking—and get in some juicy gossip while I'm at it. And on fasting-days, I've rushed off to my meal before the noon-bell sounded.'

'Well', said Repentance, 'this effort of yours to confess ought to do you some sort of credit, anyway.'

At this Glutton broke down and burst into passionate sobbing over the evil life he had lived; he followed this with a solemn vow to fast. 'However hungry or thirsty I become', he declared, 'my stomach will digest no meal of fish on a Friday till Aunt Abstinence lets me have permission. She's someone I've had no time for all my life!'

Then Sloth came forward, filthy from head to foot, with a pair of oozing eyes. 'I've got to sit down', the fellow said, 'or else I'll drop off where I stand. If I got into my bed, I tell you I wouldn't stir before I was ready to eat, except to relieve my bowels. As for the bells, they could ring on for ever!' Belching, he got out the words 'Bless me—',* thumping his bosom hard; then stretched, gave a prodigious yawn, and was soon snoring soundly.

'Come on, stir yourself, man!' cried Repentance. 'Get a move on and make your confession!'

'I can't be bothered to open an eyelid', came the reply. 'Not if my life depended on it! I can't say my "Our Father" properly as the priest intones it at mass. I know some ballads about Robin Hood and Randolph, Earl of Chester,* but I don't know any about our Lord or our Lady. I've made solemn resolutions forty times over—and completely forgotten them by the next morning. I've never carried out penance imposed on me by the priest, nor have I ever felt any great sorrow for my sins. And if I ever let out a prayer—except in anger!—what my tongue utters is miles from what I actually feel. I've spent every single day—holy days included—in idle gossip at the inn, and sometimes in church, too. The sufferings of our Lord Jesus isn't a subject I spend a great deal of thought on!

'I've never visited the sick, or prisoners in their cells. And I'd much rather hear a filthy story or watch a shoemakers' farce in summer,* or laugh at a lot of lying scandal about my neighbours, than listen to all that Gospel stuff—Matthew and Mark and Luke and John. As for vigils and fast-days, I give all that a miss; and in Lent I lie in bed with my girl in my arms till mass and matins are well and truly over. I then make off for the friars' church,* and if I get to the place before the priest's "Go, mass is finished", I feel I've done my bit. Sometimes I never get to confession even once in a year, unless a bout of sickness scares me into it; and then I produce some confused mishmash or other.

'I've been a priest in a parish* for over thirty years, but I've no idea how to read music or sing the mass, or to read the life of a saint. I'm much better at tracking down a hare in a ten-acre field than at chanting "Blessed the man" or "Blessed are all those . . .". I wouldn't know how to go through these psalms verse by verse for the benefit of my parishioners. Another thing I do know is how to conduct settlement-days and hear the reeve's accounts read, but I wouldn't be up to making out even a line or two of canon law.

'If ever I buy anything on credit, unless it's carefully recorded in writing, I let the matter slip my mind in a trice. And if they come asking me to pay up, six or seven times, I start swearing blind that I don't owe them a thing! That way I cause a good deal of trouble to poor honest fellows I deal with—I've done it a thousand times if I've done it once. And as for the people who work for me—well, there've been times enough when their pay falls overdue. Ah, your heart would bleed if you could hear the complaints they make when I'm doing the wage-packets! I really get worked up into a rage when it's time to pay my employees—and I can tell you, I utterly hate having to do it.

'Now, if anyone does me a good turn, or helps me in time of need, all I give him for his kindness is ingratitude. Behaviour like his I can't make head or tail of. You see, my own reactions are just like a hawk's (I've always been that way). You can't lure me with kindness,* there's got to be something hidden in your hand to peck at—I mean some tangible gain in it for me somewhere! And as for kindnesses my fellow Christians showed to me years ago—things they said or else refrained from saying—I've forgotten that sort of thing five dozen times. Over and over again, too, I've let good food go to waste. Meat, fish, bread, beer, milk, and cheese—you name it: I've kept them till they'd gone right off and were no use at all to a soul. When I was young, I spent my time gadding about and simply refused to learn a thing. Since then, I've had to resort to begging, thanks to this damnable laziness of mine.

> God! How I failed to rise and shine
> During that long-lost youth of mine!'*

'Didn't you repent?' asked Repentance—and for answer, Sloth passed out immediately. He remained like that till Keep-Watch Wakeful* drew water from his eyes and dashed it over his face, shouting at him over and over again:

'Sloth, you'd better watch out! Guard yourself against Despair, who's out to get you. Say to yourself, *"I am sorry for my sins."* Beat your breast and beg God for his grace. There's no vice in the world so black that it cannot be extinguished by his goodness.'

Then Sloth got himself into a sitting position, and made the sign of the cross again and again. Solemnly he resolved before God to overcome his vice. 'Every day for the next seven years', he declared, 'unless I'm prevented by illness, I'll get to church before daybreak,* and hear matins and mass, just like a monk. And I won't swallow down so much beer with my lunch that I have to miss evensong. All this I promise here in front of the cross! That's not all; if I possibly can, I'll give back everything I've obtained dishonestly since the time I reached the age of reason. And even if it means not having enough to live on myself, I won't stop till I've put everything right with everyone—not till the day I die. And with what's left over (I swear by the Chester Rood),* I'll go searching for Truth before I set eyes on Rome!'

Robert the robber* saw the words 'Give it back!'—and wept bitterly, because he *had* nothing to give back. None the less, the guilty creature said to himself: 'Christ, when you were dying on the cross at Calvary, my brother-robber Dismas* begged you for mercy. And because of those words of his, "Remember me, Lord!", you *did* have mercy. Take pity in the same way, Lord, on this Robert here, though I lack the means to make restitution, nor can I hope to earn anything through any skill I possess. No, but I beg you to grant, through your great mercy, some softening of my sentence. Do not damn me outright on the Day of Judgement for the wrongs I have done!'

I cannot tell exactly what happened to this felon, but I do know that his eyes shed copious tears.* Moreover, he acknowledged his guilt to Christ over and over again, and undertook to give his pikestaff a new coat of polish (it was named *Penance*),* and use it to walk with during the rest of his life; for he had slept with Theft, the Devil's aunt.

And now Repentance took pity on them all, and told them to kneel. 'I am going to beg our Saviour to grant every one of us sinners the grace to amend our evil ways, and to show mercy to us all. Now', he continued in prayer, 'O God, you created the world out of your goodness: you made everything out of nothing, and you fashioned man in your near likeness—and then permitted him to commit sin, bringing a malady on the whole human race. Yet all this was for the best,* as I believe, whatever the Bible may appear to imply: "O happy fault! O necessary sin of Adam!"'

'And this is the reason why: that sin was the cause that made your Son come down to earth and take flesh from a virgin in order to save mankind. Yes, through your Son, you became like one of us, sinners though we are: "Let us make man in our image and likeness" was one text; another said, "He who lives in charity, lives in God, and God in him . . .".* And then, in the person of your Son, you died as a man—on Good Friday, at the stroke of noon, you did this. Neither you, God, nor your Son, experienced death's ultimate dolour,* but our human nature bore the brunt of it all, and your Son lifted off the heavy burden and "led captivity captive". The sun, struck with sorrow at what happened, briefly became unseen and unseeing.* This took place about noon, the hour when the blessed eat, for it was then that your freshly-spilt blood fed our ancestors in the shadows where they waited: "The people who walked in darkness saw a great light." And that light, which sprang forth from you, blinded Lucifer, and blew all your holy ones into the bliss of heaven!

'On the third day after this, you went abroad in human form and Mary the sinner saw you, before Blessed Mary your mother. Surely it was as a sign bringing comfort to all sinners that you allowed this to happen so: "I did not come to call the just, but to call sinners to repentance."* And everything that the evangelists Mark, Matthew, Luke, and John set down about you was done, Lord, when you wore our coat of arms:* "The Word became flesh and dwelt amongst us." And that is why we can feel complete assurance when we turn to you in our entreaty, since you are our Father and our brother,* and ask—if it be your will—for mercy upon us. Have pity on these notorious sinners who repent now in tears for ever having angered you in any place, in word or in thought or in deed!'

Then Hope seized a horn called 'Turn, O God, and bring us back to life' and into it blew a breath, 'Blessed are those whose sins have been forgiven!' At this, all the saints in heaven chorused together:

'You will preserve both men and beasts, O Lord:
O God, how you have multiplied your mercies!'*

Then a myriad of people crowded together in throngs, raising their voices in prayer to Christ and his Virgin Mother, asking for grace to go and search for Truth—God grant that they may receive it! But none of them was wise enough to know how to get there, and in total disorder they strayed forth like animals over the valleys and hills, until, late in the day, they met someone dressed in the weird garb of a pilgrim.* He was holding a staff round which was wrapped a broad strip of cloth, that wound all about it like a woodbine plant. By his side he carried a bowl and a bag; on his hat were perched a hundred tiny phials, as well as tokens of shells from

Galicia, cross-ornaments on his cloak, a model of the keys of
Rome, and on his breast a vernicle. All these emblems were
designed to inform the world at large of all the pilgrim-shrines
he had visited. The first thing everyone asked him was, where
did he come from?

'From Sinai', he replied, 'and from the tomb of our Lord.
I've been in Bethlehem, in Babylon, in Armenia, Alexandria,
and various other places. You can tell from the souvenirs
sitting on my hat that I've gone walking far and wide in quest
of sundry holy saints, for the good of my soul.'

'Do you know anything', they asked him, 'about the shrine
of a saint called Truth? Could you give us directions to where
he is to be found?'

'Heavens, no!' the fellow replied. 'I've never seen any
pilgrim go looking for him with pikestaff and bag full of
provisions: never, I can tell you, and nowhere!'

'By St Peter!' a ploughman called out,* thrusting his face
forward. 'I know him—every bit as well as a scholar knows
his books! Conscience and Kind Wit directed me to his
dwelling. And then they made me give my word I would serve
him for ever, sowing and planting as long as I had the
strength for the work. I've been his follower for the last forty
years, sowing his seed and tending his stock, looking after all
his affairs, both within-doors and without, ditching, digging,
carrying out his orders. There are times when I sow, and
times when I thresh, pursue the tasks of a tailor, or mend
things like a tinker—whatever Truth happens to think of.
And, though I say it myself, I think he's pleased with my
work; he pays me well—sometimes more than I'm due. He's
the promptest paymaster known anywhere to the poor,* and
he never holds back the wages of his servants beyond the close
of a full working day. He's as meek as a lamb and the words
he utters are kind. If you want to know where he lives, I'm
more than willing to show you the way.'

'Piers, you're a friend!' said the pilgrims, offering to pay
him a fee.

'Not on my life!' Piers swore. 'I wouldn't accept a farthing,
not for all the wealth in St Thomas's shrine!* Otherwise
Truth would think the worse of me over the years to come.

But if you really want to get there, this is the way to take. You must travel, both men and women, through Humility, until you arrive at Conscience: there Christ may know for certain that you love the Lord your God above all else. And after this, you must refrain from harming your fellow men in any way whatever: you must treat them exactly as you would have them treat you.*

'After this, continue on your way,* following a stream called Speak-gentle-words, until you come to a crossing, Honour-your-parents. Step into the water there, and wash yourselves thoroughly; then you'll run all the more nimbly the rest of your life. And in this way, you will see a place called Never-swear-needlessly-and-never-take-God's-sacred-name-in-vain.

'Next you will reach a little field, and this you must not enter. Its name is Do-not-desire-men's-money-or-their-wives-and-do-not-cause-their-servants-any-mischief. Be careful to break no branch from any tree except your own. Two tree-stumps stand there; but don't you make a stop there. They are called Do-not-steal and Do-not-kill—press firmly on past both. Pass them on your left, and don't throw a backward glance towards them; observe every holy day with all due care, until the evening comes.

'Next, you must turn aside by a hill called Do-not-bear-false-witness. It is hedged about with silver coins and various other kinds of payment; but don't pluck anything growing there—it might well cost you your soul!

'Now you will see a place called Tell-only-truth-and-perform-what-you-say | And-never-do-otherwise-for-threat-or-for-pay. And then you'll arrive at a castle* shining bright as the sun. This manor-house is encircled by a moat, named Mercy; its walls are constructed of Wisdom, to keep Wilfulness at bay; its crenellations are Christian Faith, to strengthen and protect; and its buttresses are Believe-this-if-your-wish-is-to-be-saved.

'All the dwelling-houses within the precincts of the manor are roofed, halls and chambers alike, not with lead but with love and kindly words, such as a brother uses to a sister. The drawbridge is Pray-well-and-prosper-the-better. Every pillar is formed of penance and prayers of supplication to the saints, while the hinges the doors hang on are deeds of alms.

'The gatekeeper's name is Grace—a good fellow, truly; and his deputy is Amend-your-ways, a face well known to many. Say this to him as a password: "Truth knows truly I've carried out the penance the priest told me to do, and I'm sorry for my sins and shall carry on being so, every time they come to mind, even if I should be made pope one day. Tell Amend-your-ways to approach his master humbly and ask him to open up the wicket-gate. This is the one slammed shut by a woman's hand as it plucked the apples Adam and Eve ate raw:

> The door that Eve once caused to close
> Was opened by a virgin Rose.*

Remember—it's Grace who holds the big latchkey in his keeping, even if the king of the castle should be at rest. And if he allows you to pass through in this way, you will catch sight of Truth seated within your own heart,* wearing his chain of charity; and you must behave like a child, obeying him without grumbling, as if he were your father.

'But that's the time to be on guard against that vicious devil Anger. He's full of resentment against the one who sits within your heart, and he'll stir up inside you the fires of self-regard. The brilliance of your own virtuous acts will seem to blind you then, and as a result you'll dry up like the morning dew, the door will slam to behind you, the key will turn with a click, and you'll find yourself outside. It may be a century or so before you step inside again! This is how you might come to lose God's love—by thinking much too highly of yourself.* Obtain it again you may, that's certainly true—but only by means of his grace, not any gift you can proffer.

'However, there are seven sisters whose task it is to serve Truth constantly;* it is they who guard the side-gates of the castle. One is called Abstinence, and another is Humility. Charity and Chastity are his principal pair of servants, while Patience and Peace afford great help to many others. The lady Liberality lets in many a man, and has helped to liberate a good thousand from out of the devil's dungeon. Anyone who

is a kinsman of these seven sisters, I swear to you, will receive
a wonderful welcome and splendid hospitality. But unless you
are related to one or more of these seven—you have my word,
it will be hard going indeed for any of you to squeeze your
way in at any one of these gates, unless Grace should take a
hand and intervene.'

'Christ Almighty!' exclaimed a pickpocket, '*I* haven't any
kinsmen there!'

'Nor have I', muttered a man who kept apes, 'as far as I can
make out.'

'Dear God', breathed a wafer-seller,* 'if I knew this was
true, I wouldn't put one foot before another, if every friar on
earth were to preach his choicest sermon at me!'

'Oh yes, you would!' cried Piers, urging them to try and do
some good. 'There's a young woman here called Mercy;* she
has authority over them all. Moreover, she is the particular
kinswoman of every single sinner; and so, for that matter, is
her son. It is through the help of these two—place your hope
in them, and in no one else—that grace will be yours for the
getting; but get there in time!'

'By St Paul!' exclaimed a pardoner. 'But what happens if no
one knows me there? I'd better be off and get my box of
indulgences, my papal bull, and episcopal authorization!'

'Christ in Heaven!' exclaimed a prostitute.* 'I think I'd
better go along with you; you can say to people I'm your
"sister!"'

I've no idea *what* became of that pair.

'This would be the very devil of a journey for anyone attempting it without a guide to go with us every foot of the way!'—Such were the words in which the people began to grumble and complain.

'By St Peter!' cried Piers the Plowman, 'I've got a half-acre of land to be ploughed along the length of the main road. Once I'd ploughed and sown it, *I'd* be willing to go with you and show you the way.'

'That would mean rather a long wait!' exclaimed a lady in a veil.* 'What are we women supposed to do in the meantime?'

'Some of you', replied Piers, 'could sew up grain-sacks to prevent the wheat falling through. And you beautiful ladies with those long fingers of yours, provide yourselves silk of the best quality, so that when the need arises you can embroider priests' chasubles to adorn our churches.* My advice to you is to practise cloth-making, and teach your daughters to do so. Find out about the living conditions of people in need who have nothing proper to wear, and provide clothes for them. That is something that Truth commands us to do.* For unless the earth should prove unable to bear, my part will be to provide them their food as long as I live, because of my love for our Lord in Heaven. And I tell you that anyone who depends on food and drink to live is obliged to help the man who earns that food to work, and work effectively.'

'By Christ!' exclaimed a knight, 'he's giving us the best advice there is. But to tell the truth, ploughing isn't one of the subjects *I* was taught at school. All the same', he went on, 'show me how, and God help me if I don't at least give it a go!'

'By St Paul!' replied Piers. 'This is a handsome offer of yours. But no; I'll toil and sweat for both of us. I'm willing to work all my life because of the good will I have towards you.* But this is on condition that you, for your part, protect Holy Church and myself against those ravaging villains who destroy everything they come upon. You should also go and hunt for all you're worth. Get the hares, the foxes, and the boars and deer that break down my hedges. And go and train up your falcons to prey on the wild birds that flock to my fields and do my harvesting for me!'

The knight came forth with a courteous reply to all this. 'Piers', he said, 'I give you my solemn word that I'll do everything in my power to keep this agreement of ours, even if it means I have to resort to force. As long as I live, I'm prepared to give you my support.'

'Good!' said Piers, 'but there's one more thing I ask of you. Make sure you never cause trouble for any of your tenants, unless what you're doing has the approval of Truth. You may indeed be entitled to impose fines on them,* but let pity work out the price they are to pay, and let humility hold back your hand, whatever Meed may whisper in your ear! And even if poor men were to find some monetary means of easing their cause, don't touch it, in case it exceeds any due claim you have on them. Remember, at the conclusion of life's long year,* you'll have to hand it all back again, in a highly dangerous place that goes by the name of Purgatory. Don't be too hard on your serfs: you'll find things go all the better with you for it. A man may be your social inferior here on earth, yet in the Kingdom of Heaven he may turn out to deserve a more honourable place and a higher happiness. Think of the text that says "Friend, take a higher place!"* Have a look, too, in the crypt of a church, where the bones of the dead are kept. Can you recognize a serf from a knight there? Can you tell which is which? Keep death's lesson deep within your heart.* Never let your own tongue tell a lie; and hold in abhorrence all stories and tales except those that sing the praises of virtue and serve as lessons to instruct the men who work for you. Have nothing whatever to do with purveyors of filth, and keep your dinner-table free of people whose speech dishonours it. Grasp this clearly, my friend: they're tuning those pipes of theirs to the pitch of Hell!'

'By St James', swore the knight, 'I solemnly agree to do just what you say for every day I live upon this earth!'

'I, for my part', replied Piers, 'will dress myself in pilgrim's clothes* and travel with you until we find Truth.'

Hereupon, Piers began to don his working-clothes, some of them patched, some still in one piece, his leggings, and the mittens he wore to keep his fingers from freezing. At his back, where pilgrims carry a provision-bag, he hung his ploughman's seed-basket. 'In this', said Piers, 'I want a bushel-weight* of wheat grain. I intend to sow it myself and then set off like a pilgrim to obtain my pardon. And this I promise in Our Lord's name: anyone who helps me to plough or sow here, before I set off, will have the right to glean here in time of harvest, and enjoy what he can pick up, whatever anyone may say. And for every craftsman who knows how to live a good, honest life I shall provide the sustenance he needs. But there'll be nothing for Jack the juggler, or Whorehouse Jane, or Danny the dice-sharper, Denny the pimp, or Friar Fix-it and all that crowd of his cloth, and that goes for Randy Robin,* whose mouth needs a good rinsing. Truth once told me to state clearly that people like these "would be blotted out of the book of life",* and I should have nothing whatever to do with them. You know that Holy Church is forbidden to ask such people to pay tithes, "because their names are not to be written with those of the just". Look—they've had the good luck to get away. God help them somehow to repent!'

Piers had a wife, whose name was Work-in-time.* His daughter was called Do-as-you're-told-or-your-mother-will-scold. His son's name was Let-your-superiors-have-their-way | Don't-judge-them-or-you'll-dearly-pay | It's-God-who-has-the-final-say.

'Now that I'm old and grey', continued Piers, 'and have all that I myself need, I'm determined to go on pilgrimage with the rest. But before setting off, I'm going to have my will drawn up. "In the name of God, Amen":* here and now, I am making my will myself.

'Let the one with the best claim to it have my soul, and protect it from the Devil. That is what I believe; and until I'm required to give an account of myself before God, as the Creed states, I am relying on my record here to obtain release from my sins and remission of my guilt.*

'The Church is to have my dead body* and be the final
custodian of my bones. Was it not the priest who demanded a
tenth of all my grain and goods? For the sake of my soul, I
have always paid him on time; so surely he, in turn, is obliged
to remember me by name at mass, in the commemoration of
all the faithful departed?

'I want my wife to have everything I have honestly earned,
and nothing else besides; she is to divide it amongst my dear
sons and daughters. Even if I were to die today, all that I owe
has been paid in full; what I have borrowed I always returned
before going home to bed. As for what is left over,* I swear
by the Rood of Lucca that I shall use it to honour Truth while
I live; I shall be his pilgrim by ploughing the earth for the
benefit of the poor. My plough-pusher* will be my pilgrim's
pikestaff, separating the roots and helping my coulter to cut
through and free the furrows of weeds!'

So now Piers and the pilgrims went off to the ploughing;
and many of them helped to work this half-acre of his.
Ditchers and diggers dug up the unploughed ridges,* and
Piers, pleased with their work, praised them enthusiastically.
Other labourers, too, worked with great dedication; each
man, in his own way, set himself to one task or another—
some, for instance, to meet Piers's wishes, hoed up the weeds.
When the hour of nine arrived, Piers let his plough come to a
stand, and went to have a look at their work himself; he
wanted to see who had worked best and deserved to be taken
on again when harvest-time came round. Some of the people
he found were sitting down and singing songs over their ale;
their sole contribution to ploughing the half-acre field was
'Fol-de-rol and fiddle-de-dee'!

'Now, by my soul's peril!' Piers swore in sheer rage, 'unless
you get up right away and set to work, not a single wheat-
grain that sprouts in this place will ever help to brighten your
looks when your stomachs start to feel the pinch. You can die
of starvation, for all I care—and the devil take anyone who
sheds a tear for it!'

At this, the scrimshankers took fright, and they began to
pretend their sight was defective, or they twisted their legs to

look as if they were maimed—layabouts of this ilk know all the little tricks!—and started moaning to Piers and begging him to let them off. 'Oh, bless you, sir', they whined, 'our poor arms and legs aren't fit for working; but we'll gladly pray for you, and for your plough as well! We'll ask the good Lord to give you an abundant harvest and reward you for all this enormous kindness you're showing to us here. You see, we're in such terrible shape, we simply can't risk pushing ourselves too hard with any really heavy physical work.'

'*If* what you say is true', replied Piers, 'I'll find it out soon enough. But I've a shrewd suspicion you're a bunch of idle parasites! Truth, though, knows exactly what's what with each of you. I'm an old hand of his, and I'm under orders to tell him the names of anyone who injures any of his honest workmen. You people simply consume what others earn by the sweat of their brow. But Truth is going to teach you to drive his team—and if you don't learn, you'll have to be content with barley-bread and water from the stream.* On the other hand, those who really are blind, or crippled, or chained up in prison, will eat loaves of wheat and drink the same drink as I do, till God in his good time sends them relief from their afflictions. But you people are quite fit to work so as to satisfy Truth; so you can earn your food and wages by looking after cattle in the fields, or by protecting the crops from wild animals, or by making ditches, by digging, by threshing the sheaves, or by mixing lime-mortar or carting manure to the fields. Ah, but your lives are devoted to lying, deceit, and sloth, and if vengeance hasn't already lighted upon you, it's only thanks to the patient forbearance of God.

'No, I intend to keep my hand-outs and doles for anchorites and solitaries* who eat nothing at all between twelve today and noon tomorrow; and I'll use my money to provide clothing for those who have churches and monasteries in their charge. But none of it will go to bogus wandering hermits and itinerant gospellers* who don't know how to preach and have no licence from the bishop to do so. Only the honest ones will get their bread and broth, and enough of it at that, for it's impossible to live a proper life devoted to religion without some secure supply of what is needed.'*

At this point, Waster* flew into a rage and flung down his glove in front of Piers Plowman. A loud-mouthed Breton,* too, challenged him rudely: 'Go and piss on your plough, you goddamned bastard! Who the hell cares whether you agree to what we demand or not? We'll have your flour and your flesh when we fucking well please—just try and stop us!'

Then Piers Plowman turned and complained to the knight, asking for the protection he had offered against these villainous scoundrels and human wolves, whose fierce attacks cost everyone so dear.

'These people', he said, 'eat up everything without producing so much as a pea! If things go on like this, and my plough is forced to lie idle, there'll be no prosperity for people to enjoy'.

At this the knight, with the courtesy that was part of his calling,* gave Waster a warning, accompanying it with some good advice to boot: 'If you don't do your bit, you'll feel the full weight of the law; you have my word as a knight!'

'I've never done a stroke in my life', replied Waster, 'and I'm damned if I'm going to start now!' And he went on to declare he didn't care a damn for the law, or half a damn for the knight, or an empty eggshell for Piers and his plough. He ended by threatening to beat up Piers and his men if he ever came across them again.

'Now, by my soul's salvation!' Piers cried, 'I'm going to make you suffer—just wait and see!' And he bellowed at the top of his voice for Hunger, who heard him right away. 'Take vengeance for me on these ravagers',* he shouted, 'look how they're ruining everything around them!'

Then Hunger, without a moment's delay, put his arms out, gripped Waster round the stomach, and squeezed so hard that salt water started from his eyes. He smacked the Breton braggart so hard across the face that he looked as hollow as a lantern for the rest of his days. Hunger gave the pair of them such a drubbing that he nearly burst their bellies. I assure you they'd have been worm's meat if Piers hadn't given him a loaf of pea-flour and begged him to hold off.

'Spare their lives', he said, 'and let them share the pigs' food, or else eat loaves of beans mixed up with bran.'*

This caused the bogus handicapped such a fright that they rushed into the barns and started wielding the threshing flails for all they were worth, from dawn till it was night. Consequently, Hunger hadn't the heart to show up, thanks to a potful of pea-soup Piers had made. A whole bevy of hermits closed their fists on the handles of spades, and trimmed their copes to the length of a jacket; then off they went, workmen all with spades and shovels, and set to work digging and making ditches as a way to keep Hunger at bay. Blind men and bedridden invalids by the thousand suddenly got better, and people who had sat about begging for money underwent immediate recoveries. The very food prepared to feed horses sufficed to feed several afflicted with the pangs of hunger. Beggars in droves proved quite willing to work for nothing better than beans. Not a poor man but was perfectly content with a dish of pease-pudding for payment, and sprang forth to do Piers' bidding with the speed of a sparrow-hawk. Piers was delighted with this, and set them to their tasks, giving them food and paying them the most suitable wages he could afford.

By now, Piers was feeling quite sorry for them, so he begged Hunger to go back home to his own domain and remain there for ever. 'Thanks to your influence', he said, 'I've been well and truly avenged on these vicious layabouts. But before you go, I'd be grateful if you could tell me the best way of dealing with people who beg for alms?* I've no doubt whatever that as soon as you've gone they'll fall to their slacking again. It's simply the experience of real distress that's keeping them in line at present; they only do what I say to avoid starving. Yet, for all that, they are blood-relations of mine, after all; didn't God redeem us all together? I recall Truth once instructing me to love each one of them, and always to help them in every kind of need. I want to know now what you think would be best. How shall I keep control of them and ensure that they do some work?'

'Now, listen', said Hunger, 'and consider this a sound piece of advice. As for the sturdy, able-bodied beggars who are well able to earn their bread by working—give them what you feed dogs and horses to ensure that they survive. Nourish them with beans to stop their stomachs from swelling up with want. And if those fellows start moaning about it, tell them to go off and work; they can enjoy fancier fare when they've done something to deserve it.

'But if you meet anyone who's come down in the world through no fault of his own but sheer bad luck, or has suffered at the hands of some group of scoundrels, make it your business to find out what you can about him. Then, for the love of our Lord in Heaven, use what you have to help and support such people. Show them love by giving to them; isn't that what it means to be truly human—that "we should each bear one another's burdens"?* There are all kinds of people you can see around you who are in real need, without clothing or any source of income; help them with coin or in kind—do something to make their lot better. Love them, don't blame them; leave it to God to be their judge and decide if it's punishment they need, even when they are plainly guilty of some crime. "Vengeance is mine", says the Lord, "and I shall repay."* But if you want to find favour with God, follow the Gospel teaching and win the affection of simple, humble people; that is how you yourself will obtain grace. "Make friends for yourself", says Scripture, "with the money you have, bad though it be in itself."'*

'I wouldn't wish to offend God', said Piers, 'for all the wealth in the world. Can I do what you say without myself doing wrong?'

'Yes, I give you my word', answered Hunger, 'or the Bible's not to be trusted. Go to Genesis, that giant book which tells the tale of mankind's beginnings, and study God's command there: "In the sweat of your brow you shall till the earth to earn the bread by which you shall live."* The Wisdom books teach the same lesson—I've seen it there in the Bible: "the sluggard felt the chill—so the fields he would not till! For which reason he'll have to turn beggar, but will find no one prepared to assuage his pangs."* And St Matthew, the evangelist whose symbol is the figure of a man,* has this to say: "A wicked servant had a pound, and because he refused to do business with it, he earned his master's disfavour for the rest of his days. The master took away the

pound from him and gave it to the one who had ten pounds."
And he adds some words which continue to echo in the ears of
the Church: "The man who has shall receive, and his needs
will be met. But the man who has not shall not receive, and
no help will he get. Even what he thinks is his will I take from
him yet!"*

'Kind Wit lays it down as a rule that every man should do
some kind of work:* teaching, ploughing, labouring in
prayer. Christ likewise requires that everyone should work,
whether the life he leads is active or contemplative. In the
psalm that begins "Blessed are all those who fear the Lord",
this is what the psalmist tells us: that the man who earns the
food he eats by his own honest toil is blessed, both physically
and spiritually. That is the Bible's promise: "You will eat of
the labours of your hands."'*

'Hunger, my friend', said Piers, 'there's one more thing I
beg you. Can you give me, please, some medical advice? The
fact is that some of my workmen—and I myself, for that
matter—have been off work with stomach pains for a whole
week.'

'Oh, I know just what illness is bothering you!' came
Hunger's answer, 'you've been eating too much—that's what's
making you groan! But mark my word', he went on, 'if you
value your health, never drink before you've first eaten some
food. And, for that matter, don't eat, either, until you
actually feel a touch of hunger. That's the best sauce for
making food seem tasty. Leave some over for supper-time,
too, and don't sit too long over your meal. Better still, get up
from table before you've eaten all you feel you could manage.
And don't let Sir Excess Overmuch share your table, enjoying
your friendship; the fellow's a lecher with a tongue for tasty
morsels, and a ravenous desire for titbits of all kinds.

'If you follow this diet,* I'm ready to bet my ears that all
the doctors in England will have to take their fur-lined hoods,
and their gold-buttoned Calabrian fur-coats, and sell them off
to get a decent meal. They'll have to give up medicine—take
my word for it—and learn to work with their hands if they
want to ensure they ever eat again. Doctors? They're mostly
quacks, God help them! The main effect of their wretched
mixtures is to carry people off before their hour has struck.'

'By St Paul!' exclaimed Piers. 'What excellent sense you talk! Hunger, this lesson is a delight to listen to; may God reward you for it! You can leave now whenever you're ready, and I hope that all goes well with you.'

But Hunger said, 'I vow to God, I'm not going to budge till I've had my meal for the day—and, in addition, something to drink with it.'

'I've no money', said Piers, 'for chickens or geese or pork. All I've got is a couple of fresh cheeses, a tiny amount of curds and cream, an oat-cake and a couple of loaves for my children, baked from bean-flour and bran. I give you my solemn word, moreover, that I don't have the ingredients to fry you a platter of bacon and eggs. All I've got is parsley, leeks, and a huge supply of greens, as well as a cow, a calf, and a mare that pulls my dung-cart in the dry season. You see, that's the sort of food we've got to live on till Lammas-tide comes,* by which time I hope the fields will be ready for harvest. Then I can give you the kind of dinner I'd like to!'

At this, the poor people all went and got their peas, still in their shells, and brought beans and baked apples in their laps, along with spring onions, chervil, and an abundance of ripe cherries. This they presented to Piers to satisfy Hunger. He, however, gobbled it all up, and demanded more. In a panic, then, the poor people set about feeding Hunger, hoping to put an end to him with cabbages and peas. By now, though, harvest-time began to approach, and the new season's corn came to the markets. Then everyone cheered up, and started feeding Hunger with nothing but the best; and taking a leaf out of Glutton's book, they put him to sleep with a draught of good strong ale!*

By this stage, Waster was totally unwilling to work; instead he went loafing about, and even the very beggars turned up their noses at being offered loaves with bean-flour in them. Nothing would do but the finest kinds of bread, with names like 'cocket' and 'clear-matin', and only the purest wheat-flour would suffice. Nor would they touch your thin halfpenny beer, but only the most select nut-brown ales the brewers could offer. Landless labourers, with nothing to live on but their hands, made faces at meals of yesterday's reheated cabbage. Even penny-ale wasn't good enough for them, nor,

for that matter, a simple side of bacon. They'd put up with
nothing but fresh meat or fish, fried or baked, and it had to
be served 'piping-hot and straight from the stove!'—this in
case their stomachs should catch cold. And if a man of this
class wasn't paid a lordly wage, he'd be heard bemoaning the
time he was born to be 'a lousy bloody labourer'. One of these
lads doesn't give a twopenny damn for that adage of Cato's—
'You were born poor; bear your poverty with patience.'* So
he gets angry with God, protests against the whole order of
things, then curses the King and his Council for decreeing
laws that penalize working men. And yet, while Hunger had
the upper hand, not one of them dared to complain or take
any action against *his* 'Statute', backed as it was with a look
that stopped you in your tracks!

But I have a warning to deliver to you working men: get
hold of what you need while yet you can. For Hunger's going
to come back, and come back quickly! With him, he will
bring heavy rains, to teach a lesson to Waster and his ilk.
Within the next five years, there's going to be a famine; what
with floods and severe storms, the crops will fail. This is
Saturn's message, sent to you as a warning:*

> *When in the sun you see disaster,*
> *Two monks' heads, and a girl as master*
> *(Multiply this by eight!)—*
> *Plague will pull back, dearth sit in judgement,*
> *Dave Ditcher die for lack of nourishment.*
> *All this will happen one fine day*
> *Unless God in his goodness should say,*
> *'Hold, enough! Abate!'*

Truth heard about what was happening, and sent word to Piers that he should look to his plough-team and cultivate the soil. And he obtained for Piers and his heirs in perpetuity an absolute pardon, *a pena et a culpa*,* from all punishment and from all guilt attaching to sin. Truth's command to Piers was to stay at home and plough his fallow lands. And to everyone who made any useful contribution to his work, helping him to plough, plant, or sow, Truth granted pardon along with Piers Plowman.

Kings and knights who protect Holy Church, and justly govern those beneath them, receive a pardon enabling them to pass through Purgatory with ease and become sharers with the patriarchs and the prophets in Heaven. Bishops who live holy lives, provided they are learned in both canon and civil law, and use their knowledge to instruct the ignorant and lead people to repent, to the best of their ability, are thus described in the pardon Piers produced: they count as the apostles' equals, and at Doomsday will be entitled to sit enthroned on the high seat of judgement.

In the margin of the document there was added, for merchants, a remission of several years' punishment;* but the Pope* would not grant to them an absolute pardon. This was because they do not observe holy days properly according to the Church's rules; moreover, they use oaths like 'by my soul!' and 'so help me God!' in order to market their goods, though they can only do so with a bad conscience. Under his private seal,* however, Truth sent the merchants a letter in which he urged them to buy and sell freely, save the profits, and put them to good use. They should repair hospitals and help the sick; be active in repairing rutted roads or bridges that had collapsed; bring about suitable marriages for orphan girls, or else find places for them in convents of nuns. They should provide food for the destitute and imprisoned, enable boys to be educated at school or apprenticed to a trade, and assist religious orders with endowments that would bring them an adequate income. 'I myself', he said, 'will send you my angel Michael to ensure that no fiend will harm or frighten you at the moment of your death. If you agree to do all these things, he will protect you from falling into despair and give your souls safe conduct, to share the joys of Paradise with my saints'. This, to the merchants, was heartening news indeed, and many of them burst into tears of joy, praising Piers Plowman for obtaining this bull of remission.

The least comprehensive pardon of all was that granted to fee'd barristers. A text in the Psalms denies salvation to those who accept gifts, in particular from innocent people who don't know what wrong it is they are supposed to have done. 'Take no payment from the innocent', it says. Barristers ought to take special pains to plead for such people and help their cases forward. Their services should be recompensed by those in high position in state and church: 'Their payment shall come from kings and from princes.' But there's many a judge and juryman who will take more trouble on behalf of a pretty prostitute than do the right thing purely for the love of God—take my word for it! Yet if a lawyer does expend his energies speaking up for a poor and innocent man who has no resources and has done no one any harm; if he supports his cause without looking for payment, but offers his expertise freely for love of God—on the day *he* dies no fiend will lay a finger on him, or seek to impede the safe journey of his soul. The Psalter guarantees this in the verse, 'Lord, who shall dwell in thy tent?'*

Four basic goods* there are that cannot be sold for money: water, wind, knowledge, and fire. Our Heavenly Father granted them all as a common possession to the world as a whole. They are Truth's treasures given for the benefit of mankind, and will never increase or diminish unless God himself so ordains. Now, as for those who *do* take money from the poor for their legal services—when they approach the moment of death and desire indulgences, how very tiny the pardon they receive as they stand on the brink of the world to come! Do I falsify the case, my honourable legal friends? St Matthew knows the truth of the whole matter: 'Do to others as you would have them do to you!'*

Next in the pardon came all working people who earn a
living by their hands, get their livelihood in an honest
manner, and live in obedience to the law and in accord with
charity. These, for their humility of heart, receive the same
forgiveness that was sent to Piers. But there's no mention in
the document of people who live on alms, unless their motive
for begging is a good one. For anyone who begs or asks for
alms, without having to, is a diabolical deceiver. He defrauds
those who are really in need, and at the same time cheats the
hapless giver, who, if he knew the facts, would rather give to
someone in real distress—thereby helping those whose need
for alms is greatest. This is the lesson on almsgiving taught by
Cato: 'Take heed whom you help!', while the author of the
Historia Scholastica advises: 'Keep your alms in your hand
until you know whom you should give to.'*

There is another view of the question, however. The
blessed Gregory urges us to give to all who ask, for the sake of
the One who gives us all: 'Do not choose who to be charitable
to, lest you overlook someone who is truly deserving. It is not
certain whether charity to the undeserving may not please
God even more!'* The reason for this is, that you don't know
who *is* deserving, whereas God does know who really is in
need. So, if there is any deception involved, it's the receiver
who is the deceiver. The giver merely gives, and in doing so
settles his own account with God; the beggar, however, is a
borrower, who keeps on getting still further into debt.
Beggars, after all, are continually borrowing, and their only
guarantor is Almighty God; He alone can pay back their
creditors—and with interest to boot:

> 'Why did you not put my money in the bank
> To earn me interest while I was away?'*

So, you beggars, don't ask for alms unless you are in dire
need. For the Bible bears witness that anyone who has the
means to buy himself some bread has enough, even if he has
nothing else besides: 'He is rich enough who does not lack
bread.'* (Make a practice, too, of reading the lives of the
saints* in your spare time!) The Bible, indeed, forbids
begging, and criticizes those who go in for it in these words: 'I

have been young and old, and I have not seen the just man forsaken, or his offspring in quest of bread.'*

These beggar-men observe neither charity nor law; they refuse to marry the women they sleep with, but behave as if they were wild animals: they whinny like horses, then up and in! The children they beget are regarded as bastards. When such a child is young, he may injure his back or some other bone and as a result spend the rest of his life deceitfully sponging, along with his own brood of children. There are more physical deformities amongst those beggars than in any other group of people in the world. Those who live this kind of life may well detest the day they were born into this world, when the hour to leave it eventually comes round. But as for aged, white-haired men without the strength to help themselves, pregnant women who don't work because they cannot, the blind, the bedridden, the severely hand-icapped, lepers and suchlike who accept their disabilities without complaining—all these receive as complete a pardon as does Piers himself. Out of love for their humility of heart, the Lord God has given them their purgatorial penance here, during their lifetime on this earth.

And now, a priest spoke up, and said, 'Piers! I shall have to read your pardon. I'll translate every clause and give you its sense in English.'*

Piers opened up the pardon at his request; and I, from behind the two of them, laid eyes on the document in its entirety. It consisted of just two lines, and not one letter more, and was written down as here given, as a testimony sent from Truth:

> *Et qui bona egerunt ibunt in vitam eternam;*
> *Qui vero mala, in ignem eternum.* [1]*

'By St Peter!' exclaimed the priest then, 'I can't find any pardon. There's just "Do well and have well, and God will receive your soul" and "Do evil and have evil, and expect only this: that the day you die, the devil will take your soul!"'

---

[1] 'And those who do good will go into eternal life; | But those who do evil, into everlasting fire.'

And Piers, in sheer rage, tore the pardon in two, and said:
'*Si ambulavero in medio umbre mortis, non timebo mala, quoniam
tu mecum es.*[1]* I shall leave off my sowing, and not work so
hard, or spend so much effort bothering about what I'm to
eat. From now on, my plough will be prayers and penance:*
and even if my good wheat bread runs out, I'll weep for my
sins when I should be asleep. The Psalter tells us that the
prophet David ate his bread in penance and sorrow; many
others have done so, too. But if a man loves God faithfully, he
can earn his living without any difficulty: "Tears have been
my bread both by day and by night!" And unless St Luke is
misleading us, Our Lord teaches us by the example of the
birds not to be overly concerned about earthly happiness.
"Do not be solicitous", he says in the Gospel, showing us
examples by which to live our own lives. "The birds of the
field—who provides for them in winter? They have no granary
to turn to, yet God provides for them all."'*

'What!' exclaimed the priest to Piers. 'By St Peter, it strikes
me you've picked up a bit of education, eh? Who taught *you*
to read?'

'The Abbess Abstinence taught me my a.b.c.', was Piers's
reply. 'And later Conscience came, and taught me a good deal
more.'*

'If you were a priest', said the other, 'you could set up
anywhere you fancied as a preacher, trained in theology, and
take *Dixit insipiens*[2]* as text for your sermon!'

'Ignorant clot!' cried Piers. 'How little you must look at the
Bible! You can't often have read the proverbs of Solomon:*

> Cast out those who scoff and gibe
> Lest quarrels and disputes arise!'

The priest and Piers went on to dispute with each other,
and the noise of their exchanges woke me up. I looked round,
and saw that the sun had now travelled to the south. There I
was on the Malvern Hills, without any food or money, and I

---

[1] 'Though I should walk in the midst of the shadow of death, I will fear no evil:
for thou art with me.'

[2] 'The fool hath said in his heart . . .'

walked on my way for at least a mile, turning this dream of
mine over in my mind . . .

Many a time since then, this dream has made me ponder on
all the things I saw as I slept, and to ask, *Could such things be?*

Deep in my heart, I became absorbed in the thought of
Piers Plowman and that pardon he received, which brought
comfort to everyone; and I recalled how the priest questioned
its validity with a couple of well-turned phrases. But I've no
real taste for the business of interpreting dreams, something
I've often observed go sadly astray. Cato and the religious
authorities advise us not to take dream-interpretation
seriously: '*Somnia ne cures*'* is the phrase—don't lose any
sleep over dreams!

On the other hand, though, the Bible bears out that the
prophet Daniel interpreted the dreams of a certain king,
known to the learned by the name of Nebuchadnezzar. Daniel
said this to him: 'My lord King, what your dream signifies is,
that a foreign army is going to come and lay claim to your
kingdom. And your land will be divided amongst men of
lower rank than yourself.' And in fact, things later turned out
just as Daniel had foretold: the King did lose his realm, and
lesser men did indeed take it from him.

Joseph, likewise, had a wonderful dream in which the
moon, the sun, and the eleven stars all did him obeisance.
Jacob thereupon interpreted Joseph's dream. 'My dear son',
said his father, 'there is going to come a time of famine; all of
us—I myself and my other sons—will come looking for you
in our hour of need.' It happened as his father said, in
Pharaoh's time, when Joseph was presiding over Egypt as its
chief magistrate. Just as his father had stated, his kindred all
came to look for him there.*

All of this makes me keep thinking about the dreams—and
especially about how the priest proved that 'doing well' isn't
any kind of pardon. My own verdict was that doing well was
superior to indulgences, masses said regularly over two or
three years, and letters of remission sent by bishops.* On
Judgement Day, I concluded, it is 'Do-well' that will be

received with honour, excelling as it does all the papal pardons in the world.

The Pope does, of course, have the power to grant people a pardon which will enable them to enter Heaven without having to do formal penance. This is a part of our faith, as we have it on the authority of the learned: 'Whatever you bind upon earth will be bound in Heaven, too.' God forbid, too, that I should refuse to believe that pardon, penance, *and* prayers do indeed save souls, even souls guilty of all seven capital sins! But actually to *rely* on masses said for three years . . . my own honest opinion is, this can't be as certain a route to salvation, surely, as 'doing well'?*

For this reason my advice to rich men is this, if they rely on their wealth to pay for triennial masses: don't let that lead you into breaking the Ten Commandments without giving another thought to the matter! I warn in particular rulers, mayors, and judges, you who possess the goods of this world and enjoy the reputation of being wise: don't rely on obtaining a pardon in the form of a papal bull! At the terrible Day of Doom, when the dead are to rise and all appear before Christ to make their reckoning, the judgement will openly state what kind of life you lived here—how you administered the laws of God, and how you conducted yourself day by day. Then, even if you have a whole sackful of pardons and letters of privilege from heads of religious houses; even if you are a paid-up associate fraternity member in all four orders of friars,* with a double supply of indulgences to boot—unless Do-well* comes to your help, I doubt whether your whole stock of pardons and letters patent will amount to much more than the value of a single pie-crust!

And so I advise all Christians to call on God for mercy, and to beg his mother Mary to intercede for us with him, to grant us the grace here and now during our lives: to perform works that will enable Do-well to declare, after we die, when the Day of Judgement comes, we did as he commanded us to do!

VISION THREE

PASSUS VIII

So, dressed in coarse woollen clothes, I spent the whole of a summer* roaming about in a search for Do-well. And time and again I enquired from people that I met if anyone knew where Do-well lived.* I asked any number of people, what sort of person could he be?

Wherever I went, though, there was nobody, at any level of society, who could tell me where the man was to be found. Eventually, one Friday, I met two Franciscan friars,* university men with sharp minds. I greeted them politely, as I'd learned to do, and asked them to tell me, for charity's sake, before they went on their way, if they knew any place in the whole surrounding country which might be Do-well's home.

'Let me know', I said. 'After all, you people cover more ground on foot than anyone else in the world. You know the rural areas, courts, and all sorts of places—from the palaces of royalty to the humble houses of the poor. Doubtless you must know where Do-well—and Do-evil,* too—both live.'

'By Mary!' replied the masters, 'he lives with us. He always has, we believe, and always will.'

'I dispute that!'* I answered, in correct scholastic form, and embarked on a formal argument about it. 'It's a true premiss', I began, 'that, as the Bible says, "even the just man falls into sin seven times a day."* Well, I presume that whoever sins, does evil; but Do-well and Do-evil cannot coexist. It therefore follows logically that Do-well *cannot* reside permanently with you friars. He must, at least on occasion, be elsewhere, guiding men and women in their lives.'

'I'll tell you, my son', one of the friars replied, 'just how a virtuous man can sin seven times a day; I'll illustrate it for you by means of a little parable. A man finds himself in a boat out in the open sea. The wind, the water, and the rocking of the boat cause him, time and again, to fall down, and then get up again. The reason is that, however firmly he tries to stand, he loses his footing as soon as he moves. He still remains perfectly safe and sound, though—and that necessarily follows. If, on the other hand, he got up abruptly and made a grab for the helm, the combined force of the wind and the water would turn the boat right over, and the man's life would be lost merely through his own negligent oversight.

'Now', he continued, 'that's exactly the way it is with people during their lifetime on earth. The water is an image of the world we live in, with all its ups and downs, chances and changes. Earthly possessions are symbolized by the massive waves rolling and tossing under the impetus of the wind and storm. The boat stands for this human frame of ours, a thing fragile in its very essence. Consequently, under the influence of the Devil,* our fleshly instincts, and the mutability of the world, even the most conscientious person succumbs to sin "seven times a day".

'But—it's not mortal sins such a man commits. And this is because he's protected by Do-well, the valiant fighter Charity, who is our main support against sin. He's the one who gives man the energy to get up, and he steers the human soul. So in this way, though your body may "sink" as low as a boat in the water, your soul remains always safe; unless, that is, you yourself deliberately follow the promptings of the flesh—and, after that, the devil—and go on then to commit mortal sin, thereby getting drowned. If that is what you want, God will go on putting up with your sluggishness of spirit. After all, he gave you the power to govern your own life properly—gave it as a free gift. He gave a measure of intelligence and free will to every creature, including the birds of the air, the fishes, and the animals. But man possesses it in the highest degree and is therefore most to blame if he fails to use it to perform acts of virtue, as Do-well instructs him.'

'I simply haven't got the innate capacity to grasp everything you've been saying',* I replied. 'But if I live long enough to go on looking, I shall try to learn better.'

'I commend you', he answered, 'to Christ who died on the cross.'

'May the same Christ save *you* from misfortune', I replied, 'and give you the grace to become men of virtuous life, as long as you live on this earth!'

And so I went on travelling far and wide, walking alone through a wild, uncultivated region,* following the edges of a wood. The jubilant song of birds caused me to linger, and I lay back for a little while in a clearing, under a lime tree, listening to the delicious carolling of those birds. The cheerful sounds that came from their throats worked on me, till I drifted off to sleep there. And then I had what I imagine must be the most extraordinary dream anyone in the world has ever dreamed.

It seemed to me that a tall man, who looked just like me, came up and called me by my very own name.

'Who might you be?' I asked. 'How can you know my name?'

'You know that perfectly well', he replied. 'No one could know it better!'

'*Do* I know who you are?' I pursued.

'Thought',* he answered. 'I've been keeping you company for the last seven years.* Haven't you ever seen me before?'

'You're Thought?' I said. 'Well then, you ought to be able to tell me where Do-well can be found!'

'Do-well', he answered, 'and also Do-better, and the third of them, Do-best, are three splendid virtues*—and you don't have to go very far to find them. Take a man who speaks the truth and acts honestly, earning his living by his labour or the yield of his land; a man who's not given to drunkenness or treating people like dirt. That is someone by whose side *Do-well* walks.

'Do-better', he went on, 'does all these things, and a great deal more besides. He's as meek as a lamb and speaks kind and gentle words, helping everyone in whatever way he needs. He has taken all those money-bags and wallets that belonged to the Earl of Avarice and his descendants, he's burst them wide open, and he's made himself friends with the cash accumulated by the covetous. He has entered the religious life, and devoted himself to expounding Scripture, preaching in public on that text of St Paul's, *Libenter suffertis* ..., "You who are wise, let those who are unwise live with you; willingly do good to them, for that is what God tells you that you should."*

'Do-best stands above the two of them. He carries a bishop's crozier, which has a hook on one end, with which to draw people back from the brink of Hell. That staff of his also has an end with a sharp point; with this he thrusts down evil men who lie in wait plotting mischief against Do-well. Between themselves, Do-well and Do-better have arranged to crown one man king, to govern and protect both of them. Then, if Do-well and Do-better act against Do-best, the king can come and intervene, and put them in gaol, where they'll have to remain for ever, unless Do-best intercedes on their behalf!

'In this way, Do-well, Do-better, and Do-best, the third of them, have crowned one man to be king. His task is to protect them all, and to govern the kingdom in the light of their advice, doing nothing without the agreement of all three.'

Then I thanked Thought for all the advice he had given me. 'All the same, though', I went on, 'I swear I don't find what you say very appealing! What I really want to acquire is a more direct, immediate idea of what these things actually mean in people's experience—Do-well, Do-better, and Do-best.'

'The only person who can direct you to the place where the three of them are to be found',* said Thought, 'is Wit. Apart from him, I don't know another living soul who can!'

In this way, for the space of three days,* Thought and I went on, engaged in a debate about Do-well as day followed day. And before we knew it, we found we had met Wit.* He was tall and lean, like no one else I've known. His clothes suggested neither display nor destitution, his expression was serious and his voice quiet. I wasn't bold enough to broach any topic that might rouse him to a heated argument, except insofar as I could ask Thought to act as an intermediary between us. That way I could throw out some line of discussion that might enable me to put his powers of mind to the test; the question was how to distinguish Do-well from Do-better, and then Do-best from the pair of them.

At this juncture, Thought interposed. 'This is Will', he said, 'and this is what he wants to know. Can Wit show him where in the world Do-well, Do-better, and Do-best can be found? What this man wants to discover is whether each of them is an actual person or not. His aim is to do what the three of them want him to do.'

'Sir Do-well', said Wit, 'lives less than a day's journey from here. His dwelling is a castle which Kind* made out of four kinds of thing. It is made of earth and air mixed together and ingeniously combined with wind and with water. Inside it, moreover, with great skill, Kind has enclosed his loved one, who is as dear to him as he is to himself. *Anima** is her name, and she is an object of great enmity to a proud French knight called the Prince of this World.* His one desire is to abduct her by some stratagem, if he can. But Kind is well aware of this, and guards her all the more closely; he has entrusted her to the hands of Sir Do-well, the chief lord of this border country. Sir Do-well's daughter, Do-better, is her handmaiden, serving this lady faithfully at all times. Above both of them is Do-best, who is the equal in rank of a bishop. What he commands must be performed, since he is in charge of them all: it is by his instruction that the Lady Anima is guided.*

'However, the castle's constable, whose task is to protect them all, is a prudent knight who goes by the name of Inwit.* He has five handsome sons by his first wife: See-well, Say-well, the courteous Hear-well, Sir Work-well-with-your-hand—a powerful fellow, this one—and Sir Godfrey Go-well—a sturdy bunch of noblemen, all of them! These six have been placed in their office to look after Lady Anima's well-being, until such time as Kind should arrive or summon her to his own safe-keeping.'

'What kind of being *is* Kind?' I asked. 'Can you tell me?'

'Kind', replied Wit, 'is the one who created every kind of thing in the world. He is the father and shaper of everything ever made. He is the mighty God, who never had a beginning, the lord of life and light, of pleasure and of pain. The angels, along with every existing thing, are subject to his will; but it is man who resembles him most in features and in form. The animals, you see, came into being through a word that he uttered: "He *spoke*", says Scripture, "and they were created."* But he made man to resemble himself most closely of all; and he fashioned Eve from man's rib-bone without recourse to any intermediary. For he was absolutely alone by himself, and he said, "Let us *make* . . . ".* It's as if someone were to say: "More is needed for this than just my word; my utterance requires the active help of my power." A parallel case would be that of a nobleman who wanted to write some letters.* He had plenty of paper and knew perfectly how to write; yet if he had no pen, then, great man though he might be, those letters of his would never get written!

'And so it would appear that when God said in the Bible, "Let us *make* man in our image", he had to act as well as speak in order that his wise purpose might be expressed. And this is how man was created, through the power of Almighty God's word and action operating together, and endowed with a life destined to know no end. For God, out of the depths of his heavenly being, gave man a spiritual soul and, in his bountiful kindness, granted him true happiness—everlasting life for him and his descendants.

'That, then, is the castle which Kind made: its name is *Caro*,* which means "Man with a soul". It was brought into being through action and word together; man was made through the power of our Sovereign Lord!

'Inwit—the inner sense, or mind*—and all the physical senses are enclosed within the body in a close bond of affection with the Lady Anima, whose name means 'the principle of life'. Through every region of the human body, Anima walks and travels freely, but her central resting-place is the heart: there is her home. Inwit, however, is located in the head, and discovers by examining the heart what is good or bad for Anima, and governs her as he decides. For, second only to God's grace, the main influence on man is his mind or understanding—Inwit.

'Great misfortunes befall men who abuse their understandings—boozing gluttons, for instance, "whose god is their belly".* People like that are the Devil's slaves, and he'll get their souls in the end. For the souls of people who live lives of sin come to resemble the evil one, just as those who live virtuous lives are an image of Almighty God: "He who lives in charity lives in God."*

'How terrible it is that drink should destroy a soul that God redeemed at such a price, causing him to abandon those he created in his own likeness! "I tell you solemnly, I do not know you", says one text of Scripture; and another declares, "I have abandoned them to the desires of their hearts".* But as for the mentally deficient, who lack understanding, I have authority for saying that it is the Church which is responsible for looking after them; it is also the Church which must take care of orphan children, widows with no means of earning a living, the insane, and young girls who are powerless to fend for themselves. All these may be thought of as lacking Inwit or understanding, and as requiring instruction and guidance. I could easily go on at length about this topic, citing a number of texts in support from the four great Doctors of the Church.* St Luke's Gospel, likewise, confirms the truth of what I say.

'If a godfather or a godmother see their godchildren suffering illness and misfortune, and are able to help them, they will be punished in Purgatory unless they do so. Surely the infant who hasn't reached the age of discretion deserves more from them than merely receiving a Christian-name, at a time when he had no idea what was happening? If those in high position in the Church performed their duties properly, no Christian soul would cry out for alms at the gates of a house, or go without any bread or stew to sup on. Why, a Jew wouldn't allow himself to see a fellow-Jew go about wailing with distress, if he had the means to relieve it—not for all the goods upon this earth!* It's a scandal that one Christian should behave so unnaturally towards another, since Jews—whom we regard as fitting companions for Judas!*—assist each other in every kind of need. Why can't we Christians be as generous with Christ's treasure as the Jews are with theirs? They're becoming *our* instructors—the fact's a reproach to us all! My fear is that society at large will have to pay dearly for its selfishness!

'Bishops are going to be found at fault for the way they have treated beggars. But a harsher judgement than befell

Judas awaits the man who will patronize some foul-mouthed jester but send a beggar away because he's in rags:

Another Judas is the bishop who would withhold
The treasures of Christ from the poor man at his door.
Destruction, not charity, is wrought with gold
By a man who squanders wealth that should feed the poor!*

Someone who acts like this is not doing well; he has no fear of Almighty God, and he cares nothing for the counsels of Solomon, teacher of the wise, who said "The fear of the Lord is the beginning of wisdom."*

'The man who holds God in awe, *he* does well.* Someone who reverences God out of love, not out of fear of being punished, does better, and for that reason. But the one who does best is the man who never wastes a single word or a single moment of his time. Recall that "He who offends in one point, becomes guilty in all"!*

'Truth knows this for a fact: the saints in Heaven reserve their utmost repugnance for people who waste the time given to them on earth and, second to time, the faculty of speech. Speech is a plant that springs from grace—it is God's minstrel, heaven's proper pastime. Now our Father, in whom we trust, would never wish his own instrument to lie there idle and untuned, nor to see his minstrel waste his time gadding about from one alehouse to another.

'But as for all honest, upright men who genuinely wish to work, God never fails to grant them his grace, or the chance to go out and earn their living:

For those who seek Heaven's King
Will never want anything.*

'In the secular sphere,* Do-well can be found amongst married people living honest, upright lives; they are the ones whose efforts and earnings sustain society as a whole. It is from this order that there issue those whom we call confessors, kings, knights, emperors, scholars, virgins, and martyrs; all of these came, ultimately, from one single man. Woman was created to help man in his work, and it is for that reason that marriages are arranged through the action of an intermediary. They begin with the consent of the couple's fathers and the advice of their families, followed by the mutual willingness of the pair themselves. That is how marriage was brought into being, and God himself was its author. It is God, likewise, who testifies that marriage is heaven upon earth.

'But there are other people with deceitful and treacherous natures—thieves, liars, vandals, low types born of irregular unions. All these, in my judgement, were begotten in an evil hour,* as Cain was begotten upon Eve. The Psalter refers to vicious creatures of this kind when it says "The sinner has begotten grief, and brought forth evil".* Every descendant of that monster Cain came to a bad end. Didn't God send a message to Seth through an angel?* "My will", he said, "is that your descendants should marry only each other, and not join in wedlock with the offspring of Cain." For all that, some of them defied our Father's injunction, and formed unions between the descendants of Cain and those of Seth. At last, God became angry with what they were doing, and this is what he said: "I am sorry, now, that I ever made man!"*

'Without delay, God came to Noah and commanded him to start work at once. "Quickly!" he said, "go and build a ship constructed of planks and timbers. You yourself and your three sons, along with all your wives, must get promptly into that vessel, and stay there until forty days have come and gone. By then, a flood will have washed clean away that accursed race brought into this world by Cain. The animals that are now alive will cry out curses against the time that saw that unholy Cain come into the world. Because of what he did, all animals that haunt the valleys and hills shall die; so, too, will all the birds of the air. The only exceptions will be one pair of each species; these, inside that clinker-built vessel of yours, will find safety."

'In this instance, the children paid the full price of their ancestor's sins, and everyone came to grief because of their forefathers' wrongdoing. Now, I'm aware that the Gospel is against this view in one respect, when it says that "the son shall not bear the father's sin, nor the father the guilt of his son". Yet I find experience shows that if the father is deceitful and wicked, the son will turn out to possess his parent's bad qualities, at least to some degree. Try to graft apple-shoots on an elder tree, and it will be a miracle if you get sweet fruit from it. This must apply even more to a bad man; any son he begets can't avoid having some flavour of his father about him. Very rarely do you see it turn out otherwise: "Do men gather grapes from thorns or figs from thistles?"*

'And this, then, is how, through that damned soul Cain, disaster came down on the earth—simply because the people contracted marriages that were in opposition to God's will! That is why people who marry off their children in a similar way live to regret it. For these days, the fact is, as I've observed, there are people who embark on unnatural unions purely out of greed to get hold of property. But from such marriages come forth offspring who prove as great a source of trouble as the ones I mentioned before. It's the good who should marry the good, even when they have no goods to speak of. Doesn't Christ say "*I* am the Way, the Truth, and the Life?" Doesn't he promise us, "I can make all prosper"?*

'Ah, dear Christ! how repulsive it is when a young girl is paired with some weak, worn-out old man! Likewise when a man marries, just for her fortune, some rich widow who will never bear a child—except in her arms! Since the time of the plague,* a number of couples have formed unions marked by jealousy, unhappiness, and bitter quarrels in bed. The sole fruit they produce is abusive language, the only children to cherish, bruises and blows. If they were to set off to win the Dunmow flitch,* they'd never succeed without Satan's assistance. That bacon would slide from their grip unless they perjured themselves to get it!

'So this, then, is my advice to all Christians: don't desire a marriage based on desire for wealth (or, for that matter, rich relations). Widowers and widows, follow the same course: marry for love, not to get hold of land. That way you'll earn God's favour, and also enough to live on.

'Every layman who cannot persevere in a chaste single life, should go and make a prudent marriage, to protect himself from falling into sin.* For sexual pleasure is the Devil's lime-rod; so, while you're still young and your tool is in fighting shape, cool your heat in the marriage-bed, if you want to escape all blame:

> While in your prime, avoid the lure of whores:
> *Gateway to Death* stands written on their doors!*

'And when you have acquired a wife, take care to have sex only at the proper time*—not like Adam and Eve when Cain was conceived. For I tell you honestly, there should be no love-making between a man and woman under the wrong conditions. Unless both are pure, physically and morally, in a state of true charity towards one another, and at peace in their conscience as regards God's law, that secret, intimate act must not be performed. But if they lead lives that conform with these conditions, the sexual act is pleasing to Almighty God. For it was he who established marriage in the beginning, and it was also he himself who declared: "It is good for each man to have a wife of his own, in order to avoid lechery."*

'Those who have been conceived under any other conditions are considered base and vile, deceivers, bastards, rogues, and liars—lacking the grace to earn their keep or to gain their neighbours' good will. All they are up to is gadding about, eating their way through whatever they can lay hands on. Opposed to Do-well, they do evil instead, as servants of the Devil. And after they die, they will go and join him, unless God grants them the grace to repent while they are still in this life.

'Do-well, my friend', he concluded, 'is to do what God's law teaches.* To love both your friend and your enemy—now that, believe me, is Do-better. To give, to care for both infancy and old age, to heal, and to help—all that is to Do-best of all! So, Do-well means to fear God; and Do-better means to suffer; and out of the two of them proceeds Do-best—which can lay low the Proud One himself. I mean that Evil Will who undermines so many virtuous efforts, driving Do-well away by the power of mortal sin.'

Now Wit had a wife, whose name was Dame Study,* as lean
of face as she was of figure. She was beside herself with rage
at the way Wit had been instructing me. Glaring at him, she
declared in harsh tones: 'How very wise you must be, Wit, to
go imparting your wisdom to flatterers and half-deranged
neurotics!' She went on haranguing him in this vein, called
down curses, and commanded him to hold his tongue. 'No
more wise words to instruct idiots!' she concluded. 'Don't
cast your precious pearls before swine who have more acorns
than they know how to use.* All they'll do is slobber all over
them! These fellows far prefer pigswill to all the priceless
jewels that abound in the Earthly Paradise.* I'm referring',
she continued, 'to those whose behaviour clearly shows that
land, social standing, wealth, and all the income and leisure
you could ask for mean more to them than the entire body of
moral truths that Solomon ever uttered.

'Nowadays', she said, 'wisdom and knowledge aren't worth
a brass farthing unless Greed has passed his toothcomb
through them, the way that clothiers smooth out their raw
wool.* Can you think up some shady scheme or crooked
enterprise? Do you know how to manipulate a settlement-
day* so as best to do down an honest claimant? Then you've
got skills that will be in great demand at the council-table! It's
people like this who influence the nobility with their dishonest
advice, and manage to make honesty itself seem in the wrong.

'The holy prophet Job observes in his book that it's the
wicked who get their hands on this world's goods, and it's
those who defy the law who end up occupying the highest
places: "Why do the wicked live?" he asks. "Why do sin-
ners prosper?" The Psalter makes the same point about
wrongdoers: "Look, these people are sinners: and yet how
successful they have been in obtaining worldly wealth!"
Scripture says, "Look how they even ennoble themselves, the
scoundrels!" Yes, those whom God gives most to, give away
least to others; men with great fortunes show least regard for

the poor: "They have destroyed what you created; but the
just man—what has *he* done?"*

'Obscene jesters can count on getting paid by them for
their filthy performances, as may bawdy comedians and low
minstrels. But what about the man who has the words of
Scripture constantly on his tongue? The man who knows by
heart the history of Tobias,* the lives of the twelve Apostles,
or the sufferings Jesus endured from the Jews at the com-
mand of Pilate? Dear God! Little thanks he gets for teaching a
lesson of real value. I swear that's not how to get on in this
world!

'It's quite another story with those fellows who play the
half-wit, and live a life in deceitful defiance of God's com-
mandments. They trundle out tall stories about themselves,
spitting and spewing up a torrent of vile language. They
booze, they slobber, they get their audience to gawp at their
antics as they poke fun and spread slander about people who
won't waste a penny of their money on them! But what
do they know about music, an art that brings joy to men's
spirits? About as much as old Muggin the miller* does about
chanting the psalms in church! I swear to God, if it wasn't
that what they peddle is just pure filth, no king, knight, or
canon of St Paul's Cathedral would hand them a worn half-
penny as a New Year's present!* Ah, but nowadays the
common notion of enjoyable, entertaining music is to see it as
just a stimulus for sex, or else as a means of getting in with a
patron, or else, maybe, as so much empty din. Getting tanked
up and constant swearing are the only form of amusement
now in fashion.

'But at dinner-time in hall, when the music is over, if
people do talk about Christ, this is what they say, whatever
their education: "Have you heard that one about how two
persons of the Trinity did in the third?" This sort of stuff
they support with some outrageous line of argument, claiming
to draw on St Bernard's authority,* no less! Then they fish
out some hypothesis or other in order to try and determine its
validity. And in this vein they sit slobbering at the high table,
and when their bellies have reached bursting-point, they chew
God up in their greedy chops!*

'All the while this is going on, people in real distress have to eat their hearts out at the gate, starving, thirsty, and shivering with cold. Not a soul will come anywhere near them to ease their misery, but instead they are shooed off like dogs and ordered to get lost, quickly! People who share their goods with the needy in *this* way can have precious little love for the God who blessed them with all they possess. If there weren't softer hearts to be found among simple people than in the ranks of the rich, all who ask alms would go to their beds without a morsel to eat. Oh, God figures large enough in the mouths of these high-powered theologians, but to catch a glimpse of his mercy and kindness, you must look amongst the poor:

> I heard news of God's tabernacle in petty Ephrata,
> Found it hidden in remote country places.*

The clergy and just about everyone else jaw on endlessly on the subject of God, rolling him round about on the tips of their tongues; but it's the humble who keep him in their hearts!

'Since the time of the plague, friars and frauds like them have been dreaming up difficulties as a diversion for the sneering upper classes. Out of sheer clerical bloody-mindedness they deliver sermons at the cross outside St Paul's,* the effect of which is to undermine people's faith, so that they cease to give generous alms or feel sorry any longer for their sins. In the religious orders, and indeed in all sections of society, rich and poor alike, pride has reached such proportions that prayers have lost all efficacy as a means of stopping the plague. These days, God seems to be deaf—he can't even be bothered to open his ears. Because of *their* sins, he snuffs out little children!* And yet, these incorrigible materialists can't even take the hint from what's happening to their own number. Not even fear of the Black Death itself can make them abandon their pride! Oh no, they won't be kind to the poor as simple charity demands; instead they greedily go through their wealth, buying fancy clothes and extravagant meals. They won't give a scrap to beggars as Scripture instructs us: "Share out your bread to those who are hungry."

No, the more they earn, the more they own, the more land and servants they get control of, the less they seem willing to give away in charity!

'But the lesson of Tobias is clean contrary to this! You rich people, take note of the Bible's testimony concerning men of this sort:

> If you have much, give much; if little, still
> Take care to give that little with good will!*

What Tobias urges is this: if you have a great deal, spend it munificently, and if you aren't rich, let what you give correspond to what you earn. After all, we have no guarantee of how long we will live. These are lessons that should give pleasure to the nobility, since they bear on the right way of treating their dependants with the greatest possible generosity. Nobles shouldn't conduct themselves like wandering minstrels or friars who go searching for dinner-parties, living in other people's houses and shunning their own homes.

'Every day of the week, what a miserable place the hall is, if the lord of the manor and his wife have no desire to dine there! All the well-to-do people now make it a rule to eat by themselves in a private parlour* to avoid the company of the poor; or else they quit the main hall, which was built for people to eat in together, and use a separate room with its own fireplace. The reason is, to economize on food: they want no scraps left for others to eat up!

'I've listened to the conversation of the nobility as they sat at table over their food. They go on for all the world as if they were theologians, discussing Christ and his powers, finding fault with our Heavenly Father, who created us all, and objecting to the Church's teachings in querulous tones. "Why", they demand, "should God be prepared to put up with the antics of some damned snake? Why should he let him trick them—first the woman and then the man, so that they ended up in Hell on account of his deceitful acts and words? And why, on account of their sins, should all their descendants suffer the same penalty—death? Now"—these great men proceed to demonstrate—"the authorities have got it quite wrong, given what they tell us that Christ actually says in the Gospel, about 'the son not bearing the father's guilt'* and so forth. Why should we, living in this present time, have to rot away in the earth because of something Adam did? That's completely and utterly against reason! 'Every man must bear his *own* burden.' "*

'These are the sorts of problems stirred up by those arrogant intellectuals, who make people lose their faith as a result of brooding over what they say.—(*Imaginative, later on, will provide an answer to your question.*)*—But listen to what St Augustine says with these argumentative types in mind. His text is "Don't be more wise than you need to be!"* Don't desire to know *why* God was willing to let Satan lead mankind astray. Just put your trust loyally in what the Church teaches, and throughout your life pray to God for his pardon and forgiveness. Pray, too, for the gift of his mercy to help you repent while there's still time. As for anyone who insists on knowing the whys and wherefores of God's providence... well, I wish he'd go and stick his eye up his bum! Wanting to know *why* God permitted Satan to trick mankind... or *why* Judas was allowed to betray Jesus Christ!... *Everything* that happened did so because God wanted it* (Lord, we adore you for it!) and everything in the future will come about as God wills—whatever arguments we indulge in!

'As for those who use debating tricks to confuse people's minds about the difference between Do-well and Do-better— I hope they end by losing their hearing, since they're always out to discover just what they are! Unless a man's life is a *life* of Do-well, I can assure you he hasn't the remotest chance of getting to Do-better, even if Do-best should beckon him on as one day follows another!'

Now, when Wit had taken in what Dame Study had been saying, he became so embarrassed he couldn't lift his gaze from the ground; then, as dumb as a doornail, off he went by himself. There was nothing I could do, even though I fell on my knees, to get him to give me an atom of what he was thinking. With a laugh, he bent his head and glanced in Study's direction,* indicating she was the one I should be asking favours from.

When I grasped what he intended, I went up to Study, bowed, and said, 'Lady, I'm extremely grateful to you! I'd be honoured to enter your service and do your every wish for the rest of my life, if only, Madam, you'd teach me to know what Do-well really is.'

'A becoming modesty!' she replied, 'and I like the humble tone of what you say. So I'll direct you to my cousin, whose name is Clergy.* Within the last six months he has married someone who is a close relative of the Seven Arts. The lady's name is Scripture. These two, I expect, in accordance with my instructions, will, I'm sure, be able to direct you to Do-well.'

At this, I cheered up, like a bird at the dawning of a fine day, and felt as full of good spirits as a minstrel who's just been handed a gift of gold. I asked her to tell me the direct way to where Clergy lived. 'And', I added, 'give me some word by way of introduction, for it's time that I was going.'

'Ask for the main road', she answered, 'that leads from here to Experience-of-Sorrow-and-Joy—that is, if you really wish to learn. Ride on past Wealth, but don't stop there; for if you do, you'll never get to Clergy. You must also avoid that sensual plain called Lechery. Leave a good mile between it and yourself, over there on the left hand as you go. Then you'll come to a manor house called Guard-your-Tongue-from-Lies-and-from-Bad-Language-and-Drink. At this point, you'll catch sight of Sobriety and Sincerity, where everyone you meet will be open and frank. And in this way, you'll come to Clergy, whose knowledge covers a vast range of things.*

'Use this as your word of introduction. Say that you come from Study, who laid the basis of his education. Give my greetings to his wife; remind her that I wrote the Bible for her* and got her to study the Wisdom literature and the Book of Psalms, complete with its commentary-glosses. I also taught her logic, and after that, law, and gave her a thorough course in the theory of music.

'It was I who first set the poet Plato to his studies, and instructed Aristotle and others in the art of dialectic. I first got grammars written for the use of the young, and thrashed

them with the birch if they refused to learn! I invented the
tools used in every craft*—woodwork, sculpture, and archi-
tecture; blear-eyed as I may look, it was I who taught masons
to manipulate the spirit-level and the measuring-line.

   'But theology—now that's a subject which has landed me in
a hundred difficulties.* The more I mull over it, the more
hazy and uncertain it seems; the deeper I probe into it, the
more obscure it appears. It's not a branch of knowledge, I'm
sure, which benefits from the drawing of ever-finer distinc-
tions. Were it not for the fact that at the heart of it, love lies
hidden, theology would strike me as an utter waste of time.
But just because it sets so high a value on love, I in turn love
it; for where any study is motivated by love, the presence of
grace can always be discovered. If you are interested in Do-
well, make sure you love faithfully; for Do-better and Do-best
have both studied under Love.

   'Turning elsewhere, to the area of philosophy, this is what
I've seen in Cato's *Distichs*:

> The man of words who's hollow at the heart—
> Make him your model; art's undone by art!*

Flatter like a deceiver, and you'll succeed in deceiving those
who are false themselves. This is what Cato teaches his
followers; but it's not the lesson of Theology, if you attend to
what *he* says. Theology teaches us the exact opposite of Cato's
lesson, since he urges us to treat our fellow men like brothers,
to pray for our enemies, and to love those who spread
falsehood about us and bring them aid in their time of need—
in a word, to do good in return for evil, as God himself
commands: "While we have time, let us do good to all, but
above all, to our fellows in the faith."*

   'St Paul, whose goal was spiritual perfection, instructed the
people to do good out of love for God, giving alms to those
who asked, and especially to those who were our fellow
Christians. And our Lord himself teaches us to love those who
disparage or slander us, and not to hurt in return people who
hurt us. God himself forbade it when he said, "Vengeance is
mine; it is I who shall repay."* So, as long as you live, see

that you love;* no subject you could find to study in all the world could be so beneficial for your soul.

'Astronomy, on the other hand, is a knotty, impenetrable subject.* Geometry and geomancy are full of tricky terms, and anyone who sets out to study those three will be hard put to get anything worthwhile from them. At bottom, what they all seem to be tending towards is magic. You'll find various devices hidden away in cunning cabinets designed to deceive the spectator. If it's Do-well you're aiming at, have nothing to do with any of these things! All these arts, admittedly, trace their origin to me; I was the one who first worked out how they could be used to pull the wool over people's eyes!

'Mention all this to Clergy and Scripture when you introduce yourself; and ask them if they'll be good enough to advise you how you are to discover what Do-well is.'

I said, 'I am deeply in your debt, my lady', taking a respectful leave of her. Then, without ado, I set off energetically and didn't stop until I reached Clergy. I greeted this worthy man as the good lady had instructed me, after which I paid my respects to his wife, treating them both with ceremonious courtesy, and showing them the credentials* I had been provided with. I don't think anyone since the world began received a warmer, more hospitable welcome than I did, as soon as Clergy learnt I had been staying with Wit and his wife Dame Study. I told them straight out that I had been sent there to learn about Do-well, Do-better, and Do-best.

'Do-well', said Clergy, 'is the life of the ordinary person who believes in the Church and all the essential articles of the Christian faith.* He believes faithfully, in other words, in Almighty God, who exists from all eternity, and in his true Son, who saved mankind from Death the destroyer and from the power of the Fiend, accomplishing this through the help of the Holy Ghost, the spirit who proceeds from them both. These three are distinct Persons, though the Godhead is not many, but only One. For they are all just the One God, and each is wholly divine: God the Father, God the Son, God the Holy Spirit proceeding from both. He it is who created man and every other living creature as well.

'Long ago, St Augustine* wrote at length on the Trinity, and put all his effort into strengthening the foundations of our faith. But what authority did he draw upon? The four Gospel writers—all of them. Christ himself, moreover, as these same authorities attest, spoke of his divinity when he declared: "I am in the Father and the Father is in me; anyone who sees me, sees the Father also."* Every Christian theologian who has ever lived has found this teaching impossible to explain fully; but this is what the simplest must *believe* if their desire is to do well. You see, *no* one has ever possessed so subtle an intellect that he was able to demonstrate Christian truths by argument. Nor, for that matter, could any merit attach to belief in what is capable of rational proof:

> What is faith worth that's based on human sense,
> Or makes a God out of experience?*

'Next, then, Do-better. This consists in accepting obediently, for the sake of your spiritual growth, the whole Gospel ideal that the Church puts before you in its teaching. That, my friend, means striving your utmost—and trusting in God's mercy as you do so—to make your life and actions accord with the creed that you profess, so that appearance and reality correspond when the time of testing arrives: "Seem what you are; be what you seem to be!"* Don't let anyone draw false conclusions from observing your outward behaviour; let it truly reflect your inner spiritual condition.

'Lastly, Do-best. What this means is having the courage to rebuke wrongdoers—if you can do so as someone who is himself free from reproach. But never criticize *anyone* if you yourself deserve to be rebuked:

> If to blame others is your aim,
> Take care you remain free from blame.
> The critic falls into a trap
> When his own failings bite and snap!*

'In the Gospel, God has a harsh reproof for all who find fault with others when they themselves are far from free of faults! "Why do you see a mote in your brother's eye, when you cannot see the plank that is in your own?" Why does that trifle get you into a rage when your own major fault simply blinds you all the more? "First, then, remove the beam from your own eye."* Which one causes the greater obstruction to your vision—the tiny speck or the huge plank?

'My advice to every such unseeing idiot is—first put yourself to rights! I'm thinking here of the parish clergy, who should do their utmost in preaching and instructing all kinds of people to bring them to mend their ways. This text was recorded for your benefit, so that before teaching others the path to salvation, you should ensure your own lives lived up to that standard. The word of God can never be preached to no purpose, however: it's always efficacious in *some* way, and it might be of some benefit to you, even if it failed to get through to your parishioners!

'But nowadays, it looks, frankly, from the point of view of the world, as if the word of God is having absolutely no effect on people—educated and uneducated alike. Except in the way St Mark speaks of in his Gospel: "When the blind lead the blind, both fall into the pit!"*

'And this is the image to which the common people resort when talking about you. The plank, they claim, lies in your eyes, and thanks to your deficiencies, and the scandal of corrupt priests, motes tumble into the eyes of all sorts of people. Now the Bible clearly demonstrates, does it not, how dearly the Israelites paid for the sins of two vicious priests,* Ophni and Phineas. On account of their greed, the Ark of the Covenant came to grief and Heli's neck was broken.

'So, since you are the ones who correct other people's faults, take this lesson to heart, and begin by correcting your own! Then you'll be able to stand up unabashed and proclaim the words David set down in the Psalms: "You thought, wrongly, that I was like you.* But I will show you were mistaken, and stand my ground before you!" When that happens, the half-educated won't have the effrontery to criticize or complain or carp the way they do now. What is it they call you—"dumb dogs that don't know how to bark"?* On the contrary, they'll be afraid of saying anything to upset you or stand in the way of your work as pastors. Your mere request will rouse them to charitable acts more effectively

than a pound of silver coins. Be quite sure of this: there's
nothing they wouldn't do, inspired by the sight of your own
holy lives.

'As for the clergy who are members of religious orders: this
is the rule they should stick to, if they want to be worthy of
their calling. St Gregory, a great scholar and a holy pope, lays
down the principles of the religious life in his treatise, the
Moralia. And this is the image he uses as an example to them
to follow: "When fish are taken away from salt water or fresh
and are beached up without moisture, they simply die. In the
same way, members of religious orders flop about helplessly,
drop dead spiritually when they desire to seek out some other
place than their convent or their monastic house to live in."*
Why, if heaven is anywhere to be found here on earth, if there
is any real balm for the spirit, I can think of several reasons
for placing it in a monastery or a university. No one enters the
cloister in order to quarrel and fight; it's a place of
harmonious co-operation, given over to study and to learning.
And in a university, the home of reason, don't they make fun of
students who simply refuse to learn? But relations between all of
them are of the friendliest, since everyone's business is to help
teach his fellows.

'Now, though, the religious life has sunk to a matter of
riding about on horseback, or wandering at large through city
streets, presiding at settlement-days or buying property. A
monk will follow the hunt from one abbey estate to another
with a pack of hounds baying at his behind, for all the world
just like a nobleman born. And unless the serving-lad who
brings him a drink kneels down before him, he scowls straight
in his face and demands, "Where did you learn your
manners—eh, boy?"* What a mistake the nobility made
when they gave away their estates—land that should have
gone to their heirs—to monks who don't give a damn if it
rains on their altars! There are even a number of districts
where monastic rectors live in comfort as sole incumbents of a
parish.* But do they care about the needy? No—their
"charity" is not for the likes of them.

'But the time is going to come, my monastic friends,* when
a king will sit down and get you to make your confessions!

And then, for failing to observe the Rule of your order, you're going to end up getting soundly beaten, as Scripture says you should. Nuns, monks, and secular canons—he's going to set them all to rights and impose a penance on them to return to a strict observance of their original Rule. The nobility, higher and lower, will apply a certain heavy rod to them: the principles of the Psalm "Blessed the man . . .".* They'll get back again for themselves the estates to which their children have some claim, and they won't mince their words in telling you why:

> Some sit on horses, some hold chariot-reins;
> But see them fallen now, see them in chains!*

'And then friars, as they sit in their refectories, will pick up the keys to Constantine's treasure-chest,* which contains all the wealth that Gregory's godchildren have managed to misspend. Then, too, the abbot of Abingdon* and all who succeed him in his office will receive a sound blow from a king, a wound it will be impossible to recover from. Will this really happen, then? You whose business is to study the Bible constantly know very well that it will!

> How have oppressors come to nought?
> How has the tribute ceased to be paid?
> The Lord has broken the staff of the wicked,
> The rulers' rod that punished the people;
> He has given them an incurable wound.*

But before that king arrives, Cain must first bestir himself.* But Do-well shall strike him down, and bring his power to an end.'

'Then do Do-well and Do-better consist', I asked, 'in secular lordship and the estate of knighthood?'

'I have no wish', said Scripture, 'to start being sarcastic, but unless the authorities have got it all wrong, kingship and knighthood don't have an iota of a claim, as far as I can see, when it's a question of helping one get to Heaven. Neither do wealth or noble birth, for that matter.

'St Paul, in fact, demonstrates that it's *impossible* for the rich to get to Heaven.* Solomon, too, declares, "There's no lower object of love than lucre".* And Cato's advice is to bother about it only so far as necessity dictates: "Respect money as a means, not as an end." The patriarchs, the prophets, and the poets as well have all written counselling us not to set our hearts on wealth, and they've sung the praises of a poverty that's accepted in a spirit of patience.* The apostles testify that it's the poor whose inheritance is in Heaven, an inheritance that's really theirs by right, whereas the rich have no claim to Heaven, and can only obtain it through the merciful favour of God.'

'Oh no, I challenge you on that!' I cried with an oath. 'I know a way to refute that argument, founding my case on both St Peter and St Paul. A person who has been baptized is saved, whether he is rich or poor.'*

'That applies only in extreme cases', replied Scripture, 'for instance, with pagans and Jews. It is indeed sound enough doctrine to say *they* can be saved in that way. In those circumstances, even a non-Christian can baptize a pagan, and he, because of the true faith that is in him, will inherit Heaven when he dies as surely as any Christian. But the ordinary Christian person can't get to Heaven without something more than just baptism. This is because Christ, who died for all Christians, insisted on requiring from everyone "who wished to rise with Christ"* that they should love, practise alms-giving, and fulfil the law. This means loving the Lord God above all else, and after that your fellow Christians with a like love. The man who has faith in his salvation is *required* to love. And unless we do act in this way before the Day of Judgement, it will go hard with us when that time arrives. No use to us then the money we've put away or our fancy clothes—all moth-eaten by then—if we let beggars go naked during our lives! And what good to us then all the pleasure we took in pheasants and fine wines, while we knew about people who were in distress? Every Christian is obliged to be generous, first to his fellow Christians, and then in the same way towards unbelievers, in the hope of bringing about their conversion.

'God's commandment to people of every social rank is, that no one should ever injure another. His words are: "Never kill any creature made in my image and likeness, unless I order

you expressly to do so."* He also says "*Thou shalt not kill*
means you must be ready to put up with injury from others as
the *best* way. Vengeance belongs to me,* and I shall punish
every man for the evil he has done, either in Purgatory or in
the depths of Hell, unless the pressure of mercy stays my
hand."'

'This has been a lengthy lecture', I answered, 'and I seem
to be rather little the wiser for it! It's all very obscure, your
account of where Do-well or Do-better is to be found. You
retail a number of stories drawn from Theology's teaching:
you say that from the moment I was created, nay, from well
before it, my name was entered in the Book of Life or else
omitted for some wrong or other of mine, as the Bible says:

> No one to Heaven has ascended
> Save him that is from Heaven descended.*

Now, I swear there isn't a text in the whole of Scripture that I
believe in more whole-heartedly. For just consider Solomon,
that wise sage who wrote the sapiential books. God favoured
him with not only the gift of intellect but with all the wealth
needed to rule his kingdom and advance its prosperity.
According to the Bible, he ruled wisely and well. And who
have a higher claim as teachers of mankind than Solomon or
Aristotle? Theologians who compose treatises or sermons on
the topic of God's mercy are indebted to the writings of both;
were they not the wisest men of their day? And yet for all
this, the Church has no doubt that both are in Hell!* Now
suppose I were to live like them in the hope of winning
Heaven, even though they—for all their wise thoughts and
actions—are both of them suffering the agonies of the
damned. Wouldn't I be acting like a fool, whatever gloss you
might choose to put upon it?

'But I assure you I wouldn't find it the least bit astonishing
if many clever people failed to find favour with God. After all,
there are lots of people in the world whose main concern in
life is money, not the things of God. That's why in their time
of greatest distress—I mean, when they stand on the brink
of death—they do not receive the grace of final repentance.
This was the case with Solomon* and others like him, who

displayed great intellectual powers, though their lives, as Scripture informs us, were invariably in contradiction to these gifts. That's why great intellectuals and scholars of immense learning rarely live up to the level of their mental endowments—as they themselves freely admit: "The scribes and the pharisees sat in the seat of Moses . . . "*

'But I expect what may happen is what happened in the time of Noah,* when he built that ship of his from planks and timbers. None of the craftsmen or other labourers who worked on it were saved, only birds and animals, the good Noah himself, and with him his wife, his sons, and their wives. Of the men who built the ark not one was saved!

'God grant that this will not happen to the people entrusted to teach the faith of the Church! For the Church is a place of refuge; it is the house of God; it is a protection from the confusion of the world. It protects us as Noah's ark saved the animals—while those who laboured to build it, the deluge drowned. The conclusion I'm getting at is this. I'm referring to the clergy, the carpenters, as it were, responsible for building the Church for the Lord's livestock: "Men and beasts, O Lord, thou wilt preserve!"* On Judgement Day, there is going to be a great deluge of death-bringing fire. So this is my advice to you, the clergy, carpenters of the Ark of God, the Church: make sure that your lives and actions accord with the injunctions of Scripture; otherwise, you too might find yourselves unable to enter the ark!

'I observe that on Good Friday it was a criminal, a man who'd spent his whole life lying and stealing, who was the first to be saved,* before anyone else: St John the Baptist, or Adam, or Isaiah, or any of the prophets of old, who had lain in the Devil's clutches time out of mind. Without even having to do penance in Purgatory, a robber was saved in preference to all these, and went straight to the eternal joys of Heaven! Who was ever capable of a more vicious act than Mary Magdalen? Who actually *did* a more heinous act than David,* who wilfully plotted to have Uriah murdered? Or what about Paul the Apostle, who ruthlessly set himself to the task of exterminating the whole Christian community? And yet now it is these who occupy the highest place among the saints in heaven, though the lives they lived on earth had been wicked in the highest degree! At the same time, those whose words of wisdom fill many a learned tome, are consigned to keep company with the damned.

'What Solomon says is true, and I think it holds good for us all: "There are men who are just and men who are wise; but the deeds they do lie in the hand of God."* The wise and the virtuous: their lives are a secret the truth of which is known to God alone. God alone knows whether a person will be judged worthy of Heaven because he lived a life of love and goodness, or rejected because of the malice and hatred within him, which showed in the way he lived. Don't we recognize good-ness by contrasting it with vice? How could you tell if an object was white, if everything was black? And how could you know a virtuous man unless there were some who were evil? So there's nothing for it but to go on living with sinners (very few people, to my mind, are in fact good). There's a French proverb which says, "What you can't undo, you must endure!" God *can* turn all to good; may he have mercy on us all! Wasn't the truest word that he ever said, "*Nemo bonus*": "No human being is good"?*

'There's something as obvious as day, too, I've forgotten. Christ himself never uttered a word in praise of learning. In fact, what he said to St Peter and his chosen disciples was this: "When you stand on trial in the presence of governors and kings, take no great thought over what you are going to say.* Before rulers and judges, feel no anxiety at all. I shall put words in your mouths, and give you an ample supply of sound arguments with which to confute those who challenge your claims about the Christian faith." David, too, observes that though he had to speak in the hearing of monarchs, no one could get the better of him in the subtleties of debate. Yet in times of dire need, it has never been intellect or erudition that finally carried the day.

'The most powerful theologian who ever wrote about the Trinity was Augustine; he was the greatest of the four chief western Fathers of the Church. I remember seeing something he wrote in one of those works: "See how the ignorant scale the heavens by force, while we, the wise, remain sunk in Hell below!"* The meaning of this in plain English is clear: no one is more easily seduced from orthodoxy than brilliant scholars who read up scores of books; and no one is surer of salvation, no one is more firmly rooted in religious faith, than ploughmen, shepherds, shoemakers, and poor, ordinary working people.* It's the ignorant, the unimportant, the nobodies whose unadorned "Our Fathers" have the power to smash through the palace-gates of Heaven. And they when they die bypass the pains of Purgatory, and enter the kingdom of the blessed with nothing to help them but unadulterated faith. This, though they lived their lives with a knowledge of religion that was, you might say, less than complete.

'Oh yes, and hasn't everyone come across educated people who cursed the day they ever knew more than their Creed, or even, simpler still, just their "Our Father?" There's more than one parish priest who wished he had! I can think of cases—anyone can—of how peasants who perform services for their superiors rarely end up falling into debt, the exceptions being those in charge of their master's own property—I mean, of course, reeves of the manor and clerks of accounts. In the same way exactly, the ignorant and the uninformed seldom sink into such a depth of depravity as the clergy, the educated entrusted with watching over the treasure of Christ our Lord. By "treasure" I mean the immortal souls of men. What does the Gospel give us as God's command? *"Go into my vineyard!"* '*

After this, Scripture looked at me with disdain, and proceeded to put her own case. She roundly berated me in Latin, treating me as a trifler, and declared: '*Multi multa sciunt et seipsos nesciunt.*'[1]*

I became so upset and angry at her words that the tears flowed; and as a result, I became drowsy and soon I fell asleep.* Then I had an extraordinary dream. Right where I stood I was snatched up by Fortune* and carried off into the domain of yearning desire. Fortune caused me to gaze in a mirror that was named Middle Earth,* and then she said to me: 'Here you can see things that will make you marvel. Here you can discover what it is you desire; why, you may even (who can tell?) attain it.'

Now, Fortune had accompanying her two beautiful young women.* The elder girl was called Lust of the Flesh, and the other's name was Lust of the Eyes. The Pride of Life brought up the rear, and urged me, for fear of doing harm to my looks, not to take Learning *too* seriously.

Lust of the Flesh threw her arms about my neck and said, 'You're young and full of juice; you've many years ahead of you to devote to the love of the fair sex. Look in this mirror, and you'll see a whole range of pleasures that should make the rest of your days on earth a treat!'

The second girl spoke in the same vein. 'I'm more than happy to do what you want', she said. 'I'll never abandon your side till you've got yourself some estates, and a nice title to boot.'

'He'll find me his friend', said Fortune in conclusion. 'No one who once followed my promptings ever saw happiness trickle through his fingers.'

At this point, there appeared someone with sunken features, whose name was Old Age.* 'If *I* meet you, fellow, I swear by our Lady', he muttered, 'you'll discover that Fortune will indeed let you down—and in your hour of

---

[1] 'Many know much, who know nothing of themselves.'

greatest need, moreover. And as for Lust of the Flesh, she'll drop you completely. Then, all day and all night, you'll find yourself bitterly cursing the time you ever encountered Lust of the Eyes. And the Pride of Life will lead you on right to the brink of the precipice!'

'Oh, really? Don't give a damn for it!' This was said by Recklessness,* who stepped forward dressed in rags and tatters. 'Follow Fortune's way,' he urged, 'you've a long way to go before *you* reach old age. It'll be time enough to start feeling humble when your hair begins to grow thin. Remember what Plato the poet once said: "Man proposes, but God disposes."* If Truth's willing to vouch that you're doing well if you follow your fortune, then there's surely no risk that Lust of the Flesh or Lust of the Eyes will be in any hurry to trouble you! They won't lead you astray unless you want them to.'

'Come on, Titch!' cried Childishness,* taking me off without further ado, until Lust of the Flesh became my sole reason for living.

'Oh, the pity of it!' called out Old Age, echoed by Holiness.* 'That intelligence should degenerate into vice, and a man's will collapse in the grip of self-indulgence!'

But Lust of the Eyes promptly stepped in to cheer me up, and remained my inseparable companion for a good forty-five years.* The result was that I lost all shadow of interest in Do-well and Do-better; I hadn't the least desire to hear so much as their names mentioned. In fact, I spent far more time brooding about Lust of the Eyes than actually doing anything about Do-well or Do-better. And Lust of the Eyes did much to keep my spirits up. 'Don't *now* start having scruples about how to get rich', she said. 'Go and confess your sins to some friar or other. Take my word for it, as long as Fortune's your friend, the friars will be, too! They'll enroll you in one of those fraternities of theirs and pester their Provincial to get hold of a pardon for you. Every man jack of them will be happy to say his prayers for you, provided your pockets are up to it.'

(*Ah, but 'penance that's paid for silver pence*
Won't clear a soul of guilt—soul is not sense'.)*

None the less, this siren's words sang so sweetly in my ears that I followed her advice, until I'd left youth behind as no more than a memory, and found myself well on the way to old age. At this point, Fortune, for all her fancy promises, turned her face against me, and I was hounded down by poverty and brought to the ground. And then I discovered that my friar had become somewhat hesitant, and was starting to hum and haw over our original arrangement; and all because I said I didn't want to be buried in their friary graveyard, but rather in the grounds of my own parish church. (I'd heard Conscience say one time that it was right and proper for a man to be buried in the place where he'd been baptized.)* And because I put this point to the friars, they decided I was a fool, and cooled off noticeably towards me; all because of my honest, down-to-earth words! All the same, I expostulated with my confessor, who regarded himself as a man of real intellect.

'Frankly, brother', I said, 'aren't you behaving just like one of those suitors who sets out to marry a widow simply to get control of her property? I swear by the cross, you are! Why, you wouldn't give a hang where my body ends up buried, so long as you get my money! You know, there's something I find quite astonishing—and I'm not alone in this. I mean that your order seems altogether keener about hearing confessions and conducting funerals* than about baptizing children who are preparing to become Christians. Baptism and burial are surely both necessary; yet it seems to me a much more worthwhile thing to baptize. After all, someone who has been christened, so the authorities tell us, may reach the heights of Heaven through contrition; there's a phrase—"Contrition by itself can blot out a man's sins." But an *unbaptized* infant can't be saved in this way: "For unless you are born again of water and the Holy Spirit, you cannot enter the Kingdom of Heaven."* All right, I appeal to you, the learned: am I telling the truth, or am I not?'

At this Honest Fidelity* burst out laughing at me, because of the way I scowled as I said these words. 'What are you making such a face about?' he demanded, fixing me with his eyes.

'Ah,' I replied, 'if only I could make it known, this dream of mine! Yes, make it known to the whole world!'

'By St Peter!' he exclaimed, 'and by St Paul, as well—why ever not? I can find support in the writings of both for doing so: "Harbour no voiceless rancour against your brothers: rebuke them in the open light of day."'*

'Yes', I rejoined, 'but they're just as well able to adduce bits of the Gospel in support of *their* position: "Do not judge, so that you may avoid being judged."'*

'Really?' replied Fidelity. 'Then what use is religion at all—if no one's allowed to attack deceit and flattery? Look, the Apostle had good reason for saying "Don't harbour silent grievance against your brother".* The prophet David says just the same in the Psalms: "You thought, wrongly, that I was one of you . . . "* It is legitimate for ordinary laymen to affirm what's true if they wish it: that's their right in both canon and in civil law. But this doesn't hold for parish priests or for the higher clergy, of course. They're the ones who should avoid making public statements—even ones which are factually accurate—if the subject that's involved is somebody's sin.* Now, if something's already a matter of public knowledge, why should you feel restrained from handling it in a poem with the aim of attacking really serious evils? Of course, you shouldn't ever be the one who starts the war on whatever's amiss; even if you see something badly wrong, don't be the first to announce the fact. It's better to feel sorry that the wrong hasn't been put right.* And *never* make public what's really a private affair. Don't praise someone's behaviour just because you like him, or attack it because he's someone you can't stand. There's a good saying: "Praise little—and blame less!"'*

'What he says is quite true!' declared Scripture just then; and getting up quickly, she proceeded to deliver this sermon. But, if simple lay-people were to get wind of the argument she put forward, I'm certain it would undermine their regard for the Christian faith they are taught by the clergy. This was her theme, and this her text;* I took it all in fully.

'Many were invited to take part in a feast', said Scripture, 'and when they'd all arrived, the porter unlocked the gate and

picked out just a few to be let in, secretly; the remainder he
left to go their ways.'

I was so disturbed by this text of hers that my heart began
to beat irregularly. I found I was becoming completely
confused, and I started to argue about it with myself: was I
one of the chosen ones, the elect, or wasn't I? My thoughts
went back to Holy Church;* hadn't she received me through
my baptism as one of God's chosen ones? Christ, surely,
called us all to be saved; all we needed was to want to
come—pagans, schismatics, and Jews alike: "All you who are
thirsty", he said, "come to the waters . . ."* And what he
ordered them to do was to suck the healing drops of salvation
from sin that flowed down from his breast, and to drink down
that antidote for the spirit's ills—each and everyone able to do
so!

'It follows', I declared, 'that *all* Christians can come and
claim admission there, thanks to the blood he redeemed us by
and the baptism given us as its consequence. "The man who
believes and is baptized", says scripture, "will be saved!"*
Why, even if a Christian wanted to renounce his faith,*
common sense tells us he couldn't do so legitimately. Can a
villein, say, draw up a legal document, or sell his property
without the permission of his lord? There's no law allowing
that. What he can do, of course, is get into debt and run away
from home, wandering about irresponsibly like the perjured
rascal that he is. But sooner or later, Reason will call him to a
settlement, and soundly take him to task; and Conscience
will go through the accounts with him and expose him as
totally bankrupt. He'll then imprison the wretch in
Purgatory's fires: that will be the cost of discharging his debts
until Judgement Day arrives!—Unless Contrition is willing to
come and make an eleventh-hour plea, whether spoken in
words or felt in the heart, for mercy to be shown towards all
his offences.'

'That is quite true', replied Scripture. 'There *is* no sin that
can prevent the divine mercy from putting all to rights—
providing it has humility to help it. His acts of mercy, as the
Bible says, are the most sublime of all God's creations: "His
tender mercies stand above all his works." '*

'Who cares about books?' cried someone who had broken out from Hell.* 'I am Trajan, a loyal knight, and I can call on a pope to testify that I died and was condemned to unceasing punishment because I had never become a Christian. Scholars are familiar with the facts: it wasn't all the Christian learning in the world that was able to snatch *me* from the jaws of Hell; no, it was simply love, honest integrity, and the justice of my judgements. St Gregory was fully aware of these things, and the reason why he desired the salvation of my soul was the truth that he saw in what I did. And because he grieved for me, and longed for grace to be given to me, his request was granted, even though no prayer had been said—and I was saved! As you see, it was not because masses had been sung, but because of love, and the discovery that I had lived a just and upright life. It was these that rescued me from terrible suffering, where prayer would have been of no avail.

'You noblemen who are listening to me, consider what fidelity accomplished for a Roman emperor who, as the authorities can show, had never received Christian baptism. That pagan was not saved through the intercession of a pope, but purely and simply because of his upright life, as St Gregory himself testifies. You, the nobility, in particular, should keep this lesson in mind: meditate on Trajan's integrity, and show the same justice towards those whom you rule.

'This theme is a very difficult one; but for those of you who are members of the clergy, the *Legends of the Saints** will tell you the story more fully than I can now. But this is how faithful love and a life lived in truth forcibly rescued a pagan from the pains of Hell. Blessed be truth, which could break down Hell's gates like this, and save a pagan from the power of the Devil when neither learning nor knowledge of the principles of the faith could do so! Love and fidelity—they, now, are subjects really worth studying! The gracious volume that contains these is the book of heavenly happiness and joy. It was God who fashioned it, wrote its text with his own fingers, and gave it to Moses on the mountain, instructing him to teach it to all mankind.

'Without love', continued Trajan, 'law isn't worth a straw!*
Nor is any body of knowledge, if it comes to that—including
all the seven liberal arts. All the time you spend on them is an
utter waste, unless your motive for studying these things is
love of God, not desire to earn money or academic titles.
Their whole purpose is to enable us to love God, and to love
other people better, as a result.

'It was St John who said it (and his words are the truth):
"The man who does not love remains dead."* Believe me, his
is a state of living death! John also says that we should all love
everybody, friend and foe alike, and be as generous to other
people as they are to themselves. Someone who doesn't give,
doesn't love. God, who is fully aware of the fact, commands
everyone to do his best to love first his neighbours, then his
enemies, just as he loves himself. For we win merit by loving
those who hate us, and the highest merit of all lies in putting
ourselves out for the sake of the poor. It is their prayers that
can be of most help to us. Doesn't Jesus Christ, who is our
joy, our treasure in Heaven, haunt our lives in the guise of
poor people?* Doesn't he look out at us from their faces,
smiling with love, seeking to recognize us by our kind hearts
and caring looks, finding out in that way whether we love the
great ones of this world more than the Lord of heavenly joy?
He urges us in the Gospel that when *we* entertain, "we should
not invite our own relatives or well-to-do people of any kind
at all. But", he says, "ask the distressed, the handicapped,
the poor. Won't your friends feed you in return? Simply try
to repay you for your entertainments and your presents? That
is the way that one friend treats another. But *I* shall pay for
the poor—repay with interest the efforts of any who give the
poor food or money, and love them for my sake."*

'God, who is all-powerful, could have made everyone rich,
had he so wished. But it's for the best that some are wealthy,
while others are poor and have to beg. For all of us are
creations of Christ, enriched out of his treasury—blood-
relations, as it were, beggars no less than great nobles. This is
because on Calvary the Christian faith welled forth with the
outpouring of Christ's blood; and on that spot each of us,

redeemed by the body of one single person, became nobles, "so to speak, by birth".* Not one of us was to be counted beggar or knave—unless our own sins should bring us to that condition: "He who sins becomes the slave of sin."*

'Under the Old Law, the Bible tells us, we were called "Sons of Men", being as we were the descendants of Adam and Eve, until the death of the one who was both God and Man. After his resurrection, his title became *Redemptor*, "the one who has bought back", and we—the poor and rich alike—are his brothers and sisters, "bought back" by him. For that reason, let's love one another the way affectionate children do, with smiling and laughter. And if anyone has anything left to spare, let him use it to ease the lot of someone in need. Let *everyone* help other people—for all of us must leave this place one day. "Bear one another's burdens"* the Bible says. Let's not be mean and ungenerous with what we possess, whether it's goods or knowledge; after all, no one knows how close he may be to having to abandon both! No one should be critical of another person just because he happens to have more knowledge of Latin. And no one should go about uttering bitter rebukes; for no one in the world is without fault. Whatever the authorities may say about Christianity, or anything else, Christ declared openly to a prostitute, at a feast, that *her faith* would save her,* and salve the wound of sin.

'It follows then that faith is a reliable support, superior to both logic and law. In the *Legends of the Saints*, little importance is attached to either of these without the assistance of faith. For it takes a very long time indeed for logic to sort out a problem; and law is slow to show willing unless there's money to be had by it. If you want the plain truth of the matter, my advice to every Christian is not to get too closely involved with either. There's a passage of Scripture I know— you'll find it recorded in St John*—that derives from the teaching of Faith, Faith that has saved sinful mankind: "Whatever measure you measure by will be used to measure out to you in return." So, let us familiarize ourselves with *love's* law, just as Our Lord taught it. In the words of St Gregory—and he had our spiritual good in mind when he said them—"Better to examine our own faults and failings than to pry deep into all natural things."*

'My reason for bringing up this subject is the poor. It is, after all, in their guise that our Lord has often been recognized. Take what happened in Easter Week, when he was on the way to Emmaus.* Because he was dressed like a poor man, and wearing pilgrim's clothes, Cleophas could not recognize him as Christ—till the moment when he blessed and broke the bread that they were to eat. So they recognized by his actions that it was Jesus; but they couldn't recognize him by his clothing, nor, even, the sound of his voice. All this, I tell you, was an example to us sinners here and now to speak in a humble and gracious way, and not dress up in vain and extravagant clothes. For we are *all* pilgrims.* And God, time and again, has been encountered in the ranks of the destitute, dressed in a poor man's clothes, and looking like a pilgrim; whereas no one has ever seen him in the clothing or the company of the rich!

'St John the Baptist and other saints appeared dressed like the poor, and asked for alms* as poor pilgrims do. Jesus Christ came down into this world in the body of a Jew's daughter; and she, though she was a woman of good family, was a genuinely poor girl, and married to a poor man. When Martha made that great complaint of hers against Mary Magdalen,* this is what she said to our Lord himself: "Lord, don't you care that my sister leaves me to do all the serving myself?" And the divine answer came without hesitation, as St Matthew tells us. Our Lord expressed great esteem for Martha's attitude, as well as for that of Mary; but he gave first place to poverty, commending it the more highly, when he said: "Mary has chosen the best part, which will not be taken away from her."

'As far as I can see, every wise man there's ever been praises poverty*—provided it's accompanied by patience—as the best kind of life, much better, and countless times fuller of blessings than the way of life of the rich. Although it seems sour when you are enduring it, the after-taste is a sweet one. It's like a walnut: on the outside there is a bitter-tasting husk; but remove the shell, and then after you reach the rind comes the kernel of the nut, which is satisfying and nourishing to eat. That's what it's like when poverty or penance are patiently accepted; they encourage a person to turn his thoughts to God, and to experience a strong desire to weep for his sins, and to pray from his heart. Out of all this, mercy can grow up, and the kernel of it is Christ, who strengthens and nourishes the soul. Moreover, the man who lacks wealth sleeps much more securely than the rich man. He's much less afraid of death, of being burgled in the darkness, and that surely stands to reason. "Poor, I can play; your property makes you brood."*

'Now, even though the Bible records Solomon as saying, "Give me neither poverty nor wealth",* someone still wiser than Solomon affirms in his teaching that perfect poverty means having *no* possessions, and that is the way of life most pleasing to God. As St Luke testifies:* "If you wish to be perfect, go, sell what you have, and give it to the poor." What that means for people living in our world is this: anyone who wants to be really perfect must give up possessions or, as the Bible says, sell them and give the money to those who beg alms for the love of God. For no one who serves Almighty God has ever gone hungry, as David says in the Psalms. And to someone who earnestly desires to serve God worthily, no privation is a cause of pain: "Nothing is impossible for one who wills it!" Nor does he lack the necessities of life, or clothing of linen or wool: "Those who seek the Lord shall not be deprived of any good thing."*

'If priests had any sense, they wouldn't accept money for saying mass or matins. Nor would they accept from usurers any food, or a tunic or a cloak, even if it meant their dying of cold—not if they were really doing their duty as David describes it in the Psalms: "Judge me, O God, and distinguish my case from the sinner's."* The psalm "Trust in the Lord . . ."* has a bearing on priests who find themselves without spending-money. It says that if they work with integrity and trust in Almighty God, they will never lack the necessities of life, or clothing of linen and wool. The very claim to financial solvency, on the basis of which you receive ordination, guarantees your position.* So there's no need to

take money in return for saying masses; the person who
provided your claim to entitlement should be paying your
salary, or else the bishop who actually ordained you, if you
really deserve it!

'Why, what king ever conferred knighthood on a man
unless he had the resources befitting the status of knight,* or
had properly provided for his needs as a man-at-arms? What a
wretched knight is the man who has no lands, no noble
ancestry, and no reputation on the battlefield! And no less
wretched is the king who dubbed such a man a knight! Well,
I would apply the same criticism to all those priests who lack
both learning and a good family background, and have
nothing but a tonsure and a claim to financial support—mere
words, maybe—to meet their needs in difficult circumstances.
Such men, I believe, place their hopes of a benefice in the
mere fact of their clerical tonsure rather than in their
education or their reputation for living a virtuous life. It's a
mystery to me why bishops ordain such people priests, since
all they do is lead the laity astray.

'You know how a legal document is open to challenge in the
higher courts; if its wording contains inaccurate Latin, the
law will not recognize its validity, any more than it will if the
text contains interlinear insertions, or if portions of it have
been left out.* Anyone who goes in for adding glosses to a
legal document in that way is considered to be an ass. Dear
God! ass is the only name, isn't it, for a priest who gets the
Gospel wrong when he reads it, or misses out parts of the
service at mass or matins. "He who offends in one point
becomes guilty in all!" In the Psalms, David is addressing
such leavers-out of words when he says, "Sing praises to our
God, sing praises! For the God of Israel is king of all the
earth. Sing praises *wisely*!"

'My belief is that the bishop who creates such people
"knights of God"* will be rebuked in the presence of God for
doing so: people who don't know how to "sing wisely", or
recite the Psalms, or say their daily mass. There's no way of
exonerating either the bishop or the priest from blame; both
of them stand accused of "*ignorancia*—which excuses neither
bishops nor ignoramus-priests!"*

'I've been going on so long about the problem of uneducated priests that I've completely lost track of the subject of poverty! But poverty, when it's accompanied by patience, is assuredly a worthy theme for praise. It's a far better state of life than being rich!'

Now, there was a great deal more in this dream of mine about someone who came and argued with me in the way I've described. This is what I saw as I slept. And after this, Kind* appeared; he called me by my name and urged me to look carefully, and acquire understanding by looking at the marvellous things this world affords the beholder. And then it seemed to me that I was carried up to a mountain called Middle Earth; the purpose was to teach me from the example of every created being how I should love Kind, my creator.

I saw the sun, and the sea, and the land, and the places where birds and animals went with their mates, wild serpents in the woods, and astonishing birds with spotted plumage of variegated hues. I could see men and their mates, too, and I took in at one glance both poverty and plenty, peace and war, happiness and misery. I saw how men took meed and rejected mercy.

I perceived clearly how Reason followed all the animals in the way they ate, drank, and procreated.* After the act of mating, the animals of either sex took no notice of each other as they had when in the heat of copulation. Immediately this was over, the male animals would join the other males in the daytime; and at day's end likewise, males and females were kept apart. There was no species of cattle in which the cow, after becoming pregnant, would go bellowing after the bull; nor would the boar-pig pursue a pregnant sow. Likewise horses, dogs, and every other type of animal refrained from mounting their mates after the young were conceived.

I saw birds making nests in bushes, and the smallest one would have defied the wit of man. I marvelled at the magpie; where, from whom, did she learn to arrange the twigs where she breeds and lays her eggs? I don't supppose there's a master-carpenter able to match her nest, and I'd be amazed if any builder knew how to copy its construction! Nor was that all I found myself marvelling at. There were many other birds that concealed their eggs in secret spots under cover, in marshes and on moorland, hiding them away when they left the nesting-place, to protect them against other birds and preying animals. Some species carried out their mating up in the trees, and gave birth to their young high above ground. Some procreated by exchanging breath through their bills,* others by sexual contact. I watched the breeding-habits of the peacock. Filled with wonder, I asked myself who was their teacher? Who instructed the birds to set up their nests so high that neither man nor beast could get at their chicks?

And after this, I turned my gaze to the sea, and then up towards the stars. I saw a myriad marvels which I cannot begin to describe: in the woods, flowers of beautiful hue, such countless colours springing up in the green grass, some smelling acrid, and some sweet. It seemed like a strange enchantment. To elaborate all the species and all their shades would take up more time than I have! But what troubled and upset me above all else was this: that Reason seemed to be keeping watch and ward over the whole animal kingdom, but not over human kind, male and female. Time after time, Reason seemed to desert them, rich and poor alike. At this, I levelled a reproach at Reason, and said to him right out: 'It astonishes me—seeing how wise you're thought to be—that you don't accompany man and his mate, to save them from misfortune.'*

Reason lost no time in putting me right. 'Don't you go troubling yourself', he replied, 'as to why I put up with things or why I do not! It's no business of yours. If you know how to improve matters, do so; my task is to wait. Just to put up with things is the highest kind of virtue; it's also the promptest form of retaliation! Who has more to put up with than God?'* he went on. 'No human being, I can tell you. God could put right in the twinkling of an eye everything that's wrong in the world. Yet, for the good that's in it for some individual, he puts up with what he does, and thereby proves himself better than we are.

'The Bible', Reason continued, 'counsels men to endure: "For the sake of God, be subject to every human creature."'*

This is the way they discipline their children in France (and among our gentry, too):

> Patience is a pretty virtue,
> Cursing is a poor revenge;
> Just suffer well and say well—
> All in the end will go well.*

So, my advice to you', he declared, 'is, try and keep better control over your tongue. Before you start criticizing other people, first see if you yourself are entitled to praise. There isn't a living creature that could have created itself; now, if a man—unaided—could make himself virtuous, there'd be no grounds for criticizing *anyone*, you can rest assured! Yet you won't find more than a handful who enjoy having their worst faults pointed out before their faces!

'This is what one of the shrewd wisdom-writers says in the Bible: "Do not strive over things that are not your concern."* Whether someone is ugly or good-looking, it's not right to find fault with his physical make-up, since his features were fashioned by God himself. And this is why—because *everything* God has created is well made, as the Bible itself testifies: "And God saw all that he had made, and it was very good."* He commanded every species of living thing to multiply, and all this was for the benefit of man, whose lot is to suffer the distress of fleshly and diabolic temptation.* For it follows from the very substance man is made of that he cannot completely avoid following the bent of his nature. Cato agrees with me: "No one from fault lives free." '*

At this, I immediately blushed, overcome with shame;* and promptly woke up. How wretched I felt then at losing my dream, and the chance of finding out more! Speaking to myself, I heartily cursed the moment of my waking. 'Dear God!' I cried, 'now I think I know what Do-well is!'

And as I raised my eyes, I met the glance of someone who asked me, 'Well, what is it, then?'

'To observe much, of course', I replied, 'and endure still more. That, surely, is Do-well.'

'Had *you* endured while you were sleeping there', he said,

'you would have learnt all that Clergy knows and grasped yet
more by means of Reason;* for Reason would have brought
home to you exactly what Learning has been saying. But
thanks to your interfering, you've been left high and dry:

> Had you but held your tongue,
> A sage you'd have become.*

'Adam, as long as he said nothing, had all Paradise to enjoy
at will. But when he started prating on about food, and prying
into the depths of divine wisdom, he was thrust out from that
place. And that, Will, is how Reason dealt with you. You,
with your hail-fellow-well-met manner, praised this and
criticized that, when none of it was any business of yours at
all. This made him lose all willingness to instruct you any
further. Now, it seems, you're open to the accusation of being
proud and presumptuous;* and on that basis, Clergy will keep
well clear of your way!

'Listen: giving someone a severe telling-off is a far less
effective form of discipline than direct humiliation; that's
what will really mortify him, and lay the basis of some real
improvement. It's like when some drunken oaf tumbles into a
ditch, and people leave him lying there, and take no notice of
him till he decides to get up. If Reason took him to task then,
the fellow wouldn't take a blind bit of notice, or care a damn
about Clergy's good advice. It would be sheer malice then,
surely, to start raining blows or insults on such a wretch. But
when he's brought to his feet by sheer necessity, and fear of
starving to death, and when shame scrapes the muck off his
clothes and washes the dirt off his shins—that's when a
drink-sodden fool begins to realize what he's done wrong.'

'I wager my soul', I replied, 'it's true, what you say. Why,
I've seen it often enough myself. Nothing stings, and nothing
stinks, like open, downright, humiliating shame—something
that makes a man a social outcast. And I know why you've
been saying all this to *me*; it's because I went and sounded off
against Reason!'

'Why, yes', he replied, 'what else?'—and started to walk
away. But immediately I got up, too, and set off after him;
and asked him, if he didn't mind, to tell me his name.

'I am Imaginative',* he said. 'Though I may sit alone, I've never been inactive, in sickness or in health. Take my word for it, I've been your companion for the last forty-five years.* Many's the time I've roused you to reflect on the end of your existence—how many years have already passed, and how few remain ahead. I've made you recall the reckless abandon of your early days and plan to put things right during your mature years—in case, if you waited for old age, you might find you lacked the power to do so. For old people find it hard to put up with deprivation and penance, hard, too, to exert themselves in prayer: "If not in the first watch or the second . . ."!*

'Change your way of life while it still lies in your hands to do so! How often you've been warned by attacks of the plague, poverty, and sickness! These are the sharp rods God uses to beat his beloved children: "Those whom I love, I chastise!"* And in the Psalms, David speaks of those who love Christ when he says, "Your rod and your staff, these have comforted me". "Although you beat me with your staff", he is saying, "or with a cane or a rod, I look on this as something to take joy in, because it helps my soul to advance in virtue." And yet, here you are—dabbling in verse-making, when you could be busy saying your Psalter, and praying for those who provide the food you eat!* Aren't there already enough books telling people what Do-well, Do-better, and Do-best are? There are certainly pairs of friars enough to preach sermons spelling out what they all amount to!'*

I could see the truth of what he was saying; so, by way of justifying myself in part, I replied: 'Cato offered his son a little relief when he told him even a scholar sometimes relaxes. Well, that's what I do when I write my verses. I "find a place for pleasure amongst my pressing pursuits".* I've also heard', I went on, 'how the saints in various lands were willing to amuse themselves on occasion; they were all the saintlier for it! But of course, if someone *could* give me a

definitive account of Do-well, Do-better, and Do-best, I'd
have no desire to work at all. Instead, I'd set off to Church
and say my prayers there, never stopping except to eat and
sleep.'

'In one of his epistles',* he replied, 'St Paul demonstrates
what Do-well is. He is speaking of *fides*, *spes*, and *caritas*, of
which the greatest is *caritas*. Faith, Hope and Charity are all
good, and frequently bring men salvation; but none of them
does so as directly as does Charity. Now, there's no doubt
that someone who follows the teaching of a trusty loyal Faith
does "do well". Take the case of a married man who loves his
wife and lives by God's law while both remain alive. Or, let us
say, you're a member of a religious order, and instead of
wandering off to Rome or Rocamadour* you stay put in
obedience to your Rule; that, too, is a direct route to Heaven.
Or again, if you're in a position to marry, but have the resolve
to remain a virgin, look no further to find where holiness lies.

'What made Lucifer forfeit the happiness that was his in
Heaven above? What lost Solomon his wisdom, or Samson his
strength? Job, among the Jews,* paid a high price for *his*
earthly prosperity. Aristotle, too, and various others—like
Hippocrates, Virgil, and Alexander, conqueror of the wide
world—all came to an unhappy end. For each one of them,
money and mind alike proved fatal. Felice's loveliness be-
came a source of shame to her,* and in the same way, fair
Rosamund foully misused that beautiful body she had been
endowed with. It was on lust she lavished all her treasure.
You can read elsewhere about scores of men and women
who've spoken wise words but acted quite otherwise:

> Though eloquent in virtue's cause,
> Their lives still contradict her laws!*

'The same holds good for the rich, building up fortunes
that ultimately fall into the hands of their arch-enemies.
These people looked unmoved on the sufferings of the needy,
and failed to love them as our Lord commands; now they
suffer the loss of their own souls. What God says is, "*Give*,
and you shall receive".* That is how wealth and intelligence
have proved a snare to so many. He's an unhappy man who

has either, if he neglects to use them well: "Those who know
God's will and fail to do it will be beaten hard with a whole
rack of rods!"* Knowledge, says the Bible, engenders
spiritual pride—"puffs up the soul".* And wealth which has
not been honestly earned does exactly the same.

'Yet in all these cases, grace acts as a healing herb, a
remedy for the ailments they give rise to. Grace, however, will
only strike root amongst humble people. The only place it will
grow is patience, and poverty, amongst people who live
upright and holy lives. And, as the Gospel says, it does this as
a gift of the Holy Spirit, "the Spirit who breathes where he
will".*

'Now, learning and natural understanding are based on
observation and instruction, as Scripture makes clear to
anyone who can read: "We speak what we know, we bear
witness to what we have seen."* From "what we know"
comes "clergy", that learning which is of heavenly origin.
And from "what we have seen" comes natural knowledge,
which comes from observing a variety of people. Grace, on
the other hand, is a gift of God, and its source is God's great
love. No theologian has ever discovered how grace arises, and
natural understanding has never fathomed its ways: "No one
knows where the Spirit comes from, or where it goes."*

'Nevertheless, both learning and natural knowledge deserve
commendation; this applies especially to learning pursued for
love of Christ, who is the root of all learning. Moses bears
witness that God provided written guidance for the people of
the Old Law about the treatment of a woman caught in the
act of adultery.* Rich or poor, she was to be stoned to death.
Now, you can read about a woman who was found guilty of
that act; and yet Christ in his graciousness saved her—
through his learning! For in those characters that Christ
wrote, the Jews realized that to God's eyes they were
guiltier—and of an even greater sin—than that woman
standing there; and they went away ashamed. Learning it
was, made manifest there, that brought that woman succour.
The Church knows that what Christ wrote down saved her.
So learning *is* a source of comfort for repentant humankind;

yet to the hardened sinner, even education will prove a curse
at the hour of death.

'Again, how could bread become the body of Christ without
the help of learning?* That body is at once a healing remedy
to those in a state of grace, and a source of eternal death and
condemnation to those who die in their sins. Christ's writing
at once comforted and convicted of guilt the woman whom
the Jews brought to Jesus, but whom it was his will to save.
So, in the same way, my friends, Christ's sacramental body,
unless it is worthily received, will turn to our condemnation
on the Day of Judgement, just as his written characters
condemned the Jews.

'That is why my advice to you is, love learning for the sake
of Christ; and natural knowledge is affiliated to learning, too,
and both—take my word for it!—close relations of our Lord.
Love them, I say, if for that reason only. Both of them, you
see, are like mirrors in which we can see our faults, and, by
seeing them, set them right. They give guidance to the
educated and uneducated alike. So, never disparage logic,*
nor law and its ways; I advise you, never get involved in
disputes with the learned!

'Can a man without eyes see? Neither can a scholar "see",
unless he first acquires the skill from reading books. Books
were made by man, but it was God who taught what they
should contain; it was his Holy Spirit that provided the
exemplar indicating what men should write down. Well, just
as the power of vision enables someone to see the direction of
the road, so literacy and learning teach the ignorant the road
to reason. Supposing a blind man went armed into battle;*
would he have much chance of actually hitting his enemy with
his axe?* There's no more chance that a man equipped only
with natural reason—unless he is instructed by the learned—
could arrive, through natural reason alone, at the truths of the
Christian religion, and so achieve salvation. Christianity is
the chest in which the treasures of Christ are contained; and it
is the learned, the clergy, who keep the keys to it. They
unlock it at will, to give uneducated lay-people forgiveness for
their sins. All these have to do is be prepared to ask for it in

an obedient and submissive spirit, as a grace granted to them by God.

'You know how in Old Testament times the Ark of the Covenant* was in the keeping of the Levites. No mere layman was so much as permitted to lay a finger on that chest—only a priest, or the son of a priest, or a patriarch, or a prophet. A grievous fate befell Saul for presuming to offer sacrifice; and as a consequence of that sin, his sons also met their doom. A number of others, too, who were not Levites, accompanied the Ark, and with all due honour and reverence; but because they laid hands upon it to lift it up, these also duly paid with their lives.

'And so, my advice to everyone without exception is this: do not hold learning in contempt or set small store by the knowledge possessed by the learned just because of the sort of lives they lead. What we should *do* is accept their words at face-value, since their testimony is, in fact, true. What we should *avoid* is embroiling ourselves in bad-tempered disputes with them. What begins in a heated exchange of words will end in an exchange of blows; and you know what Scripture says: "Do not lay hands upon the Lord's anointed!"*

'The truth is that on earth the learned, the clergy, hold their responsibility from Christ. Why, even knights cannot be knighted without recourse to the clergy.* Natural understanding, on the other hand, is based on a whole range of sensory experiences; seeing the animal kingdom, feeling joy and sadness, encountering things real and things illusory. In the ancient world, people made a point of noting down the striking phenomena they observed, in order to instruct their children. They thought it the height of good sense to become acquainted with knowledge of this order. Yet knowledge such as this was of no use whatever when it came to saving man's soul; and the books containing it have never guided anyone to the happiness of heaven. Why? Because all that natural knowledge had been derived simply from various things men had observed. This science of the ancients was condemned by the Fathers of the Church, who regarded their utterances and, indeed, their entire philosophy as so much folly. Compared with the knowledge of Christ, they judged it a complete waste of time: "For the wisdom of this world is foolishness before God."*

'It is from on high that the Holy Spirit will come down,* cleaving Heaven asunder; and love shall spring out on to this earth below, to be received by the pure and discovered by the learned: "Shepherds there were speaking to one another . . ."'

'The writer of that hasn't a word to say about the rich, the merely clever, or the uneducated upper classes; what he mentions is the most erudite men in the world: "there came wise men, *magi*, from the East"*—and I'll bet you five shillings no friars could have been found there! That Child wasn't born in some beggar-man's shack but in a citizen's dwelling-house, the finest in Bethlehem: "But there was no room for them at the inn" says Scripture—and a pauper would've had no use for an inn, now, would he? So the angel appeared to shepherds and to sages, commanded them to go to Bethlehem to honour God's birth, and sang a joyous song of comfort, "Glory to God in the highest Heaven!" Rich men were snoring in their sleep when the star shone out before the shepherds, a looking-glass aglow with the hope of heaven! The learned recognized it, and they came with their presents, to do homage and obeisance to the One in whom omnipotence sat enthroned.

'Why have I been telling you all this? It's because I had taken in how you kept on arguing against learning, flinging sarcastic gibes. This is what you said:* "Of all Christians, it's the ignorant who win salvation more easily than the educated and the learned, or even those with ordinary practical understanding." And what you said *is* true of certain people, but only in a certain way, as you'll see.

'Suppose you were to take a couple of strapping fellows and throw them into the Thames without a stitch on, or anything to help one more than the other. One of them knows how to swim and dive, while the other, never having been taught, has no idea how to keep himself afloat. These two men in the Thames, then—which of them do you reckon is most afraid of drowning? The one who's never plunged in a pool and has no idea how to swim? Or the swimmer, who's safe if he wishes to be, while his companion, who has never swum, drifts away with the surge of the tide, in mortal fear of meeting a watery death?'*

'The one who can't swim, I suppose', was my reply.

'Exactly!' he cried. 'It stands to reason that someone who possesses some education, even if he sins frequently, understands more promptly how to free himself from sin, and reach salvation, than someone who's ignorant—believe me, he does, if only he really wills it! For if the educated man has his wits about him, he knows how to take comfort for his soul from the mere fact that he is sorry for his sins, even if he hasn't yet confessed them. You are aware how two of the Psalms set much store by contrition because of the way in which it chases away sin: "Blessed are those whose iniquities are forgiven, whose sins have been covered over."* This realization is a comfort to the educated man and protects him from despair—that surging river in which the Devil's temptations press a man to his limits. The ignorant man, however, daren't move a muscle until Lent arrives,* and doesn't so much as *feel* sorry till the moment for confession actually arrives! Even then, there's precious little he can say, and everything he believes about the state of his soul is determined by what his counsellor tells him. And *he* is some local cleric or parish priest who himself lacks the knowledge to instruct the uneducated. And "when the blind are leading the blind . . . "!*

'What a miserable fate to have to spend your life stuck in a slough with the ignorant! The man who sent his son to school deserves that child's undying gratitude. Spend your youth on getting an education, and it may even save your life, as well as your soul! Isn't *"Dominus pars hereditatis meae"*[1]* a heartening little text? It's managed to save a score of convicted thieves from Tyburn tree, whereas your mindless villain ends his days strung up! What sort of salvation do you call that?

'Now as for the thief *you* mentioned, who received grace from God on Good Friday:* that was because he submitted in faith to Christ on the cross, acknowledged his own sinfulness, and asked for grace from God. God is always ready to give it

---

[1] 'The Lord is the portion of my inheritance.'

to those who pray with true humility and in a genuine spirit of repentance. Yes, that thief did get into Heaven. But he didn't attain the heights of glory reserved for saints like St John, and others like him, whose merits entitled them to a higher state. It's as if someone were to invite me to a meal and then make me sit on the floor. I'd have more than my fill of food, but I wouldn't have the honourable treatment of those seated at the side-tables, let alone those placed with the guests of honour on the dais. I'd be in a position all by myself on the ground, with no table at all, just like any old beggar. This is how things stand with that criminal who won his salvation on Good Friday. He's not to be found seated with St John, or with saints Simon and Jude,* or with the virgins, the martyrs, the confessors or the holy widows. He's alone somewhere, all by himself, and gets his dinner on the ground. Remember: once a thief, always under the frown of the law—your fate in the balance at the judge's pleasure: "Never feel free of fear, even for a fault forgiven!"* How could you treat a saint and an outright thief exactly the same? It would be neither reasonable nor just to give the same reward to both!

'It's like this. Trajan, that thoroughly upright noble man, was not thrust down so deep into Hell that God could not get him out with ease. The same, I believe, holds true of the thief's situation in Heaven. *He's* in the very lowest degree of Heaven, if our faith is to be trusted; he hangs on, as it were, by the skin of his teeth—if, that is, we judge strictly by the Church's law: "God renders to everyone according to his works." But if you were to go on and ask why only *one* of those two thieves who were crucified submitted in faith, but not the other—that's a problem that remains insoluble to every theologian in the world. "Why did it seem good to God? Because his will was it should be!"*

'I'm saying this with you in mind—you who always want to know the whys and wherefores. You argued aggressively with Reason, insisted on knowing about the birds, and the animals, their mating-habits and their nesting-habits—why some up there and why others down here—just because you felt like knowing! And then about the flowers in the forest, their lovely colours so bright and brilliant, and where they got

them from; and then about the rocks, and the stars . . . and
you're still beating your brains about how the animal creation
seems to have so much intelligence . . . But neither Learning,
Clergy, nor Natural Understanding, Kind Wit, has ever
known the cause of all this.* It's known only to Nature, Kind
himself, and to absolutely no one else in the world! It's he
who provides the magpie with its plan of construction, he who
whispers in her ear how to build and breed in a dense
hawthorn thicket. It was *Kind* who taught the peacock its
special way of mating, just as he taught Adam to recognize his
private parts, and likewise taught him and Eve how to cover
them up with leaves.

'Time and again uneducated people demand of theologians:
why didn't Adam begin by covering his mouth, which ate the
apple, rather than starting with the lower part of his body?*
Yes, that's the sort of question ignorant people put to the
learned! But no divine knows—Kind alone knows why he did
so. Still, in the old days, people did indeed draw parallels and
likenesses from the animal world, as sages inform us. They
noticed that the most beautiful of birds breeds in the most
repulsive way, and when it comes to flying, is the least agile of
all birds, including water-fowl. I mean, of course, the peacock
and the peahen, which are symbols of rich men in their pride.
If you chase a peacock, it's unable to fly up high, and because
of its trailing tail you can quickly overtake it. Its meat is
horrible to eat, its feet are horrible to look at, and its cry lacks
all charm—in fact, it's hideous to listen to!

'All this is true of a rich man, too, if he holds on to his
wealth and refuses to part with a penny of it until his dying
day. The "tail" of all his life—I mean his *end!*—is a wretched
one. Just as the peacock's plumage hampers his flight, so
possessing silver pence and golden nobles burdens all those
who hang on to them till their tail is finally plucked!* And
what if, at that point, a rich man does repent? What if he rues
the day he amassed so much and made free with so little?
Then it doesn't matter how earnestly he calls out to Christ; I
believe that his voice will sound in our Saviour's ear as
raucous as the chattering of a magpie. And when his dead
body is brought for burial in the tomb, I think it will make

the surrounding area stink; everything nearby will be polluted with its poison! The peacock's feet (I gather from Avienus)* signify the man's executors: treacherous friends who won't fulfil his instructions, even if they swear to carry them out to the letter. In this way, the poet shows that a peacock is admired only for his feathers, just as a rich man is treated with respect because of his wealth.

'The lark, however, a much smaller bird, has a much more agreeable song, flies much faster than the peacock, and has a good deal more meat on it—tastier meat, at that. The lark can be compared to people whose station in life is a low one.

'These are examples given by that great thinker Aristotle,* who uses this comparison with the smallest of birds in his philosophical writings. But whether or not Aristotle is *saved*, no theologian knows for certain. There's no written authority, either, to tell us the fates of Socrates or of Solomon.* Such, though, is the goodness of God that I hope, in his mercy, he will grant rest to their souls. After all, he gave them the intellectual powers that enabled them to guide *us*. We desire to be saved; shouldn't we, then, feel all the more obliged to pray for them, because of what we owe to their writings? Our scholars would be ignorant to this day if it wasn't for what they learnt from these men's books.'

'But all the Christian authorities', I replied, 'state in their writings that *no* human being created in the divine image— pagan and Jew alike—will find salvation without the Christian faith.'*

'I deny that!' answered Imaginative, beginning to look annoyed. *"Salvabitur vix iustus in die iudicii. Ergo, salvabitur!"* [1]* And after that, he spoke no more Latin. 'Trajan', he said, 'was a just and upright nobleman who never received baptism. Yet we have it on authority that he is saved; his soul is in Heaven. There is a baptism that you receive at the font. There is also a baptism of blood, shed by the martyr. And it's a firmly established doctrine that there is, too, a baptism of fire: "There came a divine fire which burnt not, but brought illumination."*

---

[1] 'Even the just man will *scarcely* find salvation.—Which means, surely, that he *will* be saved!'

'Now, consider the righteousness of someone who has never sinned or transgressed against his own principles.* He lives according to his lights in the belief that nothing higher is to be found (for, if it could, he'd willingly embrace it). Such a person dies with the disposition I've described. God, surely, who is just, would never refuse to commend such authentic righteousness! Well, whether it will actually turn out so or not, the "faith" found in a just man's righteousness is a thing of real substance. Doesn't it contain the hope of some reward for a life lived justly? The word *DEUS* does: *Dans* "giving"; *Eternam* "eternal"; *Uitam* "life"; *Suis* "to his own"—that is, to the faithful.* There's another text, too, which says, "Though I should walk in the midst of the shadow of death, no evil will I fear".* The standard interpretation of this psalm-verse recognizes that a man of righteous life merits a reward. Intellect and wisdom', he concluded, 'were at one time the treasure men looked for in governing a kingdom. No mere wealth was held in higher esteem. It was a source of happiness; it was what it meant to be human!'*

And so saying, he vanished.

VISION FOUR

PASSUS XIII

Immediately I awoke, almost at my wits' end. And when I set out on my way, it was like a man under sentence of death. For several years after this, the life I pursued was that of a wandering beggar; and time and again, I found myself brooding deeply about this dream.* I brought to mind first how Fortune abandoned me in my hour of greatest need; what Old Age threatened to do if we ever met; how the friars kept their services for the rich, and cared precious little for those who weren't, and even made difficulties about burying your body in their graveyard unless you left them money during your lifetime or agreed to help them pay off what they owed! In that dream I'd also seen how greed got a stranglehold on clerics and priests; and I understood how lay-people, led astray by ignorant priests, run the risk of eternal punishment, unless our Lord intervenes on their behalf. My dream showed me Imaginative telling me about Kind, about the wisdom of his ordinances and his overflowing loving kindness towards the animals of earth and the creatures in the sea. I saw how he favours no living thing with 'less' or with 'more', since everything capable of movement owes its very existence to him alone. And my dream concluded with Imaginative declaring, 'The just man shall scarcely be saved!'—after which he'd passed from view in the twinkling of an eye.

I lay down and spent a long time mulling this over. At length, I fell asleep. And then—such was God's will—Conscience came, bringing me new heart as I lay there. He was inviting me to come to his manor-house, and have dinner with Learning. And because Conscience mentioned Clergy's name, I accepted promptly.* When I arrived, I noticed a doctor of divinity—someone I didn't know—who was giving Scripture a low, courteous bow. Conscience, who knew him well, gave him a warm welcome. After washing and drying our hands, we all went in to dinner.

In the courtyard outside, however, Patience was standing,* dressed in pilgrim's clothes. In the name of charity, he requested something suitable for a poor hermit to eat. But Conscience invited him to come inside, and with tactful courtesy said to him, 'Welcome, good fellow! Go and wash your hands; we're just about to start.'

The theologian I mentioned, as the most distinguished person present,* was given the place of honour; after him, came Clergy, Conscience, and Patience. I was put together with Patience as my dinner-companion, on one of the side-tables. Conscience called for the food to be brought, whereupon Scripture came and promptly served people with a variety of dishes.* These were drawn from St Augustine, St Ambrose, and all the four Evangelists, and 'they ate and drank what there was to be had. . .'.*

However, the Doctor and his companion ate no ordinary meat, but altogether finer and far costlier fare,* including soups and fancy cassoulets. They were used to doing themselves well, the cost being covered from profiteers' contributions. But their sauce was too pungent, its flavouring overdone. Its spices had been ground in a mortar called *Post mortem*,[1] a varied mix of bitter punishments. That, at least, is how it must turn out, unless they sing psalms and shed salt tears for the souls of those guilty men I mentioned:

> You who sup on the sins of men—
> Unless you weep and pray for them,
> What now you eat with a glutton's joy
> You'll vomit up in agony!*

Then Conscience politely asked Scripture to bring some bread for Patience and for me, his companion at the table. What he placed before *us* was a sour-tasting loaf with the words, 'Do penance'. And then he poured us something to drink: 'This is a medicinal draught of perseverance;* it will work', he ended, 'as long as life and limb hold up.'

---

[1] After death.

'Why, what excellent fare this is!' Patience exclaimed. 'It's a feast for a king!'

The next course to appear was 'Blessed are those whose sins have been forgiven'. This had been prepared by 'Blessed the man whom God imputes no sin to'. There followed a serving of yet another course, 'Have mercy on me, O God'; and then 'Those whose sins are covered' came, in a dish of confession uttered secretly: 'I said, I will confess my wrongs to the Lord.'*

'Bring Patience another helping', whispered Conscience in an aside; and one was duly brought for him: 'All who are holy pray to you in due time.'* Conscience entertained us with cheerful topics of conversation, like 'A contrite and humble heart, O God, you will not despise.'* Patience, for his part, was delighted with the excellent fare, and proceeded to enjoy his meal. But all the time, I was working myself up into a foul temper; the reason was the sight of that theologian at the high table, draining cups of wine at such a rate. ('Woe to you mighty drinkers of wine!')* He was eating his way through a variety of dishes—stews, puddings, tripes, wild brawn, and eggs fried in lard.

At this I muttered to myself—but Patience could hear me—'It isn't four days since this fellow was preaching, before the dean of St Paul's,* about the hardships that the apostle Paul endured: "In hunger and thirst and beaten three times with rods, and five times by the Jews, at forty strokes a time . . ." But there's one little expression that he and his like always skip over in their sermons. It's where St Paul tells the Corinthians in that epistle he wrote them, *"Periculum est in falsis fratribus"*.* That's Scripture's warning, which I'm not prepared to put into English here and now, in case it's repeated. I don't want to upset people whose virtues are really genuine; but those who know Latin can feel free to read it: *"Unusquisque a fratre se custodiat!"*[1] (Anyway, *I've* never come across one of these wandering friar-people who was ever willing to preach on that theme in English—without taking

_____
[1] 'Let everyone be on guard against a *brother*, for, as they say, there's danger in false *brothers!*'

care to put a gloss on its meaning! Yet for all that they'll preach about what good penance does our souls, and about the pains and hardships Christ suffered for man's sake. But this God-Almighty glutton', I exclaimed, 'with those plump cheeks of his, couldn't care a scrap for poor people, like us. Doesn't he "do evil", not practising what he preaches?'

Such was what I said to Patience; and there welled up in me a great desire to see those dishes and platters in front of this theologian turn into molten lead in that belly of his, set a-boiling by the very Devil himself!

'I'm going to have a little argument', I declared, 'with our friend Master Jordan Jeroboam* over there! I'll ask him to tell me what penance is—that topic he preached about not long ago.'

Patience was aware of what was passing through my mind, and winked at me to keep a hold on myself. 'You'll see in a moment', he said, 'when he can't manage to eat another thing, he'll start feeling what it's like to endure *penance*. I mean in his belly—he'll belch between every word. His stomach will begin to rumble, and then he'll yawn. Now that he's truly tanked up, he's all ready to give his theology lecture. Watch him demonstrate from the *Apocalypse of Golias*, and from the *Life and Passion of St Avereys*,* how all these dishes are good penitential fare; bacon, brawn, chicken casserole, cassoulet—not one of them's either fish or meat! And then he'll refer to a certain "trinity", and he'll get his companion* to confirm what he turned up in some chest of books—a text dealing with the friars' form of life. (But if it isn't a pack of lies from the first page on, don't ever trust what I say again!) That will be the time to press our Doctor about Do-well and Do-better, and whether Do-best is some sort of penance.'

So I sat quietly as Patience asked, and in a few moments this theologian, his cheeks burnished and glowing red as a rose, cleared his throat and proceeded to hold forth. Conscience heard him, and raised the question of a certain 'trinity', casting a look in our direction.

'What is Do-well, Professor?' I asked; 'is Do-best some kind of penance, sir?'

'Do-well?' asked this theologian, quickly taking a drink, 'That means "Don't harm your fellow-Christians—as far as you can manage."'

'Well, Professor', I replied, 'so help me, I'd say *you're* not in a state of "do-well". Why, you've been harming the pair of us here by eating up the pudding, the stew, and the other dishes, while we didn't get so much as a bite to eat! Is that how you do things in your friary hall? I'd be astonished if you didn't have a riot on your hands in place of peace and harmony—assuming the novices had the guts to complain! I'm more than willing to cash in *my* penance for yours; I'm all packed up and ready to start on "Do-well"!'

At this, Conscience put on a conciliatory expression, and threw a glance at Patience as if to say, Get him to keep quiet! Then he resumed himself by saying, 'Professor, if you don't mind my asking, what *are* "Do-well" and "Do-better"? Presumably you theologians must know.'

'"Do-well"?' replied the Doctor of Divinity. 'It means doing what the clergy teach. "Do-better"—that's someone who both teaches and works hard at it—that is, teaching. "Do-best" is applied to a person who himself actually practises what he professes and what he preaches.* "The man who both acts and instructs shall be called great in the kingdom of Heaven."'*

'Your turn now, Clergy', said Conscience. 'You tell us what "Do-well" is.'

'I have seven sons',* replied Clergy, 'who work in a castle the lord of life inhabits. They are there to learn what Do-well is. Now, until I see complete accord established between the seven of them and myself, *I* can't presume to teach anyone what it is. Why? Because someone called Piers Plowman has hung a big question-mark over all of us. He says no branch of learning is worth a brass farthing except one—*love*! And the only authorities he relies on to support his case are "Love the Lord your God" and "Lord, who shall dwell within your tent?"* Do-well and Do-better, he says, are two "infinites", and these "infinites", helped by faith, are the means to discover the way to Do-best. This it is that will save the souls of men. And that is what Piers Plowman has to say!'*

'I'm not very clear about all this', replied Conscience, 'but I do know Piers well;* and I'm prepared to guarantee *he'd* never say anything that contradicts Scripture. So let's leave this topic till Piers is here to show us what it actually means in practice. Patience, though, has travelled a great deal; maybe he knows something that the learned do not know. Christ himself seems to imply as much in saying that "The patient are victorious."'*

'Well, since you ask me', Patience replied, 'and provided I give no offence by what I say . . . ! It is "Learn. Teach. And love your enemies."* Learn, and you do well; teach, and you do better; love, and you do best. That's a lesson I once learned from a lady I was in love with (her name was—Love). "By your words", she said, "by your actions, and by your deepest heart's desire, you must love your own soul unwaveringly as long as you live. And in that way, out of love for your Lord in Heaven, you must go on and learn to love your enemy;* and you must love him under all circumstances, just as you love yourself. Cast coals on his head—by speaking kindly to him. Try to win his love by everything you do and say. Keep hammering away at him with love, until you end by forcing him to smile. And unless he gives in at last to a beating like that, the fellow deserves to lose the use of his eyes!"

'That, of course, is not how you'd treat a friend; it wouldn't be a sensible way to go on! Genuine affection, after all, doesn't ask anything from you—only, that is, the pleasure of your conversation. It's firmly wrapped up in there,* is Do-well, with that Latin half-line inscribed on lamps, *Ex vi transitionis;*[1]* and I carry it about as a symbol of that Saturday which originally established our calendar, along with the total meaning of the Wednesday of the following week. The full of the moon* provides the power of them both. As long as I have it with me, I'm always welcome.

'So—open it up! Let this theologian decide whether Do-well's there inside. For this I swear in the name of my Creator: none of these things—poverty, suffering, pain,

---

[1] 'By the power of transitivity'.

malicious tongues, cold, anxiety, bands of brigands, heat or hail, fiends out of Hell, fire or flood, or the menaces of some enemy of yours—none of them, I say, will ever harm you, provided you keep it always with you: "*Caritas*, love, is afraid of nothing!"*

'I'll go further and promise you this, as I hope to be saved: if you ask for anything, you'll succeed in obtaining it effortlessly—from emperor or empress, earl or baron, pope or patriarch. You will overcome all of these through this riddle's potency, which derives not from magic but from wisdom. You yourself will be able to make kings and queens and common people alike give you everything they own, and trust in you as the best guardian of their goods, ready to follow where you lead for the rest of their lives: "the patient *are* victorious."'

'What absolute twaddle!' the theologian exclaimed. 'It's pure minstrel-romance,* the lot of it! Why, a combination of the wisest heads and the strongest arms anywhere has had no success in establishing peace between the Pope and his enemies! Nor has a living soul been able to achieve as much between a pair of Christian kings—not on terms that would satisfy both nations!' And with that, he thrust the table from him and said in a confidential tone to Clergy and Conscience, that they really ought to get rid of this fellow Patience: 'You know what these pilgrim-types are like, I presume—past masters at telling tall stories!'*

Conscience, notwithstanding, spoke up audibly, and the tone that he adopted was a polite one. 'Friends', he declared, 'I think I shall take my leave.' And turning to Clergy he said very amicably, 'I intend to set off with Patience here,* if it's God's will that I may do so, and accompany him on his pilgrimage, till I've acquired somewhat more experience.'

'What!' exclaimed Clergy to Conscience. 'Don't say you've started hankering after New Year's gifts and odd bits of largesse!* Or have you been suddenly overcome by an urge to interpret riddles? Look, let me bring you a Bible, open at a certain book of the Old Testament; it will teach you, assuming that's what you want, the last word on this

subject—one which our pilgrim-friend Patience can't quite
have mastered fully.'

'In Christ's name, no!' Conscience answered Clergy. 'May
God repay you for your kind offer; but I assure you, I don't
feel in any way superior because of what Patience is offering
me. But it's the inner intention of the man—as well as that of
certain people here*—which has brought on in me an urge to
repent my sins. Goodwill in a human being, you see, is
something beyond all price. Nothing, however precious, can
stand comparison with sincerity of heart. Think of Mary
Magdalen: didn't she get more for that pot of ointment than
Zacheus, for all his saying "I'll give a half of all my goods to
the poor"? Isn't the same true of that poor widow-woman
with her pair of pennies, compared with all the others who
put their offerings in the Temple treasury?'*

And so Conscience began by saying goodbye politely to the
friar. He then said quietly in Clergy's ear, 'Dear God, if I
survive, I swear I'd prefer a full share of patience to half this
library of yours!'

Clergy, however, refused to take leave of Conscience;
instead he said to him in a grave voice, 'You'll live to see the
day you grow tired of wandering about, and then you'll wish
you had me to advise you.'*

'God knows, that's true enough!' exclaimed Conscience.
'But if only we could both make Patience our partner, yes,
our close bosom-companion, there's no trouble in the world
we couldn't put right!* We could bring the desire for peace
into the hearts of kings. We could convert every single nation
to belief in the one true faith—Moslems, pagans, eventually
even the Jews!'

'True enough', replied Clergy, 'I can see what you're
getting at. But I shall stick to my proper task; I'll confirm
young people and others who are adequately instructed, till
Patience has put you to the test, and brought you to a
condition of perfection!'

Thereupon Conscience and Patience, like a pair of pilgrims,*
went on their way. And, as pilgrims do, Patience carried
provisions in his knapsack: sobriety, humility of address, and

genuine faith. This would serve to strengthen him and Conscience if they should ever set foot in the lands of Unkindness and Greed—territories where the traveller finds no food. And as they proceeded on their journey, the subject that they spoke about was Do-well. Now, as I witnessed, they came across a minstrel. Patience took the initiative and addressed him; what was his trade, he asked him, and where was he making for?

'I'm a minstrel',* the man replied, 'my name is *Activa Vita*.[1] And because I take my name from being "active", I hold every idler in abhorrence! I'm a wafer-seller, I'd have you know, and my customers include many of the nobility. Yet I get few robes and fur-lined gowns from them! Now, If I knew how to tell tall stories and set people roaring with laughter, I'd certainly get the clothing and cash that end up in the hands of rich men's minstrels. But I can't tap tabors or tootle on a trumpet. I can't tell stories, or fart at will, or strike up on the fiddle at entertainments. I can't pluck a harp, and I don't know how to crack jokes, or to juggle, or play fancy tunes on the pipe. I can't stroke a psaltery or accompany myself on a guitar. So—*I* don't get any nice little presents from his lordship simply for producing my bread for sale! In fact, all I do get's a blessing on Sunday, when the priest asks everyone to say an "Our Father" for Piers Plowman and those who look after his interests. That means me—the man of action, the man with no time for idlers! Ask any honest working-man, any ploughman—who provides his wafers from one year's end to the next? I'm the one, of course!

'My bread is in great demand—from beggars and mendicants, crooks, friars, fellows with tonsures. I lay on bread for the Pope, and provender for his horse; but by God, d'you think I've ever been *provided* with a prebend, or with some parsonage that lay in his gift? Not a thing, apart from a pardon, with a lead seal* and a couple of heads in the middle! Now, if I had some educated fellow who could write, I'd get him to draw me up a complaint to the Pope. I'd ask him to send me, under his seal, a remedy for the plague! Why can't

---

[1] The life of activity, the practical life.

papal blessings and bulls put an end to these plaguey boils? "In my name they shall cast out devils; they shall lay their hands on the sick, and they shall recover."* If they *did*, I'd be double-quick making my pastries for the public; yes, as willing to work as hard as you like, getting food and drink for the Pope and all his servants—if only it really was true, that his pardons had the power to cure the sick. At any rate, I certainly believe they *should*! He has the power St Peter possessed,* agreed? Well then, he must have the pot with the ointment, too: "Silver and gold I have none; but what I have, I give you: in the Lord's name, get up and walk!"

'Still, I suppose the reason he can't work miracles is that people just aren't worthy to have God's favour.* It isn't really the Pope who's to blame. After all, no amount of blessing will do us any good if we remain unwilling to change our ways. All the masses that men say can't bring about peace among Christian nations until pride has been totally stamped out! And the only way that'll happen is through a famine. Look— before *I* can turn flour into bread, I have a fair bit of sweating to do, right? Many's the cold morning this has to happen, if people are going to get enough to eat. So, before my wafers get made, there's a lot of hard grind to be gone through—and by me.

'The whole of London, I'll have you know, is rather partial to these wafers of mine; they certainly look sour when they can't get them! Yes, it's not long since the whole population was feeling pretty sorry for itself—when the bakers' carts stopped rolling in from Stratford with their bread. Beggars would burst into tears, then, and even your labouring men began to feel just a wee bit anxious. People won't forget those days in a great hurry! The year of our Lord thirteen hundred three-score and ten, to be precise—when Chichester was Lord Mayor of London.* There was a drought in April that year— and were my wafers scarce!'

Now, I swear that during this I was looking very closely at our active man, Haukin. So, for that matter, was Conscience, and in particular at what he was wearing. He had on a coat of Christian faith* as it is held and taught by Holy Church. But in several places it was covered with a variety of stains. Here

it was stained with pride, and there with angry, violent
words—scolding, mocking, and unreasonable behaviour. In
dress and demeanour Haukin held the world in disdain. He
was always pretending to be something he wasn't, or to
possess what he didn't; that was his heart's desire. This is
why he goes around boasting and bragging, backing it all up
with audacious oaths. Yet all the while he's absolutely
unwilling to take criticism from another person; he considers
himself so special, such a rare sight to set eyes on, that he's
utterly unique, a paragon of piety. Dressed up like a hermit,
he's the founder of his own order* (membership: one)—a
religion without any rules, and so no reason for obedience!
Lambasting the erudite and the ignorant alike—he's
outwardly in love with honesty, but in his soul, a liar. His
mind and his senses equally were given over to fantasizing and
brooding about how to get known as cock of the town.

He was always interfering with other people's affairs. He
wanted everyone to think him the cleverest of men, a past
master of his craft and a deep thinker to boot. A really rough
rider of horses—especially mares; tremendously attractive,
utterly trustworthy, pious as they come, and pure as the
driven snow; endowed with superb good looks and a fine
physique. At once the most skilful of singers and so clever
with his hands. Generous to a fault—but only for people's
good opinion, of course. If he gives alms to the poor, he
makes quite certain everyone hears about it. He has
practically nothing in his purse or in his chest, yet he'll walk
about looking like a lion, with the airs of an earl. The boldest
of beggars, his boasting is backed by nothing; gossiping at
every street-corner and tavern, describing in detail things he's
never seen and swearing they're all of them absolutely true.
He carries on and crows about feats he's never accomplished
and various achievements he's never approached. This is how
it will go:

'Look! You don't believe me, eh? You think I'm inventing
it all, do you? Well, ask what's-his-name here, and who-
d'you-call-'em there—they'll tell you what I've been through
and what I've seen, the fortunes I've made, the things I've
experienced, and the very high-class people I'm connected

with.' Now this was his sole concern: that people should
know about things he'd said and done—anything to win him
popularity and praise. But—'If I set out to please men, I
could not be the servant of Christ Jesus', and, in another
text—'No man can ever serve two masters!'*

'Dear Lord, Haukin!' cried Conscience at this point. 'This
coat of yours—your best—it's covered all over with spots and
splotches! The thing's badly in need of a proper wash!'

'You're right', admitted Haukin, 'whichever angle you look
at it from—back, front, or from either side—you'll find it a
mass of creases and filthy stains.'

He turned round as he spoke, and I had a good look. It was
ten times filthier, in fact, than it seemed at first! The thing
was bespattered with anger and malicious thoughts, with
hostile feelings and the insulting language that sparks off and
kindles conflict: there was all the lying and constant carping
of a tart tongue quick to foment a quarrel. Everything bad he
knew about anyone, he simply had to blurt out. He railed at
people behind their backs and wished them the worst of luck.
What he knew about Will, he couldn't keep back from Wat;*
and if Wat knew something, Will had to know it forthwith.
With that deceitful tongue of his, he could turn the best of
friends into bitter enemies. 'One way or other', he said, 'by
the power of words or else by physical force, I've managed to
get my own back in the end—and if I haven't, I've gone on
anyway snipping away at myself, inside, like a tailor with a
pair of scissors, cursing away at everyone I could think of.'
'His mouth is full of cursing and of bitterness; labour and
sorrow lie under his tongue.' And another text declares:
'These sons of men, their teeth are like weapons and arrows,
their tongues like sharp-edged swords.'*

'There's not a soul', he went on, 'that I'm capable of feeling
lasting affection for; and no one trusts me because of the tales
I tell. When I fail to come out on top, I get so depressed I
start to suffer from cramp, or sometimes from pains in the
chest; or else I shake all over during these bouts. Sometimes I
get a fever that may last a whole year, and then I pour scorn on
all spiritual remedies and turn instead to a sorcerer for help.
No man of the Church—not Christ himself,* so help me!—
can hold a candle to the Cobbler of Southwark or old Mistress

Emma of Shoreditch. God's word, I tell you, never did me
any good; it's through a charm I've been lucky enough to
recover!'

Looking at his coat more carefully, I could see how it was
soiled with the sin of lechery. It would start with lustful
looks; every time Haukin met a girl, he made suggestive
signs, the idea being to lure her on to sin. With another, he'd
kiss her hard or start groping beneath her smock, till the pair
of them were thoroughly aroused. They would end up, then,
going the whole way. He kept this up even on fast-days,* on
Fridays, and at times of abstinence like vigils; it made no
difference whether the season was Lent or any other—to him,
all times of the year were just the same. For people like this,
there was no closed season on copulation; the only limit they
acknowledged was their appetite. And what happens when
that, too, is played out? Then they turn to salty stories about
the cavortings of lechers and their whores, and beguile their
old age recalling their sordid exploits.

Then Patience noticed that in places Haukin's coat had
grown grimy with unbridled greed for material things. Goods,
not God, were the object of this fellow's affections. His every
fancy was given over to ways of obtaining wealth:* whether
by using false weights and measures or else by bearing false
witness. His practice was to lend money for the chance it gave
of getting his hands on the security deposited, not in order to
forward an honest man's efforts. All his wits he devoted to the
challenge of cheating people. He was skilled in adulterating
the goods he sold and then cleverly disguising the deception.

'Yet', he exclaimed, 'the stuff I sold had the very lowest
quality mixed up in it; what a splendid con I thought that
was! And if my neighbour had a servant or an animal more
valuable than my own, there were no lengths I wouldn't go to,
to get my hands on it! And if there turned out to be no other
way of getting the thing, I ended up eventually by stealing it.
I'd simply pick his purse or pick his lock. Night and day I
was constantly on the prowl, amassing what I've got by
unlawful means.

'Or let's suppose I was ploughing. I'd encroach so close that
I'd manage to pinch a foot, maybe, or a furrow's breadth of
soil from the strip of land belonging to my neighbour. Or say

I was harvesting: then I'd reach over myself—or maybe order my reapers to do it—and sickle in sheaves of corn I'd never planted!*

'Again, if anyone ever borrowed from me, he certainly paid for it! Either he gave a present or two under the counter, or handed over a regular fixed-rate payment. Whatever *he* felt about it, my aim was a profit. But I was an absolute skinflint when it came to helping my own family and friends. But if anyone did buy my wares, I'd go at it hammer and tongs till he agreed to pay a penny or two more than the thing was worth. I'd go still further and swear blind it had cost *me* much more than I was asking.

'On holy-days at church, hearing mass, God knows it never crossed my mind to ask him forgiveness for my misdemeanours. In fact, if I did feel sorry, it was for my lost profits, not the sins of my flesh. If I actually had committed a mortal sin, I felt far less anxiety than I did over some loan I thought wouldn't be repaid—even if the date of repayment was still far off. But if, somehow, I *did* manage to do a fellow Christian a good turn, I'd start suffering from a bad conscience about that!

'Sometimes I had to send my agents* across the water to Bruges, or despatch an apprentice to Prussia to see to my interests there—some matter, maybe, involving foreign exchange. All the while I was waiting, I found no relief from worry in going to mass or matins, or, for that matter, in any kind of amusement. I couldn't start saying an act of contrition or an "Our Father" without my thoughts straying to my money worries; I couldn't concentrate on the love of God or the comforts of his grace.' 'Where your treasure is, your heart is also.'*

Yet more was to come. That greedy creature had dirtied his garment with blasphemous language and horribly muddied it with lying assertions, taking God's name in vain without any need; swearing like this without ceasing had worked on his coat like floods of sweat outpoured. Haukin had, moreover, consumed more food and quaffed more drink than human digestion was designed to cope with. 'And often enough', he said, 'I've paid the price of indulgence by falling ill; and then

I've been terrified of dying in mortal sin.' As a result, he
would collapse in despair, believing himself beyond salvation.
That, in fact, is the sin of sloth, sluggish inertia of spirit that
nothing can serve to shift. Even divine mercy is impotent to
help someone who dies in that miserable condition!

  . . . What, then, are the branching ways down which a man
is borne down to sloth? It begins when he feels no remorse for
his wrongful actions, expresses no contrition for them, but,
on the contrary, fails to carry out the penance given by the
priest. He offers no alms, fears no sin, lives in defiance of the
Christian religion, and refuses to observe any of its
commandments. To him, every day is a holiday, and life one
long, unceasing carnival. He has no ears for any words—
unless they are dirty ones. If anyone refers to Christ, or the
things of the spirit, he gets in a rage and insists on 'a bit of
fun'. As for penance, or the poor, or the sufferings of the
saints—he loathes such things and anyone who mentions
them. These are the limbs down which men slide into sloth; I
warn you, watch out for them!

  Listen, you nobles especially—men and women, and yes,
even prelates—with your licensed jesters, flatterers, and liars.
You enjoy listening to these people because you expect them
to make you laugh—but *woe to you who are laughing at this
moment . . .!** You give them food and tips, yet say a flat 'no'
to the poor. I fear greatly for you when the moment of death
approaches, and you find those three groups of men have
brought you to a grim conclusion, no laughing matter: 'Those
who acquiesce in evil are just as guilty as those who act it, and
deserve an identical punishment.'*

  The patriarchs and prophets who preached the word of God
saved men's souls from Hell through the discourses they
delivered. In the same way, flatterers and fools are the Devil's
disciples; and through *their* utterances, they entice people into
the vices of the flesh. But it's the duty of the clergy, who are
acquainted with Holy Scripture, to inform the nobility what
the prophet David says about such people. These are the
Psalter's words:

The man who acts proudly will have no place in my dwelling;
He who speaks evil will not prosper in my sight!*

No filthy buffoon should gain a hearing, public or private, in any household where people of discretion live. I can quote you God's own testimony for this! Nor should arrogant scoundrels earn the least recognition from a noble man or woman.

Now, minstrels of the king's household find a warm welcome from the clergy and the nobility alike; they receive attention on account of the respect that is owed to their royal master. Surely, then, oughtn't the rich to be that much readier to receive the utterly destitute, who are the minstrels of the King of Kings? This is just what God says himself in St John's Gospel: 'The man who despises you, despises me.'* So this is my advice to you rich people when you are entertaining: for the benefit of your souls, admit 'minstrels' of this kind! Let some poor man sit at your table instead of a licensed fool, and invite some learned cleric who can teach you about our Saviour's passion, and in that way rescue your soul from your enemy Satan. Let him sing you the grave tale of Good Friday: there's no scope for flattering you there! Make some blind man your comedian, some disabled woman your table-wit; let them call out for 'bounty!' in the presence of our Lord, and add lustre to your honoured name!

Here, then, are three kinds of 'minstrel' who can really make a man laugh when it matters most—at the moment of death! What solid consolation they will hold out then for a man who attended to them gladly throughout his days on earth. These are the minstrels who cheer a man's spirit, fanning hope that he *will* be worthy to join the blessed in Heaven, because of the way he acted in this life. But flatterers and fools with their filthy stories will conduct those who patronized them to Lucifer's celebrations. *Turpiloquium*[1]* is the opening phrase of that terrible tune the Devil draws from the fiddle-strings of Hell!

... These are the ways in which Haukin, the active man, had sullied his coat. At length Conscience, as politely as he could manage, proceeded to make him feel guilty for neglecting it: for failing to give it a decent wash, or even to run over it with a brush!

[1] Dirty talk.

'I've only got one cloak* at all!' exclaimed Haukin. 'I'm hardly
to blame if the thing's all mucky and rarely gets a clean: I
even have to sleep in it at night! That's not all, I've got a wife
and servants and children'—

      I have married a wife and so I cannot come . . .*

—'All of these help to mess it up time after time, whatever I
say about it. It *has* been to the laundry—during Lent and at
other times; the soap used was sickness, which penetrates
pretty deeply! I've also had financial setbacks, and the effect
of those was to make me chary of offending God or any decent
soul—at least as far as I could manage. I duly received
absolution from the priest, and he gave me a penance for my
sins: I was to be patient, feed the poor, and confine my
covetousness to preserving my integrity as a Christian. For all
that, God knows I couldn't keep the thing clean for an hour
on end. It was always getting dirty somehow—by looks, or by
some thoughtless thing I said. Some way or other by an act,
or a word, or some wish deep inside me, I was sure to get
muck all over it from one end of the day to the next!'*

    'I'll show you', replied Conscience, 'how to make your
contrition effective, so you can scrape every kind of dirt off
this coat of yours. The starting-point is a heartfelt *sorrow* for
sin. Then, with the help of a confessor who knows what he's
doing, Do-well will wash the coat and wring it out—*confess*
your sins. Then Do-better will steep it in a solution of lye and
make it as brilliant as genuine scarlet cloth. Then he'll dye it
good and fast with goodwill and with God's grace of
repentance. After that, he'll send you off to *satisfaction*,* to
dry your garment out in the sun.

    'And Do-best will keep it clean from every unkind act. No
insect will ever cover it with spots, no moth will ever eat it,
and for the rest of your life no evil creature, fiend or fellow
mortal, will besmirch it. There won't be a herald or harp-
player with a smarter costume than our active man, not a

minstrel held in higher esteem by every kind of person than our wafer-seller Haukin, the man whose life is one of practical activity: all this, if you do as I instruct you!'

'As for me', spoke up Patience, 'I'll provide the dough you require, even when there's no plough to till the earth, and also the flour that's needed to feed people in the way that will best benefit their souls. Even if no grain of wheat were to grow, no grape to deck the vine, I'd furnish food for everyone alive—yes, and enough food, too. No one will go without anything he needs. We shouldn't be too concerned about our bodily requirements. Doesn't Scripture say, "Do not be anxious about what you are going to eat?" And doesn't God "feed the birds of the air"? It is "the patient who win the day"!'*

This made Haukin laugh, with a mild oath. 'Good God, man', he said, 'I don't see much future for any man who puts his trust in *you*!'

'No?' replied Patience—patiently—and out of his haversack drew some food; it offered real nourishment to every living creature. 'Look', he said, 'if our faith is to be trusted, there's livelihood enough to be had here! No creature was ever endowed with life unless some means to live was also provided, in some shape or form. Start with the earthworm under the dank soil; then the fish that live in the water; the cricket, at home in the fire; the curlew, a bird whose flesh is the finest (being fed on air alone); and animals that eat grass, grain-stuffs and fresh roots. All these creatures are a symbolic lesson to us that man, too, is capable of life through a trusting faith and love. God himself assures us of this: 'Whatever you ask the Father in my name, I will do." And in another place he says: "Man does not live by bread alone, but by every word that proceeds from the mouth of God."'*

I, however, looked to see what this nourishment was that Patience was praising so. It turned out to be a section of the 'Our Father'—none other than the words 'Thy will be done'!*

'Take this, Haukin', said Patience, 'and eat it when you get hungry, or when you feel numb with cold or parched with thirst. Then you'll feel no pain from fetters, or from some suffering: for the patient *are* the ones who win the day. Just remain master of your eyes and your tongue, your powers of smell and touch, all your five senses; then you need never worry about wheat, or wool, or linen, or drink. You won't be afraid of death because you'll die at peace with God, whether you die from hunger or from the heat—let it be as he wills! In fact, if you live by his teaching, the shorter the life you're given to live, the better!

> The man who loves our Saviour's law
> Will treat this world as so much straw!*

'You see, it was through God's breath that the living creatures came into being and spread across the earth: "He spoke, and they were created." Doesn't it follow logically, then, that men and animals alike *live* through God's breath? That's what Scripture claims in the words we say at grace before meals: "You open your hand and fill every living creature with your blessing."*

'It's recorded that there was a period of forty years when people managed to live without carrying out any cultivation; and water welled up from the hard rock for man and beast alike to drink his fill. And in the time of the prophet Elias, the heavens remained closed, and no rain fell. You can read in the Bible how for several years people succeeded in living without ploughing the land to grow their food. There's written authority, too, for the story of those seven people who slept for seven hundred years. *They* survived without eating at all—and eventually they awoke!*

'Well now, if human beings were to live as the law of moderation requires, there'd never again be any shortage of food among Christian people, if Christ's own words are to be relied on. No—it's our *un*natural behaviour that creates a condition of dearth in a Christian nation, just as over-abundance engenders pride, amongst poor and rich alike. But moderation*—that's a thing of such value it could never cost too much! Just think of the disastrous calamity that befell the people of Sodom; didn't that result from an excess of eating and sheer idleness?

> Too much leisure and too much food
> Encouraged evil's vilest brood!*

Because they rejected moderation in food and drink, those people were led to acts of grave evil that brought delight to the Devil himself; and as a consequence of their horrible sins, vengeance fell upon them, and each of the cities of the plain disappeared into Hell!

'That's why we must pursue moderation, and make faith our protecting shield.* It's through faith, as we know deep within us, that contrition comes; and contrition expels mortal sin, and makes it venial, something that can be pardoned. Even if a man had lost the power of speech, his inward sorrow could save him, and lead his soul to the happiness of Heaven; all that's required is for faith to testify that during his life he believed in the Church's teaching. So it follows, then, that contrition, faith, and conscience fundamentally make up Dowell; and when oral confession proves impossible, these operate as surgeons in the fight against mortal sins.*

'However, verbal confession is something still more efficacious, especially if a man feels inward contrition. You see, oral confession *destroys* sin, however serious it may be. Through a full confession to a priest, sins are "killed", whereas contrition merely diminishes their gravity, making them something capable of being forgiven. (This is what David says in that psalm-verse about our sins "having been covered over".) Satisfaction, finally, goes to the very root of the matter: it both slays sin and removes the remains; it makes mortal offences vanish completely, just as if they'd never been committed. Thereafter, they are neither seen nor felt, but appear like wounds that have healed without leaving a trace.'

'Where does *Charity* live, though?'* asked Haukin. 'Never in my life have I heard anyone mention him—and I've travelled quite a bit in my time.'

'Have you come across total honesty? Humility of heart? Self-control in speech? That's where you'll find Charity. He's the man entrusted with looking after God's household!'

'Is patient poverty', asked Haukin, 'more pleasing to our Lord than the wealth a rich man has earned, honourably, and properly disposed of?'*

'Can you find such a man?' replied Patience. 'If you can, let's lose no time in praising *him*!* But though you can read about rich men in every part of the world, I've never heard of one who didn't go in mortal dread of the approach of death— not one who, when the day of reckoning drew near, didn't prove to be deeply in arrears, rather than being free of every debt. The poor man, on the other hand, has a good case to present. He can show by recourse to reason alone that he *deserves* to have the Lord's good favour; after all, he's claiming what is his lawful right!* Someone who's never known happiness in his life can ask for it at the hands of a just judge; and this is what he can say: "Look at the birds and animals, and the wild serpents in the woods, which know nothing about the joys of heaven. You compel these creatures to endure the rigours of winter, until sheer want has made them nearly tame. But then, you send them the summer, the ultimate delight they're capable of—a time of 'heavenly joy' to every creature, wild and tame alike."

'It follows, then, that the poor and destitute, like the animals, having spent their whole life in pain and deprivation, can look forward to some recompense. Unless God sent them *some* kind of happiness, some time or other—either here on earth or in another place—why, nature itself could never allow it! What a wretched existence such people would have been made for, with no happiness *ever* in store for them!

'Even the angels who are now in Hell knew happiness at one time, and Dives enjoyed the sweet things of this life—*la dolce vita*. Just the same is true of human beings who were rich: they and their wives along with them enjoyed a life of pleasure. It's extraordinary, to judge by the standards of common sense, how God should be willing to shower his bounty on so many people before they have actually earned it. Yet that *is* how God treats some of the rich; and it seems a pity to me! In being paid here they are, so to speak, getting their Heaven on earth—living in luxury without stirring so much as a finger. But when a man of this sort dies, he forfeits God's favour,* as David says in the Psalms:

The rich have slept their sleep and have found nothing . . .
Their joy is like the dream of one who wakes,
For in your kingdom you will make them—nothing!*

'It's pitiful, that wealth has the power to tear a man's soul from Christ's loving embrace, at the very moment a man breathes his last!

'Servants who get paid their wages in advance are constantly ending up in need. And take men who eat their dinners before they've done their stint, a decent day's work: these people rarely die in credit, either. It's only after a workman has finished the job that you can really see how well he's done it, and so what he deserves to be paid. He certainly should not get paid in advance, in case the work turns out unsatisfactory.

'I'm applying all this to the case of you, the rich. It doesn't look as though you'll get heaven during your life on earth and, after that, another heaven to follow! That would be as if an employee were to be paid his wage in advance and then went on to claim more, just like the man who hasn't had his yet but waits for the end of the day to get his payment. My rich friends, this simply cannot be—unless St Matthew* has got it all wrong about what God really desires: "To start *and* end in pleasure—that's too much!"*

'On the other hand, if you rich people are moved by pity* to look to the needs of the poor, if you live by God's law and treat everyone justly, then Christ, out of his gracious kindness, *will* stand by you in the end, and will provide "double payment"* to those whose hearts have really been open to compassion. It's like when a serving-man receives his pay before starting work, but then, when he's done the job and done it well, goes on to get a further reward on top—a coat, say, in addition to the wages agreed on. In some such way, Christ grants Heaven to those who are rich as well as to those who are not—provided they live lives filled with compassion for others. And everyone who performs his allotted task as he should, receives a double payment for his efforts: on earth, that is forgiveness of his sins; in the next life, Heaven.

'But, judging by what the saints say in their writings, it's a rare occurrence,* God's actually granting this twofold reward to a wealthy man. The rich have a very enjoyable time of it here, with their food and their clothes, just like the wild animals in the merry month of May, and the pleasures last right through the period of summer. But towards Midsummer Day,* beggars find they are having to sup without bread; and for them, winter is a much harsher time. Then they are forced to go wet-shod, suffering severely from hunger and thirst, bitterly scolded and abused by the well-to-do. It makes you weep to hear the things they say!

'Now, Lord, send these people summer, give them *some* sort of happiness! After they leave this life, grant them Heaven, since they have had to live here in such want. (You could, after all, have ordained that no one was poorer than anyone else, and everyone equally intelligent and discerning— if you had wished it!)* Take pity, too, on rich people who care nothing for these prisoners of yours—ungrateful, many of them, for the wealth you endow them with. None the less, Lord, in your kindness, send them the grace to change their ways! They seem immune to the blows of famine, to drought, floods, heat, and hail, if they only have health. Here, they lack nothing they fancy or desire!

'But poor people, Lord, these prisoners of yours in their dungeons of wretchedness—comfort them, Lord, those poor creatures for whom nothing but misery results when there's famine or drought, all their days on this earth! In winter they suffer from lack of proper clothing, and even in summer rarely enjoy a full meal. Christ, bring the comfort of your kingdom to these distressed subjects of yours. Don't the clergy testify that you bring comfort to *every* creature, when they say those words of the prophet, "Turn back to me, and you shall be saved"?*

'This is how Christ, through his own nobility of nature, preached to robbers and thieves, rich and poor, prostitutes and rogues—to every kind of person. You taught them, Lord, to receive baptism in the name of the Trinity, and through that christening to be cleansed from every kind of sin. And you taught, too, that if through negligence we fell into sin again, we should acknowledge it and confess it, and beg for your mercy, and through these means repent, as often as we desire.

'And what if the Evil One should object to this, and start to cause us agony in our conscience? We should immediately take our deed of acquittal and thrust it before the Devil's eyes

to read: "Let it be known to all, that through the Passion of
Our Lord . . ."* That way we can drive back the Devil, and
prove to him that we have a surety—Christ. However, the
parchment on which this deed of release is inscribed must be
poverty, genuine patience, and a total seamless faith. The
parchment finds no place for self-exalting pride; what above
all it requires from everyone is to be inwardly poor.
Otherwise, everything we could possibly do would be utterly
pointless: saying strings of "Our Fathers", doing penance,
going off on pilgrimage to Rome—unless what we spend on
all this springs from a source of sincere faith deep within us.
Failing that, *all* our labour is lost—just look at how people's
names are engraved in the windows of friars' churches*—if
the very foundation we are building on is unsteady. That's
why Christians should share their wealth and not just greedily
look to their own advantage.

'There are seven sins* from which we are constantly under
attack; the Devil brings up the rear and does his best to help
them. But it's *wealth*, these fiends have discovered, is the
quickest way to lead men to their ruin. For where wealth
rules, respect follows, does it not? And *that* rouses a glow of
pride, in poor and rich alike. The rich man, though, is
respected thanks to his wealth, whereas the poor man goes to
the back of the queue. Yet this same poor man, perhaps, is far
better endowed with intelligence and wisdom; and those are
qualities far superior to riches or high rank, and far more
highly esteemed in the court of Heaven. Again, the rich man
has a great deal to account for, and has to tread a very delicate
path. Riches are a frequent obstacle on the straight road to
Heaven; isn't it "impossible for a rich man to enter the
kingdom"?* The poor man, on the other hand, pushes on
ahead with only a rucksack to weigh down his back: "for their
works follow them . . ."* And this he does with the bustling
eagerness of a beggar, confidently claiming eternal happiness
because of his poverty and penance: "Blessed are the poor, for
theirs is the Kingdom of Heaven!"*

'Moreover, Pride gets the upper hand much more easily
amongst the rich than amongst the poor; it finds some lodging
either in the master or his man! But in the state of poverty—

provided patience is also to be found there—Pride has no power. Indeed, *none* of the capital sins can find a foothold there for long or get any real mastery over poverty, *if patience accompanies it*. Think how the poor are always quick off the mark to make themselves agreeable to the rich; how submissively a poor man does what he's told, just for the sake of having the rich man's scraps! But submissiveness and self-assertion are absolutely opposed to one another, aren't they? In every aspect of life, each one is sworn enemy of the other.

'Then, if Anger wrestles with a poor man, he ends by getting the worst of it. Suppose a dispute arises: the poor man hasn't much strength, and if he starts to complain or make a fuss, things are going to turn out badly for him. You see, someone who depends on others for his food and wages *has* to be humble and *has* to watch what he says!

'Gluttony next. If *he* should start bothering Poverty, he's going to get precious little for his efforts. After all, Poverty's income simply won't stretch to buying fancy foods; and however much he may want to drink decent beer, he can't change the fact that his bed's a cold one. He's forced to lie there in discomfort, all twisted up, no nightcap on his head; and when he tries to stretch, he feels underneath him straw, not sheets. So, the price for him of indulging in gluttony and sloth is—what? Sheer misery when it's time to get up! He's so cold he feels like crying (sometimes, maybe, he even weeps for his sins)! The fact is, Poverty can never really live it up without something to spoil his pleasure, as part of the bargain; maybe, too, there's some real pain to boot.

'Or Greed; what if *he* wants to grab hold of Poverty? They can't get properly to grips with each other—and especially not round the neck. Everyone knows Covetousness is a rough customer, with hands and arms of a very long reach indeed. Poverty, though, is just a little chap who barely comes up to his middle. There's no sport to be had out of a pair so badly matched in height—none worth watching, anyway. And even if Avarice wanted to afflict the poor, he's got very little scope for doing so. Poverty has nothing but bags to put his goods in; but Avarice goes in for big cupboards and chests with iron bands. What about the problem of being burgled? There's nothing to boast about in having broken open a beggar's sack, is there? Not compared to a coffer bound with steel!

'Lust, too, regards Poverty with distaste, since he's hardly liberal with his cash, and he doesn't go in for choice food, and very rarely gets the chance to drink wine. What about those wretched brothels, too, the "stews"?* They'd fall in ruins if they relied on nothing but poor men to provide their customers. The tiles would soon he falling off their roof-tops!

'And then there's Sloth. Even if Poverty *does* give in to Sloth, and fail to serve God properly, the trouble he'll have will quickly teach him a lesson. He'll be forced to reflect that his one support is God—*there's no one else!* He's God's servant, as the Lord himself declares; it's to his retinue that the man belongs. And whether this is actually true of his case or not, at any rate he wears the trappings of Poverty; and that was the garb in which our Saviour brought about the salvation of all our race.* That's why all poor people who really *are* patient can ask, nay claim happiness in Heaven, after this earthly existence is at an end.

'But now, think how much stronger and bolder a claim can be made by someone who *could* have had what he wanted: lands, social advantages, sexual pleasure. Yet for love of God he abandons it all, and lives the life of a beggar. He's rather like a girl who leaves all for the man she loves—mother, father, all her family and friends—to go and make her life with her chosen spouse. Now a girl whom a man gets on those terms is really worth his affection—much more than one who came to him by an "arrangement", with first the agreement of the various parties involved, and then a role in it somewhere for hard cash! That's what it's like for someone who renounces possessions and undertakes to be patient: what he contracts is a marriage with Poverty.* And Poverty is a relation of none other than God himself; yes, a kinswoman—the tie is as close as that!'

'In God's name, then!' Haukin now exlaimed. 'I've been listening to you singing the praises of this Poverty. But what, I ask you, Patience, does "poverty" *mean?*'

'*Paupertas*', answered Patience, speaking in Latin, '*est odibile bonum**—good, yet hateful. It's the removal of all worries, possession of property *sans* reproach. It's God's gift, and good health's smiling mother. A trouble-free road, controlling hand of wisdom. Business where there's no loss-sheet; and, amidst the vicissitudes of fortune, a pure felicity free from the smallest care.'

'I can't make head or tail of all this!' cried Haukin. 'You're going to have to spell it out in plain English.'

'It's pretty hard', replied Patience, 'to explain all I've been saying in simple language. But I'll try my best to get what I can across—provided you on your side make the effort to follow!

'Poverty, then, is the basic virtue* that pride is most implacably opposed to. So there's good reason for thinking it a "good": because everything is that tends to put off pride. Just as contrition is a source of comfort (this is something your conscience is fully aware of), sorrowful in itself, but at the same time a spiritual support, so, strictly speaking, poverty *is* a penance to the body, but at the same time brings happiness to the soul. To the spirit, it is like pure, health-giving air, just as contrition is a source of strength, a *"cura animarum"*—what that means is, "a guardian of our souls". That's why poverty's "a good thing—but something that's found hateful".

'To go on: poverty is rarely called on to bring in a legal verdict, and no poor man finds himself obliged to judge others by sitting as a justice of the peace. A poor man can't get elevated to the high office of mayor, nor can he serve as a minister of the crown. It's not often that a poor man's required to impose punishment on other people. So poverty is *"remotio curarum"*—and that means "the removal of anxieties". So people in the condition of poverty are capable of carrying out God's command: "Do not be a judge of any man."*

'A poor man rarely gets hold of a great deal of money except by coming into a lawful inheritance. He doesn't make profit out of using false weights or measures that haven't passed the test of inspection. Nor does he borrow from his neighbours a jot more than he's well up to repaying. That's how poverty is *"possessio sine calumnia"*—"ownership without blame".

'The fourth point is this: poverty is a condition of life that benefits the soul; it protects from sin, but there's more still that it does. Poverty restrains the sexual instincts from any number of foolish errors, and thus it becomes an additional source of strength: "*donum Dei*"★—a gift of God himself.

'The fifth feature of poverty is that it's the mother of good health, man's friend in time of temptation, and for the foolishly ignorant, a lover who's totally chaste: "*sanitatis mater*".★

'The sixth aspect of poverty refers to it as a path of peace: this enables poverty to journey through somewhere as perilous as Alton Pass★ without the risk of being set upon by robbers. You see, wherever poverty travels, he's followed by peace; the less baggage he trails with him, the more confident he feels within—"A poor man meets a thief but goes on singing."★ Oh yes, he can remain without concern even if he falls amongst a band of brigands. That's why Seneca says, "*Paupertas est absque sollicitudine semita*"★—a path through life free from anxiety.

'And so to the seventh feature of poverty. Poverty is a deep source of wisdom, taciturn and reserved of speech as he is. For powerful men are unwilling to favour poor ones, and give little heed to what they argue. Oh yes, the man free from the itch for money can *afford* to tune his tongue to truth alone;★ hence, call poverty "wisdom's tuning-teacher"—"*sapientiae temperatrix*".

'The eighth mark of poverty is this—that it stands for honest effort at all times, and refusal to take more than one truly deserves. And if a poor man's engaged in trade, he doesn't think it a loss to win people's love by putting the goodwill of men before pure profit. Hence "*negotium sine damno*", "loss-free business".★

'In its ninth aspect, poverty is sweeter than any sugar to the soul. For the poor man himself, patience serves as bread, sobriety is sweet drink★ and a worthy physician to him when he's sick. This is what I learnt from Augustine, whose learning was acquired for love of God—that poverty is a blessed state of life in which man's body and his spirit alike are not dogged and harried by an endless ruck of affairs:

"*absque sollicitudine felicitas*"—"happiness", that is, "free from worry". Now may God, who gives everything good, give rest to his soul; for he was the first to teach us the meaning of poverty!'

Then Haukin the active man cried out in anguish: 'Why didn't I die and go off to my grave a minute after I had been baptized? What have I done for Do-well? It's so *hard*', he went on, 'to live, and to have to go on sinning! Sin—it constantly shadows you night and day!' And he collapsed into a deep melancholy, tears brimming over at his eyes,* and cursed the time he did any action that might displease our good and loving God. He almost fainted, so passionate was his sobbing, and time and again he let out anguished sighs: why had he ever possessed land, or estates, large or small? Why had he ever had power over anyone other than his own self?

'God knows', cried Haukin, 'I'm not fit to wear clothes at all—no shirt, and no shoes—except to cover the shame of my putrid flesh!'

And with that he went on crying out for mercy, weeping and lamenting; and with the sound of his sorrowing, I awoke.

VISION FIVE

PASSUS XV

But after I woke, it was a very long time indeed before I could get any proper grasp on the nature of 'Do-well'. My understanding would grow, and then decrease, till I ended up reduced to a state of idiocy.* Then there were people who criticized me for the way I lived—but few who had a good word to say for it. They thought of me as a worthless ne'er-do-well; didn't I refuse to tug the forelock to the gentry, or show proper respect to anyone, if it came to that?—folk in furs with silver necklaces, senior barristers, people of that ilk. Not once could I bring myself to say, 'I hope God is treating you kindly, sir!' or incline my head in a courteous bow. The result was that everyone thought I'd lost my mind; and so, mindless, I started to rave—till at length Reason took pity on me, and rocked me into a sleep. And then, as if by magic, I caught sight of something fashioned out of a fine-drawn substance,* without any tongue or any teeth. This creature held forth to me about my destiny, my origin, and my nature. At length, I put him on his word to tell me, for the love of Christ, if he was a being that Christ our Lord had created.

'Oh, yes', he replied, 'and in many places I *am* "Christian"*—a familiar figure at Christ's court and, in some measure, related to him. No matter how late the hour is when I knock, neither the door-keeper Peter, nor Paul with his sword in hand, will willingly deny me entrance there.* Midnight or noon my voice is so little a stranger's, that everyone in his palace welcomes me warmly.'

'What name do they know you by', I asked, 'these people in Christ's court?'

'*Anima*', he answered, 'is my name, "the Soul",* because I *animate* the body. But as that which wills and desires, I bear the name of *Animus*, "Intent". As the power that acquires and possesses knowledge, I am called by the name *Mens* or "Mind". When I face God in prayer and meditation, my title then is *Memoria*, "Recollection". Making moral judgements, and acting as Truth instructs me, my appellation is *Ratio* or, as we say in English, "Reason". Perceiving what others say, I am called *Sensus*, the power to know and understand the fundamentals of every practical skill. Now, when I make decisions, negative or positive—to do something, or to hold back from acting—I am called "Conscience", God's secretary and accountant. In my capacity to love sincerely both the Lord God and my neighbour, my name is "Faithful Love"— *Amor* in Latin. But when I'm on the point of departing from my body, leaving it as a lifeless corpse behind me, I become a voiceless ghost—my name *Spiritus*.*

'St Augustine and St Isidore were the ones who together drew up this catalogue of my names. But you can take your choice of what to call me—now that you know them all.'*

'Well!' I broke out, unable to keep a straight face, 'you rather remind me of our worthy bishops. Don't they go around trailing a long list of titles? There's "Prelate" and there's "Pontiff" and "Metropolitan", "Bishop", of course, "Pastor"—and a whole pile besides!'

'Fair enough', he replied, 'now I see what you're after. From what you say, I suppose you'd like to find out exactly why bishops have all those names. And why I have all mine, for that matter!'

'I would indeed, sir!' I answered. 'I hope no one will be offended by my saying this, but what *I'd* like to have is a complete fingertip knowledge of every branch of learning under the sun—and, for good measure, the various crafts and skills!'

'In that case', he said, 'you're a long way from perfection. One of Pride's men-at-arms, that's what you are. It was just such a desire as yours that caused Lucifer to fall from Heaven:

> I am going to plant my right foot in the north
> And be like God Almighty from henceforth!*

But don't you realize', he continued, 'that it would be completely contrary to nature, and totally at variance with reason, for anyone other than God to know *every*thing!

Solomon protests against those who think that way; listen to
how he pours scorn on their reasons: "Too much honey is
harmful to a man; too much idle curiosity about the majestic
ways of God brings down His might upon deluded man!"*

'In plain English, for those who speak nothing else, this is
what Solomon means. If you eat too much honey, it cloys
your stomach, doesn't it? Now supposing you open your ears
to twice the amount of virtuous doctrine as the next man—
what then? Unless you *live* twice as well, the doctrine just
does you double the amount of harm! This is how St Bernard
puts the same thought:

> Blessed the man who reads the Sacred Book
> And bends his will to make its *verba*[1] work!*

It was greed to grasp at knowledge, seize upon sapience, that
thrust Adam and Eve out of Paradise:

> Craving for knowledge stripped Man bare
> Of glorious lasting life, to which he was heir.*

Now, honey is hard to digest and lies heavy on the stomach,
does it not? It's the same with someone who's restless to
know, by means of his reason, the fundamental workings of
God's sublime power. An attitude like this creates a barrier to
the operation of divine grace. Why? Because at the heart of it
lies pride and a greed, thoroughly carnal in its nature, that
resists Christ's wisdom and the teaching of all the learned:
"Wisdom means being no wiser than you should be!"*

'Listen to me, you friars and university men—you who
preach sermons to simple unlettered people. As you are
holding forth about the Trinity, you stir up thoughts that are
totally beyond grasping. The result, as often as not, is to
undermine the faith of the ordinary man. It would be far
better if the learned—most of them, anyway—gave up that
sort of preaching; they should instruct people about the Ten
Commandments, or the Seven Deadly Sins, and the various
offshoots of those sins, which set men on the highway to
damnation.* You should talk about the ways in which the five

---

[1] Words.

senses are misused—and not just by others, but by friars too!
How? By bothering far too much about what you wear, and
by showing off your high-falutin scholarship—something you
do for display, not out of fervent Christian love. Oh, but the
common people have no doubt what I'm getting at is the
truth. It's the great ones of this world you're intent on
pleasing.* How promptly you honour people who pay money!
And yet:

Let them wallow in confusion, those worshippers of wood!
Why adore hollow idols? Why follow falsehood?*

'Have a look at the Gloss's commentary on that verse, my
learned friends. I may be a simple-minded fellow, but if I've
got this wrong, you're free to lead me to the stake and set me
alight! As I see it, you don't mind taking alms from anyone—
usurers, prostitutes, money-grabbing traders. And who do
you bow your head to? Mighty magnates who count out coins
in your palms—even though that's contrary to the rule you
profess. But let me appeal to the words of Christ himself;
what was it *he* said to his disciples? "Do not be respecters of
persons."* (Now, there's a subject on which I could fill a fat
volume!) But on the matter of parish priests, who *are* directly
responsible for the Christian community, I shall air my
thoughts, for the sake of the truth itself. And anyone with
ears to hear, let him listen!
'It's from the Church itself that holiness and virtue spread,
through the lives of just men who teach the law of God. But
in exactly the same way, it's from the Church that every evil
also emanates, wherever there are bad priests and bad
preachers and teachers. You can see what I mean from a
parallel—trees in summer-time. Some have their branches
covered with leaves, while some have none; there's something
wrong in the roots when you get such branches. It's the same
with the priests and preachers of the Church: they form the
root of that sound faith under which the community can be
governed. But it stands to reason that where the root is rotten,
there can never emerge any flower, or fruit, or lovely green
foliage.

'Ah, if only you men of learning would give up your craving for fine clothes and instead be kind and generous with what belongs to Christ! That's how the clergy *should* be. If you were men of honour, who spoke the truth and led decent lives, if you detested the sound of obscene conversation, and refused to accept tithe-offerings from dishonest ploughmen and crooked traders ... ah, how hard it would be then for simple uneducated people *not* to follow your teaching and be converted from a life of sin! They'd do so all the more readily from seeing your example than from hearing your preaching, when you don't yourselves practise what you preach. What that looks like is hypocrisy!

'There's a Latin text on this topic that compares hypocrisy to a dunghill covered with snow but crammed with snakes inside; it also likens this vice to a whitewashed wall with a filthy interior.* Yet that's just about how it stands with so many priests, so many preachers and clergy in high positions. How splendidly white you all look, with your fine talk and your fine clothing! But underneath it all, your actions and the real motives behind them are more of a piece with the wolf than with the shepherd!* Just listen to what St John Chrysostom says on the subject of clerics and priests: "All good comes forth from the Temple; so also does every evil. If priests live lives of integrity, then the whole Church will flourish; but let *them* grow corrupt, and all the faithful will begin to wither. If priests live sinful lives, the people as a whole will turn to sin. Now, when you notice a tree that's colourless and drooping, you know its root is diseased; so when you observe a community without moral discipline, devoid of religious fervour, you can know for certain there's no health in the priests!"*

'All that is set down in Latin; but if the common people knew what it meant, I'd be very surprised indeed if every priest within sight didn't give up wearing swords and fancy ornaments, and rest content with rosary-beads and a prayer-book under his arm! Look, here's Father John and there's Father Geoffrey, wearing a belt with silver buckles, a sword or a knob-hafted dagger with gilded studs! But it's the Breviary that's the one proper tool of his trade, out of which

to recite the psalm, "I will please the Lord...".* For all
that, a service-book is the last thing he wants to be seen with;
that's not all—if he's not paid good money, too, such prayers
as he says he'll say with a bad grace.

'Ah, you poor simple people, how much money you waste
upon the clergy! Still, when it comes to cash that's acquired
anyway by underhand means... isn't it just the workings of a
wise Providence that it ends up in the hands of dishonest
men? I'm thinking of those clerical rogues who preach only
for payment, as well as the whole gang of executors, sub-
deans, and summoners (each complete with his concubine, of
course). Money that was got by fraud is scandalously spent:
it's pimps and prostitutes who reap the benefit of such
property. Meanwhile, the people of God are deprived of it all,
and die in abject penury and distress.*

'But what actually happens to the goods left behind by
parish priests and avaricious clerics? All too easily it finds its
way into the safe-keeping of spendthrifts. Or else, if maybe
those people die intestate, straight away in comes the bishop
and his crew, who manage to have a fine time of it with his
wealth. But this is what they say: "What a tight-fisted miser
the fellow was! Never put by a penny of his to help cousin
or stranger; devil take his soul! Look at the mean-minded
way he ran his own household. Here's the money the old
skinflint stowed away; we might as well spend it all enjoying
ourselves!"*

'Exactly the same fate lies in store for everyone who's mean
with his money—it makes no difference whether he's learned
or simple. Off go his goods once the fellow is a ghost! But it's
not like that with a truly good man. God himself sees how
sincerely *he's* mourned. Real tears are shed for a generous
spirit whose board groaned with the evidence of his bounty.
People won't let such a man pass from their minds; we
remember him with our prayers, with deeds of penance, and
by our own charitable actions.'

'Charity?' I interjected at this point. 'What *is* charity?'

'It's something quite childlike', came his answer. '"You
cannot come to the Kingdom without becoming like a
child."* I said "child*like*" not "childish", not lacking in

sense. It means possessing a will that is *free*—that is, generous.'

'Ah, but where do you find a friend with a "free" heart such as you speak of? I've lived in the world, and my own name is "Long Will";* but *I've* never found real charity, wherever I may have looked for it. Oh, people feel plenty of compassion for mendicants, or for the poor; everyone's willing enough to lend where they're sure they'll be repaid. But as for charity—the virtue St Paul praises as the highest, the one that's pleasing to God above all else . . . Charity which isn't "puffed up, or ambitious, and never seeks its own"* . . . Dear God, I've never seen the man who didn't seek his own, who didn't sometimes covet things he had no need for—or *take* them, for that matter, if he got the chance! According to my clerical friends, Christ is to be discovered everywhere; but I've never seen him more distinctly than my own reflection in a looking-glass. "We see now through a glass, darkly; but then, face to face"*—yes, that applies well enough to charity! It's not something you can win like a trophy in a prize-fight, or the profit in some business operation.'

'No', he replied, 'charity has nothing to do with business, or with asserting your claims, or with saying "I want, I want, I want!" Charity takes as much satisfaction in a single penny as in a pound of gold. It's as content with a gown made of coarse grey wool as with a fine jacket of choice scarlet or silk from Turkistan.* Charity rejoices with everyone who is happy, and is kind, too, to people who are evil. He's generous and loving to every one of God's creatures; not one of them ever feels his curse. Charity doesn't *know* how to bear a grudge, and he has no desire to tell lies, or to laugh anybody to scorn. Everything people tell him he happily takes on trust as being the truth; and he puts up uncomplainingly with every kind of misfortune. It's not earthly wealth that he longs for but the happiness that lies only in Heaven.'

'But does Charity *have* any income, or any property? Does he have any rich men among his friends?'

'Charity cares not a jot about what he earns or what he owns; this is because he does indeed have a friend—one who looks after him, and has never let him down in his hour of need. I mean Thy-Will-be-done,* the person who perpetually provides for him. If Charity has supper, his sole dish is Hope-in-the-Lord.* He knows how to draw the "Our Father" and colour the picture in with "Hail Marys".* Sometimes he makes a practice of going on pilgrimage: but it's to places where you will find the poor, and prisoners, his aim being to relieve and release. And even when he's unable to bring them food, he carries a sustenance that's even sweeter: the love our Lord commands us to show—care and concern for the conditions that they live in.

'When Charity has had his fill of these labours, there are other times when he goes and works in a laundry, maybe for some twenty minutes or so. Now he turns his thoughts to the time of his youth, and ponders that period when Pride used to hold sway. All its trappings he bundles up together, gives them a thorough soaking in his breast, then squeezes them out and beats them hard with a psalm: "I laboured in my groanings every night..."* Lastly, he rinses them out in a bath of warm water from his eyes. And as he does all this, Charity sings; sometimes he says in tears, "a contrite and humble heart you will not despise, O God".'*

'Ah, Christ!' I exclaimed, 'I wish I knew the man! There's no one in the world I'd *rather* know!'

'But you'll never see him in person', he replied, 'without the help of Piers Plowman.'*

'But the clergy who look after the Church', I returned, 'do *they* know him?'

'The clergy?' he said, 'they too have no knowledge of him—except through actions and words. But Piers Plowman has a deeper insight into the heart of a man's intention, and into the reasons why men suffer: "And God saw their thoughts..."* After all, there *are* people whose hearts are full of pride, though they exercise the utmost discretion in their talk, and are most obliging towards city magnates and the nobility. It's these same people who turn up their noses at the poor; they glare like lions if you find fault with them! Oh, yes—you'll also find mendicants who *appear* to be devoted to a life of prayer, with lamb-like expressions and the true saintly demeanour. But what is all this poverty of theirs? Just a means of getting a free meal without having ever to lift a finger! It's not penance and the quest for holiness.

'So, you can never recognize Charity through his outward appearance or his air of learning; not even through his words and actions, but only through the *will*. And what that is, no living creature knows—save Piers Plowman, "Peter, that is, *Christ*".* You won't find him amongst layabouts and wandering hermits, or in the company of anchorites who carry collecting-boxes on their belts. These people are all deceivers by profession; damn the whole crowd of them, and devil take anyone who supports them!

'No, Charity is God's champion in the fight; yet he's as courteous as a well-mannered child, the brightest and most sparkling guest at table. It's the love deep in his heart that gives him all his delightful conversation; it's this that makes him good company, this that makes him a constant joy to be with. But that's how Christ himself tells us to behave: "Don't be gloomy-solemn", he says, "like hypocrites!"* Yes, I've seen Charity going clad in silk, and I've also seen him in the coarsest clothing: in rough grey wool, but also in furs, sometimes wearing a suit of gilded armour. But whatever he wore, he gave alms cheerfully to those in need.

'Think of Edmund and Edward*—kings, both of them, but also held up as saints: Charity walked unceasingly by their side! But I've also seen Charity singing mass, and reading psalms and lessons. I've seen him on horseback, and I've seen him in rags and tatters. I can't say I've ever come across him, however, asking for alms as a beggar! Ah no, more often I've found him in expensive clothes, wearing a cap, his head shaved and anointed. True, he was once to be found in friar's robes; but that was ages ago, in the time of St Francis; he's rarely seen in that Order since those days!*

'The fact is, he *is* in favour with rich people, and he's happy to accept gifts of clothing from them—provided they live lives free of guile and deceit: "Blessed the rich man found without a blemish."*

'Charity will also set foot in the courts of kings, where the council consists of just and honest men. But where they have made a bosom-friend of Greed, Charity refuses to show his face. He rarely has anything to do with scurrilous gossips at court, because of what goes on there—the squabbling, the backbiting, the scandal, and the lies.

'Charity doesn't turn up in Consistory Hall before the bishop's officer, because that's where proceedings last for ever unless someone is paid a bribe to speed them. Church courts are the places where marriages are made and unmade for cash down:* learned canon lawyers there ignobly set asunder a union put together by Conscience and Christ!

'At one time, Charity was accustomed to find a home amongst archbishops, bishops, and other great men of the Church; these would share out to the poor their portion of the earthly treasure of Christ. But now Greed holds the keys to the chest and keeps that treasure for his own relations, his executors, and his servants, not forgetting some for their offspring, too.

'I'm not passing judgement, God knows, on any one individual, or group of people; no, I beg his grace for *all* of us to amend our lives and follow Charity! If you do come across him, you'll know him by his bad manners. You see, he doesn't curse and swear, he doesn't boast or fling praise about, carp or compliment or go around with grim looks. He doesn't solicit, or crave, or clamour for more; he says—"In peace I shall sleep and find my rest."* The main sustenance on which he survives is a love that is nourished by Christ's passion. He doesn't ask alms or beg for money, nor does he borrow loans at interest. He never injures anyone, or hurts people by the things he says.

'Now *that* is the generous gentleness of spirit that should prevail among Christian people. Whatever afflictions come upon them, they should hold fast in their hearts to this truth: whatever they might be suffering, God, for our sakes, suffered more. And he did it as an example to us to suffer, and not look for revenge against our enemies for the treacherous way they treat us. That is the will of the one who is our Father. It's plain to everyone, isn't it, that if God *had* so willed it, Jesus would never have been betrayed by Judas and given up to be crucified by the Jews. St Peter and St Paul would never have been imprisoned, or undergone martyrdom

as they did. No, our Lord suffered as an example to us to
suffer in our turn. And this is what he told those who were
willing to suffer: "To suffer, in the end, is to succeed."

'Let me show you what I mean', he continued, offering me
a number of authentic instances. 'The *Golden Legend**
recounts the lives of the saints, telling what they underwent in
the way of penances, deprivation, and suffering: from hunger,
from the heat, and from every kind of illness and affliction. St
Anthony, St Giles, and other desert saints* lived in the
loneliest places amongst wild animals. Monks and mendicants
lived in mountain-hollows and caves, in complete solitude,
rarely exchanging a word with each other. However, none of
them—Anthony, Giles, or any hermit of that time—received
what he lived on from lions or leopards; they were fed, so the
authorities tell us, only by the birds of the air. The one
exception was St Giles, who used to summon a female deer to
him; he kept alive on the milk of that harmless creature. But
he didn't have it every day to satisfy his hunger, only, as the
Legend informs us, on rare occasions. As for Anthony, he had
a bird that used to bring him the bread he lived on; and when
he had a guest to entertain, it was God who provided for them
both.

'Paul, the first hermit, enclosed himself in a dense screen of
moss and leaves, so that no one could see him. And for many
years he was fed by birds of the air, till he founded the order
we now call the Austin Friars.* And Paul the apostle,* when
he had done preaching, made baskets, and earned what he
needed by working with his hands. Peter fished for his food,
as did his companion Andrew; they sold some of their catch,
and some of it they cooked, and that is how they earned their
keep. Mary Magdalen,* for her part, lived on roots and dew,
but her real sustenance was to meditate, and to contemplate
God the Almighty. It would take me more than a week to list
every one of the people who lived in this way year after year,
out of the love they had for our Lord.

'Yet there was never a lion or leopard that wandered
through the glades, no bear or boar or any other wild animal,
that did not fall at their feet and wag their tails! I believe that
if *they* had had the power of speech, they'd have fed those

hermits even before the birds did. Now, those animals showed the saints every helpful service of which a beast is capable—licking their feet and lowing as they moved through the clearings. Yet for all that, it was not by means of fierce wild animals that God sent them their food, but only through the agency of birds. What this symbolizes is—that the humble should be supported by the gentle.* In other words, virtuous laymen are the ones who should provide for people called to the religious life: those who live righteously should sustain the ones who seek a life of sanctity. Then the nobility would lose their taste for vice—men and women alike. They'd be reluctant to exact more than their due from tenants, if they found friars turning down their offers of alms and urging them instead to take the money back where they'd got it from!

'We, ourselves, are God's fools,* living in expectation, until birds bring us the food we are to live by. Listen, you who profess the religious life: if you get a decent helping of stew and bread, and a modicum of cheap ale to drink, and meals that run to one course only, you're indeed getting enough—at least as far as your rule tells me you should. This is what Job has to say on the matter:

> Will the wild ass bray when he has grass?
> Will the ox bellow before a full manger?
> Compared with beasts, you men stand condemned:
> For them, simple sufficiency suffices;
> Excess is the origin of *your* vices!*

'If only laymen were familiar with this Latin text—how careful they'd be about who they gave their gifts to! They'd spend five or six days taking advice before conveying property rents into the safe-keeping of monks and canons. It's a great pity, my noble friends, that you listened to such *bad* advice and alienated from your own descendants the property that your ancestors left *you*! To get them to pray for you, you gave money to those who are already rich—orders that were founded, endowed even, for no purpose except to pray for others!*

'Is there *anyone* alive now who actually lives out the words of the prophet: "He has distributed, given his goods to the poor"?* If there *is*, I suppose it must be these poor friars of ours. What they obtain by begging they spend on building—with some left over for themselves and those who work for them. These indeed take from those who have, and give to those who have not!

'But what about you clerics, knights, and well-to-do citizens? Many of you act like the man who had a forest full of fine trees, but went on planning how to plant more and more in it. You well-off people give robes to those who are well-off themselves, helping your helpers where no real *need* exists. You're like someone who fills a barrel with water from a running stream, then carries it forth to keep the Thames from going dry! That, my rich friends, is exactly what you are doing, laying on clothes and food for people who are every bit as comfortable as yourselves. These are the ones whose lot you want to ease!

'But surely, if religious orders do have wealth, they should make it their business to lay on hospitality for beggars, not for well-to-do city merchants. I have this on good authority:

> To deprive the poor of their own is sacrilege;
> To give to the wicked is to make sacrifice
> To devils! Monks, though needy, do not take
> What's given you—rather, give; it's privilege
> And not privation to have what may suffice.*

'And so: my advice to every Christian is this. Mould yourselves in the shape of Charity. For Charity—there's no disputing it—is the means of lifting the burden of guilt that every conscience carries; souls can be freed from Purgatory by the power of his intercession! But there's something seriously wrong with those whose task it is to look after our religious life. What happens as a result is that the community is weakened and its faith undermined. You've come across those coins called "Luxemburgs":* they contain base metal, yet they look like the real thing. The imprint on these coins is authentic enough; it's the metal that they're made of that's debased. Well, that's how it stands with some of our current clergy: they speak the right words, bear the sign of baptism, and the tonsure of ordination, the proper impress of the King of Heaven. But the metal—that is, the human soul—has lost its purity through habitual sin. The consequence is, it seems, that nobody loves his neighbour any longer; no one seems to love our Lord, if it comes to that. For what with war and crime and all these unpredictable changes in the climate, experienced seamen and learned scholars alike have lost their faith in the movement of the heavens, and likewise in what the natural philosophers teach us.

'Every day now you can see it.* Astronomers who used to forecast coming events end up making errors. Time was when sailors on shipboard and shepherds looking after their flocks could tell from observing the skies what was going to happen. And ploughmen who tilled the land would tell their masters, from the quality of the seed they were given to sow, what kind of crops they could expect to obtain. They could advise them what grain to sell, what to consume, and what to keep by. Now everyone's getting it wrong, on sea and on land alike: shepherds, seamen, and farmers who work the land. None of them has any notion now how to go about things, or what skills to practise.

'Astronomers these days are completely at a loss; they find the weather keeps turning out exactly opposite to what they'd calculated. Grammar, the very foundation of all learning, utterly baffles the children who try to study it. If you look carefully, none of our educated people today know how to write verses that scan or produce a decent piece of composition. There's not one human in a hundred who can translate a text, or read a letter in any language save Latin or English.*

'Look at any level of society you like. I'd reckon we'd all get a shock to find any headmaster in post except Doctor Deceit and his deputy Mr Flatterer. What about those with the highest university honours—I mean doctors of canon law and theology? These are the people who should have mastered every known branch of available knowledge. They should be able to refute arguments, and resolve every intellectual problem.* And yet—it makes me blush to think of it—if you were to press them hard, they'd prove unsound both in philosophy and in physic.

'All this fills me with apprehension about our priests missing out bits, as some do, when they say mass and the offices. Well, if they do skip over parts—as I hope, of course, they don't—our faith will be sufficient. I'm thinking of that text the clergy sing on the feast of Corpus Christi: "Faith alone suffices"*—to ensure the salvation of ordinary lay-people, as it does in the case of Mahometans and Jews.

'Ah, what a pity, though, that our instructors don't live the sort of lives they tell *us* to! If they did, wouldn't lay-people be that much more unwilling to offend God? As for the Moslems, their religion already has something in common with ours. Don't they believe in and love one all-powerful divine Person, just as we Christians, educated and simple alike, all have faith in one God? Yes, Christians and non-Christians alike, all believe in a single Creator God. But it was a human being, Mahomet, who led the Moslems of Syria into infidelity. Notice how he did it.

'This Mahomet had been a Christian;* failing in his ambition to become pope, he set off and made his way to Syria. Having a mind of some ingenuity, he tamed a dove, feeding it day and night on grains of wheat that he placed in his ear. Now, whenever this clever fellow went out and preached, the dove would come to his ear looking for food: such was the spell Mahomet had placed upon it! In this way, he made people fall to their knees before him as he was preaching; for he gave them his solemn word that the dove which used to visit him in this way came from heaven as God's messenger* to Mahomet, telling him what he should teach the people. And that is how Mahomet, through a crafty device of his, and the assistance of a white dove, led men and women into heresy. As a result, in those regions, the learned and the lay-people alike all adhere to the faith that Mahomet taught.

'That is how God allowed the Moslems to be deceived—by a Christian cleric who had gone spiritually astray. But . . . I'd be taking my life in my hands if I dared tell the truth about the *English* clergy!* The dove they feed is called Greed, and they've gone and adopted Mahomet's way of living. Now no one cares for integrity any more.

'Anchorites, hermits, monks, and friars, because of the holy lives they lead, are spiritually the equals of the Apostles. Now surely God our Father, whom we trust in, would never wish his ministers to take alms from cruel oppressors who persecute honest men? Rather, they should follow Anthony, Dominic and Francis, Benedict and Bernard, too, whose original teaching was to live frugally in simple dwellings on the alms they received from good and honest men. Then, through the holiness of their lives, grace would grow and put forth shoots, and people who suffered from all kinds of illnesses would feel better, in body and in soul, through the help of their prayer of intercession. If those who pray are themselves living lives of virtue, their prayers and self-denial must be efficacious in reconciling all who are at strife: "Seek", says Scripture, "and you will find!"

'Don't housewives say that "Salt's a great preserver"? But remember the Gospel: "*You* are the salt of the earth."* Doesn't Christ call the leaders of his Church—assuming, that is, that they are holy men—salt for the souls of Christians? "But if *salt* loses its savour, by what means is it to be salted?" Now fresh meat or fish, whether boiled or baked, is obviously going to be tasteless without salt. The same is surely true of the souls of men who never see churchmen setting a good example! Yet isn't it the Church that should point the highway to Heaven, act as a guide, carry the banner boldly, encourage the stragglers, and provide a model to follow?

'Eleven men* once converted the whole world to the true faith. To my mind, it should be that much easier now to win over every kind of person—considering how many teachers *we* now have. There are priests, preachers, a pope at the head: these should be God's salt to preserve men's souls!

'At one time, England and Wales were entirely pagan,* until Gregory sent missionaries to this country to preach. Augustine baptized the king at Canterbury and, as we can read in the histories, the whole of that region was converted to the Christian faith, and paid honour to the cross of Christ. They baptized multitudes and spread the faith more through the miracles they performed than by dint of delivering lengthy sermons. Yes, Augustine accomplished this as much through the power of his actions as through the impact of his saintly preaching. That is how he conveyed to people what baptism and the Christian religion meant.

'You've seen cloth that comes straight from the weaver.* It isn't fit to wear till it's been scoured and beaten under foot or in fulling-stocks. It has to be thoroughly washed, and carded with teazles, tucked and stretched, and only then can it come under the tailor's hands. It's much the same with a child delivered from its mother's womb. Until it has been baptized in the name of Christ and confirmed by the bishop, it remains heathen as far as Heaven is concerned, and there's nothing that can be done to save its soul. The very word "heathen" derives from *heath*—uncultivated land.* It refers to un-inhabited wastes where only wild creatures survive, animals unbroken and untrained, that roam about never having felt the hand of man.

'You remember St Matthew's account* of a man who gave a feast one time? He didn't feed his guests with venison or roast pheasant, but with fowls that flocked around him and followed him when he whistled: "See my oxen and fatlings have been killed, and everything is ready." And it was with the flesh of calves that he fed the people who were dear to him.

'The calf stands for purity of life in those who administer God's laws. Just as a cow nourishes the calf with mother's milk until it is fully grown, so love and integrity sustain the righteous. Virgins and men of gentle spirit yearn for the works of compassion, in the same way that the calf yearns for sweet milk: that is how right-living men long for mercy and truth. Now, by the hand-fed birds you should understand the lay-people; these are slow to exercise charity unless they are taught by the example of others. Chickens in a yard will come flocking when you whistle; it's like that with people whose minds remain in a crude and undeveloped condition. These will acquire charity and faith only by imitating the conduct of the educated, and then forming their own opinions and beliefs on the model of their words and their actions. Those birds hope to find food by following the whistling; in the same way, the common people hope to win Heaven by looking to the guidance of the learned. And the man who gave the feast symbolizes Almighty God himself, who grants happiness to all men through his grace. By means of great storms and untoward events he warns us, as if with a whistle, indicating thereby his will for us. And his purpose is to do us honour, and feast us in Heaven on everlasting food.

'Parish priests and clergy, who are the leaders of the Church, have a good life here without a tenth of the effort expended by an honest working-man; and they have their defenders, who'll be wroth with me for writing in this vein. But I have for my authority St Matthew and St Mark, and also the psalm, "Lord, remember thy servant... We have heard of God's tabernacle in Ephrata".* What pope or bishop these days, though, actually carries out what Christ commanded?—"Go out into the whole world, and preach the Gospel to every living creature."*

'Isn't it shameful that people have gone on so long, continuing to profess their faith in Mahomet? Yet numberless prelates have been consecrated by the Pope; there are bishops of Nazareth, of Nineveh, of Nephthali, and of Damascus.* Why then, since these people desire the name of bishop, don't they follow Christ's exhortation? Why will they not set out on their mission as pastoral bishops, preaching the Passion of Jesus, ready to live and die in accordance with his own words: "The Good Shepherd* lays down his life for his sheep"? In saying that, Christ surely intended the salvation of people such as the Moslems. It was with Christian and heathen alike in mind, too, that he said, "Go into my vineyard!"*

'Now the Moslems, the scribes and the Jews all share part of what we believe; so it ought to be easier to convert them, surely, if anyone made a serious effort to put across the doctrine of the Trinity. Scripture says, "Seek, and you will find!"* After all, the Moslems pray to Almighty God, and they have a genuine belief in him; only it is Mahomet they rely on as a mediator between them and God. So those nations have a real faith, but a false mediator; and that is a great misfortune for upright men who have to live under the rule of

Islam. It's also a terrible reflection on the Pope and those prelates he consecrates, who go round with titles like "bishop of Bethlehem" or "bishop of Babylon".

'When the Son of Heaven's High King was sent down to earth, he worked many miracles to lead men to repentance. He thereby provided a solid argument to show that salvation cannot be achieved except by means of his mercy and his grace, through our own penance, suffering, and genuine, unqualified belief. Christ took his human nature from a virgin, and so became our "metropolitan".* And it was with the blood from his heart that he baptized and enlightened everyone who had a deep desire for faith. Since that day, numbers of saints have endured mortal agonies; they have given their lives to spread the faith in many different lands—in India, in Alexandria, in Armenia, and in Spain. They have died painful deaths for the sake of what they believed. To protect the Christian faith, St Thomas* died a martyr, out of love for Christ, at the hands of cruel Christians! His was the cause of justice in this kingdom and in kingdoms throughout the whole of Christendom. Through the death of St Thomas, the Church received a signal honour: he stands as a model, a resplendent mirror for every bishop—for none more so, I'd say, than those appointed bishops in territories under Moslem sway. Those men shouldn't spend their time hopping about all over England consecrating altars, poking their noses into parish priests' affairs, and hearing confessions without the local bishop's leave. Doesn't Scripture say, "Do not put your sickle into another man's corn"?* And in the Roman Empire, many a man was martyred for Our Lord's sake, before the faith could win recognition and Christ's cross be honoured.

'It is a harrowing experience to read about the lives of just and virtuous men in the past. They mortified their flesh severely, renounced their own desires, and went poorly clad in regions far remote from their own people. They slept on stony beds, with no book to read but the book of conscience,* and with no earthly comfort to cheer their spirits—nothing whatever but the Cross! And yet in those times poor and rich alike enjoyed peace and abundance to the full. Now, though, the painful experience is to hear how the red noble is revered

more highly, and received with greater honour, than the cross
of Christ*—which put down death and the power of mortal
sin! And in these days, what do we have? War. Misery.
Would you like to know why? Because of greedy desire to
have a cross—a crown stamped in gold! The only cross
honoured by rich men and religious orders alike is the one
that stands imprinted on groat and noble. On account of
their greed to get hold of that cross, the Church's clergy are
heading for a fall like the one the Templars* had. I tell you,
the time is coming fast!

'Do you recall, my learned listeners, how the people I've
just mentioned attached more value to wealth than to virtuous
living? The facts are such I hardly dare to utter them! Those
Templars were a religious order on whom Reason and Right
agreed in pronouncing a well-deserved sentence of doom.
Listen, you clerics—because of your covetousness, it won't be
long before they likewise pass judgement on those who
possess the property of the Church, and turn you out of office
for your pride: "He hath put down the mighty from their
seat . . ."*

'Take this as certain, you bishops—if Knighthood, Kind
Wit, the Commons, and Conscience join together in a loyal
compact, you'll forfeit forever the dominion you hold over
your lands. And then you'll have to make a living like the
Levites of old, as God's word proclaims—"By the first-fruits
of the land, and by tithes."*

'When the emperor Constantine,* in an act of generosity,
endowed the Church with property, servants, landed rights,
and income, they say the voice of an angel was heard at
Rome, crying out aloud: "Thanks to this Donation, the
Church has today drunk deadly venom, and all those who
exercise St Peter's power have been poisoned!" What we need
now is an antidote capable of restoring the health of the
higher clergy. Nowadays, those whose duty is to say prayers
for peace are hindered from doing so by the burdens of
worldly wealth. You, the nobility, take over their territories, I
say, and let them live on tithes! If possessing goods is a poison
that corrupts the clergy, wouldn't it be a good thing to relieve
them of it—for the sake of the Church? That would be to

clear their veins of the venom, before some worse calamity befall us. If our priests lived holy lives the people must perforce turn from sin; whereas now, they defy God's laws, and hold our religion in contempt.

'Every consecrated bishop carries a cross, in token of his obligation to travel through his province visiting his people. His duty is to preach to them, and teach them to believe in the Trinity, to nourish them with spiritual sustenance, and provide for the poor who are in need.* But there are texts in both Isaiah and Hosea that have a bearing on your case. They imply that no man should become a bishop unless he possesses food, both for the body and also for the soul, to give to those who are in need of it: "In my house there is neither bread nor clothing; do not, then, make me ruler of the people!" Hosea says, speaking of the sick and the infirm: "Carry the tithes, all of them, into my barn, so that there may be food within my house."*

'But we—we are Christians, believing in the cross of Christ, steadfast in our faith, with a clergy to hold us to it, us and those who come after us! The Jews, too, live by the law of justice, a law that God himself incribed in stone, because it was unchanging, and destined to endure for all time. ("Love God and your neighbour"*—isn't that the entire Judaic law?) God gave that law to Moses, telling him to teach it to the people, until the coming of the Anointed One. And that is the law they believe in, and hold to be the best. Now, in addition to the Law, they were given knowledge of Jesus, who taught them the Faith, Christian faith. They knew that he was a holy prophet, who saved multitudes from terrible sufferings. Many a time they saw him perform miracles, wonderful works of power.* Once was when he feasted the people, five thousand of them, with only two fishes and five loaves; that feeding was clear evidence to them that he was the Messiah, as he appeared. And then he raised up Lazarus, who had been placed in the tomb, and lay there buried, stone dead and stinking. In a ringing voice of power he summoned him: "Lazarus, come forth!"* And he made him rise and walk there before the Jews. For all that, they solemnly declared on oath that, to do this, he had resort to witchcraft! Whereupon they made it their business to destroy him. But it was only themselves that they destroyed. He, through his patient endurance, brought all their strength to nothing: "the patient win the day!"

'The prophet Daniel foretold the ruin of the Jews:

> When the Holiest comes, whom God shall send,
> Then your anointed state will reach its end.*

Yet those miserable people still think of Christ as a *false* prophet, his doctrine so much deception. They pour scorn upon it, to a man; they still expect the coming of one who will save them. Their learned rabbis go on to this day looking for the signs of a Messiah—Moses, maybe, come back from the grave!

'Nevertheless, it remains true that all of them—Pharisees and Scribes, all the adherents of the Jewish faith, and of Islam, too, hold together in one single faith: they all of them worship God the Father.* So both Moslem and Jew are familiar with the first sentence of the Christian creed: "I believe in God the Father Almighty." Surely, then, the bishops of Christian lands should strain every nerve to teach them, stage by stage, to accept the second?—"And in Jesus Christ, his only Son." After that, they can go on to articulate the words—"And in the Holy Spirit"—and come out and affirm "the forgiveness of sins"—yes, and eventually tell it out to the end: "the resurrection of the body, and the life everlasting. Amen!"'

'Now, bless you for this magnificent discourse of yours!' I exclaimed. 'For the love of Haukin the active man,* I shall think myself your devoted friend for life. All the same, though, I'm still very confused about exactly what "Charity" really means.'

'I'll tell you the truth about it', he replied. 'It's a tree, a very special one indeed! Its root is mercy and its trunk compassion. The leaves are trustworthy language, the law of Holy Church. The flowers are gentle words and kind looks. The tree itself is called "Patience"*—a humble simplicity of heart. And this is how, through the efforts of both God and virtuous men, there grows upon it the fruit of Charity.'

'To get just a glimpse of that tree', I replied, 'I'd be prepared to travel two thousand miles. And to be able to eat my fill of its fruit, I'd give up every other kind of food. Lord!' I exclaimed, 'but does anyone know where it's found growing?'

'It grows in a garden', he said, 'which God himself created. That tree's root is found right in the centre of man's body. "Heart"* is the name of the arbour it grows in, and care of the garden, the hoeing and the weeding, are entrusted to *Liberum Arbitrium*,[1]* under the authority of Piers the Plowman.'

'*Piers the Plowman*!' I echoed—and from sheer joy at hearing his name mentioned, I fell at once into a deep faint.* For a long time I remained there in a love-dream; and, at long last, it seemed I caught sight of Piers the Plowman, who proceeded to show the whole place to me. He invited me to look closely at the tree, from top to bottom; and as I did so, I at once became aware that there were three props supporting it from underneath.

'Piers', I said, 'may I ask you why these props have been placed here?'

[1] 'Free Choice'.

'To protect the tree from falling under the force of the winds', he replied:

'When the just man falls, he escapes injury
Because the Lord's hand is stretched out to support him.*

These winds',* he went on, 'would nip off the blossoms in springtime, were it not for the support of these props. For people who set their hearts on the truth, the world has the appearance of an evil wind. This wind bears in its wake greed, which creeps in among the leaves, offering a variety of enticing prospects, by which it almost succeeds in nibbling off all the fruit. When that starts to happen, I strike out with the first of these supports—and this is "the Power of God the Father".

'The flesh, too, is a fierce wind, and in the time of blossoming blows such violent gusts of sensual desire as to rouse men to look at sights that lead to folly. After the sights maybe come words, and lastly actions, the canker-worms of sin, which eat through the blossoms down to the bare leaves. Then, when this happens, I turn to the second prop—"the Wisdom of God the Father", which means the Passion of our Lord Jesus Christ, and the potency within it. It is by means of prayer, penance, and meditation upon our Saviour's suffering that I am able to protect the tree, until I see the fruits have set and are starting to mature.

'And then at this point the Devil arrives; and he tries to destroy my fruit with every cunning stratagem at his command. He tugs away at the root, and he throws missiles at the upper branches—unkind neighbours, quarrelsome slanderers, squabblers, and wranglers. Against the trunk of the tree, he places a ladder whose rungs are made of falsehoods; and at times he makes off with the blossoms before my very eyes. Sometimes, though, he's prevented by Free Choice, whom I myself have authorized as my deputy to guard the tree with care. Understand that

> He who sins against the Spirit
> Will never have his sins forgiven—

which amounts to saying

He who sins through his own free choice
Fails to resist sin as he should.

'But when the Devil, the Flesh, and the World creep up behind me together, threatening to steal my fruit, Free Choice seizes on the third plank and strikes the fiend to the ground. This he does entirely through the Holy Spirit's grace aiding him; and in that way at last I get the upper hand.'

'God bless you, Piers!' I exclaimed. 'How beautifully you describe the virtues in them, the special powers each possesses! But I have a whole swarm of questions in my mind about these three props here. What wood did they spring up in? And where did they grow? They all seem to be of equal length—not one of them is smaller than another. And as far as I can make out, they've sprung from a single root, and all appear exactly the same size and colour.'

'That, as it happens,' said Piers, 'is the very truth of it. I'll tell you without further ado what the tree is called. The ground out of which it grows is called "goodness";* and in saying that, I've told you the name of the tree. What it signifies is the Trinity.'

He then fixed me with a look of such intensity that I refrained from pushing my questions any further. Instead I asked, as tactfully as I could, if he'd explain to me what the fruit was that hung there in such lovely clusters.

'Down at the bottom here', he replied, 'if need arises, I can pick the marriage-fruit—a good, juicy fruit, this. Further up there, grows the widow-fruit, in quality like a fine Cailloux pear. But the uppermost boughs produce the truest, most delicately flavoured crop of all—the maiden-fruit, equal in excellence to the angel-apple. These are the very first to ripen; they achieve their sweetness without ever swelling up; and these fruits will never turn out sour!'*

I begged Piers then, would he pull down an apple and let me sample its flavour? Piers reached up to the top,* and the fruit started to scream. He tugged at widowhood, and it began to weep. But when he laid a hand on matrimony, it made such a din, let out such a sorry screeching, that *I* felt sorry for it as Piers shook it. And this is the reason why: as each one tumbled down, the Devil appeared and picked up all the apples together, the big ones and the little ones alike—Adam, Abraham, the prophet Isaiah, Samson, Samuel, and St John the Baptist. With not a single person to stand in his way, he carried them off as bold as brass, and set up for himself a store of virtuous men in a place called Limbo.* This region forms the verge of Hell, a place of darkness and fear where the Devil holds sway.

Then Piers, in sheer rage, grabbed one of the props, and struck out at him, come of it what might—it was the Son, through the will of the Father and the grace of the Holy Spirit—to try and get back the spoil from that cowardly thief, and steal back from him the fruit he had stolen.*

And then the Holy Spirit, through the mouth of the angel Gabriel, spoke to a humble creature, a virgin whose name was Mary. He said that Jesus, the son of Justice,* was going to make his lodging within her chamber, till the time of time's fulfilment should arrive:* the moment that Piers' tree would flower and bear fruit. When that came, Jesus would enter the jousts for it, and do his utmost to settle by trial-at-arms who was to have the fruit—the Devil or himself.

The virgin humbly consented to the angel's message, answering him with courtesy in these words: 'Here I am, God's serving-maid, ready to carry out his will, in which there can be no sin. "Behold the handmaid of the Lord; let it be done to me according to your word." '*

And Jesus rested in that young woman's womb for a period of forty weeks, growing into a child within her body. Then, after this, he learned the skills of battle,* in readiness to face the Devil well before the appointed hour arrived. Piers the Plowman noted the coming of that hour, and gave him lessons in the physician's art, in order to enable Jesus to protect his life. Thus, even if his enemy should wound him, he would know how to cure himself. And he led Jesus to try out his skill as a doctor upon the sick, till he qualified as a competent practitioner, able to deal with every emergency. He then went out looking for sick men and sinners alike, and healed both the sick and the sinful, the blind and the maimed; and he turned loose women from vice to a life of virtue: "For it is not the healthy who need a physician, but those who are ill."*

The leprous, the dumb, people afflicted by bloody fluxes—
these were the ones he cured, time and again. None of these
acts did he think of as a miracle, except for the time when he
healed Lazarus,* who had lain dead for four days in his grave,
and made him rise up and walk amongst the living. But
before he worked this miracle, he was deeply moved with
sorrow, and tears welled up in his eyes, a thing seen by many
who were present. Those who witnessed the event declared
there and then that Jesus was the Physician of Life, and Lord
of Heaven above. But the religious authorities amongst the
Jews violently opposed this claim, declaring that Jesus
performed these acts of his by means of sorcery and recourse
to demonic power: 'You have a devil within you!' was what
they said.

'Then you and your children with you are low-born slaves',
came his reply, 'and *your* "Messiah" is Satan, as your own
words testify. Have I not brought salvation to you and your
offspring, your own bodies and even your very livestock?
Brought relief to the blind? Fed you with fishes and five
loaves, and left behind whole basketfuls to eat?'

Jesus delivered a stinging rebuke to the Jews; he threatened
to thrash them with a knotted cord, overthrowing the stalls of
those who trafficked in the Temple or plied the trade of
money-changer within it. In full sight of those who stood
there he cried out, so that everyone could hear it: 'I shall
overthrow this Temple, lay it low! And three days later, I
shall rebuild it afresh, as spacious and grand—or even
grander—in every detail, as it was before. Listen to what I
tell you! You must call this building the place of prayer and
devotion: "My house shall be called the house of prayer." '*

At this, a flood of fierce hostility welled up in the Jews.
And at once they set about scheming and planning his death,
as soon as the time was ripe. Day by day they waited for their
chance, until at last one presented itself, on a Friday
preceding the feast of the Passover. On the Thursday before
that, when he was eating supper, Jesus spoke these words: 'I
have been sold to the Jews by someone among you. That man
shall rue the time he betrayed his Saviour, whether he did it
for money or for some other cause.' At this, Judas made a

vehement protest; but Jesus insisted it was none other than himself. 'It is you', he said, 'who are speaking to me at this moment!'

Then that evil man got up and left to keep his assignation with the Jews. He arranged with them a sign by which they would recognize Jesus. It's a sign which to this day is too much in evidence—a kiss from smiling lips that conceal the contempt deep in the heart within. That was the way of Judas, who betrayed his lord that day. 'Hail, Master!'* said the villain, went straight up to Jesus, and kissed him, springing the trap in which the Jews would kill him.

Jesus now spoke to Judas and the Jews: 'What treachery I find in your sweet words, what deceit in your embrace, what bitter-tasting venom in your laughter! Ah, Judas—you will come to stand as an emblem of betrayal in the eyes of all mankind. But a worse fate still awaits you, my friend; for your villainy will rebound on your own head:

It must be that evil things will come;
But woe to the man through whom the evil comes!*

I know I have been betrayed into your hands; but leave my apostles in peace—let them go unmolested!'

And this is how he was arrested on that Thursday night of shadow and murk, through the agency of Judas and the Jews. His name was Jesus; and on the Friday next, for the sake of mankind, he would enter the lists at Jerusalem, and fight there to win the happiness of the whole human race. On the cross upon Mount Calvary, Christ did battle against death and the Devil,* and put an end to the power of both; dying, he destroyed our death, and turned dark night into day!

At this very moment I awoke; and rubbing my eyes, I scanned the horizon in every direction, eagerly looking for Piers the Plowman. Like a man bereft of the use of his reason, I wandered all over the region, looking and looking for Piers the Plowman, searching for him in one place after another.

And then, on mid-Lent Sunday, I met a man with hair as white as may-blossom. His name was Abraham.* I began by asking him where he came from, then who he was, and where he intended to go.

'I am Faith', said that man, 'it would hardly befit me to tell a lie. I'm a herald-of-arms belonging to the household of Abraham. I'm in search of a man whom I saw once—a fearless knight whom I recognized by the coat-of-arms he wore.'

'What sort of insignia does this warrior wear?' I went on to ask. 'As you hope for Heaven, tell me.'

'His device is three men in one body;* none of them is taller than the others, and they are all of the same power as they are of the same dimensions. All perform the same actions that each performs severally, and yet each one acts entirely by himself. The attributes of the first are power and majesty, which appertain to him as the creator of all things; the name that is uniquely his is "Father", and he by himself is a single, distinct person. The second person, proceeding from that lord and father, is called Truth, "the Son";* he is the guardian of every creature possessing intelligence, exists from all eternity, and has no beginning. The third, who is also a person, separate and distinct, is called the "Holy Spirit"; he is the light of everything that has life, on land or in water, bringing strength to all created beings, the source of all happiness and joy.

'So three attributes belong to a person claiming the status of a lord. One of these is "power"; another is "means", some intermediary through which that power can be expressed— both his own and his agent's—and also something which both experience or sustain. So God, who had no beginning, but choosing the moment that seemed right to him, sent out his son in the role of a servant, for a period of time. His task here was to labour until he had brought his offspring to birth: children of charity, Holy Church their mother. The patri- archs, the prophets, and the apostles were those "children"; and Christ, Christianity, and all Christians* make up "Holy Church". What this signifies is that man must believe in one God who, as it pleased him, revealed himself in three persons.

'But can this really be true, though? The human condi- tion itself shows that it can; for the states of marriage,*

widowhood, and virginity, emblematizing the Trinity, all
stem from a single human being—Adam, the father of us all.
Eve took her origin from him, and the offspring they had
arose from the two of them. Each is the others' joy in the
severalness of the three Persons. Both in the heavenly domain
and here on earth there is but one unique name for the three.
Likewise, human nature, the human substance, arises out of
the married state, and this represents the Trinity symbolically
as the object of orthodox belief.

' "Power" is to be found in matrimony, because it increases
the race. Now, if this isn't too bold a thing to say, that fact
makes it an authentic symbol of the Heavenly Father, who
made all to begin with. The Son (to use the same daring
figure) clearly corresponds to the widow: "My God, my God,
why have you forsaken me?"* This means the Creator became
a creature in order to know by experience what both were.
But have you ever heard of a widow who had not first known
marriage? It was no more possible for God to be man without
having a mother. Well, a widow who hasn't been married is
a contradiction; and so, too, a marriage without children
scarcely deserves the name: "Accursed the man who has not
left offspring in Israel!"*

'And so, human nature in its totality subsists, we may say,
in a trio of persons—a man, his spouse, and the offspring
born from them. I solemnly swear that this makes up a single
species from one act of begetting. Such may be said to be the
relationship between the Father, the Son, and the Free Will
that comes from them both: "the Spirit proceeding from the
Father and the Son."* He is the Holy Spirit of them all, and
they all are but the one single God.

'It was thus that I saw God one summer-time,* as I was
sitting in the porch of my house. I got to my feet and bowed
to him, giving a courteous greeting. What I saw was three
men—and I offered them the warmest of welcomes. I washed
their feet and dried them, after which they dined on calves'
flesh and the finest bread, and shared my inmost thoughts.
Between us there exists a covenant of total trust, of which I
could speak if I should wish. By way of initiation, he
subjected me to a trial, to see if I loved him better than Isaac,

my son and heir, whom he commanded me to slay. He knew how much I loved him; he will surely hold it to my credit! Of that I'm quite certain in the depths of my heart; and so too is my son.

'Afterwards, because he required it, I circumcised my son: indeed, I myself, together with all the male members of my household, shed our blood for the sake of that Lord of ours; and we hope to bless the hour in which we did so. All my trust, all my faith, repose firmly in this belief, because he himself made a promise to me and my descendants: of land, dominion over it, and everlasting life. But he granted someting more, in addition, to me and my descendants. He granted us mercy for our sins, however often we should ask for it: "As you promised to Abraham and to his seed for ever."*

'And then he instructed me to make sacrifice, worship him by the offering of bread and wine;* and he called me the foundation of his faith, through whom he would save his people, protecting from the Devil all who believed in me.

'In this way, I have acted as his herald, both here on earth and in Hell, strengthening many an anxious soul who looks for his coming. And so', he concluded, 'I am now in quest of him—for I recently heard from a man who has baptized him:* John the Baptist was that man's name. John has told the patriarchs, the prophets, and the others who were waiting there in darkness, that he saw here on earth the one who would save us all: "Behold!" he said, "the Lamb of God, who takes away the sins of the world!"'

I was filled with astonishment when I heard these words, and also on seeing the spacious robes he wore. For there, clutched to his breast, was something he carried, over which he made a sign of blessing. Looking within the folds of his garments, I saw a leper* lying there, rejoicing in the fellowship of the patriarchs and the prophets.

'What are you looking at?' he asked. 'What is it you want?'

'I'd like to know', I replied, 'what that is in your bosom.'

'Look!' he answered, and allowed me to see it.

'Lord have mercy!' I exclaimed, 'this is indeed a gift of great value! What royal lord is it intended for?'

'It *is* a precious gift', came his reply, 'but the Devil has staked a claim to it—and, for that matter, to me as well! No pledge', he continued, 'can obtain our release, and no man can stand surety for us, or rescue us from his power. No manner of bail can win a way out from the Devil's prison-yard, until the one I am speaking of shall come. "Christ" is the name of the one who will one day deliver us from the dominion of the Devil. And the pledge he will lay down is something worth more than any of us deserve: no less than his own life in exchange for ours! Without that, I would have to lie there for ever, and these in the folds of my garment with me, until a lord such as he comes to our rescue.'

'The pity of it!' I cried. 'Can sin so long hold out against God's powerful mercy—mercy whose power could set all things right for us all?'*

Hearing what he had said, I burst into tears.* But as I did so, I saw someone else speedily run forward, taking the same road down which he had gone. I asked him straight away where he had come from, what his name was, and where he intended to go. And he, without delay, proceeded to tell me.

'I am *Spes*', he said, ' "Hope", a spy sent out in search of a knight: the one who gave me my orders on Mount Sinai,* authorizing me to rule all kingdoms under them. I am carrying the document with me now.'

'Is it sealed?' I asked. 'Is your authority open to inspection?'

'No, it's not sealed',* he replied. 'I'm looking for the one who has charge of the seal—which is the cross of the Christian faith, with Christ hanging on it. And when the document has been sealed with it, I know for a fact that the Devil's time of dominion will have come to its end.'

'Let's have a look at your letters', I said, 'and find out what the law has to say.'

At this, he produced his letters-patent, a piece of solid rock on which was written a couple of phrases, and a gloss, as follows: *Love God and your neighbour.** This, I assure you, was the text itself—I managed to get a good look at it. The gloss was inscribed in splendid letters of gold: 'On these two commandments depend the whole of the Law, and the prophets.'

'Is this all of it, your Lord's laws?' I asked.

'Yes, indeed', he replied. 'And I guarantee that anyone who acts in accordance with what is written here will never suffer any harm from the Devil, or fear in his soul the death of the soul. For, though I say it myself, I've managed, thanks to this charm,* to save myriads of people, men and women.'

The herald I mentioned confirmed what he said. 'He's telling the truth, as I've several times discovered. Look, here in my robe lie wrapped those who did believe in that charm of his: Joshua, Judith, Judas Maccabeus—to say nothing of another sixty thousand or so whom you can't see here!'

'It's really astonishing, what you say!' I rejoined. 'But which of you is really telling the truth?* And which one am I to put my trust in, when body and soul are at stake? Abraham here tells me that he saw all three persons of the Trinity—

separate, clearly distinct from one another, yet all three of them only one God. That is what Abraham taught me, and he claims to have saved those who held that belief and repented of their sins. He can't say for certain how many they are, but a good number are wrapped there in his cloak. Very well, then, why do we need yet another law, since the first one is enough to save us and win us happiness? But now, along comes *Spes*, and informs us he's seen just such a law; but *he* says nothing about the Trinity having given his document to him. What it says is to believe in *one* all-powerful Lord, to love him, and then to love everyone as myself.

'Well, the way it looks to me (or to anyone, for that matter) is like this. A fellow who's obliged to walk with the help of a stick—one stick, I say—is obviously much less infirm than someone who requires *two* sticks to walk with! Now, I swear it's pure common sense, surely, that it's easier to teach plain, uneducated people one lesson than two, when such people find *any* lesson too hard by half. And it *is* hard—very hard— for anyone to believe Abraham's words; but it's a good sight harder still to love a scoundrel! It's easier to *believe* in a three-personed God, when the persons involved are all worthy of love, than to *love* worthless layabouts and be kind to them, just as if they were decent, honest people. I suggest you clear off', I concluded, addressing *Spes*. 'Good God, man! anyone who got to know your law wouldn't stick to it for much longer than a minute!'

As we went along the road, talking to each other, we caught sight of a Samaritan.* He was mounted on a mule, and riding at a smart pace in just the same direction that we were going. He had come from a place called Jericho, and was jogging along at speed to a joust that was to be held in Jerusalem. He came abreast with the herald and Hope together, at a point in the road where a man lay who had been set upon by robbers and left lying wounded. He was unable to get up and walk, or even move a hand or foot, or do a thing for himself. In fact, he seemed scarcely half-alive, stripped as bare as a bodkin, and abandoned far from any hope of assistance.

Faith was the first to see him, but he stepped smartly aside, and wouldn't come any nearer than nine ridges of a ploughed

field! Then Hope came tripping along after him, Hope who
had made such a great ado about helping all and sundry with
the aid of Moses's commandments. When *he* saw the poor
fellow, he recoiled as if he'd had the shock of his life, like a
duck when he catches sight of a falcon approaching. But as
for the Samaritan—the moment his gaze alighted on the man,
he got down from his mount and, leading it by the reins, went
up to him to examine his wounds. Feeling his pulse, he
realized that the man was in mortal danger, and unless he
received treatment instantly he would never get up again.
Promptly, then, he opened up the two bottles he was
carrying, and cleansed the man's wounds with wine and oil.
He dressed the cuts with the oil and bandaged his head; then
he wrapped him in his cloak, and took him on his mount to a
small village, the name of which was *Lex Christi*, "the Law of
Christ".* It lay a good six or seven miles away, in the
direction of the new market. He lodged the man in an inn and
called the innkeeper.

'Take this man', he said to him, 'and look after him until I
return from the jousting. Look, here is some money to pay for
treating his wounds.' And giving him two silver pence to
cover the cost of his keep, he said: 'If there's any further
expense on his account, I will settle it with you later. I cannot
stop now', he concluded and getting up on his mount, rode
off in haste down the highway to Jerusalem.

Faith hurried on in his track and tried to join him, and *Spes*
put on a spurt to see if he could catch up with him and speak
with him before they reached the city. And when I saw this, I
too did not delay. I set off at a run in pursuit of that
Samaritan, who had such a fund of compassion in his heart,
and asked him to take me on as his serving-man.

'It's very kind of you', was his reply. 'But no; think of me
rather as your friend, as your companion—especially', he
finished, 'when you are in need.'

I thanked him, and went on to tell him that Faith, and his
companion *Spes*, had both run away at the sight of that pitiful
wretch who had been robbed by thieves.

'Don't be too hard on them', he replied. 'The help they can
give is of little use anyway. There's no medicine in the world

that can restore the man to health. Faith can't, neither can our excellent friend Hope, so badly have his wounds started to fester. What he needs is the blood of a child born of a virgin.* If he were to have a bath in that blood, be baptized in it, as it were, and then be encased in a plaster made from that infant's agony and pain—*then* he might be able to get up and walk. But he will never recover his full strength until he has eaten the child entire, and drunk up all his blood. You see, no human being has ever journeyed through that desolate wasteland without being robbed or set upon, whether he was riding or on foot; no one, that is, except Faith, his companion *Spes*, and myself—and now you too, and all who do as we do.

'In these woods', he went on, 'an outlaw lurks, hiding beneath a bank. From there he can see everyone, and observe who is at the front, and who is bringing up the rear, and who is on horseback; you see, he considers a mounted man tougher prey than someone travelling on foot. He saw me, the Samaritan, coming up behind Faith and his companion, on my horse named *Caro*,* "Flesh", which I got from human nature. And then that scoundrel's courage deserted him, and he went and hid himself in the depths of Hell. But I give you my word for it: before three days are over, that villainous thief is going to be bound fast in chains. Never again after that will he trouble anyone who travels down this road. "Death, I am going to be the death of you!"*

'When that happens, Faith shall become a forester here, and range about through the woods. His task will be to act as a guide to ordinary people who are unfamiliar with the region; he'll show them which road I took, and where the path that leads to Jerusalem lies. Hope's duty will be to assist the innkeeper to look after the sick man as he is getting better. And all those who are too weak and exhausted to receive Faith's instructions will be brought along by Hope's loving attention (of which his letters patent have something to say). And as they come to accept belief in Holy Church, Hope will find them a place of rest and recovery, until I have won healing and salvation for all the sick. Then I shall come back and pass through this region once again, bringing strength and support to every ailing soul that asks for it, or wants it, or

raises his voice to call out. You see, in Bethlehem the child
has been born who is going to save by his blood everyone who
lives in Faith and follows the teaching of his companion.'

'Ah, my kind master!' I cried, 'am I to believe as Faith
and his companion both instructed me? That there are three
distinct everlasting divine persons, all three of them but the
one God? That is what Abraham taught me. And later Hope
commanded me to love the one God with all my strength, and
next to love every single human being just as I do myself; but,
above all, to love the Lord our God!'

'Place your trust', he replied, 'your unshakable faith in
Abraham, that herald of arms. And as Hope commanded you,
I command you likewise: love your fellow Christians in just
the same way that you love yourself. And if you find objec-
tions to this, whether they arise from some inner scruples or
from the claims of common sense, or else from the arguments
heretics propound, counter them by showing them your hand.
For God, you know, can be compared to a hand;* listen and
find out how this may be so.

'The Father was, from the first, like a *fist*, with one finger
bent, until he saw fit to unbend his finger, and put it forth, as
an extension of the palm, in whichever direction that it should
be required. The palm itself is the whole hand, and also puts
out the fingers, to carry out whatever task the hand purposes.
This makes it, we can safely say, an accurate emblem of the
Holy Spirit of Heaven: he resembles the *palm*. The *fingers*,
that are free to bend and perform actions, make an apt symbol
of the Son, who was sent down to earth. He, as the palm
instructed, made direct, intimate contact with our Lady, the
Virgin Mary, and assumed from her his human nature: "He
was conceived of the Holy Spirit."

'The Father, then, resembles a fist with a finger capable of
touching anything the palm judges worthy of contact—"for I
will draw all things to myself."* And so, all three of them are
only one, as is the case with a hand, three distinct aspects that
appear one in the manner of their representation. The palm,
for instance, puts forth both fingers and fist; from which it
directly follows that the person we call the Holy Ghost reveals
the reality of both the Father and the Son. Likewise, you

observe how a man's hand keeps a firm grasp on things by
means of four fingers and a thumb acting in accord with the
palm; well, that is how the trinity of Father, Son, and Spirit
hold the whole wide universe in themselves*—the sky, the
air, the water, and the earth, Heaven and Hell and all that
they contain. And so—there's no need to believe anything
else!—three realities are present in our heavenly Lord;
though each of them is distinct, they have never been
separate, any more than a hand could have movement in the
absence of any fingers.

'To go on: just as my fist, when closed, is my hand in its
entirety, so the Father, the maker and creator, is in himself
fully divine: "Thou art creator of all things . . .",* and in
him, the power of creation resides in its totality. My fingers,
that can draw and paint, also constitute a complete hand;
carving and designing, too, are skills that pertain to the
fingers. So, by way of analogy, the Son can be thought of as
the Father's wisdom, and as being fully divine with the
Father, not less so and not more. The palm, too, is the hand
in its essence, although its capacity is distinct from that of the
clenched fist or the actively working fingers. For what
especially pertains to the palm is the potentiality of extending
the joints, opening the fist, and taking what the fingers pick
up, and also of letting it go, when it grasps what the fist and
the fingers want. The Holy Spirit, therefore, is God, neither
greater nor less than the Father or the Son, but of the same
power. And all of them are one God only, one as my own
hand is a unity—my fingers outstretched or folded, my fist,
and my palm, all of which make up only a single hand,
however I may alter its shape.

'However, if someone is injured in the very centre of his
hand, it goes without saying he won't be able to hold any-
thing. This is because the pain felt in the palm is such that the
fingers lose their capacity to close and form a fist; they have
no power to seize, or clutch, or grip, or hold. Now, if the
centre of my hand should be injured or pierced, I'd become
incapable of holding anything I picked up. However, if my
thumb and fingers had their skin stripped off, as long as there
was no great pain felt at the centre of my hand, I'd be able to

function in all kinds of ways: I could move things about, or make repairs, even though my fingers were throbbing, every one of them.

'Reasoning on these lines', he continued, 'I can find grounds for concluding that the sin against the Holy Spirit is beyond absolution on earth or anywhere else: "He who sins against the Holy Spirit shall never have forgiveness for his sin."* This is because someone who commits that sin pierces God, so to speak, "in the palm". As I said, God the Father is like a fist, the Son like the fingers, while the Spirit is, as it were, in the place of the palm. So, anyone who sins against the Spirit would seem to injure God in the spot where his power of holding firm is located; it's as if he desired to *extinguish* God's grace.*

'The Trinity, you see, can be compared to a torch or a taper;* in these, a wick lies embedded in wax, and from the two there springs forth a flame of fire. You know how the wax, the wick, and the heat-principle itself combine to produce a lovely flame of fire, that can help men to see who have to work by night. In the same way, the Father, the Son, and the Holy Spirit generate among the community that love and faith which purge the sinfulness of all kinds of Christian people. Now, sometimes you will see a torch abruptly extinguished—the flame blown out, but the wick still glowing, barely smouldering, without any fire or light. That's how the Holy Ghost appears—still God, but "grace devoid of mercy"*—towards every unnatural creature who lusts to destroy that upright love and life the Lord God created.

'Now, for men who have to stay up late working on winter nights, glowing coals are less welcome than a blazing bundle of hemlock-stems, or a brightly shining candle. In the same way the Father, the Son, and the Holy Ghost together cannot offer grace, or the forgiveness of sins, till the Holy Spirit first starts to glow, and then flames up into life. The Holy Spirit, though, can be no more than a glowing ember, until true love bends over him and blows. When this happens, he flames up before the Father and the Son, making their power melt, until it dissolves into mercy. You can see this happen in winter, when icicles on the house-eaves, under the sun's heat, dissolve into liquid drops and vapour in the space of a mere minute.

'So then, it is the Holy Spirit's grace that melts into mercy the Trinity's awesome power; but only for those who are merciful themselves, and not for anyone else! You know how wax placed on a hot coal will flare up immediately on contact, bringing relief to people who sit in the dark unable to see. In just the same way, God the Father has the will to forgive people with humble hearts, if they repent of their sins with real sorrow, and make amends, paying what they can by way of restitution. For even if they fall short of complete satisfaction, provided they die intending to make all good, the divine Mercy will mark their humble intent, and itself make up what remains still owing.

'The wick of a torch, when it makes contact with fire, produces a heat-giving flame that cheers up everyone as they sit there in the gloom. So Christ in his gracious courtesy—if only humankind will ask for mercy!—is willing to forgive and to forget our offences. And that isn't all; he is prepared to go on praying to God his heavenly Father in order to obtain his forgiveness.

'But even if you spent four centuries trying to strike a spark from a flint, if you lacked touchwood to light from it, tinder, or matches, all your labour and all your lengthy effort would be wasted. No spark could ever produce a fire unless there was something to kindle! In the same way, the grace of the Holy Spirit, even though he is indeed God, is a grace empty of mercy if it encounters the lovelessness of humankind.* This is something to which Christ himself bears witness: "I say to you solemnly, *I know you not!*"*

'If you treat your fellow Christians uncharitably, then nothing else you do will be of any use to you. You can pray, give alms, perform penitential acts from dawn to dusk, obtain every pardon and indulgence that's to be had, from Pamplona* to Rome; but if you're unkind to your fellow human-beings, the Holy Spirit will not hear you or help you. And how could he? For what uncharitableness does is to extinguish him, so that his light cannot shine forth, his fire cannot burn or blaze up bright, such a fierce tempest does unkindness unleash. Am I speaking the truth about this? See what the apostle Paul has to say: "If I speak with the tongues of men and of angels, but have not love, I gain nothing."*

'And so, listen to my warning and take care—you who are wise in the ways of the world, and you who have money, and minds to think with. Look to your souls, be sure to govern them well! Here is my advice to you: take care not to lack love towards your fellow Christians. It's true that many of you rich men are alight, but you're not ablaze; you are worthless beacons that cannot catch the eye! But—"Not everyone who cries *Lord, Lord* will enter Heaven!"* Think of Dives,* who died and was condemned because he never showed kindness in giving food or alms to people in need. I advise every rich man to take note of his case, and offer your wealth to God, the source of all grace. For what is going to happen to those who fail in kindness towards God's people? The only fate I expect for them is to spend eternity in the same place as Dives.

'Unkindness, then, is the contrary element which, so to speak, puts out the Spirit's grace—grace that springs from the very nature of God. For human inhumanity *un*makes what the generous kindness of God has created. Take the example of robbers without any conscience—Christians, these, but what unnatural ones!—who out of greed or resentment will kill a man for his goods, destroy him by words or, if need be, with their hands. What these evil monsters are destroying is something that belongs to the Holy Ghost himself. I mean life, mean love, the flame that burns in man's body! For every good man, too, can be compared to a torch or a taper, burning in honour of the Blessed Trinity. And I believe, in all conscience, that someone who murders a good man is destroying a light more precious to our Lord than anything else that exists.

'There are, to be sure, a number of other ways in which men sin against the Holy Spirit; but of them all, this is the very worst.* To destroy, knowingly, out of sheer greed, a human being whom Christ redeemed at so high a cost! How could such a man ask for mercy? And what good could mercy do him, if he was bent malignly on annihilating mercy itself?

'Nothing stands closer to God than innocence; and this is what it cries out night and day: "Vengeance! Vengeance! No forgiveness for those who wiped us out, those who spilled our blood, those who uncreated us, as it seemed: *Revenge, Lord, the blood of all just men!*"*

'Yes, that is what real charity demands—*vengeance, vengeance*! And since Holy Church and Charity insist so strongly upon this, I could never accept that *God* would love someone who lacks charity—loathes it, even—or take pity on him, however long he prays.'

'But supposing', I said, 'that I had been a sinner, and was now on the point of death. If now I do feel sorrow for having offended against the Holy Spirit, and if I confess my sins, cry out for grace to the Creator of all things, and if, with real humility, I ask for his mercy—could I not be saved?'

'Yes', replied the Samaritan, 'it is possible. You *could* repent in the way that you describe, so that through your turning from sin God's justice might in turn be transformed into pity. But in point of fact, does experience bear it out? Very rarely indeed do we see a man who was found guilty in the royal courts being let loose when Reason rightly condemns him—just because he now repents! No, where Reason is the injured party, the charge is so overwhelming that the king simply *cannot* exercise mercy;* not, at any rate, till both parties have come to an agreement, and justice is meted out to both, as the Church's written tradition has it:

> Your sin will never be forgiven
> Till you give back what you have stolen.*

'But that is exactly how it will go with people who live their whole lives doing nothing but evil, and leave off only when life is about to leave *them*. At that point, the terrible despairing that they feel serves to keep grace firmly at bay, so that the very thought of mercy is unable to make way into their minds. The hope of good, which ought to be a support, turns into an expectation of the worst, into despair. And this is not due to the impotence of God—his being incapable of putting right all that is wrong. His mercy, as Scripture says, is indeed greater than the sum total of mankind's evil acts: "His

tender mercies are over all his works."* But before his justice
can be transformed to pity, some sort of restitution is
required; and for the man who is quite without means to
make it, his sorrow takes the place of satisfaction.

'There are three things,* according to the Bible, which will
force a man to run away from his own house. One is a
monstrous shrew of a wife who proves impossible to control;
the husband is so terrified of her tongue that the fellow has no
choice but to bolt! Then again, if the roof has come away, and
it's raining right down on his bed, he'll hunt high and low for
somewhere dry to sleep. But if the smoke from a smouldering
fire gets him in the eyes, this proves a worse affliction than a
shrewish wife or a damp bed. For the effect of the choking
fumes is to make his eyes smart so badly he's almost blinded,
while his throat grows hoarse and he starts to cough and
curse: "God blast the buffoon who brought in such mouldy
wood! Why the devil didn't he blow the bloody thing till it
burnt properly?"

'This is how you should interpret these three things I've
mentioned. The wife is our recalcitrant flesh, that refuses all
our efforts to discipline it. For the tendency of man's physical
nature is, always, to fight against the spirit. Whenever it gives
in to sin, it finds some excuse or other: "The flesh is weak",
or "God easily forgives and forgets our sins, if only we ask for
mercy and resolve to improve!"

'And then there's the rain that falls on us as we're trying to
get to sleep. What this stands for is the sicknesses and griefs
that we ought to put up with, in the spirit of the teaching of
St Paul: "My power is made perfect in infirmity."* Even
though men complain bitterly at their pain, and lack patience
in accepting it, common sense tells us they've some excuse for
complaining—the simple fact of the sickness that they suffer.
At the end of their lives, therefore, it won't be hard for our
Lord to have mercy on them, however poorly they may have
put up with their lot.

'But as for the acrid smoke that gets into our eyes: what
that means is the greed and the unkindness that extinguish the
mercy of God. For unkindness is absolutely contrary to
everything that is reasonable and right.* There's *no* one who

is so sick or miserable or wretched that he's incapable of
loving, if only he wants to; or unable to open his heart and
feel good will or speak one kind word; or wish and desire
mercy and forgiveness for every human being in the world; or
love them all like himself, and amend his own state of soul in
doing so.

'I can't delay any longer!' the Samaritan cried; and spurring
his mount, he rode off like the wind. And, as he did so, I
awoke.

VISION SIX

PASSUS XVIII

Shirtless and shoeless now I made my way along, for all the world as if I cared nothing for the cares of life. Like an idle wastrel, I let my days drift by, until I grew tired of it all and my sole desire once more was to sleep. I lazed about until the season of Lent arrived; and then I sank into a long and lasting slumber. There I lay snoring soundly, until Palm Sunday.* I dreamed continuously about children crying out *Glory, praise and honour*, and about older people chanting *Hosanna* to the accompaniment of the organ. And I dreamed of the passion that Christ endured in order to redeem us all.

Then along came riding someone mounted on an ass, barefoot, looking like the Samaritan and also, partly, like Piers Plowman. He had no spurs and carried no spear, but he seemed spirited and alert, as a young man should be on the day he comes to be dubbed a knight and win the right to adorn his slashed shoes with spurs of gold.*

At a casement window up above Faith appeared and shouted out: 'Look! The Son of David!'—just as a herald does when knights in search of renown ride forth into a tournament. And the old Jews who lived in Jerusalem sang out for joy: 'Blessed is he who comes in the name of the Lord!'*

At this I asked Faith what all the sudden activity meant. Who was coming to take part in the tourney at Jerusalem? 'Jesus', was his reply. 'His purpose is to get back something the Devil has laid claim to—the fruit that belongs to Piers Plowman.'

'Piers! Is he here?' I asked. With a look of secret complicity he answered, 'This Jesus, noble as he is, intends to joust in Piers's coat of arms,* wearing his helmet and armour, human nature. In order that he—Christ—should not be recognized as God himself, he will bestride his steed of war clad in the simple jacket of the ploughman, Piers. But not a single blow he receives in his human frame will injure at all the divine nature that comes to him from the Father.'

'But who is going to joust against him', I asked, 'the Jews or the scribes?'*

'Neither', he said. 'His opponents will be the Devil, and the unjust sentence of death that is to be passed on him. Death's boast is that he will wipe out and bring low every living thing on land or water. But Life declares this is a lie, and is laying down his own life as a pledge; despite all Death can do, he will rise to his feet within three days. Then he will recover Piers Plowman's fruit from the Devil, and put it where he pleases. He will bind Lucifer and beat that monster Death down into the dust: *"I, even I, shall be your death, O Death!"* *

And then Pilate arrived with a great crowd of people, and took his seat in the place of judgement; he was to see how bravely Death would perform, and to adjudicate the rival claims of both. But Jews and judge alike were hostile to Jesus, and the whole court let out angry cries of 'Crucify the fellow! Crucify him!'* A man then stood up to make a formal accusation before Pilate. 'This Jesus', he said, 'has been making fun of our Temple, laughing it to scorn. He claims he can destroy it in one day, and then rebuild it in another three—yes, that's what he said, this man who stands here before you! Rebuild it, he says, to the same scale, in every last detail just as it was before!'

'Crucify him!' yelled one of the officers. 'I swear the fellow's a sorcerer, take my oath on it!' Another cried, 'Take him away!' Then, gathering some pointed thorns that grew on a tree, he set about making a crown out of it. That vile scoundrel then thrust the crown viciously down upon his head. 'Hail, master!' he snarled in tones of hatred, and started to hurl spear-like reeds at him.

Then, using three nails, they nailed him naked upon the cross; and putting a poisoned drink* on the end of a pole, they held it up to his lips, inviting him to sip the bane that would end his life on earth.

'If you're so clever', they cried, 'help yourself now! You're Christ, are you, the son of a king? Well, then, come down

from your cross. Then we'll believe that Life is indeed your
friend—a friend who will never willingly let you die!'

'It is finished', said Christ, losing consciousness, like some
poor wretch, all his colour drained away, who breathes his last
in the dungeon of a prison. And then he let his eyelids fall,
the Lord of life and of light. Daylight shrank in terror; the
sun was darkened. Walls stirred from their bases and split
asunder. A shudder ran through the whole wide world. At
that terrifying noise, the dead rose up from where they lay
buried in the depths of the earth, and began to proclaim the
cause of that ceaseless storm. 'A fierce battle is going on!' cried
a corpse. 'Here in this darkness Life and Death are locked in
a desperate struggle to slay each other. No one will know for
sure who has won till dawn has broken early on Sunday
morning.' And with those words he sank back into the
ground.

There were some who affirmed that this man, who had met
his end with such noble dignity, was divinely begotten:
'Truly, the Son of God!'* Others, however, insisted he was a
sorcerer. 'Wouldn't it be wise', they said, 'to find out for sure
whether he is really dead or not, before he is taken down from
the cross?'

Now, two thieves had also been put to death on crosses
beside Christ, as was the common practice at that time. One
of the soldiers' officers stepped forward and first broke the
legs of both of them, then their arms. But not one of those
vile creatures dared to touch the body of the Lord; he was a
knight, the son of a king, and so at that hour Nature's God
decreed that no base ruffian should be so bold as to lay a hand
upon him. A knight, however, came forward, carrying a spear
with a sharpened point.

His name, tradition tells us, was Longinus,* and he had
been blind for many years. He was standing there in the open
before Pilate and the rest; and now, against his will, that
sightless Jew Longinus was brought by force to enter the joust
against Jesus. This was because every single one of them,
horseman or foot-soldier, lacked the courage to lay a finger on
his flesh, or take his corpse from the cross. All but the blind
knight, who thrust him through the heart.

The blood came spurting out. It ran down the spear-shaft and shot back the bolts of blindness on the knight's eyes. He fell at once to his knees and begged for mercy. 'Jesus, Lord!' he wailed. 'It was no wish of mine to inflict that hideous wound upon you. Ah, I am sorry for it, with all my soul! For what I have done, I place myself in your power. But Jesus, Just One, pity me, pity me!' And with these words, Longinus's tears burst forth.

But Faith set about fiercely denouncing the treacherous Jews: wretches, he called them, whose lives would be spent under a perpetual curse. 'Vengeance fall on your heads,'* he cried, 'for this infamous, utterly evil act of yours! To make a blind man attack someone who was unable to move—that was as low a trick as anyone has ever thought up. Ah, you damned villains, do you call it any act worthy of a knight, to maltreat a corpse in any way at all? But no, despite that terrible wound he endured, Christ is the one who has carried off the prize. Look how this hero of yours, your champion knight, ran to acknowledge total defeat and put himself in the mercy of his master! But when this darkness lifts, Death will have been overcome; you will have lost, you despicable wretches; and it is Life who will hold the upper hand. That state of freedom you now enjoy will give way to one of slavery. You and your offspring will descend to the status of villeins, never again to prosper, never to have the right to possess a freehold in the land, or even to thrust a plough into the earth. Instead you will languish, barren, producing nothing, and earn your living by practising usury, something that God's own Law roundly condemns. Now as the prophet Daniel foretold, your time of prosperity has reached its end. You have forfeited all right to an independent kingdom; for Christ has come:

> *When God shall send his Holy One,*
> *Then will your sovereignty be done!'**

Filled with fear at these awesome events, and frightened also of the treacherous Jews, I withdrew into the darkness of a descent into Hell; and there, believe me, I saw, according to the Scriptures,* what seemed a woman, walking along the highway from the region of the west, with her eyes looking in the direction of Hell. The name of that girl was Mercy, a humble, kind, and ladylike soul with a voice that was gentle and soft. Straight opposite her, from the eastern quarter, her sister (as I took her to be) came walking slowly along. Beautiful and chaste, her name was Truth. She, thanks to the power that invested her, was totally immune to fear.

When these young women, Mercy and Truth, came abreast, each asked the other about these extraordinary events—the noise, the darkness, the sudden dawn, and the shining light that was hovering in front of Hell.

'I'm utterly amazed at what's happening', exclaimed Truth, 'and I'm on my way to find out what this astonishing business can mean.'

'Don't be astonished', said Mercy, 'what it means is *joy*. There was a woman named Mary, a virgin, but also a mother, though she had never had intercourse with a man in all her life. She became pregnant through a word from the Holy Spirit, and through his grace. Within her womb the child grew, and she brought him into the world free from all trace of sin. Now, as God is my witness, what I say is the truth!

'Thirty years have gone by since that child was born; yes, he it was who suffered the pangs of death this very day, round about the hour of noon. That is the reason for this eclipse that has blotted out the sun. What it means is that man shall be released from the dark, even as this dazzling light strikes Lucifer blind. Over and over again, the patriarchs and the prophets spoke of these things. They declared that man would be saved by a man, through the assistance of a virgin; they said that a tree would be the means of regaining what was lost because of a tree; and that through a death, what Death had brought low would be raised up high again!'

'What you are saying is utterly absurd' replied Truth. 'Adam and Eve, Abraham, and the rest of the patriarchs: how can you possibly imagine that this light could bring them up here? Release them from Hell? I suggest you shut up, Mercy—you're talking complete rubbish! Look, the real facts of the matter are well known to me (I am Truth, after all): whatever once enters Hell *never* comes out. Prophet?

Patriarch? Job was both, and what he says flatly contradicts what you've been saying: *"there is no way of being saved from Hell!"* '*

Mercy's reply was couched in tactful words. 'My hope', she said, 'that they *will* be saved draws on the facts of common experience, as my argument will show. You are aware that amongst poisons, the scorpion's is the deadliest of all. No antidote for a scorpion sting exists, except to take a dead scorpion and apply it to the wound. When this is done, the power residing in the creature cancels out the deadly effects of the original poison. Well, I'm ready to wager my life upon it: that's how this death will succeed in destroying all that Death first accomplished through the Devil's temptation. So, just as man was led astray through the cunning of a deceiver, so Grace, which brought all into being in the beginning, will make the end of it all a happy ending, by deceiving the deceiver—a splendid twist:

> That God by stratagem should foil
> A shape-shifting Destroyer's guile!'*

'Let's put an end to all this!' rejoined Truth. 'Look—I think I see something approaching us at great speed, coming from the frosty regions of the north. Yes, it's Justice! Let's leave off now for a moment; she will be bound to know more than we do, since she existed before either one of us did.'*

'That', agreed Mercy, 'is true. 'And I can see Peace coming from the south with a smiling face, wearing a robe of patience. For a long time now, Love* has been longing for her, and what I believe has happened is simply this: Love has sent her a message explaining what all this means—the light we can see here hovering over Hell. She is the one who will tell us.'

When Peace in her dress of patience came up to the pair of them, Justice greeted her with the deference due to one so richly attired. She entreated Peace to tell her where she was going and who she planned to meet in those festive robes of hers.

'I intend', she replied, 'to go and welcome a myriad people

whom I have been debarred from seeing for so long, because
they lay enshrouded in the shadow of sin. I mean Adam and
Eve, Moses, and the many others who occupy Hell. Mercy
will burst into song, and I shall dance to the song; you too
join us, sister! Jesus has won the tournament, and now the
dawn of joy begins to break:

> Sundown shall be a time of sadness
> But smiling day will bring in gladness.*

'Yes, Love, my heart's dear darling, has indeed sent me
written word, and this is what he says: I and my sister Mercy
are going to be the salvation of mankind. God, he said, freely
assigned to Peace and to Mercy the right to stand guarantors
for man, now and for all time to come. Look', she went on,
'here are the letters, open for all to see!* A psalm-verse
affirms "I shall have peace, and sleep in rest";* it stands as a
guarantee that these terms will never be set aside.'

'What?' exclaimed Justice, 'you must be out of your mind!
Either that, Peace, or else you're dead drunk! Do you really
believe this light can unlock Hell's gates, and save man's soul?
Sister, don't even imagine it for a moment. At the start of all
this, God himself pronounced judgement on Adam and Eve,
and on all their descendants after them. The sentence was that
they must inevitably die—and there an end—and remain in
torment for all eternity, if they but touched one particular tree
and ate its fruit. But Adam in due course broke this ban of
God's: he ate the fruit, and in doing so effectively abandoned
God's love and guiding wisdom, at one and the same moment,
to follow instead the promptings of the Devil and the desires
of his mate, all in sheer defiance of his own reason. I, Justice,
am totally at one with Truth in this when I say, their
punishment must *never* have an end; they are quite beyond
any possible help from prayer. So let them grind their teeth
on the morsel they bit off, and don't let us get heated arguing
over it. There's no cure for the evil they brought about when
they ate that mortal mouthful of theirs!'

'For all that', came Peace's rejoinder, 'I shall pray that their
agony may end, and that their pains will turn to joys at the

last. Indeed, had they never suffered, they would never have
known what happiness really was. No one, in fact, who has
never been truly wretched *can* know what happiness is. Can
someone who has never gone without food understand how
fierce the pangs of hunger are? If night never came, could
anyone properly appreciate the light of day? And suppose
there was no death for all of us in the end; what rich man
living in the lap of luxury could have the remotest idea what
grinding poverty means? Now, then: God created every-
thing as an act of sovereign goodness, and he took on human
nature, from a virgin, in order to save mankind. More, he let
himself be betrayed so as to look straight into the bitter face
of Death—Death which unravels every care, the bringer of
repose. No, I am certain of it: until we first experience *too
little* we can have no notion what *enough* really means.*

'So, then: God in his goodness established Adam, the first
man, in a condition of contentment, a state of perfect joy. But
he went on to let him sin, let him feel sorrow, so as to
know by direct experience the nature of that bliss. Later, God
put himself at risk, took the adventure of assuming Adam's
humanity. Why did he do this? To discover, in three different
places, what Adam had gone through: in Heaven, on earth,
and now at last in Hell. He, who knows happiness in its
plenitude, now enters Hell to learn the last word in woe.

'This is the destiny stored up for those people: their foolish-
ness and sin will teach them not only the meaning of anguish,
but also that of a joy that has no ending. In places where
peace has always prevailed, no one can really understand what
war is. In the same way, no one can know what it is to be
happy unless he first learns the lesson at the rough hands of
Alas!'

And now there appeared a creature who had two enormous
eyes. The name of this venerable elder was Book,* and when
he spoke it was in a good round tone of voice. 'By God's
body!' declared Book, 'I'm ready to go on oath: when this
child was born, there appeared a blazing star. The whole
community of the learned were in agreement about what it
meant: that a child had been born in the town of Bethlehem
who would save the soul of man and destroy sin.

'That is not all', declared Book. 'All the physical elements testify to the truth of this.* The upper air was the first to reveal that he was God, creator of the universe; for the heavenly powers laid hold on a comet and set it alight like a torch in honour of his birth. That light was the Lord's train when he made his descent to earth. The element of water also acknowledged his divinity, when it submitted to let him tread upon it. The apostle Peter saw him walking on water, recognized who it was, and cried out aloud, "Bid me to come to you over the water!"* And see how the sun scarfed up her light when she saw in agony the One who made sun and sea! Lastly the claggy earth: heavy with sorrow that he should be ready to suffer, she shuddered like a thing alive and shattered her robe of rock.

'Yes! Even Hell itself could not hold out, but opened wide as God endured his pangs, and loosed from its maw the sons of Simeon,* who thus became witnesses of the crucifixion. So now Lucifer, little as he may like it, must believe it: a mighty giant* with his battle-engine has managed to beat down into the earth every opponent and adversary of Christ. I, Book, give you my solemn word: I stand prepared to be thrown into the flames if Jesus does not rise from the dead, all human powers restored to him; cheer his mother, comfort his people and free them from the depths of despair; and, last of all, dismantle and dissolve the certainty of the Jews that it is they who are indeed the victors. As for them, unless they are ready to do homage to his cross, acknowledge that he has risen from the dead, and put their faith in a new Law—then, body and soul alike, they are lost and done for!'

'Enough of this! No more!' exclaimed Truth. 'What do I hear and see? A spirit addressing the guardians of Hell's gate, giving them a command to unbar the entrance: "*Lift up your gates, you princes!*"* From out of that light a voice shouts to Lucifer: "Rulers of this region, open! Unbar! Here at hand, his crown on his head, stands the King of Glory!"'

At this, Satan let out a groan, and spoke to the demons who were defending Hell. 'It was a light like this', he said, 'that carried off Lazarus* against our will. A horrible calamity is upon us. This king, if he forces his way in, will carry away

the whole human race and take them with him to where he
took Lazarus once. If no one says him nay, he will shackle me
fast in chains! For a long time now the patriarchs and
prophets have been speaking about this, saying that a lord like
this, robed in radiance, was coming to lead them all out of
this place.'

'Listen!' cried Lucifer, 'I know him, this lord who comes in
light, though it is a long time since I did know him. Death
has no power to do this lord any harm, nor have the crafts and
stratagems of a devil. His way is, to go where he wishes. But I
warn him to be on guard: he'll find trouble here! If he takes
what is mine by right, he will be guilty of robbing me by
force. After all, these people are here with just cause, and for
a very good reason indeed. Good and bad alike, they belong to
me body and soul. Didn't he himself say it, the ruler of
Heaven? That if Adam ate the apple, all would have to die
and make their abode in torment with the demons. That was
the threat he uttered. Now then, since he who is Truth itself
did indeed speak these words,* and since I have held sway
here for seven thousand years,* I am convinced that his own
decree will not allow him to deprive us of the least jot that is
ours.'

'That may well be true', said Satan, 'but it does not make
me the least bit less afraid. Think—did you not get your
hands on them by a trick? You broke into his garden and sat
on the apple tree in the guise of a snake. Then you urged
them to eat; at least, you found Eve alone by herself and told
her some story or other—a pack of lies and innuendoes, every
word of it. That's how you got them ejected and finally sent
down here to this place. You can hardly claim to have got
them fair and square when the truth of it is you had to resort
to deception.'

'But God can't be deceived!' cried the demon Goblin.
'There's no tripping him up! We have no genuine claim on
them since their condemnation was brought about by means
of a treacherous piece of deception.'

'Indeed', said the Devil, 'my fear is that Truth does intend
to carry them off. For some thirty years now, by my
reckoning, he has been going about the place preaching. I

have made efforts to tempt him to sin, and once I even asked him whether he was God, or the Son of God. His answer was a short one!* And so, as I say, he has gone about the place for the last thirty-two years. Now, when I took this in, I approached the wife of Pilate in a dream in order to warn her what sort of person Jesus was.* The Jews, you see, hated him—and now they have put him to death. But what *I* wanted was to prolong his life, because I was convinced that if he died, his soul would never allow any glimpse of sin to appear before his eyes. Why? Because while he was still a living, flesh-and-blood man he would go about saving men from their sins, on condition only that this is what they freely desired.

'And now I can see it: a soul is coming, gliding towards us, clothed in a glorious radiance. I know it, I know it—it must be God himself! Look, my advice is to get away from here—all of us—and quickly! I tell you, it would be better to disappear into nothingness than have to endure the sight of him. Lucifer, thanks to your lies, all our prey has now slipped from our grasp. It was all your fault in the first place that we fell from the summit of Heaven.* It was all because we believed those stories of yours that we all fled the place in your company. And now, thanks to this final deception of yours, we have lost Adam, and with him, I'm sure, all the regions we rule over, land and water alike. *"Now shall the Prince of this World be driven out!"* '*

Once more the Light commanded them to open up, and Lucifer answered: 'Who is this? A lord you say—lord of what?'

The Light answered without delay: 'The king of glory, that is who I am—the lord of might, of strength, of every kind of power, the lord of virtues. You, proud peers of this land of shadow, open these gates immediately, so that Christ may enter, the Son of Heaven's Sovereign!'

And even as he breathed those words, Belial's bars flew off, and for all their efforts to defend the place, Hell's gates burst open wide.

Then patriarchs and prophets, the people in darkness,* sang out the song of St John the Baptist, *'Behold the Lamb of*

God!'* Lucifer was so dazzled by the blinding radiance that he quailed before the sight. But the lord gathered up into his light the people whom he loved, and spoke to Satan. 'Look', he said, 'here is my soul in payment for the souls of all who have sinned. I am giving it to save those who are worthy. Mine they are; do they not come from my hand? So surely my claim upon them is the stronger one! It is true that according to my own law, which is based on reason and justice, if they ate the apple they had to suffer death, every one of them. But I made no demand they should stay in Hell for ever. It was your trickery that led them to do what they did; you got your hands on them through deceit, and in no way by the justice of your claim. For in my royal demesne, in Paradise, covered beneath the shape of a serpent, you treacherously snatched from me something I held most dear.

'Yes, indeed, it was in a reptile's form, with the face of a female,* you carried out that felony upon my property. Now, according to the ancient law, it is permitted to use deception against a deceiver. Very good sense it is, too! "An eye for an eye and a tooth for a tooth."* Well then, a soul shall be payment for a soul, and sin shall remain with Sin. And I, as man, intend to put right everything that was done wrong by Man. Under that old law, a limb for a limb, a life for a life constituted satisfaction; well, it is by the principle of that law that I stake my unrestricted claim from henceforth to Adam, and to every one of his descendants. The destruction Death wrought upon them, my death will repair, quickening and strengthening the life that sin had quenched. That simple law of "one for one" necessitates that grace should wipe out guile. So, do not suppose, Lucifer, that I carry mankind away in defiance of the law. On the contrary, I have both justice and reason to support me in ransoming back my subjects: "I did not come to destroy Law but to fulfil it."*

'Now, you snatched away my people from my domain without any claim to justify your action; and what a treacherous, felonious act it was! But the principle of "one for one"—that and that alone—has shown me the way to win them back by the payment of a ransom. So, what you procured through deception has been repossessed by means of grace. You, Lucifer, in the shape of a loathsome serpent, obtained by a trick creatures most dear to God. Now I, the lord of Heaven, in the likeness of a human being, have paid you back your deception by courtesy of grace. One act of guile against another! And just as Adam and the rest had to die because of the effects of a single tree, so Adam and the rest will be given back life once more, through the agency of one particular tree. The Deceiver has been deceived, he has come to grief in the toils of his own deception! So now the tide of your guile has turned against you, and the flood of my grace is swelling to the full. "He falls into the pit he dug himself."* Now you are free to savour yourself that bitter draught you brewed. Doctor of death, come, drink your own potion down!

'But I am the lord of life, and my drink is love. To obtain that drink I underwent death today. So fierce was my battle for the sake of man's soul that even now I am still feeling thirsty. There is no drink that can drown my dryness, none that can ever slake my thirst; not till the time of vintage comes in the valley of Jehoshaphat.* Then I shall drink wine freshly pressed from fully ripened grapes—the resurrection of the dead. And when that hour falls, I shall come as a crowned monarch, accompanied by angels; and I shall liberate every living soul from the clutches of Hell.

'Before me all the devils will wait, the greater and the less, and stand ready to do my bidding, whatever it may be. But when that comes about, my very nature will plead with me and urge me to show mercy towards mankind. We are brothers by virtue of the blood we share, though not all of us have been united as brothers by baptism.* But all those who are my brothers in both senses—by blood and by baptism— will not be condemned to a death that knows no ending: "Against you alone, O Lord, have I sinned."*

'Even on earth they do not hang a criminal more than once, even if he should be guilty of high treason.* And if the king of the country should happen to come at the moment a criminal is suffering execution, or some other form of punishment by the law, the law requires that if the king happens to see him, he should grant him his life. But say that I, the King of Kings, should appear at the time condemnation is being passed upon the wicked? Then if justice demand I should look upon them, it lies wholly within the scope of my grace whether or not they should die for the wrongs they have done. And suppose there are any circumstances that might mitigate the seriousness of their sin? I have it in me then to exercise mercy while at one and the same time dealing out justice, and without contradicting the truth of what I have said. But what if Scripture insists that I should punish the wrongdoer? "No evil should go unpunished and no good unrewarded."* In that case, they will go to my prison Purgatory; there they will be completely cleansed, washed totally clean from their sins, until a voice cries "Hold, enough!"* and ends it.

'My mercy will be made manifest towards myriads of my brothers and my sisters. A man, after all, may be able to endure the sight of his blood-relations pierced by the pangs of hunger and the sharpness of the cold, and remain untouched in his heart. But surely he could never see his own blood bleeding, without being stirred to pity at the sight?'

*I heard most secret words it is not granted to men to speak.**

'But while in Hell my strict rule of justice shall hold sway, my mercy it is that will judge mankind as they stand before me in Heaven. For surely I would be an unnatural kind of king if I did nothing to help my own kindred? And above all in a time of supreme need, when help is most urgently required: "Enter not into judgement with thy servant, Lord."* Thus', our Lord concluded, 'it is wholly in accord with law that I should wish to lead my beloved subjects from this place; did they not believe that I would come? But as for you, Lucifer, you must pay dearly for that lie you told to Eve!' And as he said this, he shackled him in chains.

Astaroth* and the whole crowd of them huddled away in corners. They did not dare come face to face with the Lord, not even the most fearsome fiend among them all. They had no choice in the matter: they let him lead away those he wanted and leave behind those he did not.*

Then armies of angels struck their harps and sang:

> Flesh sins, flesh frees from sin;
> Our Lord is King, God-flesh-within.*

And Peace played on her pipe a lovely anthem in verse:

> Breaking through cloud the sun shines clear above;
> So, after bitter enmity, does Love!*

'After the heaviest downpour', said Peace, 'isn't the sunshine brightest? The weather never turns warmer than when the clouds have shed their moisture. It is just the same with love and friendship: love is never more fervent, friendship never more firm, than when conflict and trouble are over and done with, and love and peace hold sway. This world of ours has never known a war, never experienced wickedness of such savagery, that it could not be transformed into dimpling laughter by the power of Love—if that was what he wanted. And now, through the power of patience, Peace has kissed goodbye to every danger.'

'Let's call it a day!' cried Truth. 'Dear Lord, what you're telling us can't be denied. So let's embrace and kiss to show we are all at one!'

'And let no one', added Peace, 'so much as see we have quarrelled. Nothing is beyond the power of the One who can do all!'

'Oh, what you say is true!' replied Justice, and gave Peace a courteous kiss, which she graciously returned. In this way they sealed an accord that would last "for ever and for ever without end".*

> Mercy and Truth have embraced;
> Justice and Peace have kissed.*

Then Truth blew a blast on a trumpet and chanted *Te Deum Laudamus*,* 'God, we praise you!' Love carolled in jubilant notes to the music of a lute:

> How sweet it is, how lovely when we see
> Brothers and sisters living in unity!*

These gracious young ladies, singing their melodies, danced in a ring together until day broke, and the Easter bells rang out Christ's resurrection. And as they sang, I awoke.

I called out loudly to Kit my wife and my daughter Calote.*
'Get up!, I cried, 'do honour to Christ's resurrection! Creep on your knees to his cross, and kiss it as if it were a precious jewel. Wasn't it the cross that carried the sacred body of our Lord to save us? The cross strikes terror into the Devil himself. Such is its power that where its shadow falls, no fearsome spirit from Hell has power to walk!'*

VISION SEVEN

PASSUS XIX

And so I awoke, and wrote down my dream. Then I put on my best clothes and set off to church to hear mass from beginning to end, and to receive Holy Communion.* But about halfway through mass, during the offertory procession, I again managed to drop off to sleep. And all of a sudden, I had a dream about Piers Plowman. He was stained with blood from head to foot, and carrying a cross he entered and stood before everybody, his features the living likeness of our Lord Jesus.

At this, I called to Conscience to tell me the truth. 'Is this Jesus?' I asked, 'who fought in the jousting, and was put to death by the Jews? It's either he or Piers Plowman! But who painted him all red like this?'

Conscience replied, kneeling down to do so. 'These are indeed Piers's arms that he is wearing—his heraldic blazon and his coat of arms. But the one who has come like this, all covered with blood, is Christ, bearing his cross, the victorious hero of all Christian people!'

'Christ?' I asked. 'Why do you call him that?* Didn't the Jews speak of him as Jesus? And didn't the patriarchs and prophets foretell that every creature on earth was to kneel and bow the head when anyone spoke the divine name of *Jesus*?* Well then, surely no name can be compared with "Jesus". And there *can* be no other name that we need to call upon at all times. Why, the pitch-black fiends themselves are scared of its sound, and sinners find comfort and salvation in that name. Now you are calling him Christ: why, may I ask? Is "Christ" a more potent title, or a worthier one, than "Jesu" (or "Jesus"), who is the fount of all our happiness?'

'You're well aware', replied Conscience, 'if you're able to reflect at all, that one and the same person may be a knight, a king, and a conqueror. It's an excellent thing to have the name of "knight", because people treat you with respect and do you obeisance. The title of "king" is finer still, because a king has the power to dub men knights. But to be called a "conqueror" is something that's only given as a special privilege, requiring both inner valour and outward graciousness in the man. For a conqueror can use the territory he gains to turn simple commoners into nobles, and to degrade free men from their status to that of slaves, should they prove unwilling to accept his rule.

'The Jews, who were people of an honourable stock, treated Jesus with contempt, rejecting his teaching and his commandments alike. Now they have sunk to the level of mere serfs. Everywhere you look, there's not one who doesn't live like a lowly villein, loaded down with levies and harsh taxes. Those, however, who listened to John the Baptist, and became followers of Christ, now enjoy the status of franklins,* and complete freedom through the baptism they received; through Jesus, they have acquired a near-noble rank. Jesus, you see, was baptized, and at Calvary wore a crown upon the cross, as King of the Jews.

'Now, a king is expected to protect his realm, and a conqueror to maintain his dominion and be bountiful, by virtue of that conquering act of his. But that is just how Jesus treated the Jews: he redeemed them from sin, and taught them the faith that leads to eternal life. He defended them against hideous diseases that burn and waste away, against diabolic possession, and errors of belief. And at that time he was called "Jesus' by the Jews, their honoured prophet, the king of their realm, and wore a crown of thorns.*

'Next he went on to win a victory upon the cross, like a noble conqueror. Death had no power to destroy or to defeat him; but he rose from the dead like a royal victor, and plundered the depths of Hell. And it was then he received the title, "conqueror of the living and the dead", because he granted the happiness of Heaven to Adam and Eve, and also to many another, who had languished hitherto as Lucifer's serfs. But he seized that loathsome spirit, the lord of Hell, and shackled him in iron chains, where he still lies to this day. Who was braver, more daring than he? He poured out his heart's blood to win freedom for all who obey his law. So,

since he deals so generously with every one of his faithful
subjects, giving them dwellings in heaven after they die,
surely he well deserves to be called a conqueror! And that is
what the name "Christ" signifies.*

'However, the reason why he is now here like this,*
carrying the cross on which he suffered, is to teach us by
means of it, so that when we are tempted, we can use it as a
fighting-weapon to protect ourselves from falling into sin. By
looking on his pain, we can learn that anyone who desires
happiness must submit himself to suffering and deprivation,
and be willing to endure much affliction in his life.

'But let me say more about the way in which Christ won
that title. The truth is indeed that his name was originally
Jesus. When he was born in Bethlehem, as Scripture tells us,
and assumed his human nature, kings and angels brought him
precious gifts in order to give him the honour that was his
due. First, angels came down from Heaven, and kneeling
sang "Glory to God in the highest!"* They were followed by
kings, who kneeled in turn, and offered incense, precious
ointment and gifts of gold. They were not looking for favour,
or some reward in return; they were simply doing him
homage as the absolute ruler of earth, sky, and ocean. And
afterwards these rulers returned to their domains as directed
by the angels. In all this, there was fulfilled the prophecy you
alluded to before: "At this name *Jesus* every creature in
Heaven and on earth shall bow the knee and worship."

'And they did! At his birth, all the angels of Heaven
kneeled. And earthly wisdom in its entirety was found there
in the person of those three kings. What they offered him was
reason, justice, and compassion; that is why the learned men
of that time gave *them* the name of *Magi**—"masters of
wisdom".

'The first of those kings brought the gift of reason,
mystically signified by the incense.* And then the second
offered righteousness, the companion of reason, symbolized
under the guise of gold. Do we not see a likeness between
gold and justice, both of which last for all time? And reason,
which is what is right and true, is properly figured by that
noble perfume. Lastly, the third king came and, kneeling

before Jesus, offered him a present of pity, represented by the resinous gum. For doesn't myrrh signify "mercy", gentleness shown in words of loving kindness? So, at one time, material things of this world that we value highly were offered by those kings, who came from three different countries, and kneeled down there before Jesus.

'However, in spite of all these precious gifts, our royal lord Jesus did not become a king or conqueror then. It was not until he had grown up to the full stature of a man, and even then it demanded manifold skill. But that is only right for a conqueror, who needs to master a wide range of skills, stratagems, and various kinds of knowledge, if he wants to make his way as a leader of men. And that is just what Jesus accomplished in his lifetime, though it would take a long time to describe it all. But there were times when he suffered, and times when he went into seclusion. Sometimes he stood his ground and fought, at others he took to his heels. And on occasion he gave alms, and restored people to health, giving them back their limbs, or even life. What he willed, he performed. Being a conqueror by his very nature, Jesus went on with his work, till he had finally won all those for whom he shed his blood.

'During his early years, at a wedding-feast in Judaea,* Jesus turned water into wine, as Scripture records: and with that act the Divine One, in his loving kindness, began to "do well". Wine is a symbol of religion, and sanctity of life; but the religious law of that time was defective, because men did not love their enemies. Yet that is the counsel—yes, the command, too!—which Christ gives us all, learned and simple alike: to love our enemies. So at that feast, as I've said, for the first time our Lord in his mercy and goodness began to "do well". And then the name he was known by was not "Christ" simply, but "Jesus"; for he was a young man filled with wisdom, *filius Mariae*, Mary's son. For it was in the presence of his mother Mary that he worked that miracle. Why? So that she would be the very first person of all to put her faith firmly in him as one who had been begotten through the grace of God, and not through the action of any other person. But he did not perform that act by means of some kind of knowledge in his possession; he accomplished it simply by the power of his word, in accordance with the nature he received from his Father; and there he took the first step in "doing well".

'When he had grown somewhat older, and now no longer with his mother present there, he made the lame run and gave vision to the sightless. With two fishes and five loaves, he fed a crowd of more than five thousand people, all of whom were feeling the pinch of hunger. And in this way he brought relief to those in distress, and won for himself, wherever he went, a still more exalted name, that of "Do better". For, through his actions, he enabled the deaf to hear and the dumb to speak, and brought healing and succour to all who sought his mercy. And then, as a result of these acts of his, the common people of that land called him "Jesus, Son of David".* The reason was this: David, in his own day, had been the bravest of heroes, so that the young women of Israel would sing in their rejoicing:

> For every thousand Saul had slain,
> David slew ten times again!*

That was why, wherever Jesus went, they would greet him as "Jesus of Nazareth, son of David!" No man, they held, was so worthy as Jesus himself to be made chief ruler of the kingdom of Judah, or supreme judge in all the land of Israel.

'At this, Caiaphas and others among the Jews were filled with hostility against him, so that day and night they set about plotting ways to bring about his death. And at Calvary, on a Friday, they crucified him; and afterwards they put his body in a tomb, ordering it to be guarded by armed soldiers against any of his friends who might come by night to take it. This was because a prophecy had come to their ears that his sacred body would rise from the grave and go to Galilee, where he would bring joy to his apostles and his mother Mary. This was what people believed was going to happen.

'Now, the soldiers who were set to guard the body themselves admitted what happened: that just before dawn, angels and archangels came and, kneeling before the body, proclaimed in chorus, "Christ has risen from the dead!"* And immediately he rose, stood before them all as a living man, and then went out with the angels from the tomb.

'The Jews entreated the soldiers not to say a word about all this, but to put it about that a large band of his followers had come up and cast a spell on them as they kept guard, and in that way had stolen the body of Jesus.

'But Mary Magdalen encountered him on the road to Galilee—divine and human, fully alive and looking straight at her. And she, wherever she went, exclaimed in loud tones, "Christ is risen!" And that is how it became known that Christ had conquered, and was now fully restored to life again:

> Was it not fitting that Christ should suffer this,
> So as to conquer and enter into bliss?*

(And it goes without saying that what a woman once knows cannot be kept a secret from the world!)

'Peter came to know about it, and set off with James and John to look for Jesus. With them went Thaddeus and ten others, including Thomas,* who would be the apostle of India. Now, as all these were prudently gathered together in a house, the door of which was tight shut and bolted fast, Christ came in to Peter and his apostles, the door, I say, being locked, and the gates as well. And "Peace be with you", he said to them.

'He took Thomas by the hand and, showing him where to place it, allowed his fingers to feel the living flesh of his heart. Thomas touched it, and gave tongue to these words: "My Lord and my God! You are my God, Lord Jesus; I *do* believe! You did, truly, endure the pain of death, you will come to judge us all, you really are alive here before my eyes—living now, and for all eternity!"

'Then Christ, with gentle courtesy, replied.

' "Thomas", he said, "because you have faith, and because you truly believe this, may you be blessed now, as you shall be in eternity. And blest in soul and body may those be who never will set eyes on me as you are doing now, and yet faithfully trust that it is true. I love them and I bless them,

the 'blessed who have not seen and yet have believed' ."
'And when all this was finished, Christ went on to "do best". He gave power to Piers, and granted him a pardon.* To men of all sorts and conditions, he gave mercy and forgiveness; to him he gave the power to absolve people from every kind of sin, provided that they came and met the terms of Piers the Plowman's pardon: *Redde quod debes*—"Pay what you owe."

'And so, this is how Piers, once the conditions of his pardon have been met, has the power to bind and to loosen upon earth, and also in another place, and to absolve men from every sin—but not, of course, from the obligation to make the satisfaction that is due.

'Immediately after this, Christ ascended into heaven. There he lives, and from thence he will return at the end of time, and generously reward every person who indeed "pays what he owes"—pays well and truly, as someone of complete integrity must wish to. But if anyone does not pay, our Lord's purpose is to punish him. Everyone is to be weighed on Judgement Day, both the living and the dead. The good will find God, and in Him every happiness; but the evil will dwell in misery without end!'

This is how Conscience spoke to me about Christ and his cross, urging me to kneel down before it. And then, as it seemed to me, there came to Piers and his companions one who was the Spirit of God, the Comforter and Advocate.* Like a lightning flash he fell upon them all, enabling them to understand the nature of all tongues. I was astonished at who it might be, and shook Conscience by the arm; I was frightened by the radiance and the fiery form in which the Paraclete hung there hovering above them all.

Kneeling, Conscience replied: 'This is the messenger of Christ. He comes down from God Almighty, and his name is "Grace". Kneel, now', he went on, 'and sing a hymn of worship and welcome, if you know it: *Veni Creator Spiritus*,* come Holy Spirit!'

And I did sing that song, along with hundreds of others, joining my voice with Conscience's to cry out, 'God of grace, give us your help we pray!'

And now Grace proceeded to accompany Piers Plowman, urging him and Conscience to assemble the whole community together. 'Today', he said, 'I intend to share out my grace, in different forms to every living person who has the use of his five senses. It is a treasure that will enable them to live to the very end of their days; it is a weapon of war that will never let you down. For Antichrist* and his armies are going to bring trouble on all the world, and they will overwhelm you, Conscience, unless Christ brings you aid. There will also come a crowd of false prophets, flatterers, and deceivers, who will exert spiritual sway over kings and nobility alike. And then Pride shall become Pope, supreme governor over all the Church, with Greed and Unkindness as cardinals to counsel him. And so', ended Grace, 'before I go, I intend to leave you weapons and wealth with which to withstand when Antichrist assaults you.' And saying this, he gave each man a grace with which to find his way, so that never would he be harassed by Idleness, or by Envy or Pride: 'the forms of grace are various, their Spirit one.'*

To some men, Grace gave intellectual power, the faculty of argument and debate, with which to earn a living in this world: preachers, priests and students of the law. These were to live an honest life through the labour of their tongues, and use their minds to instruct others in accordance with what Grace was willing to teach them. Some he taught skills based on the use of their eyes, so as to win a livelihood in trade, out of the merchandise that they bought and sold.

He instructed some in the arts of agriculture and fishing, a form of work which is honourable and honest. And he taught some men to work the plough, to dig ditches and thatch roofs, and to earn their keep in that way, by following his teaching.

Some he taught to engage in computing and dividing, or in teaching the skills of arithmetic; some he taught the art of design, and the preparation of pigments. Some he taught to forecast future events, working out well in advance whether things would turn out badly or well; that is the function of astronomers and learned men of science.

Others still he taught how to mount on horseback, and win back ill-gotten goods, using force to do so, and applying tough Folvillian methods,* if need be, to obtain redress from hardened criminals.

To some, Grace imparted the desire to achieve detachment from the cares of this world, living in humble simplicity of spirit, and devoted to praying for the whole Christian people. But there was one lesson that he taught to all of them: to be faithful, whatever their trade, and to love one another. He forbade them all to quarrel and stir up dissension.

'Some ways of earning a living', declared Grace, 'may be more refined than others, but you can see the truth of the matter yourselves. Is your particular craft a salubrious one? I could just as easily have ordained you one that left you with dirty hands! Remember', Grace admonished, 'that *every* skill lies within my gift. Be careful then, each of you, not to find fault with each other; love one another like your own sisters and brothers. Does one of you know more than all the rest? Let him aim to be foremost in humility. Crown Conscience your king, appoint Skill your superintendent; and follow his advice in obtaining what you are to wear, and what eat.

'I am making Piers Plowman my agent and my officer. His duty will be to keep an account in his register of every item of debt, each "Pay-what-you-owe". Here, on this earth, Piers is to be my provisioner and ploughman;* and, to be able to cultivate *truth*, he is to have a team for his ploughing.'

Thereupon, Grace gave Piers his plough-team, consisting of four well-built oxen. One of them was Luke, a generously proportioned and gentle-looking animal. The second was Mark, and Matthew a third—both of them powerful beasts of work. With them he yoked John, a noble animal, the choicest member of Piers's whole plough-team, of finer quality than all the rest.*

In addition, Grace generously provided Piers with four working horses, whose task was to harrow the fields when the oxen had done ploughing.* One was called Augustine, another Ambrose; and then there was learned Gregory, and holy Jerome. These four followed Piers's team to teach the faith, and in very little time had gone all through Scripture with the teeth of the two harrows they drew—the Old Testament was one, the New the other.

Grace also gave Piers his seeds, the Cardinal Virtues;* these he sowed in men's souls, afterwards enumerating their names. The first seed was called 'the Spirit of Prudence'. Whoever ate it would be able to envisage beforehand the way in which a course of action would end, before he actually embarked upon it. This is the virtue that teaches us to buy a long-handled ladle, if our aim is to keep an eye on a pot of broth and keel off the fat from the surface.

The name of the second seed was 'the Spirit of Temperance'. Whoever fed off this seed acquired a temperament of such a kind that he never ended up swollen, whether from over-eating or from stress. No mockery or insult could disturb his self-control; nor could an increase in his fortune, brought about by his success in trade. He would never allow himself to be upset by words thrown out in idle thoughtlessness. Nor would he ever let a suit of clothes artfully tailored and cut be seen on his back, nor spicy food from the hand of a master-chef diffuse its choice flavours on his palate.

The third seed sown by Piers was 'the Spirit of Fortitude'. Anyone who ate that seed always had the stamina to endure every suffering sent by God, every ailment and every other trouble. No false rumours or scandalmongering, and no loss of worldly goods, could plunge him into such deep dejection that he abandoned his cheerful spirit of hope. He remained strong and steadfast in the face of all opprobrium, holding his ground with patience, supported by the prayer, 'Spare me, O Lord!', and shielding his heart with Cato's sound advice: 'Be of brave heart when you are wrongly blamed!'*

The fourth seed Piers planted was 'the Spirit of Justice'. Anyone who ate the fruit of that seed would always remain at rights with God, going in fear of nothing except deceit. Deceit works so darkly, that at times even honesty becomes invisible to the scrutiny of Justice. But, for all that, the Spirit of Justice never jibs at bringing guilty men to the gallows; it will even correct a monarch if he slips off the right path into criminal ways. For when Justice sits in court in a judge's person, he cares nothing for the anger of a king. Never has he swerved from the letter of the law through fear of some great nobleman's intervention, or even, if it came to it, the threat of death. In spite of bribes, entreaties, or interference from the sovereign, his aim has been to act with impartial fairness, as far as his capacity permitted.

These were the four seeds Piers planted; and after that, he drew his harrow over them—the Old Law and the New. This would enable love to grow up in the midst of these four virtues, and at the same time uproot the vices.

'It's a common thing', said Piers, 'wherever you go, to see rest-harrow and other weeds choking the crops in the fields where they flourish together. That is just what the vices do to the virtues! And so', he continued, 'everyone who can should harrow their native understanding of Scripture under the guidance of these doctors of the Church, and cultivate the cardinal virtues in accordance with the tenor of their teaching.'*

'Before your seed starts growing towards ripeness', said Grace, 'erect a building for yourself to store your grain in.'

'I swear to you, Grace!' cried Piers, 'you'll have to provide the wood and plan the construction of that storehouse before you leave.'

So Grace gave Piers the cross on which Christ suffered on Calvary to save mankind,* together with our Lord's crown of thorns. And with the baptismal blood he shed on the cross, Grace mixed a kind of cement, and called it 'mercy'. With this, he went on to lay a solid foundation; out of the agony of our Saviour's passion, he now erected a wall of wattle and lime, then raised a roof made up of the whole of Scripture. He called the house Unity—'Holy Church' in English.

After completing this work, Grace built a cart called Christianity,* to carry Piers's sheaves of corn back from the fields. To draw the cart, he provided horses, Contrition and Confession, and established Priesthood to oversee the work. He himself, meanwhile, accompanied Piers from one end of the world to the other, cultivating truth, the fields of faith and Holy Church's law.

So now—here Piers is at his ploughing.*

Pride caught sight of him, and assembled a huge army,*

intending to harass Conscience and the whole community of
Christians. The Cardinal Virtues he intended to blow down,
breaking them apart and biting their roots in two. Into the
field he despatched Presumption, his chief lieutenant, and his
spy Kill-Love, otherwise called Backbiter.

This pair approached Conscience and the Christian com-
munity, and delivered them a message: the seeds that Piers
had planted, the Cardinal Virtues, had no hope of surviving!
'Piers's barn', they declared, 'is going to be broken into,
and everyone inside Unity—including you, Conscience—is
going to have to get out! Your pair of horses, Contrition and
Confession, and that cart of yours, the Creed, will be given
a smart new coat of paint—sophistry, it's called.* It will
cover them over so effectively that Conscience won't be able
to tell, from the evidence of Contrition or Confession, who is
a Christian and who is a pagan! For that matter, men of
business who handle money won't have the slightest idea
whether the profits they make are lawful or unlawful, or
tantamount to usury.'

Dressed in the pied paraphernalia of cunning, Pride
advanced to battle, by his side a member of the nobility whose
sole aim in life was bodily pleasure. 'Let's live a life of
unbridled luxury, going through the whole catalogue of the
vices!' cried Pride. 'If we use our wits, we can strip society
bare and spend the whole lot in one go!'

Then Conscience addressed the whole Christian com-
munity.

'This is my advice', he said. 'Let's make our way into Unity
without a moment's delay, and let's remain there. Then let's
pray that peace will prevail in Piers Plowman's barn. I know
for certain that we haven't the strength to oppose Pride,
unless we have Grace with us as our ally.'

At this, Kind Wit came forward, to show Conscience what
he should be doing. In ringing tones, he ordered the whole
Christian community to dig a deep ditch all around Unity, so
that the Church would be able to stand surrounded by
holiness, like a fortified tower. So Conscience issued orders to
every Christian, to dig a great moat as a protection for Holy

Church and its defenders. In response, every kind of
Christian repented, and turned away from sin; the only
exceptions were the prostitutes, as well as a juror and a
summoner who were steeped in habitual perjury. That pair
knowingly sided with the guilty, and lied on oath without
turning a hair, so long as there was money in it for them.

But apart from those hardened sinners I just mentioned,
there was not a single Christian in possession of his faculties
who did not help, in some measure, to make holiness grow
and increase. Some did this by saying prayers, some by
pilgrimages, others by means of private acts of self-denial, or
else by giving alms. And then the waters of sorrow for the
sinful deeds they had done sprang up like a fountain, a
smarting flood that flowed out from men's eyes.* It was the
sincere piety of ordinary people, and the purity of the clergy,
that enabled Unity, the Holy Church, to stand firm, rooted in
sanctity.

'What do I care now', cried Conscience, 'if Pride comes to
attack us? I feel confident that the Prince of Pleasure will be
stopped dead in his tracks for the season of Lent, at least!*
Come', he continued, 'Christians all, and eat! You've worked
loyally throughout the time of Lent. Now here is the conse-
crated bread, and under its form the body of Our Lord. Grace
has given Piers the power to bring this about through the
words of God himself; and people are bidden to eat it as a
means to their salvation, once a month or as often as they
have need, provided only that they have met the requirements
of Piers the Plowman's pardon—"pay what you owe."'

'What is this?' came the general reply. 'Are you telling us
we've got to return whatever we owe anybody before we can
go to Communion?'

'Yes, indeed!' said Conscience, 'and the Cardinal Virtues
agree with me about this. Everyone must forgive one another,
as the "Our Father" requires: "And forgive us our trespasses,
as we forgive those who trespass against us."* Then you can
receive absolution, and after that, go to Communion.'

'Oh yes?' exclaimed a brewer.* 'Just see if *I* will! By God,
I'm not going to be ordered about by the Spirit of Justice, and
I don't care how long you go on about it! Christ Almighty,

Conscience—d'you think I'm going to stick to the straight
and narrow while I'm able to sell the last mouldy drops at the
bottom of the barrel, or pretend there's good strong ale in it
when there's nothing there but mild? That's my way—just
following my instincts! I've no time to go grubbing about for
handfuls of holiness. Stop rabbiting on about this "justice"
stuff of yours, Conscience! Stuff it, will you?'

'You damned worthless layabout!' Conscience cried. 'God
help you, brewer my friend, or you haven't a hope! The Spirit
of Justice is the single most important seed Piers planted; if
you don't live by its teaching, your chance of salvation is nil.
Unless Conscience and the Cardinal Virtues form the food
that people *live* on, just take my word for it, they're utterly
lost—every single living soul among them!'

'Then', piped up an ignorant vicar,* 'there're quite a few
going to end up "lost", *I'll* tell you! I'm a parish priest of this
Church of ours, and no one's ever knocked on my door who
could tell me a single thing about "Cardinal *Virtues*", or cared
a feather for Conscience, I can tell you! I've never known a
cardinal who hadn't been sent by the Pope; and when that lot
show their faces, it's us—the clergy—who've got to foot the
bill: meals, fancy clothes, plus feeding for their horses and the
whole crowd of crooks who bring up the rear. "Day by day
and every day in the week" the man in the street goes
moaning to his neighbour: "What a bloody mess the country
gets into every time these cardinals roll in! Wherever they end
up, the whole town turns into a brothel overnight. Dear God!'
continued the vicar, 'that's why I don't want to see any of
your cardinals turning up amongst these good people of mine.
Why not let their holinesses carry on hob-nobbing with the
hook-nosed fellows at Avignon, eh? You know the old saying,
surely: "If you want to be a saint, stick around with the
saints!" Or there's always Rome; doesn't their rule actually
require them to stay there, and look after the relics in the
shrines? As for your good self, Conscience, the right place for
you is the royal court; go there, my friend, and stay there. Let
this "Grace" that you're always going on about give the clergy
a little bit of his guidance. And Piers, with those ploughs of
his—the new one and the old—let *him* be made emperor of

the World.* Then everyone would really turn into proper
Christians!

'There's surely something badly wrong with the Pope,
when he should be helping people, saving their immortal
souls, not paying mercenaries to kill their bodies!* I've
nothing but goodwill towards Piers, though, because
everything that *he* does is done for God:

> God will send his rain, we trust,
> Both on the wicked and the just.*

God's sun shines every bit as brilliantly on a wicked man's
fields of wheat as on the crops of the kindest person on earth.
Piers, likewise, puts as much effort, I know, into growing
food for layabouts and whores as for himself or those who
help his labours—the only difference being that he's served
first. So, that's why I bless Piers Plowman, who's always
sweating and struggling for us all: the dregs of society or the
salt of the earth—it makes no difference in the end to *him*.
Worship God, I say! He created everything, the good things
and the bad ones alike, and he's willing to put up with sinners
until the time is ripe for them to repent. But God, dear God,
put the Pope right! He's busy plucking the Church bare! He
insists on telling our king that he's the "guardian" of the
whole Christian people; yet he doesn't give a damn if
Christians are robbed and killed! He even pays armed men to
shed Christian blood, in open defiance of what the whole
Bible teaches. Look it up in the Gospel of St Luke: "Thou
shalt not kill: *Vengeance is mine*, says the Lord."* It looks as
though he couldn't care less what happens, just so long as he
gets his own way.

'Ah, Christ have mercy, and rescue those cardinals! Change
that worldly acumen of theirs into spiritual wisdom to enrich
not the body but the soul!* The ordinary people', he con-
cluded, 'don't care twopence about what Conscience tells
them, or the Cardinal Virtues either, unless they suspect
there's something in it for them. But they have no qualms
about economizing on truth. Most people now regard the
virtue of Prudence as just sharp practice under another name;

in fact, it appears that all those illustrious virtues seem to have been transformed into vices. Everyone you meet has hit on some crafty method of concealing sin, and even manages to deck it out as shrewdness combined with straightforwardness!'

Then a nobleman who was there burst out laughing. 'Blow me down!' he exclaimed. 'To my way of thinking, it's perfectly right and proper for my reeve to get his hands on every last thing that's going—whatever my accountant or steward *advise* me to take, after looking over all the accounts and records. I can tell you, the Spirit of Understanding was hard at work when they looked at the manorial rolls!* And the Spirit of Fortitude also did its bit when it came to collecting—whatever the tenants may have felt about it!'

At this point, there entered a king, who swore by his crown: 'I was crowned king to govern the people of this land, and defend the Church and the clergy against lawless men. Now, if I'm lacking the wherewithal to do so, it seems to me perfectly lawful to take it, wherever it lies conveniently to hand. After all, I am "head" of the law!* The rest of you are just "limbs" of the body politic, but my position is right at the top. And it's because I'm the head of all that I'm able to protect you all: I am the mainstay of the clergy and master of the commons. Now, what I take from you two I take because the Spirit of Justice instructed me to do so. Remember, I am the one who judges you all! So I, at any rate, can go and receive Communion with confidence because I *never* borrow anything, and the only demands that I make on my subjects are the ones my position entitles me to make.'

'Fair enough', said Conscience, 'provided you *do* protect your people and rule this kingdom of yours justly. In that case, it is only right and proper that you should have what you ask for, in accordance with the requirements of law.

> But yet, what's yours is given you in trust,
> Not to be spent to gratify your lust!'*

The vicar had a long journey home, and took his leave politely. Just then, I woke from my sleep, and wrote down my dream.

VISION EIGHT

PASSUS XX

After I awoke, I carried on down the road; but I walked with
a downcast look and a heavy heart. I had no idea where to
stop and find something to eat and, as midday approached, I
encountered Need.* He accosted me with a rude, abrupt
greeting. 'You skulking layabout!' he said, 'why couldn't *you*
find some excuse for the way you live, just like the King and
all the rest of them? This is what you could have said about
the clothes and food *you* took in order to survive: it was all in
line with the lesson inculcated by the Spirit of Temperance!
After all, you were taking no more than Necessity taught you.
Well, Necessity has no law, and can never end up in debt,
on account of three things it takes to keep body and soul
together. And what are they? One is food, if people refuse
him any, and he hasn't a penny to his name, a friend to vouch
for him, or any belongings left to put in pawn. *If* that's the
case and he gets hold of something to eat by irregular means,
it's clear enough he's not committing a sin. Likewise, if he
acquires clothes that way, being in no position to pay for
them, Need will stand surety for him without any ado. And if
he feels like a drink, surely the law of nature would require
him to drink from the nearest dish, rather than die of thirst!
Well, in these cases Need, through dire constraint, can help
himself to anything as if it were his own. He needn't bother
about Conscience or the Cardinal Virtues—except for the
Spirit of Temperance, which he must take great care to
observe.

'Why, none of the virtues come anywhere near Tem-
perance!* Not Justice, and not Fortitude either. The Spirit
of Fortitude often runs awry; time and again, it resorts to
excessive measures, punishing one man too severely, and
being too indulgent with another. It certainly causes people
far more trouble than it has really any business doing. And as
for the Spirit of Justice—it's a matter of passing judgements

that please the King's Council and the mass of people, whatever the man on the sharp end of it feels! And the Spirit of Prudence ends up missing the mark in all kinds of situation; it makes no odds what he supposes would happen if he wasn't there to foresee the future! Supposition and speculation, no matter how shrewd, hardly add up to "wisdom". "Man may propose, but it's God who will dispose!"*

'You see, God is the one responsible for all virtues; and Need is closer to God than anyone else.* This is because he instantly humbles a man, making him as amenable as a lamb, through the sheer force of deprivation. Yes, Need necessarily compels the needy to acquire humble hearts. Why do you think the philosophers of old renounced all that they owned? Because they *wanted* to experience need. That's why they lived in utter destitution, and had no desire to be rich.

'And God himself really gave up his unfathomable heavenly happiness, and came down to take on a human nature, and so experience need. Such was the need he felt in various places, Scripture tells us, that on the cross itself he spoke these words in his agony:

> Foxes and birds can creep, or fly,
> To a hole, or to a nest,
> Fishes with fins swim ceaselessly,
> Yet have some place to rest;
> But Need has taken hold of me,
> Forcing me to endure
> The vinegar of agony
> To make joy's sweetness sure!

So, don't be reluctant to stand your ground, and endure need, since the One who made all the world was himself a willing prey to need. Never has anyone known such need, and never did anyone die a poorer man!'

When Need had done rebuking me in this vein, I dropped off to sleep immediately. And I had an extraordinary dream, in which Antichrist* appeared in human shape.

He took the crop of truth by its upper part and, tearing it up by the roots, brusquely left it lying there upturned. He then sowed the seeds of deception, causing it to sprout luxuriantly and minister to men's desires. In every region he entered, he hacked away the truth, making deceit flourish there with a power that seemed almost divine.

The friars walked in that devilish creature's wake, because he lavished robes on them. The religious orders did him obeisance with a peal of their bells, and whole communities came out in droves to welcome the tyrant and his train of followers. The only exceptions were the fools.* These poor half-wits actually preferred to die rather than go on living when good faith was put down. And so, like the deceiving devil he was, Antichrist established his rule over everyone at large. Only the humble and holy, who were not afraid to suffer, resisted all forms of falsity, and opposed those who practised it. And if any king or royal council, of clergy and lawyers, saw their deceit yet offered them aid and comfort, they got from those fools a shower of denunciation.

In this way, Antichrist soon had hundreds serving beneath his colours. Pride carried the banner, aided and abetted by a nobleman whose sole aim in life was sensual delight. He set out against Conscience, the protector and leader of all true Christians, and against his companions the Cardinal Virtues.

'My advice', said Conscience then, 'is, come with me, you fools! Inside Unity Holy Church, and there we'll make a stand. Let's shout out loud for Kind to come and protect us fools against the devil's minions;* let's do it for the sake of Piers Plowman. Raise your voices now, and summon the whole of society into Unity! That is where we must hold our ground, and fight against these offspring of the Fiend.'

Then Kind heard the cry of Conscience, and came down from the planetary spheres. Ahead of him he sent his harbingers: fevers and blood-flows, coughs and heart-pains, cramps and toothaches, colds and sores and pus-filled scabs, boils, tumours, and burning fever-fits, insane seizures and a myriad vile diseases. These, making up the foraging party sent by Kind, fastened their claws in the scalps of all and sundry, till scores of people had dropped down dead within seconds.

Cries were heard—'Look out!' and 'There's Kind, with his grim companion Death; they're coming, coming to destroy us every one!'

The pleasure-loving nobleman shouted out at the top of his voice; he was calling for a knight named Comfort to come and carry his ensign. 'To arms! To arms!' was his cry, 'every man for himself!'

Then, in a shorter time than it takes for minstrels to strike up their melody, before the heralds-of-arms had called out the names of the nobles, these men came face to face with white-haired Age. Right in the very front rank he stood, carrying the banner in front of Death; that office belonged to him by right. Then came Kind, his hands filled with the tormenting wounds made in men's flesh by pestilential boils, and wiped out myriads of people, striking them dead with virulent infections. After him, Death came in haste, and dashed down into the dust kings, knights, emperors, and popes. He left not one standing, simple and subtle alike; no one he struck straight between the eyes was left the strength to stir a second longer. Many beautiful women, together with their bold and knightly lovers, swooned their last in Death's sad embrace.

Conscience, out of kindness, begged Kind to hold his hand and wait, to see whether people would abandon pride in their hearts, turn, and become real Christians again.* Kind, at this, held off, to see if people *would* indeed repent. But when this happened, Fortune proceeded to flatter those who had survived, few as they were, promising them a long life ahead. He sent Lechery amongst men in every walk of life, married men and unmarried alike, and assembled a huge force to make an attack on Conscience.

This Lechery struck with a smiling face and words vibrating with sinister undertones; his weapons were idleness and a flaunting style. In his hand he carried a bow with broad-headed shafts, the feathers seductive promises and hollow declarations of devotion. Breathing dubious phrases and suggestions, he brought distress to Conscience and his troop, whose office was to teach in the Church.

Next Greed entered the field, and started scheming how best to defeat Conscience and the Cardinal Virtues with him. His armour was a hunger to have gold, for which he lived the life of a miser, hungry for food. His weapon was profits earned by underhand means, and kept hidden from sight by the same means—deceiving people with distorted accounts or even outright falsehood. In the assault on Conscience, Greed's follower was Simony. His sermons led the people to accept as prelates men who were committed to Antichrist, to preserve the monetary value of their office. In the person of an aggressive nobleman, Greed made his presence felt in the King's Council. Kneeling openly to Conscience in the royal court, he managed to oust Good Faith and to establish False in his place. And then, without so much as a blush, he flung down his glittering coins before him, and swept before him much of the sound good sense that had once graced the parliament at Westminster. He galloped up to a judge and jousted in his ear, unseating true justice with a word—'Take this for your trouble, my learned Lord!' Then he made off directly for the archbishop's court, where he converted Civil Law to Simony, and proceeded to line the palm of the archbishop's deputy. Then, in return for a fur-lined cloak, he dissolved lawful marriages before the death of one of the two partners, and engineered opportunities for divorce.

Conscience let out a loud groan at all this. 'Oh, God!' he exclaimed, 'if only Greed stood on *our* side, as a Christian! Look how he fights—steadfast and unstoppable, as long as there's a penny left in his purse!'

At this, Life burst out laughing,* and set about having his clothes cut in the wildest and most extravagant of fashions. He armed himself briskly in shocking talk, and said: 'Holiness? Why, you must be joking! Courtesy? I can't afford that sort of thing. Honesty? He's just a poor downtrodden peasant. Now Liar—there's a fellow who'll get on!'

And so Life came bouncing back again, simply because of a short run of luck, and spurred on ahead in the company of Pride. He didn't give a jot for any kind of virtue; nor was he the least bit worried by the carnage Kind had wrought, nor cared that in the end he would come back, and then kill every

creature on the earth, leaving only one—Conscience—alive.
Life let all this pass him by, and got himself a girl. 'Don't you
worry', he told her, 'as long as I've got my health and plenty
of heart for living the high life, you needn't be scared of
dying, or trouble your little head about growing old. You can
forget about all that gloomy nonsense; I tell you, there's no
such thing as sin!'

This was the tune to which Life and his lover Fortune
proceeded to tumble,* and in due course their embraces
engendered a graceless scion. This scoundrel, whose destiny
it was to do a great deal of harm, was called Sloth;* yet he
grew to full size at astonishing speed, and took as his spouse
Despair, a professional prostitute. Her father was a juryman
who had never managed to tell the truth under oath: Tom
Two-Tongue was the man, at every trial bent to the fingertips!

Sloth was a cautious combatant in the field; so he designed
a sling, and with it fired off fits of despair in a volley, to
the radius of a dozen miles around. This made Conscience
anxious, and he called out in a loud voice for Age; he asked
him to fight Despair, and try to frighten him off.

Age took a grip upon Hope and, setting off without delay,
drove off Despair and engaged Life in combat. But Life took
fright and ran off to Physic for support, asking him for some
remedy that might help.* He paid handsomely and Physic,
naturally, was delighted; but all he got in return was a paltry
placebo. Life, though, went on believing in the medical pro-
fession; he looked to it to prevent the onset of Age, and send
Death packing with a set of prescriptions for drugs!

But now Age headed directly for Life, and eventually he
struck a doctor in a fur-lined hood, who collapsed with a
stroke and was dead within three days.

'Now', exclaimed Life, 'I see that surgery and medicine are
utterly useless in the battle against Age!' So, seeking health
in another quarter, he cheered himself up by riding off to
Revelry. It was a splendid spot for entertainment: 'Castle
Comfort' was its name in the old days. But Age wasted no
time in pursuing him, and managed to run over *my* head in
his passage, so viciously that he left a visible mark.* He had
made my head go bald in front and on top!

'You're an ill-bred fellow, Age!' I exclaimed. 'Completely lacking courtesy, that's what you are! Since when did roadways run over men's heads? If you'd a shred of good manners, you'd first have asked my permission!'

'Permission—you lazy poltroon!' he replied, and lambasted me with old age. He hit me under the ear, and left me nearly deaf. He gave my jaw a pounding, and knocked out my backteeth, then shackled me with gout till my legs could barely move. My wife took pity on my troubles, and fervently wished that I was in Heaven. My member, which was the reason why she loved me, and which she was very fond of feeling—especially at night as we lay naked in bed—whatever I tried, had lost the power to pleasure her. Old Age, helped by her, had worn it to nothing.

As I sat there, sunk in gloom like this, I saw Kind pass by and Death drawing ever nearer. I started to shake with terror, and cried out to Kind: 'Set me free from this miserable state I'm in! Look how that grizzled old Age has been dealing with me! I beg you, Kind, give me my revenge.* I'm longing to be quit of this place!'

'Revenge?' he answered. 'If that's what you're after, get inside Unity and stay there till I call you. And before you leave, make sure you've mastered a skill.'

'Tell me, then, Kind', I asked, 'what *is* the best skill to learn?'*

'Learn to love', replied Kind, 'and as for the rest, forget them!'

'But how will that get me a living wage? How will it get me my food and my clothing?'

'If you love properly, you'll never go short of clothing or of food—no, not as long as you live.'

So, there and then, I took Kind's advice, and made my way through Contrition and Confession, until I arrived at Unity. And there, I found Conscience in command, placed as protector over the Christian community. They were undergoing a severe siege from seven mighty giants,* who had forged an alliance with Antichrist and were now pressing hard against Conscience.

Sloth made a vicious attack now with his sling. Accompanying him there came five-score of vain and stuck-up priests. They were wearing cut-away jerkins, pointed shoes, and ball-handled daggers with stiletto blades. All were Greed's men to a man, and their sworn foe was Conscience.

'Mary in heaven!' swore a scandalous Irish priest,* 'as long as I get paid, I care less for Conscience than I do for a decent pint!'

He was echoed by sixty or more from the same part of the world, who fired whole quiverfuls of broad-headed arrows, horrible oaths like 'By Christ's bloody nails!' In this way, they nearly brought Unity and holiness level with the ground.

Conscience called out at the top of his voice: 'Help me, Clergy! Otherwise I'll be ruined by these corrupt priests and prelates in the Church!'

His cry was heard by the friars, who duly came to help; but since they had little grasp of their profession, Conscience gave them up as a bad job. At which, Need approached and informed him that their real reason for coming was simply greed:* what each was after was to get his hands on a parish.

'And it may be the case', he said, 'that having no endowments, and so being badly off, they're ready to flatter the rich to make a living. But, after all, they *choose* an ascetic life—cold, deprivation, and poverty. Well then, let them eat what they've freely bitten off; but don't give them parishes to look after! It's no surprise, of course, if people who live by begging are prompter at lying than those who work for their keep and give alms to beggars. All right, then; since friars have renounced earthly enjoyments, let them go on and live as beggars do, or else eat only what the angels feed on!'

Conscience could not help laughing at this advice, and turned to cheer up the friars with some kind words. He summoned them all in and spoke to them. 'My worthy friends', he said, 'you're all welcome here in Unity, which is our Holy Church. But there is just one thing I ask of you. Be sure you remain in unity with yourselves! Never be envious of anyone, clergyman or layman, but live by the requirements of your Rule. For my part, I guarantee you food, clothing, and the basic necessities of life. You won't be short of anything, provided that you give up the study of logic and, in its place, learn to love.* Wasn't it for love that Brother Francis and Brother Dominic abandoned power, and property, and learning? Yes, it was for love—of holiness!

'Now, if it's parish livings you desire, there's a lesson Kind is prepared to teach you. God, he will say, created all things in due proportion, fixing their number at a figure not to be exceeded:

> He reckons the stars by number
> And calls them by their names.*

Kings and knights, whose task is one of protection, have officers below them, each in charge of a definite number of men. And, no matter how hard a man may labour, the paymaster will never hand over his wages unless his name appears in the payroll of properly enlisted men. Anyone else involved in the field is regarded as a robber—"pillager" and "plunderer" are their names—and in every part of the land, they're roundly cursed!

'Monks, nuns, and all who have taken religious vows are required by the rule of their Order not to go beyond a definite number. In every walk of life, the law strictly requires a fixed, definite limit to be observed. The one and only exception is the friars!* Very well, then', concluded Conscience, 'God knows it's simply contrary to common sense and decency to pay wages to you, when your numbers have grown completely out of control. Heaven's number, you know, is an even one; but Hell has no limitation on its numbers! That's a good reason for insisting firmly that your names should be entered in a register, and your numbers should be formally recorded, with an official notary to witness that the total is neither more nor less!'

All this reached the ears of Envy; and his instruction to the friars was to go to university to study logic and law—and, of course, contemplation too.* Let them compose their sermons on the basis of what Plato and Seneca taught—and demonstrate that everything on earth should be owned in common.

Ah, but anyone who teaches this to the common people is, I am convinced, a liar! God himself made the law that he taught to Moses: '*Thou shalt not covet thy neighbour's goods*.'* But how badly they observe this in the parishes of England! Our parish priests, whose duty it is to hear the people's confessions, are called 'curates' because their business is to know their parishioners, and to *cure* them. They are obliged to impose penances on them, and cause them to experience, when they undergo confession, shame, that should follow sin. But it's *fear* of shame, in fact, that sends them scurrying off to the friars! It's just as it is with people who have a law-case pending in the court at Westminster, and borrow money in order to meet their expenses. Off they go with it, and then write back to their families and friends saying they're sorry they can't repay them yet, or promising one more year will see them through. But yet, while they are actually there, they spend the money—other people's money—having a good time and living it up. Well, that's how it is with many of these people who go and make their confessions to you friars. People, for instance, like jurymen and executors. These will hand over to the friars a part of their ill-gotten gains, and get them to pray for the good of their souls. Meanwhile they have a good time with the other part—earned, of course, by the efforts of somebody else! But the debt left behind by the dead man remains unpaid till Judgement Day!

Envy was incensed against Conscience for saying this,* and resolved to support the friars in the universities, while Greed and Unkindness continued their campaign against him. Conscience remained in Unity Holy Church, and placed Peace in charge of the gates, with orders to keep them shut firm against slanderers and gossip-mongers. Hypocrisy, with them, launched a heavy attack, fighting fiercely in the precincts of the gate. Together they inflicted scores of savage wounds on wise teachers who had taken the side of Conscience and the Cardinal Virtues.

Conscience summoned a doctor* who was skilled in hearing confessions, and asked him to tend the infirm and those who had suffered the wounds of sin. Shrift prepared a biting medicinal ointment, compelling men to do penance for the wrongs that they had done. His aim was to ensure that the terms of Piers's pardon—'pay what you owe'—were properly met.

But some of them found this physician not to their liking. These wrote off asking if another surgeon was available within that beleaguered fortress—one who, they hoped, knew how to practise a less painful method of healing. Sir Give-me-a-life-of-lechery lay there, letting out groans, acting for all the world as if a Friday spent fasting would finish him off for ever. 'Somewhere in this place', he said, 'is a doctor with a nice gentle touch. He knows far more about medicine than this fellow, and he puts on a plaster with such a considerate manner! His name is Friar Flatterer; he's a physician and a surgeon rolled into one.'

Contrition then said to Conscience: 'Have him brought here to Unity. Several of our people have been badly hurt by Hypocrisy.'

'But there's no need!' replied Conscience. 'I can't think of a better doctor than a parish priest, a confessor, or a bishop; only Piers Plowman,* whose authority extends over all of them. He, of course, is entitled to grant indulgence, unless their debt of unpaid penance prevents it. Well', he went on, 'I suppose, since you seem to want it so badly, I can let Friar Flatterer* be brought to see to the sick.'

When the friar heard about this, he hurried off to a noble lay-patron for a letter of recommendation. It requested permission for him to be empowered to act like a priest within his own parish-limits. Bearing his letter, he confidently called on the bishop, and got his written authority to hear confessions in any district he entered.

And so he set out to the place where Conscience was and knocked at the gate. Peace, the porter of Unity, opened up, and without more ado, asked him what he wanted.

'To tell you the truth', replied the friar, 'the business I come on is your benefit and your health. I want to talk to Contrition; that's the reason I've come.'

'He's sick', said Peace, 'and so are several others. Hypocrisy has injured them, and they're going to have a hard time getting better.'

'I'm a surgeon', answered the friar, 'I'm a dab hand at concocting cures. Conscience knows me well; he's fully aware of what I'm able to do.'

'Let me ask you', said Peace, 'before you go any further. What is your name? Come on now, don't conceal it.'

'But of course!' replied the friar's companion. 'The name's Sir Piercer-of-your-private-places.'*

'Oh, yes?' exclaimed Peace. 'Then for God's sake, clear off! I don't care about your medical qualifications, but unless you know how to practise healing, you're not going to set foot in this place! I knew a fellow with that name some eight years or so ago. He came, dressed as you are, to a manor-house I happened to be staying at, and doctored my worthy host— yes, and his lady wife to boot! In fact, in the end, when the head of the house was away, he applied his stuff so skilfully to our women that some of them said some pregnant things about it!'

For all this, though, Good Manners* got around Peace.

'Open the gates', he ordered. 'Let in the friar and his companion, and give them a decent friendly welcome. It's just possible, if he keeps his eyes and his ears open, he may find a way of teaching Life something worthwhile: to bid farewell to greed, to take good heed of death, to leave the path of pride, and give the kiss of peace to Conscience, and get Conscience to do the same for him.'

And so it was that, thanks to Good Manners, the friar was admitted; and coming through to Conscience, he greeted him politely.

'You're welcome here', was what Conscience said. 'Do you know how to cure sick people? Contrition is here—my cousin—lying wounded. Do something to help him, would you? Have a good look at his wounds. The plasters his parish priest laid on are causing him great pain, as are the dressings; but he insists on leaving them on, however long it takes, and is absolutely against changing them yet. He's letting these stinging plasters of his stay on from one Lent to the next.'

'Oh!' said the friar-confessor, 'that's *much* too long! I'm confident, though, that I can put things right.' And saying this, he went up, examined Contrition's wound, and gave him

a plaster. It was this: 'Pay me in private and I'll pray for you!
I'll spend my whole life praying for those you're bound to. I'll
enrol you, and your good lady as well, as honorary members
of our fraternity,* for a small sum, a very modest payment.'

This is how he went his rounds collecting, glossing over
sins as he gave his absolutions. Eventually Contrition had
completely forgotten to shed tears for his evil acts and to stay
awake praying, as once his practice had been. Such was the
comfort brought to him by his confessor that he simply gave
up feeling sorrow—sorrow, which is the supreme cure for
every kind of sin.

Sloth saw this, and so did Pride and, stirring up all their
determination, they now began to launch a fierce assault.
Conscience cried out once more for Clergy to come to his aid,
and called on Contrition to come and defend the gate.

'He's lying drowned in a daze',* said Peace, 'and so are a
number of others. This friar has cast a spell on them with his
treatments. His plasters work so subtly and so smoothly that
these people have lost any fear they had of sinning!'

'Dear Christ!' cried Conscience. 'I'll become a pilgrim,
then. I shall walk as wide as the distant horizon's bounds, and
hunt the whole earth for Piers the Plowman.* He is the only
one who can put down Pride. These friars must find some
source of income to live on,* since it's need that drives them
to flattery and makes them into enemies of Conscience. Kind,
avenge me now!* Give me good luck, give me good health,
until I can find Piers the Plowman!'

His final plea was a piercing cry for Grace.

It rang on in my ears, till I awoke . . .

APPENDIX

LANGLAND'S ALLITERATIVE VERSE

The alliterative long-line of *Piers Plowman* is a traditional verse-form that goes back to Old English poetry. Its development was interrupted in the early twelfth century and it seems to have been consciously revived in the south-west Midland area towards the middle of the fourteenth century. Outstanding examples of works composed in this form include *Winner and Waster* and *Sir Gawain and the Green Knight*. *Piers Plowman* is their equal in technical skill and virtuosity, as the appended extract amply illustrates.

The alliterative line falls into two half-lines divided by a caesural pause. Its standard form (Type I) has two alliterating stressed syllables in the first half and two stressed syllables in the second half, only the first of these carrying alliteration. An example is l. 314 in the passage below:

> Eft the *l*íght bad un*l*óuke, and *L*úcifer ánswerde

where the stresses are marked and the alliterating syllables are italicized. Alliterating stressed syllables are called 'full staves', while those syllables that have stress but no alliteration are called 'blank staves'. In scansion, a full stave is indicated by the letter *a*, a blank stave by *x*, and the caesural pause by a diagonal line. Thus, l. 314, like the majority of lines in the extract, may be scanned *aa/ax*. In a variant of Type I, there may be alliteration on the fourth stressed syllable as well, as in l. 321 (scanning *aa/aa*), and in another, there are three stressed syllables in the first half-line, of which only the first two are full staves. Examples are ll. 338 and 347, scanning *aax/ax* (in l. 338 the third full stave is formed by elision of *the* and *Olde*).

The extract also illustrates two rare variants of the line. In one (Type II), three stressed syllables in the first half-line carry alliteration and both stressed syllables in the second half are blank staves. Thus, line 359, alliterating on vowels, scans *aaa/xx*. In another variant (Type III) there is alliteration in both half-lines but on only one stressed syllable in each half. This reduced form is illustrated at l. 350, which scans *ax/ax*, the alliterating sounds being the vowels *ín* and *álle*.

Generally, staves occur in words of independent semantic status (lexical words such as nouns, adjectives, verbs, and adverbs). But l. 350 shows Langland's willingness occasionally to make a full stave fall on a purely functional word (a grammatical word such as an article or a preposition). A more striking example is ll. 358–9, where full staves are formed twice in succession from the word *a*, because of the special emphasis it bears through referring to the Tree of the Fall. At other times, though, grammatical words may carry alliteration but the stress is deferred to the first, second, or third syllable following. Thus, in l. 367 the alliterating sound in the second half-line is *f* in *for* (which alliterates with *f* and *th* in the first half-line, *th* having like *f* a /v/sound in Langland's speech). But *for* does not carry stress and is a 'mute' stave. The stress falls on *soule*, and in this special variant a new alliterating sound is introduced on the fourth (usually blank) stressed syllable (*s*). This type of line may be scanned *aa/(a)bb*, and is called the 'transitional' or 'T'-type.

In addition to exploiting several metrical patterns, Langland achieves variety in his versification in a number of other ways, which this extract exemplifies. He groups pairs of lines alliterating on the same sound, as at 358–9, 361–2). The blank fourth stave of a standard Type I line may anticipate or 'trigger' the stave-sound of the line immediately following, as at 338/9 (*g*) or 371/2 (vowel). In special circumstances, Langland may use a rhyme, which stands out in sharp relief in this predominantly unrhymed verse-form. Examples are the full rhyme *sake*: *slake* at 367–8 or the internal para-rhyme *light*: *laughte* at the end of l. 326. Most striking of all, and providing one of the hallmarks of Langland's craft as an alliterative 'maker', is his use of macaronic lines, in which a Latin second half joins with an English first half to make up a perfect alliterative line of standard type (ll. 323, 370).

An extract from B, Passus XVIII, ll. 314–72 in the original Middle English (*see pp. 220–2 of the text*)

Eft the light bad unlouke, and Lucifer answerde,
'*Quis est iste?*   315
'What lord artow?' quod Lucifer. The light soone seide,
'*Rex glorie,*
The lord of myght and of mayn and alle manere vertues—
Dominus virtutum.
Dukes of this dymme place, anoon undo thise yates,
That Crist may come in, the Kynges sone of Hevene!'   320
And with that breeth helle brak, with Belialles barres—

For any wye or warde, wide open the yates.
    Patriarkes and prophetes, *populus in tenebris*,
Songen Seint Johanes song, *'Ecce Agnus Dei!'*
Lucifer loke ne myghte, so light hym ablente. 325
    And tho that Oure Lord lovede, into his light he laughte,
And seide to Sathan, 'Lo! here my soule to amendes
For alle synfulle soules, to save tho that ben worthi.
Myne thei ben and of me—I may the bet hem cleyme.
Although reson recorde, and right of myselve, 330
That if thei ete the appul, alle sholde deye,
I bihighte hem noght here helle for evere.
For the dede that thei dide, thi deceite it made;
With gile thow hem gete, ageyn alle reson.
For in my paleis, Paradis, in persone of an addre, 335
Falsliche thow fettest there thyng that I lovede.
    'Thus ylik a lusard with a lady visage,
Thefliche thow me robbedest; the Olde Lawe graunteth
That gilours be bigiled—and that is good reson:
Dentem pro dente et oculum pro oculo.
Ergo soule shal soule quyte and synne to synne wende. 340
And al that man hath mysdo, I, man, wole amende it,
Membre for membre [was amendes by the Olde Lawe],
And lif for lif also—and by that lawe I clayme
Adam and al his issue at my wille herafter.
And that deeth in hem fordide, my deeth shal releve, 345
And bothe quyke and quyte that queynt was thorugh
      synne;
And that grace gile destruye, good feith it asketh.
So leve it noght, Lucifer, ayein the lawe I fecche hem,
But by right and by reson raunsone here my liges:
Non veni solvere legem set adimplere.
    'Thow fettest myne in my place ayeins alle reson— 350
Falsliche and felonliche; good feith me it taughte,
To recovere hem thorugh raunsoun, and by no reson ellis,
So that with gile thow gete, thorugh grace it is ywonne.
Thow, Lucifer, in liknesse of a luther addere
Getest bi gile tho that God lovede; 355
And I, in liknesse of a leode, that Lord am of hevene,
Graciousliche thi gile have quyt—go gile ayein gile!
And as Adam and alle thorugh a tree deyden,
Adam and alle thorugh a tree shal turne to lyve;
And gile is bigiled, and in his gile fallen: 360

Et cecidit in foveam quam fecit.
Now bigynneth thi gile ageyn thee to turne
And my grace to growe ay gretter and widder.
The bitternesse that thow hast browe, now brouke it
    thiselve;
That art doctour of deeth, drynk that thow madest!
'For I that am lord of lif, love is my drynke,   365
And for that drynke today, I deide upon erthe.
I faught so, me thursteth yet, for mannes soule sake;
May no drynke me moiste, ne my thurst slake,
Til the vendage falle in the vale of Josaphat,
That I drynke right ripe must, *resureccio mortuorum.*   370
And thanne shal I come as a kyng, crouned, with aungeles,
And have out of helle alle mennes soules.

(By permission of Messrs Weidenfeld & Nicolson.)

EXPLANATORY NOTES

Biblical references are to the Vulgate, of which the Douai Bible gives an English translation. Where they differ from the standard English translations, the alternatives are given in parentheses.

1   *one May morning . . . Hills*: dream-visions are traditionally set in Maytime. The Malvern Hills are the setting of the waking-sequence with which the Prologue begins in all versions, and are mentioned again at the close of the second vision.

    a tower . . . a dungeon . . . a field: the landscape symbolizes Heaven (the tower), Hell (the dungeon), and 'middle earth' (the plain between them).

2   *those sons of Judas*: a class of bawdy tale-tellers whom Langland sharply distinguishes from true minstrels (players of musical instruments).

    the fellow who utters . . words: Eph. 5: 3–5.

    St James . . . Rome: the shrines of St James at Compostella (Santiago de Compostela in north-west Spain) and of the martyr-saints (especially St Peter) in Rome, the most frequented of the European pilgrimage-centres in the period. Pilgrims had a poor reputation for telling fanciful stories about the wonders they had supposedly witnessed on their travels.

    Walsingham: the shrine of Our Lady of Walsingham in Norfolk, second in popularity among English shrines to that of St Thomas Becket at Canterbury.

    all four orders of friars: the Dominicans, Franciscans, Augustinians (or Austins), and Carmelites. Many were university graduates (*masters*), but, being vowed to poverty, resorted to various means, from mendicancy to hearing confessions, to earn a living. The personified Charity may be intended to represent St Francis, the renowned exemplar of this virtue, and thus (metonymically) his order of friars.

    a pardoner: whose portrait may have suggested that of Chaucer's in his *General Prologue*, was empowered by the Pope to grant an indulgence remitting all or part of the penance imposed for sins by the ordinary local clergy. He was not supposed to preach, but Langland states that pardoners did so with the connivance of the parish clergy and without the bishop's permission.

3   *the plague*: the 'Black Death' of 1349, and subsequent lesser epidemics (see p. xxii), reduced the population by perhaps as much as a third, leaving many parishes unable to support their clergy with tithe-payments.

    Lent: during the penitential season the spiritual ill effects of absenteeism were especially felt, as the laity were obliged to make their confession and go to communion at least once a year, and particularly at this time.

3   *grand sessions*: the Last Judgement, or 'Great Doom', a scene often depicted in vivid detail on the chancel arches of churches.

the power 'to bind ...': the Petrine Privilege, or 'Power of the Keys', was based especially on Christ's words to St Peter in Matt. 16: 19.

4   *four Cardinal Virtues*: those on which the moral life turns (Lat. *cardo*, 'hinge'), are Prudence, Temperance, Fortitude, and Justice, described more fully in Passus XIX (p. 233 ff.).

as for the cardinals ... powers: perhaps an oblique reference to the French cardinals who elected an antipope, Clement VII, in 1378, thereby precipitating the Great Schism, which split the unity of Western Christendom. Langland seems to be expressing doubt as to whether the College of Cardinals, whose office it was to elect the Pope, are really the source of the absolute authority claimed by the popes as successors of St Peter.

Kind Wit: 'Native or Natural Intelligence', the power in human beings through which they establish a civilized way of life and a social order.

each ... own: the basic principle of distributive justice is central to Langland's beliefs about social order.

5   *You say ... wages fairly*: the anonymous (Latin) verses spoken by the angel express Langland's ideal of true Christian justice as law tempered by mercy, that is, human law should be administered with an eye to the Last Judgement, when kings themselves will be judged (cf. 'grand sessions', above).

a goliard: the *goliardi* were Latin verse-satirists whose name was popularly linked with *gula*, 'gluttony', and 'Golias' (the supposed founder of their 'order'). See also p. 140 and note.

Precepta ... legis: a maxim from Roman Law which the ignorant laity do not understand, but which effectively deprives them of their customary rights and allows the King to rule as a tyrant. Its doctrine is at variance with that of both the goliard and the angel.

a bevy of rats ... out: the fable of the cat and the mice had been used with topical application by Bishop Brinton in 1376. Here Langland is speaking of the general difficulty of attempting to impose constitutional restraints upon royal power. The active rat and the 'leave-well-alone' mouse may allude to particular members of the Commons in 1377, when the boy-king Richard was 10 years old (the 'kitten'). The cat is presumably John of Gaunt, the king's uncle and guardian.

6   *Woe ... child!*: Eccles. 10: 16.

7   *Mistress Emma*: may be the dubious 'wise woman' of Shoreditch (p. 145).

Alsace . . . Gascony . . . Rhine wines!: provided much of the wine imported into England.

La Rochelle: a major port north of Bordeaux on the Atlantic coast.

8 *A lady with a beautiful face*: the beautiful woman is a traditional image of the Church based on Apoc. (Rev.) 12: 1 and Eph. 5: 25–7. This is the supernal Church or heavenly Jerusalem to which all Christians are called and into which they are received at baptism, but she is not to be identified simply with the institutional Church made up of sinful men and women, or with the clergy collectively. The figure may also owe something to that of other authoritative female personifications, such as Philosophy in Boethius's *Consolation of Philosophy*, Reason in Jean de Meun and De Guilleville, and Nature in Alan of Lille.

Truth: God as both the real, the object of reason, and the faithful one, the object of trust and love (Middle English 'Treuthe' means both). The idea is biblical: see e.g. Ps. 30(31): 6, John 14: 6 and 17, 18: 37.

three things . . . in common: the notion of the three necessities of life is part of Natural Law. The virtue that observes this law is temperance, and the sin that breaks it is excess. This theme is taken up again by the character Need in Passus XX (opening).

what happened to Lot . . . drink: Lot's incest with his daughters (Gen. 19: 31–6) is instanced as a breach of the law of nature occasioned by the prior sin of excess.

9 *just enough . . . the real remedy*: the notion of 'just enough' or 'measure' is that of the virtue of temperance, which is later to be developed at length in Passus XIX.

world . . . Devil . . . fleshly nature: the enemies of man's spiritual nature (which is destined for eternal life with God in Heaven) are the flesh (his own bodily appetites), the world (the pleasures of earthly existence), and the Devil (the active spirit of evil identified with Satan and the fallen angels).

Your soul . . . heart: the text is uncertain and means either 'and that destroys your soul, so keep that lesson in your heart' or, as here preferred, 'Your soul sees what is happening, and tells your heart' (that is, your reason informs your will what is the right thing to do).

Who did the inscription . . . refer to . . .: see Matt. 22: 17–21. The right use of material wealth becomes a major theme of the poem.

10 *Wrong*: a name of the Devil which characterizes his fundamental nature; the notion of him as father of lies and murder is based on John 8: 44.

an elder-tree: presumably became associated with Judas in legend because its stems are hollow and an apt symbol of treachery.

God is Love: from 1 John 4: 8, which also states that one who does not love does not *know* God. Langland thus closely identifies true knowledge of God with a condition of the will, a major theme especially in the third vision. Truth is something to be lived, not just 'known' or 'known about' in the abstract.

11 *King David . . . the order of knighthood*: Langland envisages the armies of King David and the hosts of Heaven alike in terms familiar to him from the medieval order of knighthood. Like Chaucer and other contemporaries, he sees 'treuthe' in the sense of 'unswerving fidelity to the pledged word' as the special duty and virtue of a knight.

I shall set my foot . . . forth!: Isa. 14: 13–14, traditionally taken to refer to Lucifer, the chief of the angels. Hell was thought to lie 'downwards and northwards', a cold, dark region far from the sun (for the use of light as an image of God, see Passus XVIII).

12 *Too little . . . youth*: the couplet translates a traditional Latin proverb. The theme of wasted youth is taken up at the opening of Passus XII and in XV (pp. 126, 166).

He taught Moses . . . virtues: the Mosaic Law is identified by Christ with *love* of God and one's neighbour (Matt. 22: 37–40). Divine love as motive for the Incarnation of Christ is made explicit in John 3: 16–17.

13 *you will be weighed . . . here*: Luke 6: 38; Langland is alluding to the Last Judgement. The first part of the verse is quoted on p. 127 below.

St James . . . letter: the third chapter of St James (vv. 14–26) is seminal for Langland's thought throughout the poem. The quotation is from v. 26.

15 *your left hand*: the *left* had traditional associations of 'badness', and it is also the north, the 'devil's quarter' (see note to p. 11, 'I shall set . . .', above).

a woman . . . in a magnificent robe: the description of the woman in scarlet and gold suggests the Whore of Babylon (Apoc. (Rev.) 17: 4–6), the antithesis of Holy Church, the woman of Apoc. (Rev.) 12: 1 (see note on p. 8, 'a lady', above). She may also signify, at another level, Alice Perrers, the mistress of Edward III, who married William of Windsor, the king's deputy in Ireland, in 1376.

Mademoiselle Meed: the title 'maiden' for Meed in the original is ironical in the light of what is to follow about her sexual activities; the translation 'mademoiselle' aims to hint at this. Meed is simply reward, good or bad; her name's ambiguity is what helps to make Meed such a dangerous character.

Fidelity . . . Falsity: Fidelity stands for all honest men and the principle of righteous living, Falsity for all dishonest men, and the principle of guile and treachery, especially as embodied in the Devil. Fidelity has a brief comment on p. 40 and an important speech on p. 114.

Like father . . . good fruit: the common proverb is underlined and illustrated by a text from Matt. 7: 17; the following verses amplify the doctrine of the need for good works in the Epistle of James, quoted on p. 13 above.

16 *his gracious daughter... spouse*: Holy Church claims to be God's daughter because the Church was founded by Christ, the Son of God; 'Mercy' covers all merciful people.

Caritas: charity or supernatural love, third and greatest of the 'theological virtues'; the antithesis of the carnal or worldly love of Meed's followers.

Lord, who shall dwell... mountain?': Ps. 14(15): 1, which goes on to praise the just man and condemn those who practise usury and take bribes.

Great numbers of people... nuptials: the list covers all ranks of society; *summoners*: officials who summoned defendants for trial in the church courts; *beadles*: constables and town-criers; *bailiffs*: manorial officials, much suspected of venality; *purveyors*: officials who bought provisions for the king and made underhand profits.

Simony: a personification of the sin of profiteering out of buying and selling church offices (see Acts. 8: 9–24 for the story of Simon Magus). He here seems to be a canon lawyer, associated with his lay counterpart, Civil Law.

17 *Guile*: here probably the Devil, whose deed of endowment gives Meed and False a marriage portion of allegorical 'territories' covering the deadly sins of envy, wrath, greed, lust, gluttony, sloth, and their root-sin, pride. These 'places' may be compared with those in Passus V (pp. 61–2). They denote spiritual conditions and acts.

Usury: here 'lending at exorbitant interest', which was forbidden to Christians.

fasting-day rules: the Church allowed only one solid meal, and that not before noon, on the eves of feast-days, Fridays, and weekdays in Lent.

18 *the sufferings of Purgatory*: strictly speaking, those who committed deadly sins and and died without confessing them would not have a chance to purge them in Purgatory buy would go straight to Hell.

Wrong: here the evil principle embodied in human form. Langland happily mixes personifed abstractions like Wrong with type-figures like the pardoner, reeve, and so on.

Pauline: an order of friars, of whom little is known. Generally friars were not also pardoners. Like Chaucer's celebrated pardoner, this one is a type of venality (cf. also the miller below).

Theology: the personified principles of the Church's teaching in their developed and systematized form; his understanding of the true nature of meed is to be presumed authoritative, although unlike Holy Church he exists in this world, on the same plane as the other allegorical figures.

Amends: the 'true' parent of Meed in the sense that (heavenly) reward is reserved for those who repent of their sins and make amends for them. This is why Theology can say that Meed is 'lawfully born': he is referring to what ought, ideally, to be the case.

18   *The labourer . . . reward*: Luke 10: 7; refers to the reward due to those
      who do God's work.

19   *Conscience*: an important character in the poem, is traditionally the
      voice of God in the soul, a figure of authority.

      florins: a gold coin worth six shillings, introduced by Edward III.

20   *provisors*: clergy appointed directly to benefices by the Pope. The
      suggestion here is that they used bribes to obtain their wishes.

      Archdeacons: the Church courts were responsible for dealing with cases
      involving sexual offences but also with other breaches of canon law
      such as usury, of which the variety here (*usuria occulta*) was a
      fraudulent trading-transaction that concealed the issue of an interest-
      earning loan. The archdeacon presided over the diocesan court.

      Truthfulness: (*soothness* or *veritas*), who appears only here, may
      represent the perspicacity or insight of the just or 'true' man.

      the King: a type-figure of what a king *ought* to be; in the years of the
      poem's composition he would have called to mind Edward III (d.
      1377) rather than the boy-king Richard II who succeeded him.

21   *Dread*: stands for the fear and apprehension of the various villains
      awaiting the outcome of Meed's trial.

23   *Westminster's . . . denizens*: a separate city at this time, the centre of
      government and administration as well as the royal courts. It was a
      natural centre both for litigants and educated men seeking employment
      or preferment through the influence of lay nobles and high churchmen.

      No ignorance . . . getting on: the power of bribery is strong even
      amongst the learned. This theme of the corruption of *clerkes* becomes
      important in Vision Three.

24   *a confessor . . . a friar*: corruption of the confessional by the friars,
      adumbrated on p. 2, is here exemplified at length, and is repeated in
      the poem's climactic scene (pp. 252–4). It forms the heart of
      Langland's attack on the moral decay of the institutional Church. The
      friar's hostility to Conscience is echoed in the final Passus (p. 254).

      noble: a gold coin worth a third of a pound.

      you could rest assured . . . by that route!: the friar is guilty of simony (see
      note to p. 16 above) in offering Meed spiritual gains in exchange for
      money, as is she in attempting to buy salvation with gold.

      prone to lust: Meed's special concern with the deadly sin of lechery
      associates her with the Whore of Babylon; see note to p. 15, 'a
      woman . . .'.

      an honorary sister . . . Order!: Meed hopes to benefit from the prayers
      of the friar's community through joining it by means of 'letters of
      fraternity', a form of membership of the order offered to lay-people for
      a consideration. The same offer is made by another friar at the end of
      Passus XX (p. 254).

25 *What does God think ... benefactions?*: this singular authorial intervention suggests the strength of Langland's hostility to the friars as promoters of a 'carnal' or wordly attitude to religious matters.

Do not let your left hand ... doing: Matt. 6: 3, part of a warning against hypocrisy, a form of spiritual pride which forfeits 'reward' (cf. Matt. 6: 1) or meed from God.

a fortune in retail trade: Langland's target in attacking retailers is the practice of making excessive profits through 'cornering the market' in goods essential to life. Langland assumes there is a 'just price' for commodities which it is sinful to exceed, regarding exploitation of the poor as one of the gravest of sins.

26 *Ignis devorabit ... munera*: 'Fire shall devour the tabernacles of those who love to take bribes' (Job 15: 34).

Conscience: defined in Passus XV (p. 167) as the power to make (moral) decisions in the light of God's law, is here personified as a knight. He functions both as the faculty in general and as the king's conscientious lay advisers.

his counsellors, spiritual and temporal: the Great Council was made up of the great nobles and bishops, representing the lay and spiritual estates of the realm. The largest estate numerically (the commons) was not represented.

your father's fall ... promises: the allusion is to Edward II, father of Edward III, who was king when Langland first wrote these lines in the A-text—at the time the present text was composed, Richard II, grandson of Edward III, was probably already crowned (1377). Edward II was murdered in 1327; but the allusion to hollow promises has more relevance to Edward the Black Prince (d. 1376), Richard's father, who had failed to get payment from Peter of Castile for helping him to recover his throne.

poisoned popes: Pope Benedict XI was thought to have been poisoned in 1306; but there may be a more general allusion to the temporal endowment of the Church by the emperor Constantine as a spiritual 'poison' (see note on the reference in Passus XV, p. 185).

27 *groats*: a large silver coin worth fourpence, introduced in 1351.

your own privy seal: letters bearing the king's personal seal were sent to authorize chapters when electing an abbot, or bishops when appointing to a benefice; but a provisor could circumvent them by securing a prior claim on the basis of a papal bull, procured with the help of monetary payment or meed in the right quarters.

where Meed enjoys ... king: an allusion to Edward III's mistress Alice Perrers, whose name is punningly hinted at (Middle English 'perree', precious stones) and occurs at Passus X, line 12.

settlement-days: ('love-days') were set aside for amicably settling disputes in the manor-court, and furnished occasion for recourse to 'meed'.

28   *kill a king*: an allusion to the murder of Edward II, father of Edward III, after he had been forced to abdicate by Parliament in 1327.

  such trouble in Normandy: Meed alludes to the Normandy campaign, identifying Conscience with the policy adopted by Edward III of abandoning his claim to the throne of France in exchange for Aquitaine and a sum of 3 million crowns (Treaty of Brétigny, 1360). She accuses him of being too cowardly to face the hardships of war, such as the severe hailstorm of 14 April 1360, and contrasts the meagre copper utensils carried off by the returning English with the wealth and power that would have accrued to Edward had he maintained his claim.

29   *proper for a King . . . to give rewards*: in this speech Meed applies the term 'meed' to *every* kind of payment made by one person to another, whether in money or in kind.

30   *there are two forms of 'meed'*: in his reply Conscience distinguishes between 'meed' as God's reward for virtuous living and 'meed' as recompense for wrongdoing, which he associates with his adversary.

  Lord, who shall dwell . . . He who walks . . . justice: Conscience quotes verses 1 and 2 of Ps. 14(15), the same authority appealed to by Holy Church in Passus II (see p. 16), to develop his view of truth or integrity as the antithesis of false 'meed'. This clearly aligns him with what Holy Church represents, in opposition to the worldly corruption embodied in Lady Meed.

  robes of a single hue: the white robe of integrity alludes to that worn by the just in Apoc. (Rev.) 3: 4–5, and also to Holy Church's robe of white (p. 8).

  He who does not give . . . man: Ps. 14(15):5; usury was regarded as a grave sin by the medieval Church.

31   *In their hands . . . gifts*: Ps. 25(26): 10, the preceding verse of which foresees damnation for those who do evil for 'meed'.

  I say to you . . . reward: Matt. 6: 5, which in fact refers to hypocrites who seek recognition from men for their prayers and almsgiving; but Conscience aptly applies it to clergy who accept *payment* for discharging what is their duty as servants of the Church.

  appropriate wage . . . act of exchange: Conscience recognizes two categories of lawful payment, wages for work and payment for goods; he apparently omits *profit*, which theologians allowed to merchants for the risk incurred in trade.

  the story of King Saul: the account here is a heightened retelling of the story in 1 Kgs. (1 Sam.) 15. The ancestors' 'evil deeds' are their attacks on the Israelites in the wilderness (see Exod. 17: 8, 16).

32   *every last implication . . . example*: Conscience implies a parallel between Saul's fate and what might have befallen Edward III had he persisted in the war against France out of greed. Other details of the biblical

account, such as the command to annihilate the Amalekites, are presumably not to be pressed. Conscience here seems to be speaking more generally for the poet, too, echoing his comment at the end of the rat and mice fable in the Prologue.

Kind Wit: see note to p. 4 above.

the time is coming . . . kingdom: Conscience's prophecy may be a general vision of an ideal state of affairs to come in the Last Days, rather than having a strict contemporary application, as a close parallel between Saul and Edward III, David and the young Richard, is hard to establish. David was anointed by Samuel in 1 Kgs. (1 Sam.) 16: 13 after the latter had killed Agag.

Honest Fidelity: the moral principle of Justice or Righteousness, especially as operative in the domain of public and civil life. The original name, 'Lewte', may be rendered in most contexts as 'Honest Fidelity'; see also at 40 below, and note.

Real Love: 'Real' here translates original 'kynde', which means 'true to its proper nature or essence'.

the Jews will be struck with wonder . . . earth: an allusion to the Jewish expectation of the Messiah (believed by Christians to have been fulfilled in the person of Jesus), which would be accompanied by the reign of universal justice and peace.

They shall turn . . . ploughshares: Isa. 2: 4; refers to the Last Days and the Final Judgement as understood in the Old Testament.

33 *I shall please the Lord*: Ps. 114(116): 9; one of many attacks on worldly priests who neglect their office of prayer for the pleasures of country sports and so fail to 'please the Lord'.

The King's Court . . . Chapter Court: the four courts named are respectively the high courts for criminal justice, for civil actions, for church affairs coming under the archbishop's jurisdiction, and for ecclesiastical matters covered by cathedral or monastery chapters.

True-Tongue: the personification of the just man of the Psalms, the appropriate person to be a judge in Truth's court; cf. p. 16 above.

Nation shall not lift . . . nation: the quotation completes the verse quoted on p. 32 above, ending 'neither shall they be exercised any more to war'. Conscience's stance of favouring peace with France forms part of his overall vision of an end to all war.

a turn for the worse: this riddling prophecy cannot be deciphered with certainty, but the signs and portents are meant to have a generally 'apocalyptic' feel. Sun, moon, and arrows are associated in the prophecy of Habacuc (3: 11), and the ship may be an image of the Church in the Last Days. The moon may be the paschal full moon, and the overall sense may be summarized as follows: 'When Christians really show a readiness to die for what they believe in, the Mahometans and Jews alike will prove willing to acknowledge the truth of the Christian religion.'

33   *A good name . . . wealth*: the first verse of Prov. 22, a chapter concerned with righteous living. The implication is that virtue will triumph over wealth in the good times to come.

Honorem . . . munera: Meed's quotation is from the same chapter of Proverbs as Conscience's (v. 9); but she gives only the first part of the sentence, which on the face of it countenances 'meed'.

33–4   *omnia probate . . . tenete*: the quotation, from 1 Thess. 5: 21, occurs in the context of a discussion of various manifestations of religious gifts, such as prophecy; all of them are to be 'tried' or examined, only the valid and authentic are to be approved. Conscience's 'lady' was one who took the text (in its partial form) as a licence to do what she pleased. The translation 'a few . . . severe' tries to capture the original, which was probably *felle wordes* (with pun on *fele* 'several').

34   *Meed carries off the souls . . . it*: the second half of Prov. 22: 9 threatens damnation to those who accept bribes (after admitting that to *give* 'presents' may indeed lead to success for the giver). Conscience subtly extends the condemnation to the giver, too, by using a word (*taketh*) which can mean both 'give' and 'accept', as the translation attempts to convey.

35   *Reason* is, as defined by Anima in Passus XV, the power to make (moral) judgements (cf. p. 167). His rank as a bishop only emerges at the opening of Vision Two.

Cato is possibly the fourth-century author of the *Distichs*, quoted towards the end of Passus VI (see p. 74) and in several other places, and stands for everyday practical morality or common prudence.

True-Tongue: not the authoritative figure of Conscience's prophecy (p. 33 above) but a personified contrary to Liar, False's companion (p. 17 above).

my horse Endurance: Reason's allegorical horse recalls the imagery of Passus II (p. 19), in which False's retinue rode on a variety of mounts.

Warren Wise . . . Clevercraft: (the latter 'Witty' in the original), embodiments of *worldly* prudence, out to manipulate the legal system for profit.

Exchequer and Chancery: the Exchequer Court dealt with what we should call 'tax law', the Chancery with equity, especially the resolution of grievances that arose from cases heard in other courts.

36   *Destruction and wretchedness . . . There is no fear . . . eyes*: the quotations form the end of Ps. 13(14): 3, which deals with evildoers who have no fear of God.

his son the Prince: if a direct allusion is intended here, it must be to Edward the Black Prince, who died in 1376, leaving his heir Richard to become king on the death of Edward III in 1377. 'Prince' is added in translation.

Peace: who represents the ordinary law-abiding citizen, is to be distinguished from the Daughter of God in Passus XVIII, but reappears as the porter of Unity in Passus XX (p. 252), where once again he protests but is eventually prevailed on to compromise. Parliament is here envisaged not as the Commons in assembly so much as the Great Council meeting as a court to hear complaints and petitions from individuals.

37 *a notch on my tally-stick*: the stick was split in two halves for buyer and seller to retain a record of the transaction; the notch was all Peace seems to have got from Wrong by way of 'payment'.

Wrong is a concrete manifestation of the evil principle personified in the other world as the Devil (in Holy Church's words on p. 10 above). Each wrongdoer is, as it were, Satan's representative on earth. See p. 18.

Wise is the character earlier mentioned on p. 35, and speaks as if he were a consultant giving legal advice.

38 *... answered Reason*: Reason's long speech envisages a day when the total moral and spiritual regeneration of the country has been achieved: only then will it be safe to relax the strict punitive demands of the law.

39 *Lord, remember ... :* the general idea is that each of the religious orders should 'remember' their true calling as they sing the antiphon 'Remember, Lord'. St Benedict was the founder of monasticism in the West (sixth cent.), St Bernard of Clairvaux founder of the Cistercian Order (twelfth cent.), St Francis of Assisi founder of the Friars Minor (thirteenth cent.), not an enclosed monastic community. The 'preachers' who immediately follow may be the Dominicans ('Order of Preachers'), or more generally all priests whose duty was to preach. See Introduction, pp. xvii–xviii.

St James's shrine: the popular pilgrimage-shrine of St James in Compostella, north-west Spain (Galicia). He deprecates repeated visits and implies a preference for 'spiritual' pilgrimages, that is, works of virtue like visiting the sick as prescribed in the Epistle of St James (cf. Holy Church's words at the end of Passus I, p. 13).

Rome: the Papal Court, which at this time was actually at Avignon. Reason has in mind clergy taking money abroad to bribe papal officials to help them obtain preferment in the Church.

Dover: travellers abroad could be examined at the port of Dover to see if they were carrying gold or silver unlawfully.

a payment of pure humility: Reason echoes the King's words on p. 38 above: he denies the principle of meed (monetary payment) where only spiritual satisfaction is appropriate.

39   *No-evil meets Unpunished . . . fee!*: the couplet is in Latin in the original
       and enunciates the rule that the innocent must not be afflicted and the
       criminal must not prosper.

40   *the legal profession . . . ploughmen*: Reason's attack echoes Conscience's
       on p. 32 above: if legal justice obeys the moral law, there will be no
       scope for crime, and hence none for lawyers.

       Kind Wit agreed: his agreement with right reason here shows he is
       much closer to Conscience than to the 'worldly' wisdom embodied in
       Warren Wise and Clevercraft.

       Honest Fidelity: here a personification of the King's loyal subjects as a
       collective concept as much as the abstract principle of justice (see note
       to p. 15 above).

41   *the Commons*: refers to the whole estate of the common people of
       England, but also includes their parliamentary representatives at
       Westminster.

       let all of us keep together!: the King's declaration at the end is that he
       will rule his land under the guidance of his own reason and conscience
       working together, and also with the advice of those in whom the
       principles they denote are embodied—his upright counsellors in
       Church and State respectively. Since Reason is shown at the opening of
       the next passus as a bishop, it seems fair to assume that Conscience
       (called a 'knight' on his first appearance, on p. 26 above, stands for the
       secular estate of the nobility.)

42   *I now stirred from my slumbers*: the perfunctory waking interlude serves
       as a mere bridge-passage from the first vision to the second, which
       continues the themes of the first (political and social) on an individual
       (moral) plane.

       preach to the whole realm at large: Reason's identity as a bishop is now
       revealed: he holds what may be a crosier with a cross at the top.

       The recent plague: the great plague known as the Black Death reached
       England in 1348, and further outbreaks occurred in 1361–2 (the
       period of the A-text) and 1375–6 (the period of the B-revision). Like
       other contemporary commentators, Langland sees diseases and natural
       disasters as punishments for past and warnings against future sin. See
       Introduction, p. xxii.

       the strong south-west wind: occurred on Saturday, 15 January 1362,
       during the second outbreak of plague, and lasted five days.

       Waster: a 'type-name', perhaps traditional, since Langland envisages a
       destructive parasite rather than the rich profligate of the earlier poem
       Winner and Waster (c.1352).

       Petronella: another 'type-name', for a vain woman.

43   *the ducking-stool*: was a traditional village punishment for notoriously
       shrewish women.

Spare the rod... child!: Prov. 13: 24, which continues: 'but he who loves him corrects him betimes.' All the Wisdom books of the Bible were traditionally ascribed to Solomon.

If you lead lives such as you urge us... heart?: Reason here identifies himself with the laity, though he is still speaking in his symbolic role as the chief bishop of the realm.

take over the management... order: the threat of royal intervention here anticipates the *prophecy* of Clergy in Passus X (see pp. 104–5), but Langland is advocating right observance of the religious life, not its suppression.

44   *I say... know you*: Matt. 25: 12, in the parable of the ten virgins, one of two speaking of the Second Coming of Christ at the Last Judgement.

St Truth: not a person but the personified principle of a life lived in accordance with the will of God ('Truth').

Repentance: embodies the surge of penitent feelings evoked by the sermon; Will is both the human faculty, here collectively that of the folk of the field, in which the power to sin or refrain from sin resides, and also a wry allusion to the author's name and his fictive counterpart in the work.

Petronella: the only one of the deadly sins who is female, and one of two to be given a personal appellation (cf. p. 47 below, where the name recurs); The extreme brevity of the account of Pride, which was regarded as the root sin, may be due to Langland's having presented a type of Pride already in Vision One in the figure of Lady Meed.

Lust: the brevity of the description may also be due to so much of it having been dealt with in the Lady Meed section (see esp. p. 24 above). The Virgin Mary is the special patron of chastity, and Saturday was a day of special devotion to her. The penance of avoiding excess food and drink as leading to lust recalls Holy Church's exemplum of Lot in Vision One (pp. 8–9 above).

Envy: for Langland, both resentment at others who have what one does not have and hostility against them for having it (= Lat. *invidia*). It covers our idea of 'hate' and partially overlaps with Wrath. Envy's sin includes delight in others' misfortunes, pleasure in stirring up trouble, and an inability to wish anyone well (that is, the total absence of love or charity).

Mea culpa: part of the prayer of penitence at the opening of mass (the *Confiteor*) rather than the formula for private confession to a priest.

like those the friars wear: Langland associates the friars with envy on p. 250.

46   *my whole body... inside me*: the 'psychosomatic' effects observable in the envious—the secretion of bile and a constant fretful indigestion.

46   *I'm always sorry!*: Envy can no more understand the right meaning of
       'sorrow' than he can pray for others' good; cf. Greed's problem on p.
       50 below).

       lectors: friars who read a scriptural text and then preach a homily on it,
       'glosing' the meaning so as to render its hard moral demands
       acceptable to those with power and wealth.

47   *private boudoir-confessions*: to an amenable friar made possible an 'easy'
       absolution (cf. Chaucer's *General Prologue*, 221–4) and the avoidance
       of shame involved in facing one's own parish priest (an element of the
       act of penance Langland regarded as an important deterrent to sinning
       again).

       the friars are eating into their portion: Anger refers to the quarrels
       between friars and parish priests occasioned by the latter's resentment
       at their 'spirituality' (the income arising from performing church
       offices, including hearing confessions) being eaten into by the
       preaching friars (the result being the decline of 'spirituality' in the
       modern sense).

       a cook in her kitchen: the metaphor shifts from grafting (p. 46) to
       cookery as Wrath continues his exposure of the all-too-human world of
       (here, female) religious communities.

       The whole chapter: the members of the convent assembled in a regular
       formal meeting would have to consider the case of Petronella's
       pregnancy before it came before the archdeacon in the ecclesiastical
       court, which dealt with such matters.

47–8   *a prioress must never be ordained . . . lives*: the hearing of nuns'
       confessions by the abbess of a convent was forbidden by Pope Gregory
       IX (1227–41). The observation here could be authorial, as it is echoed
       at a later point (see Passus XIX, p. 231), but is appropriate coming
       from Anger.

48   *a pretty strict watch on my cronies*: the favourable account of discipline in
       the monasteries is in sharp contrast with the strong criticisms of the
       friars voiced earlier and at many other points in the work.

       he gave me absolution: the reference to *me* is not a lapse from dramatic
       propriety but another reminder that all the sins are those of Will (the
       representative sinner). The original puns on 'wilne' (the verb
       translated 'aim at'), literally 'desire, will (to)'.

       Greed: translates 'coveitise', strictly the desire for possession, but
       Langland's description shows he clearly has in mind the other aspect of
       the sin called in Latin *avaricia*, miserliness. Greed is shown in
       traditional terms as a wretched old man who has spent his life in
       unlawfully acquiring riches, by one means or another, in a number of
       trades and mercantile activities.

49   *Weyhill*: near Andover, Hants, and Winchester both had an important
       autumn fair.

I got in with the cloth-merchants: Greed stretched the fabric in a frame to make it appear longer, but weakened the material in the process. His wife's trick was twofold: to use material which had been loosely spun and was therefore easier to rack or stretch once woven, and to weigh wool with a false weight, thus paying the spinners for only one pound's worth while getting $1\frac{1}{4}$ pounds (and thus tricking those she had already instructed in the art of fraudulent spinning). Greed's own steelyard gave accurate measure, but trading regulations banned it (as the device was open to fraudulent abuse), prescribing only the scales or balance.

She would dilute . . . tipple: the trick with the ale involved giving customers a sample of the best brew (four times the price of the cheapest) but actually filling their jugs with a mixture of good and less good while out of sight.

Walsingham . . . guilt!: on Walsingham see note to p. 2 above. Bromholm Priory, also in Norfolk, had a reputed relic of the True Cross set into a great crucifix.

50   *restitution?*: Greed's error uses a (perhaps understandable) difficulty in grasping the meaning of penitential terminology as an emblem of deeper spiritual obtuseness; cf. Envy's even grosser mistake about 'sorrow' on p. 46 above.

Norfolk: here stands for a region at some distance from the capital; but Greed's resolve to go on pilgrimage to two Norfolk shrines suggests that Langland thought of him as a Norfolk man (his oath, translated as Cockney, is Norfolk dialect in the original). Norfolk people seem to have had a reputation for close-fistedness.

usury: Greed learnt to make money from lending at exorbitant interest by living among the Jews (the practice was forbidden to Christians) and the financial community of Lombards in the City of London, who had developed in particular various methods of transferring capital abroad at a profit. He became devoted to the cross imprinted on coins rather than the cross of Christ (avarice, not charity).

loans in kind . . . nobility: Greed took pledges from impoverished noblemen and then bought them himself (at a cheap price) in order to supply them with the ready cash they desired.

bills of exchange . . . bullion to Rome: the Lombard bills of exchange were an early form of credit transfer that obviated the necessity of actually transporting gold abroad. Money due in Rome was paid in England and the corresponding sum disbursed in Rome on production of the bill or credit-note. The operation allowed ample scope for making a profit.

for the sake of . . . protection?: Greed complains that he got scant gratitude from needy nobles to whom he advanced cash; but he managed to acquire some of their costly wearing-apparel given in pledge when they failed to pay up on the day. The allusion to gloves is to the practice of making a gift-offering to the master of one's trade on taking up with him as an apprentice to the craft.

51　　*Compassion . . . cats*: Greed again fails to understand the terminology of Christian love. He 'skins' his neighbours in need rather than helping them with his surplus wealth.

God will never grant . . . money!: this, the severest denunciation of any of the sins, is a measure of Langland's abhorrence of covetousness, which he sees as a fundamental sin against the fundamental Christian virtue of charity.

Seek fancy foods . . . friend: the proverbial couplet, praising simplicity of life as against luxury, anticipates the praise of poverty in Passus XIV.

The guilt will cling . . . back: this quotation from St Augustine's Epistle 153 underlines the vital importance of restitution, part of 'the work of satisfaction' needed if sacramental penance was to be efficacious.

52　　*Have mercy on me . . . truth!*: from the opening and eighth verses of the fourth penitential psalm, Ps. 50(51), the standard medieval gloss on which took it to mean that God would punish sin and demanded that sinners seeking forgiveness should show mercy to others. This is one of the leading ideas in the poem.

Cum sancto sanctus eris: the Latin quotation is from Ps. 17(18): 26: 'with the holy you will be holy, with the innocent, innocent; . . . and with the wayward, you will likewise go astray.'

Misericordia . . . eius: the answer to Greed's despair on regarding the enormity of his sin is the thought from Ps. 144(145): 9, the sense of which in context is that God's merciful kindness is shown in all his actions; but it was commonly interpreted to mean that mercy was God's supreme attribute, and this is Langland's understanding here and in Passus XVII and XVIII.

you have no genuine means . . . breakfast: Repentance means that everything Greed possesses has been obtained by underhand means; his genuinely 'honest' wealth is nil.

make restitution to: if it is too late to restore ill-gotten goods to the actual owners, Greed should hand their value to his spiritual father, the bishop, who will be able (and is obliged) to apply them to some worthwhile, charitable end. God's spiritual treasure, on which alone he should rely, is of course 'mercy' and 'truth'.

53　　*hot spices*: could be chewed without formally breaking the rule of fasting; they would also make Glutton thirsty, as the brewer is aware.

Cicely Shoemaker . . . Griffin the Welshman: the motley crew in the tavern include prostitutes from Cock's Lane and an incompetent priest (*Pridie*, a phrase from the consecration prayer, was the point at which a priest who had forgotten the bread and wine had to recommence mass).

a game of barter: Hick and Clement have their hood and cloak valued and with Robin's help make an exchange, Clement paying the agreed difference in value with a drink (probably for everyone).

54   *the hour of evensong*: mention of evensong and the Our Father point up Glutton's failure to do his religious duty and the length of time he has been drinking in the tavern since setting out to mass that morning.

attack of sloth: the sin of gluttony was traditionally thought to lead directly to that of sloth, beginning in indifference and ending in despair.

I've sworn . . . a thousand times: loss of rational control through drink (which Holy Church had warned could lead to lechery and worse—see Passus I, pp. 8–9) here results in breaking the second commandment: these are the 'mighty oaths' of p. 53; cf. also Chaucer's *Pardoner's Tale*, C. 638 ff.

55   *Bless me*: ('father, for I have sinned'), the opening words of the penitent to the priest in making confession. Sloth's sin undermines the attempt at repentance as radically as did Glutton's.

Robin Hood . . . Earl of Chester: this, the earliest reference to Robin Hood, like that to another popular twelfth-century hero, the Earl of Chester, suggests Sloth was a devotee of minstrels in taverns, where such stories were recited.

56   *a filthy story . . . farce in summer*: Sloth's idleness and impiety make him easy prey to the minstrel-purveyors of bawdy matter attacked in the Prologue (p. 2).

the friars' church: the implication is that the friars would not mind if Sloth put in only a token appearance before the end of mass, whereas his parish priest would rebuke him severely for it. Proper attendance at mass on Sunday was obligatory under pain of grave sin, as was confession at least once a year.

a priest in a parish: Sloth is here imagined as an idle and ignorant priest, unable to live by the standards of virtue outlined in Ps. 1 and 127(128), and therefore unable to instruct his parishioners. He is familiar with customary manorial law (because there's something in it for him) but ignorant of the laws and rules of the Church he represents. The passage may allude to the low standard of clerical education and general spiritual calibre in the years after the Black Death, which killed nearly half the clergy of England.

57   *lure me with kindness*: the hawk's lure was made of leather and feathers, to resemble a bird; sometimes the falconer put a piece of meat in it, the 'tangible gain' Sloth has in mind as a motive for any action.

God! How I failed . . . mine!: a proverbial expression of regret over an ill-spent youth.

Wakeful: the name alludes to Mark 13: 33, a warning to be prepared for death and judgement.

57   *I'll get to church before daybreak*: Sloth resolves to get up at dawn and drink nothing between noon and 3 p.m. Sleep, caused by laziness and alcoholic stupor, is the vice that keeps him from a moral and devout way of life.

the Chester Rood: a great cross that formerly stood on Rood Island in the Dee at Chester.

58   *Robert the robber*: stands for a specific sin of which the particular penance is appropriately to restore property; but he also symbolizes, like Will at the opening of the confession-scene (see p. 44), all sinful humanity in debt to God for its offences and needing salvation by Christ.

my brother-robber Dismas: the 'Good Thief' of Luke 23: 40 was given the name Dismas in the apocryphal *Gospel of Nicodemus*, a source Langland also drew on for the Harrowing of Hell sequence in Passus XVIII. His words 'Remember me, Lord, when you come into your kingdom' (v. 42) bring hope to those in the final moments of life, when it is too late to make reparation or rely on anything but God's mercy. Christ's answer at v. 43 offers encouragement to the worst offender and staves off despair.

shed copious tears: Robert's tears echo those of Will (see p. 44 above) and bring the confession proper to an end. (The prayer that follows expresses confidence in God's mercy to those who repent.)

his pikestaff . . . named Penance: Penance, specifically sacramental confession, is the support by which sinners must make their way through life. Theft is the devil's aunt because theft was the first sin committed by the fallen angel Lucifer, and the one of which Christ accuses him in Passus XVIII (see p. 221).

all this was for the best: Repentance means that despite the apparent calamity of Man's fall as described in Genesis, the subsequent Incarnation of Christ made the fall a paradoxically 'happy' one, since it required God to become man in order to save man. The quotation is from the great *Exultet* hymn sung at the Easter Vigil service on Holy Saturday.

Let us make man . . . He who lives . . . him: the two texts quoted (Gen. 1: 26 and 1 John 4: 16) are complementary: the completion of man's creation in God's image occurs with his becoming like Christ, God-made-man, through the supernatural virtue of charity.

Neither you . . . nor your Son . . . death's ultimate dolour: Repentance means that God the Father did not 'die' (he cannot) and neither did the divine nature present in the person of Jesus Christ, God the Son. But Christ's human nature *did* die, and thereby liberated man from eternal death, the penalty of sin. The quoted passage (Eph. 4: 8) looks forward to Christ's act of leading Adam and the just of old out of Limbo in Passus XVIII (see p. 225 below).

59 *The sun . . . became . . . unseeing*: these lines allude to the darkness that
covered the earth when Christ died, lasting from the sixth to the ninth
hour (i.e. 3 p.m., but *nona hora* in the Gospels being misunderstood as
midday; see Matt. 27: 45, for example). Langland envisages Christ's
blood passing through the earth below the cross and descending to
where the patriarchs wait in the darkness of Hell; they are the 'blessed'
who repeat that act as they daily feast in Heaven. The quotation from
Isa. 9: 2, familiar from its use in Advent, is especially apt in reference
to this event, which is fully described in Passus XVIII, where the
quotation again occurs (p. 220).

Mary the sinner . . . I did not come . . . repentance: Mary Magdalen,
emblem of a great repentant sinner, was the first to see Christ after his
resurrection (Mark 16: 9). The lesson of this is again the mercifulness
of God to sinners, as the quotation from Luke 5: 32 affirms was the
aim of Christ's coming.

when you wore our coat of arms: the notion that Christ's human nature
was like the coat of arms worn by a knight going to battle is developed
more fully in Passus XVIII (see p. 210). The quotation is from the
prologue to St John's Gospel (1: 14).

our Father and our brother: God is man's father as his creator, his
brother through having assumed human nature in the Incarnation;
both are important themes to be fully developed in Passus XVIII.

Turn, O God . . . Blessed are those . . . You will preserve . . . mercies!:
Hope's exultant cry is a quotation from Ps. 70(71): 20 in the form it
has in the mass, where it occurs at the end of the opening or
penitential section in the old rite. The idea of a 'horn of salvation'
occurs in Ps. 17(18): 3, closely linked with the notion of hope in God.
The second quotation (Ps. 31(32): 1) is the breath of life of the sinner
whose hope has been restored through forgiveness. The third, from Ps.
35(36): 7–8, again stresses the universality of God's saving mercy
towards all his creation.

dressed in the weird garb of a pilgrim: the folk of the field have set out in
search of Truth, a spiritual reality, but encounter an all-too-material
'professional' pilgrim. He carries souvenirs or 'tokens' of the shrines he
has visited—pewter phials from Canterbury, mementoes of St Francis
at Assisi, shells emblematizing a miracle of St James at Compostella,
cross-symbols from Jerusalem, St Peter's keys from Rome, and an
image of the face of Christ supposedly imprinted on the handkerchief
with which St Veronica wiped Christ's face on the way to Calvary.
Sinai was the mount on which Moses received the Ten
Commandments; of the other, less well-known shrines, Babylon, near
Cairo, had a church commemorating the Flight into Egypt; Armenia
refers to Mount Ararat, the resting-place of Noah's ark; Alexandria
was the site of St Catherine's martyrdom.

60 *a ploughman called out*: Piers on his appearance asserts his relationship
with two powers of man's rational moral nature already familiar from

the first vision. He has never travelled abroad but follows Truth by heeding laws and principles that every man has by nature.

60   *the promptest paymaster . . . poor*: Truth's prompt payment may be contrasted with the dilatory meanness of Sloth towards his workmen (p. 56 above). He means that, since virtue is its own 'reward', its payment is instantaneous.

St Thomas's shrine: Piers's pointed allusion to the shrine of St Thomas at Canterbury, rich with pilgrims' gift-offerings, shows how 'Truth' is a form of spiritual wealth which cannot be acquired for money. The 'pilgrimage' to the shrine of Truth, being moral and spiritual, is purely interior, although the allegorical description Piers uses makes it seem an adventurous and hazardous journey, as indeed it turns out to be.

61   *love the Lord your God . . . treat you*: Piers's directions begin with Christ's great double commandment to love God entirely and one's neighbour as oneself (Matt. 22: 37–9, 7: 12).

continue on your way . . .: The journey involves mention of several of the Ten Commandments—the fourth ('Honour-your-parents'), the second ('Never-swear . . .'), the ninth and tenth ('Do-not-desire . . .'), the seventh and fifth ('Do-not-steal . . . kill'), the sins they forbid being left on the 'left' or evil side, the third ('observe every holy day'), and the eighth ('Do-not-bear-false-witness').

a castle: this is the tower of truth glimpsed at a distance in the opening of the Prologue. It is the inner spiritual condition (cf. Luke 17: 21) which leads to ultimate reward in Heaven with God. This condition requires faith, penance, and prayer. The way into Heaven is through the action of grace and conversion, which follows from it.

62   *The door that Eve . . . Rose*: from an antiphon to the Blessed Virgin Mary from the Office of Lauds on the Monday within the octave of Easter. Mary opens the door to Heaven closed by the sin of Eve, both through giving birth to Christ and through continuing to intercede with him for sinners.

within your own heart: Truth is to be found within the soul, garlanded with love; the two virtues are for Langland indissociable.

thinking . . . of yourself: Piers's warning against Pride is now directed at a higher level than Reason's at the beginning of this Passus. The converted soul becomes prey to *spiritual* pride, a sin possible only to those who have left behind the grosser worldly sins and set out on the pilgrimage to virtue and holiness.

seven sisters . . . serve Truth constantly: the seven virtues protect the soul against their contraries (the seven deadly sins, each recurring in subtler but no less deadly guise). Without the help of *positive* virtuous qualities, the soul cannot progress.

63   *a pickpocket . . . a man who kept apes . . . a wafer-seller*: the three pessimists are representatives of those whose sin is habitual, a kind of trade. Haukin later, in Passus XIII, is a wafer-seller.

Mercy is an indirect name for the Virgin Mary, as Truth is for God.

a pardoner . . . a prostitute: they give up the quest for truth as they have too much to lose by persisting (cf. p. 238 below).

64   *a veil*: covering head and chin was worn by ladies of rank and by nuns.

embroider . . . churches: fine English needlework (*opus anglicanum*) was highly esteemed.

something that Truth commands us to do: Truth's command is implicit in the commandment to love one's neighbour as oneself, but explicit in Matt. 25: 36 (cf. also Jas. 2: 15–16). It is one of the 'corporal works of mercy'. Feeding the hungry, which Piers undertakes to do, was another.

the good will I have towards you: Piers expresses content with his lot and displays no hostility to the social classes above him, provided they fulfil their own obligation to protect and foster the basic work of society—feeding itself by agriculture.

65   *entitled to impose fines on them*: the various customary fines and dues were a heavy burden for the tenant-farmer; Piers urges not the abandonment of traditional prerogatives but a humane exercise of rights that recognizes their conditional nature; cf. Grace's words later in Passus XIX (p. 234).

the conclusion of life's long year: the notion here is that just as an earthly tenancy is renewable annually, so earthly privilege is a kind of lease with a fixed date, the end of one's life.

Friend, take a higher place!: from Luke 14: 10; but cf. also Jas. 2: 3.

Keep death's lesson . . . heart: the lesson (that Death levels all) graphically enacted in Passus XX (see p. 245).

pilgrim's clothes: his ordinary working-clothes, an apt symbol of the difference between the 'spiritual' pilgrimage to Truth (that is, living rightly) and literal pilgrimages to one shrine or another. No special 'journey' is planned, only an inner preparation for the encounter with God at death.

66   *a bushel-weight*: 8 gallons dry measure, enough to sow a half-acre.

Jack the juggler . . . Randy Robin: the list here consists of people whose vice is not an occasional failing but a deliberately practised (and profitable) occupation.

blotted out of the book of life: from Ps. 68(69): 29, echoed in Apoc. (Rev.) 3: 5 (the idea found as early as Exod. 32: 32). The Church did not accept tithes from income earned immorally.

Work-in-time: the allegorical names of Piers's family denote ideal types of industry, obedience, and respect for authority.

In the name of God, Amen: the standard formula for making a will. He is preparing for death, but it was also usual to make a will before setting out on a normal pilgrimage.

66   *I am relying . . . guilt*: Piers states clearly his belief that he will be saved or justified by his works, not just by his faith, the doctrine of Jas. 2: 24.

67   *my dead body*: having left his soul to God, he leaves his body to the Church, to which he had dutifully paid tithes, expecting to be remembered in the *Memento* prayer for the faithful departed in the Canon of the mass.

what is left over: the remaining third of his estate, after the widow has received one third and the second third has been divided amongst the children. The famous wooden Rood of Lucca Cathedral showed Christ crowned. Piers swears by it, but he is not going there on pilgrimage.

plough-pusher: a pointed or forked implement for clearing the ground of weeds.

unploughed ridges: earth thrown up by the action of the plough became full of weeds and required digging over.

68   *barley-bread . . . stream*: this very plain fare contrasts with the expected food—wheat-bread and ale.

anchorites and solitaries: generally recluses who shut themselves up in small rooms (anchor-holds) and depended for their sustenance on charity. Other solitaries and hermits might live in forests. Anima describes the solitaries' life in Passus XV (see pp. 184–5), stressing the duty of virtuous laymen to look to their bodily needs.

wandering hermits and itinerant gospellers: both had a bad reputation for dishonesty and deception.

secure supply of what is needed: a key thought of Langland's, echoed in Conscience's final words in Passus XX (see p. 254).

69   *Waster*: a 'destroyer' more than a 'spendthrift', here comes into focus after being glimpsed from afar in the Prologue (p. 1) and referred to again in Piers's plea to the knight (p. 64).

Breton: Bretons seem to have had a contemporary reputation for rude boastfulness.

courtesy . . . calling: an expected attribute of a knight; cf. Chaucer's *General Prologue*, line 46. His pledged word or 'trouthe' carried great weight and is no idle threat.

these ravagers: may be a reflection of social conditions after the plague, when a scarcity of labour put up wages and induced some labourers to refuse to work at all rather than accept the pre-plague levels fixed by the Statute of Labourers (1351).

beans mixed with bran: food which was fed to horses; see p. 70 below.

70   *dealing with people who beg for alms?*: the question of whether giving alms to beggars encourages sloth becomes an important issue.

71   *We should . . . bear . . . burdens*: Gal. 6: 2; refers in context to putting up with one another's faults; but Langland takes it—more literally—to refer to material needs.

Vengeance is mine . . . repay: Deut. 32: 35, but the thought is influenced by the surrounding context of the previous quotation (see Gal. 6: 1), which concerns *not* judging the faults of others, through remembering one's own.

Make friends for yourself . . . itself: Luke 16: 9; the meaning in context is that Piers should not think of the true deserts of those he helps but simply use what he has (which has no intrinsic value) to help others, and leave the question of ultimate desert to God.

In the sweat . . . live: Gen. 3: 19.

the sluggard . . . pangs: Prov. 20: 4; expresses an important conviction of Langland's.

the figure of a man: an early tradition identified the four beasts of Apoc. (Rev.) 4: 7 as emblems of the four evangelists, Matthew being figured by the man.

72   *A wicked servant . . . yet!*: from the parable of the talents in Luke 19, the first part summarizing the parable and the second quoting from v. 26. Langland was also thinking of the parallel account in Matt. 25, which uses the same word for 'lazy' as the preceding quotation from Proverbs.

Kind wit . . . work: plain common sense, as well as the law of God, demands that all should work, either actively or by a life of prayer.

Blessed are all . . . You will eat . . . hands: Ps. 127(128): 1–2; the righteous man will prosper; Hunger interprets it to mean that the man who works is blessed—a view of labour that is to be questioned by Piers himself in Passus VII (see p. 79).

If you follow this diet: Hunger teaches the same doctrine as Holy Church in Passus I (see pp. 8–9). Doctors only get rich because people fail to exercise temperance: it is excess that causes illness, as well as leading to other sins like sloth and lust.

73   *. . . the dry season. . . . till Lammastide comes*: between the dry season of March and next harvest (Lammas or loaf-mass was 1 August, when a loaf baked from the new wheat was offered at mass) all Piers has to live on is the foods mentioned, the corn from the previous year having been exhausted.

Glutton's book . . . strong ale!: despite Hunger's warnings, the people resort to excess (recalling Gluttony from the previous passus). Their fickleness with regard to one virtue (temperance) demonstrates the recurring or cyclical character of sin and repentance.

74   *You were born poor . . . patience*: the *Distichs of Cato* was a fourth-century collection of moral maxims which was studied as a school text-book. The doctrine Langland instances here is one he will develop fully in Passus XIV through the character Patience. Poverty here signifies, not destitution, but a life of sufficiency. Langland is critical of the demands for higher wages stimulated by the shortage of labour, and his reference to Hunger's 'statute' implies that the laws restraining

wages were becoming ineffective and that only actual want could control excess.

74   *Saturn's message, sent to you as a warning*: the enigmatic and ominous prophecy associated with the planet Saturn is of famine, which will be sent to punish the sins of gluttony and sloth, just as plague had been sent to punish pride (see p. 42). No satisfactory explanation has been given of the details of the prophecy, though the first three calamities specified are all examples of natural disorder, and the conclusion implies that the dearth is inevitable, given the way that things now stand with the common people of the land (cf. the similar forecast of mishaps for the Church in the Prologue (see p. 2).

75   *an absolute pardon, a pena et a culpa*: according to penitential theory, all guilt was forgiven in sacramental confession and only canonical temporal punishment could be remitted by means of a pardon or indulgence. But it came to be popularly supposed that a pardon absolved from guilt (*culpa*) as well as punishment (*pena*), and this was why pilgrimages, for which pardons might be granted, had become popular, especially at the end of life. *This* pardon is granted for the 'pilgrimage' of living a virtuous life.

In the margin of the document . . . punishment: mention of the merchants as 'in the margin' indicates the difficulty Langland found in placing them within the traditional social scheme of knights, clergy, and peasantry.

the Pope: slightly confusing, since this pardon has been sent from *Truth*; but Langland doubtless has in mind the difficulty for merchants of receiving even a conventional papal pardon, given that their way of life was itself prone to so many habitual failures to observe the Church's law. Alternatively, he may be saying ironically that an ideal pope would refuse the merchants pardon, but the actual one would not.

Under his private seal: the privately sealed letter is a symbolic way of providing a 'let-out' for merchants prepared to use their profits for socially beneficial works; it avoids sanctioning their more dubious practices.

76   *Take no payment . . . Their payment shall come . . . Lord, who shall dwell . . . tent?*: the first quotation is from Ps. 14(15): 5, the third from Ps. 14(15): 1. The source of the second is unknown.

Four basic goods: the four goods include three of the Four Elements, but not of course earth, which can be bought and sold (in the form of land).

Do to others . . . you!: Matt. 7: 12; if the lawyers want a free pardon from God, they should give their services freely to their neighbours.

77   *Take heed . . . Keep your alms . . . give to*: from Cato's *Distichs* (short maxim 17) and from the twelfth-century compilation by Peter Comestor retelling sacred history (from the story of Tobias).

Do not choose... even more!: actually from another of the great Western fathers of the Church, St Jerome, from his commentary on Eccl. 11: 6 (Migne, *Patrologia Latina (PL)*, xxiii, col.1,103).

Why did you not put... away?: Luke 19: 23, the parable of the talents quoted on p. 71 above.

He is rich enough... bread: from Jerome, Epistle 125 (*PL*, xxiii, col. 1,085).

reading the lives of the saints: because they lived on the bare necessities of life; see Passus XV (pp. 176–7) on the details of what sufficed for the saints.

78 *I have been young and old... bread*: Ps. 36(37): 25; the criticism of begging is only implicit.

I'll translate every clause... English: notwithstanding the bevity of the pardon, the preceding amplification has been a spelling-out of the terse contents in the light of actual conditions of the day. A literal pardon would have been in Latin.

Et qui bona... eternum: clause 40 of the Athanasian Creed, echoing Matt. 25: 46.

79 *Si ambulavero... mecum es*: this quotation from Ps. 22(23): 4, like those below, is in Latin in the original. The purpose is not to claim that Piers is *learned* but to indicate symbolically that he knows Truth 'every bit as well as a scholar knows his books' (see p. 60 above).

My plough will be prayers and penance: Piers here takes a new decision; where before he would be a 'pilgrim by ploughing' (see p. 67), he now sees the need for a more directly and explicitly religious activity. He will spend his last days 'putting first things first', but he is not rejecting manual work in principle and in entirety.

Tears have been my bread... Do not be solicitous... for them all: from Ps. 41(42): 4 and Matt. 6: 25 respectively (also in Luke 12: 22). If one puts spiritual concerns first, God will look after one's material needs; Piers is anticipating the holy hermits of Anima's discourse in Passus XV (see pp. 176–7).

Abstinence taught me... a good deal more: that is—'I learnt the elements of the Christian life from self-denial, then went on to higher studies by listening to my conscience.'

Dixit insipiens...: Ps. 13(14): 1. It continues 'there is no God'. The priest adapts the quotation to make it a criticism of Piers's supposed presumptuousness in interpreting scripture, though a layman.

the proverbs of Solomon: Solomon was credited with authorship of the Wisdom books of the Bible, including Proverbs; the verse quoted is Prov. 22: 10.

80 *Somnia ne cures*: from the *Distichs of Cato*, ii. 31; the quotation goes on—'for while asleep the human mind sees what it hopes and wishes for.'

80 *The Bible bears out . . . look for him there*: the two Biblical passages set its religious authority against Cato's secular one. Nebuchadnezzar's dream occurs in Dan. 2: 36 ff., but it is actually Belshazzar who loses his kingdom (Dan. 5: 30). Jacob's reaction to Joseph's dream in Gen. 37: 10 is in fact an indignant one, but 37: 11 describes him as mulling over the matter, and by implication taking it seriously.

masses said regularly . . . bishops: masses for the repose of a person's soul said for two or three years after his death. The bishops' letters are licenses to preach indulgences.

81 *The Pope does . . . 'doing well'?*: the essence of the argument here seems to be that pardons sent from the Pope are only efficacious if received with the right disposition; the notion that they can be a substitute for penance is not a proper interpretation of the quoted text from Matt. 16: 19 on which the 'Petrine privilege' (the supreme penitential authority of the Pope) was based. What Langland is against is any mechanical or unspiritual view of salvation rather than pardons and intercessory masses in principle.

a paid-up associate . . . friars: membership of a fraternity enabled a person to benefit from the prayers of the religious house in question.

Do-well: the idea of doing well has become personified as a character who is to become the object of Will's quest in the next vision.

82 *So . . . whole of a summer*: the opening of this waking sequence evidently refers to the summer season following the May with which the poem opened.

Where Do-well lived: Will regards the idea of doing well (an activity, expressed by a verb) as if it were a concrete individual, an embodied person (expressed by a proper noun).

Franciscan friars: in England, especially at Oxford, they had included the greatest theologians of the time, Duns Scotus and William of Ockham.

Do-evil: a fleeting *ad hoc* personification of the idea contained in the Pardon (again as a verb); see p. 78 above. Will's 'innocent' remark is perhaps not without a hint of sarcasm.

I dispute that!: Will argues with the university friars in the classic disputation-form of the scholastic tradition; the friar who answers uses an exemplum-analogy of the kind more common in sermons than in disputations, perhaps indicating a refusal to accept Will's implied claim to the status of a scholastically trained clerk. None the less, the aim is to establish a *distinctio* between two senses of *sins* in the manner appropriate to a scholastic reply to an argument.

even the just man falls . . . a day: Prov. 24: 16. The inevitability of sin is a key idea of Langland's, recurring in Haukin's lament at the end of Passus XIV (see p. 165) and implied in Imagination's warning in Passus XII (see p. 135 and note).

83   *the influence of the Devil*. . . : the friar's doctrine echoes that of Holy
      Church in Passus I (see p. 9 above), but the 'moral minimalism' he
      goes on to expound is doubtless Langland's understanding of the
      penitential laxity with which friars were often taxed. His warning
      against mortal sin echoes Holy Church's on p. 10, but he goes further
      in implying that, since venial sins are inevitable, they do not greatly
      matter.

      the innate capacity. . . *saying*: Will's answer is not unironic; he can
      understand the argument, but does not find it a satisfactory answer to
      his question.

84   *a wild, uncultivated region*: Will has returned to the lonely nature-
      setting typical of medieval dream-vision poetry. The birdsong serves
      the same sleep-inducing function here as did the flowing stream in the
      Prologue (see p. 1).

      Thought: being Will's own 'reflection', Thought resembles him
      physically in the dream (on his nickname 'Long Will', see p. 172, and
      p. xiv). Langland seems to have understood Thought as equivalent to
      Latin *mens*, the power which knows (cf. p. 166, and C. XVI. 183).

      seven years: the period may stand for an indefinite, unspecified time or
      else hint at the period from the beginning of the age of reason (age 7
      traditionally) to that of the commencement of university studies
      (around 14)—that is, the years of schooling.

      three splendid virtues. . . : Thought's definitions present (very roughly)
      Do-well as an honest and upright layman, Do-better as a charitable
      religious, (cf. p. 174) and Do-best as a holy and authoritative bishop.

85   *You who are wise*. . . *you should*: 2 Cor. 11: 19.

      where the three of them. . . *found*: Thought takes Will's desire for
      'direct' knowledge as a request to 'meet' the three Do's 'in the flesh' as
      it were.

      three days: perhaps another indefinite period; but the 'third day' was
      frequently used in the Old Testament as 'the critical, decisive day', a
      sense underlying the description of Christ's resurrection on the third
      day (cf. 1 Cor. 15: 4), and Langland may have in mind the resolution
      of an internal crisis in the encounter with Wit or Understanding.

      Wit: both 'the power that perceives and grasps' and 'the content of that
      which is so understood'; he combines traits of *Sensus* and *Racio* in
      Anima's account of the soul's faculties in Passus XV, as well as
      something of *Mens* (see p. 166). The most basic sense was 'the power
      of physical sensation'; but from his studious appearance and
      demeanour, Wit suggests rather 'the understanding which comes as a
      result of rational thought'.

87   *Kind*: not Nature, but Nature's creator, God, the 'nature' that
      originates all other natures; see also Passus XI (p. 122 and note) and
      XX (p. 244). The four elements found in nature were thought to

combine to make man's body, the summit of physical creation. Fire is
here probably denoted by 'wind' (= *aether*, the fiery upper air).

87   *Anima*: the soul as life-principle, here personified as a female character
loved by God in the manner of a chivalrous king (a traditional image
found in *Ancrene Wisse* and in lyrical poetry). The character Anima
who appears in Passus XV is male, but defines the meaning of his
name in exactly the terms of the present allegory (see p. 166).

the Prince of this World: a title for the Devil, from John 12: 31; see also
p. 220, where the verse is quoted in full. His guise as French knight is
a reflex of popular hostility to a stock type of haughty, proud
demeanour.

he has entrusted her . . . guided: the allegory envisages Anima as the ward
of a king (God) entrusted to a great lord; but though the meaning of
Do-best is explicit, the precise social or objective reference of Do-well
and Do-better is not clear (they are perhaps respectively the lay estate
collectively, and the clergy).

Inwit: the warden of the castle is the power of rational self-control and
moral choice, signified by a name broad enough to cover also the 'inner
senses' (such as imagination). Inwit's sons are not 'the senses' as such
but 'the right uses of the senses' (that is, moral not just physical
forces).

88   *He spoke . . . created*: Ps. 148: 5; the animals needed only God's *word* to
come into existence.

Let us make . . . : Gen. 1: 26 stresses God's *action*, needed because man,
unlike the animals, has an immortal soul made in God's image.

A parallel case . . . letters: in the analogy the paper stands for the earth
from which man was made, the knowledge of writing for God's
wisdom, and the pen for his active exertion.

Caro: properly just 'flesh', but Langland uses it to mean 'living body'
as at p. 201 (see below and note), or, in effect, 'man's physical nature'.

Inwit—the inner sense, or mind: the very wide sense of Inwit here covers
both 'perception' (or understanding) and 'judgement' (including moral
responsibility). Both are weakened by sins of the flesh such as
drunkenness (cf. the exemplum of Lot in Passus I, pp. 8–9), which
illustrates abuse of Inwit).

whose god is their belly: Phil. 3: 19; gluttony is a form of idolatry.

89   *He who lives in charity . . . God*: 1 John 4: 16; cf. Holy Church's words
on p. 10, giving the words immediately before those cited here.

I tell you solemnly . . . I have abandoned them . . . hearts: the two texts
describing God's repudiation of sinners at the Last Judgement are
from Matt. 25: 12 and Ps. 80(81): 13 respectively (echoed in Rom. 1:
24).

the four great Doctors of the [Western] *Church*: Ambrose, Augustine, Jerome, and Gregory. The Luke allusion may be to Acts 6: 1, but Langland may be thinking of Jas. 1: 27, echoing Deut. 16: 11–14.

a Jew . . . this earth!: Langland's knowledge of mutual support amongst Jews is presumably at second hand, since they had been expelled from England in 1290 and did not return until the later seventeenth century under Cromwell.

whom we regard as fitting companions for Judas!: the view of the Jewish people as collectively responsible for the death of Christ, and therefore as sharers in the guilt of Judas, was a common one, based on such texts as Matt. 27: 25. Faith expands on the historical disabilities of the Jews in England and elsewhere in Passus XVIII (see p. 213 below). But Langland does not criticize them for anything except refusal to believe in Christ; his criticism is directed against Christians who fail to live up to their beliefs in the way the Jews live up to theirs.

90   *Another Judas . . . feed the poor!*: these sayings may derive from the *Compendium* of Petrus Cantor (twelfth century).

The fear of the Lord . . . wisdom: Ecclus. 1: 16; also in Prov. 9: 10, Ps. 110(111): 10.

The man who holds God in awe, he does well: Wit's first *definition* of the three Do's is an 'internal' one—obedience from fear, obedience from love, total self-dedication to God's will. The account on p. 87 above (see note), not strictly a definition, had presented the triad in objective, outward terms.

He who offends . . . in all!: Jas. 2: 10; it recurs on p. 121 in Passus XI in a context of omitting words from religious services and legal documents, and here some manuscripts have 'one word' for 'one point', making St James's injunction altogether more stringent (James says that one serious sin destroys a man's goodness, Wit that a single fault, however small, suffices to do the same; possibly Langland meant that a small fault, however *seemingly* trivial, could have grave consequences).

For those who seek . . . anything: Ps. 33: 11 (34: 10), close in spirit to Piers's words on p. 60 above.

In the secular sphere: Wit's second definition sees Do-well as the objective state of holy matrimony, contrasted with irregular, unholy unions. To count as virtuous, marriage has to reflect a proper inner disposition.

91   *an evil hour*: a time of penitence to which Adam and Eve were believed condemned after the Fall, according to the apocryphal *Life of Adam and Eve*. Before its end, they came together and Cain was conceived.

The sinner . . . evil: Ps. 7: 15; this lies at the basis of Langland's view (see ibid.) that wickedness is, in a sense, hereditary.

91   *God send a message to Seth through an angel?*: the interpretation of Gen.
6: 2, 4 (the source of this passage) derives from St Augustine through
Peter Comestor's *Historia Scholastica* (twelfth century), making the
sons of God and the daughters of men respectively the offspring of
Seth and of Cain.

I am sorry, now, that I ever made man!: Gen. 6: 7.

91–2 *The son shall not bear . . . Do men gather grapes . . . thistles?*: the first
quotation is from Ezek. 18: 20, echoed in John 9: 3, the second from
Matt. 7: 16. In its immediate context, the latter refers to the
recognition of good and evil men by their actions, but the following
verses (17–19), which stress the respective natures from which the
actions proceed, lend support to the use of the text here. Langland's
view of heredity is not purely biological, though he clearly believes
temperament and propensities to be transmissible; he also has in mind
the influence of a parent's character in the early upbringing of the
child. Both the Ezekiel and John texts deny that a just or innocent
person should be punished for a parent's sins, not that temperament is
inheritable and example influential.

92   *I am the Way . . . I can make all prosper*: the first quotation is from John
14: 6, the second Langland's own addition. As on p. 90 above (see
note), Langland uses the text as a guarantee of God's material support
for those who put doing His will first.

Since the time of the plague: Wit may be referring to the various
outbreaks of plague in the 1360s rather than the initial attack in
1348–9. Population had begun to decline again in this period.

the Dunmow flitch: a side of bacon awarded at Dunmow in Essex to a
couple married for a year who could truthfully say they had never
quarrelled.

to protect himself from falling into sin: echoes 1 Cor. 7: 2. A lime-rod was
a twig smeared with glue for trapping birds.

93   *While in your prime . . . doors!*: traditional verses based on Prov. 7: 27.

only at the proper time: the forbidden times for intercourse were days of
compulsory fasting and the times of a woman's periods.

It is good for each man . . . lechery: the quotation from 1 Cor. 7: 2 is
treated as having the same divine authority as Gen. 1: 28, 2: 23–4,
God's establishment of human marriage in the Garden of Eden.

Do-well . . . teaches: the final two definitions of the three Do's see them
as 'obedience'; 'suffering and charity'; 'active pastoral care'. The
power of Do-best, equatable with, but not in itself identified with, that
of a bishop, is seen as the major active force resisting the power of the
Devil at work in human wills through the means of sin.

94   *Dame Study*: stands for grammar-school education and the university
study of the arts—that is, the disciplines preparatory to philosophy
and theology.

Don't cast your precious pearls . . . use: an allusion to Matt. 7: 6; for the preceding verses see p. 163 below.

the Earthly Paradise: popularly supposed (on the basis of Gen. 2: 12) to be rich in gold and precious stones. See *Pearl*, ll. 73 ff.

has passed his toothcomb through them . . . wool: the purpose of this action is 'to see what is in it for them'; education is valued only if it can be 'smoothed' into a means of earning money.

settlement-day: see note to p. 27 above.

94–5 *Why do the wicked live . . . Why do sinners . . . Look, these people . . . They have destroyed . . . done?*: the first quotation is from Job 21: 7 and continues, 'why are they advanced, and strengthened with riches?' The second is from Jer. 12: 1. The first Psalm quotation is from Ps. 72(73): 12, followed by Study's comment ('Scripture says . . .'). The second is from Ps. 10(11): 4.

95 *Tobias*: whose book is in the Vulgate, is instanced as an Old Testament figure of exemplary life, a model for edification.

old Muggin the miller: as in Chaucer, a type of the crude, unspiritual man.

a New Year's present: it was customary to give presents such as clothing to servants and retainers on New Year's Day.

St Bernard's authority: Bernard of Clairvaux (1090–1153), theologian, mystic, and monastic reformer. He held the older view of the Incarnation which underlies Langland's own treatment in Passus XVIII, that is, that God allowed the Devil to kill the innocent Christ, thereby forfeiting his claim over the guilty Adam and his descendants. The view quoted is a blasphemous travesty of this.

they chew God up . . . chops!: anticipates the satire of the gluttonous doctor of divinity in Passus XIII; see esp. p. 140.

96 *I heard news . . . country places*: Ps. 131(132): 6, Ephrata being Bethlehem, as in the famous prophecy of Mic. 5: 2. God's presence, symbolized by the Ark of the Covenant in the Old Testament and by Christ's birthplace in the New, is recognized in the charity of the simple and poor.

the cross outside St Paul's: the great cross north of the east end of Old St Paul's was a popular place for open-air sermons, especially by celebrated preachers. It was at St Paul's, possibly at the cross, that Will heard the doctor of divinity preach on penance (see p. 139).

Because of their sins . . . children!: the allusion appears to be to the outbreak of 1361–2, known as the *mortalité des enfants*, because it especially took a toll of children. Study relates the attacks of plague to pride, as Reason had done in Passus V (cf. p. 42) and laments the ineffectiveness of prayers as Haukin is later to do in Passus XIII (see p. 150).

96-7   *Share out your bread . . . If you have much . . . will!*: the first quotation is
        from Isa. 58: 7, the second from Tobit 4: 9; both passages occur in a
        context stressing the spiritual value of almsgiving.

97   *by themselves in a private parlour*: Langland criticizes this new practice
        because it undermines the rich man's incentive to give to the poor out
        of his surplus.

98   *the son not bearing . . . guilt*: from Ezek. 18: 20 (cf. John 9: 1-3); see
        note to p. 91 above.

        Every man . . . burden: Gal. 6: 5; here torn out of context, and
        overlooks the earlier verse 2, which stresses the mutual responsibility
        of Christians.

        Imaginative will provide an answer . . . question: Imaginative appears at
        the end of Passus XI (see p. 125) and gives his 'answer' in Passus XII.

        Don't be more wise . . . be!: Rom. 12: 3; Paul goes on to recommend
        'wisdom unto sobriety', that is, a restraint upon one's desire to find
        answers to every religious question. Augustine attacked the desire 'to
        know a thing as it is in itself' in his *On Baptism*.

        Everything . . . because God wanted it: Study's mention of Augustine
        and her stress on the inscrutable supremacy of God's will recall the
        teaching of Archbishop Bradwardine, who opposed Ockham and his
        followers earlier in the century. See Introduction, p. xxiii.

        glanced in Study's direction: Wit means that Will has sought knowledge
        or understanding by too direct and precipitate a route; it is 'wedded'
        inseparably to study or intellectual discipline, and cannot be got by any
        other way.

99   *Clergy*: (or Learning) is wedded to Scripture, an allegorical way of
        saying that the object to which the learned, that is the 'clergy', should
        be devoted is the Word of God: all worldly or secular learning is only a
        means to reaching that end. The Seven Arts leading to the degree of
        Master were the formal arts of the *trivium* (grammar, rhetoric, and
        logic) and the substantial, largely mathematical ones of the *quadrivium*.
        Only then could the student proceed to the study of the Bible in the
        Faculty of Theology. As this was the pursuit of those destined for Holy
        Orders, our clergy, the image of marriage to represent the relationship
        is apt.

        Ask for the main road . . . things: Study's use of 'signpost-allegory' here
        recalls Piers's directions to the pilgrims earlier in Passus V; see pp.
        61-2). Wealth and sex as temptations to fall off from learning are
        appropriately on the *left* side, as was Lady Meed in Passus II (see p.
        15).

        I wrote the Bible for her: Study does not claim authorship of the Bible
        (that is, divine inspiration) only the practical, literary skills that
        enabled it to be written down and transmitted.

100   *the art of dialectic . . . every craft*: Study's activities cover not only philosophy (studied in the higher levels of the Faculty of Arts) but also the practical arts (or crafts), which were learned in the craft-guilds, not the universities.

      theology . . . a hundred difficulties: Study's reservations over theology are due to its being the proper object of Clergy, not of the student in arts, and also to the unease felt at the time about the speculations of more radical thinkers on deep and obscure topics like God's foreknowledge and human free will.

      The man of words . . . art!: Cato's *Distichs*, i. 26, expressing a typical piece of this-worldly prudential morality in contrast with the Christian doctrine of charity that Study recognizes as the basis of theology.

      While we have time . . . faith: Gal. 6: 10, asserting the doctrine of charity at the basis of all Christian learning or 'clergy'.

      Vengeance is mine . . . repay: Deut. 32: 35, but Langland probably has in mind Rom. 12: 19, which quotes it in a context of urging forgiveness of enemies and the repayment of evil by kindness.

101   *see that you love*: an injunction later repeated by Kind in Passus XX (see p. 248).

      a knotty, impenetrable subject: Study wryly acknowledges that the skills she has communicated to men are capable of being used for bad ends. Geomancy is the art of divination by means of earth, dots, and geometrical figures written on the ground. Neither it nor alchemy was, of course, an academic subject, but students trained in the arts sometimes gravitated towards them as a means of making money.

      [Will's] credentials: his having studied the arts and lived a sober and virtuous life while doing so. This accounts for the friendly welcome by Clergy, who recognizes his readiness to embark on the pursuit of Do-well through studying the Scriptures.

      the life of the ordinary person . . . faith: Clergy defines Do-well as belief in God and Christ, Do-better as living out one's belief by charitable acts, and Do-best as actively opposing sin (the last perhaps implying a formal right to do so deriving from Holy Orders).

102   *St Augustine*: his treatise *On the Trinity*, in fifteen books, was completed in AD 417.

      I am in the Father . . . sees the Father also: the first clause of the quotation is John 14: 10, the second 14: 9. An important text for the doctrine of Christ's divinity.

      What is faith worth . . . experience?: the statement that faith is above empirical proof is from another of the four great Western Doctors, Gregory the Great (*c.* 540–604).

      Seem what you . . . be!: from *Homily* 45 on St Matthew, wrongly attributed to St John Chrysostom.

102   *If to blame others . . . bite and snap!*: from a pair of anonymous Latin verses in Leonine form (i.e. hexameters with internal rhyme).

103   *Why do you see a mote . . . First, then, remove . . . eye*: Matt. 7: 3, 5, make a slightly different point from the above—the need not to criticize others' failings when one's own are greater. But Clergy's stance, while not ruling out the possibility of moral satire, is stricter than that of Fidelity in Passus XI, who is, however, speaking of what is permitted to a layman, and who sounds like a layman himself (see p. 114). He is not, however, muzzling criticism as such: as the following critique of priests shows, Clergy, as the spirit of learning and the clerical vocation, is unsparing of faults, and has a right to be.

When the blind lead . . . pit!: Matt. 15: 14, an attack on the Pharisees. The implied comparison with the Christian clergy is disturbing.

the sins of two vicious priests: the account in I Kgs. (1 Sam.) 4 (see esp. 11, 18) tells how Ophni and Phineas, the sons of the priest Heli, were killed in battle and the Ark lost to the Philistines. Heli fell and died when he heard the news. Since the two men had stolen the sacrificial meats, arousing God's wrath, they are an apt warning to the clergy who misuse their privileges through greed.

You thought, wrongly, that I was like you: the words of Ps. 49: 21 are spoken by God, but aptly made a possible affirmation for the just man to adopt. The preceding verses (16–20) deny the right of the unjust man to attack the faults of others.

dumb dogs that don't know how to bark: Isa. 56: 10; this and the following verse, an attack on the Jewish priesthood, are apt as a warning to Christian clergy against sloth and greed. Clergy's argument for the primacy of a holy priesthood anticipates Anima's in Passus XV (see p. 170).

104   *When fish are taken away . . . house to live in*: the passage expresses a widespread traditional idea, and is found in various sources, including ch. 21 of the *Golden Legend*, which Langland draws on in Passus XV (see p. 176), though not in the *Moralia in Job*. Pope Gregory is a suitable authority to invoke, however, since he sent Augustine to England in 597, thereby introducing the Benedictine monastic rule at Canterbury. See also p. 105, 'Gregory's godchildren'.

unless the serving-lad . . . boy?: it was customary for a serving-man to kneel before someone of the rank of knight; see Conscience's reference to this on p. 226.

There are even a number of districts . . . parish: Clergy envisages parishes where the rector was either an absentee or else exploited the income from his living as if he were a secular landlord, without regard to the needs of his parishioners. A number of churches were in the gift of an abbey or greater priory.

But the time is going to come, my monastic friends . . . : this famous threat of possible intervention by the king and the nobility was taken by sixteenth-century Protestant readers as a prophecy of the Reformation. But Clergy has in mind not the dissolution of the monasteries but their reform, something which had happened before in the history of the Church (for example, in the tenth and twelfth centuries). See Introduction, pp. xii, xvii.

105 *Blessed the man . . .* : Ps. 1: 1, which goes on to attack the wicked.

Some sit on horses . . . chains!: Clergy applies Ps. 19: 8–9 to the wealthy monks who ride about like lords.

Constantine's treasure-chest: the emperor Constantine (d. AD 337) endowed the Church with land, something Clergy sees as the original or model of the endowment of monastic orders by lay lords. The monks are Gregory's godchildren in that he was himself a monk before reluctantly agreeing to be made pope. The reference to the friars implies that they will be the first to benefit if the monks *are* dispossessed.

the abbot of Abingdon: Abingdon Abbey was one of the wealthiest in England. The reference to Cain below gives the lines an 'apocalyptic' feel, but the threat none the less sounds more now like a prediction.

How have oppressors come to nought . . . wound: the quotation from Isa. 14: 4–6 refers to the tyranny of the king of Babylon. Clergy wittily identifies the tribute Israel paid him with the tithes and rents paid to the monks, and makes the incurable wound inflicted by Babylon into one which God himself will inflict.

Cain must first bestir himself: Cain is a 'type' of Antichrist, who was expected to return to earth in the last days; but he is not mentioned in the actual description of the latter in Passus XX, and may here simply stand as a general symbol of the disorder and upheaval that are to precede the drastic overhaul of the Church by a reforming king. On 'type', see Introduction, p. xxxvi.

St Paul . . . Heaven: an allusion to 1 Tim. 6: 9–10.

There's no lower object . . . lucre: Ecclus. 10: 10 (the next verse warns of the brevity of earthly power). The quotation from Cato's *Distichs*, iv. 4 is less austere, recognizing the utility as well as the dangers of money.

106 *poverty that's accepted in a spirit of patience*: Clergy here anticipates the teaching of Patience in Passus XIV; see p. 162.

A person who has been baptized is saved . . . poor: Will may allude to 1 Pet. 3: 21 or Gal. 3: 27–9; both texts assert the efficacy of baptism, but not its total sufficiency, a view Scripture promptly contradicts, distinguishing the narrow cases in which baptism *does* suffice, for example, on the point of death, when a non-Christian may in faith ask even another non-Christian to baptize him.

who wished to rise with Christ: Col. 3: 1; cf. also v. 10, which insists on charity; cf. below, 'man . . . is *required* to love'.

106–7 *Never kill any creature made in my image . . . do so*: this is based on Exod. 20: 13, the exceptions envisaged being direct commands such as that to kill Agag instanced by Conscience in Passus III (see p. 31).

107 *Vengeance belongs to me*: from Deut. 32: 35, quoted earlier by Hunger in Passus VI (see p. 71), and shown to be no idle threat by the Samaritan in Passus XVII, especially as punishment for murder (see p. 207).

No one to Heaven . . . descended: John 3: 13, referring in context to Christ himself. It is not a statement about predestination, nor have either Clergy or Scripture mentioned it (both see Do-well rather in terms of charitable action). Will's use of the text, though somewhat wilful, moves the debate from the question of what *doing* well is to that of whether knowledge, and so learning, is necessary for the grace of salvation to be made available. His 'book of life' allusion is to Apoc. (Rev.) 20: 15.

the Church has no doubt that both are in Hell!: Will's conclusion follows from the standard doctrine that baptism was necessary for salvation (see, e.g. John 3: 5); neither Solomon nor Aristotle had, of course, been baptized, and their exceptional intellect therefore tells neither for nor against the possibility of their salvation.

This was the case with Solomon: Will's critique associates his lapse into idolatry (see 3(1) Kgs. 11: 1–11) with desire for wealth, and also with his intellect. His line of thought is perhaps influenced by Col. 3: 5, which identifies greed with idolatry, and his recollection of Study's denunciation of those who value wisdom and knowledge only for the money it can get them (see p. 94).

108 *The scribes and the pharisees . . . Moses*: Matt. 23: 2, where Christ's point is that his hearers should follow what the rabbis or teachers of the Law actually teach, but not what they do; the parallel with the position of the contemporary Christian clergy is clear enough.

what happened in the time of Noah: the story of the 'just and perfect' Noah is in Gen. 6–9. A verse of 1 Pet. 3: 20 (which occurs before that on p. 106 above) is an early instance of the identification of the Christian Church as the New Testament 'antitype' of Noah's ark of salvation. Will's analogical reasoning here, like that of the friar in his parable of the boat in Passus VIII (see pp. 82–3), is rhetorically impressive but theologically suspect.

Men and beasts . . . preserve!: Ps. 35(36): 7; 2 Pet. 3: 10–12 describes the fiery end of the world and another text, Matt. 24: 37–9, also describing the sudden arrival of the last day, explicitly recalls the Flood.

a criminal . . . was the first to be saved: Will alludes to Christ's promise that the thief would be with him in Paradise that day (Luke 23: 43). This gave him 'priority' over the patriarchs and prophets in Hell, from Adam to John the Baptist.

a more heinous act than David: David's murder of Uriah is described in 2 Kgs. (2 Sam.) 11; Mary Magdalen was seen as the archetypal sinner because of the 'seven devils' cast out of her (Mark 16: 9), interpreted as the seven deadly sins; Paul's early persecution of the Christians is described in Acts 7, 9. All were of course *repentant* sinners, and their cases do not argue for or against the value of learning.

109   *There are men . . . God*: Eccl. 9: 1 leaves it as a matter known to God alone how the wise and the just will stand in the world to come.

Nemo bonus . . . good?: Will again twists the sense of the quotation, which is from Luke 18: 19. Christ is contrasting man with God in saying no man is 'good', and even refusing to accept the term of himself.

When you stand on trial . . . say: based on Mark 13: 9, 11; the reference to David is an allusion to Ps. 118(119): 46. Both texts support better than his earlier examples the need for dependence on God's grace rather than one's own intellectual powers.

110   *See how the ignorant . . . below!*: from the *Confessions*, Bk. VIII, ch. 8.

ploughmen, shepherds, . . . people: the mention of 'ploughmen' aligns Will's position here with that of Piers in his dispute with the priest at the end of the Pardon scene in Passus VII (see pp. 78–9), from which 'clergy' in the person of the priest emerged with little credit.

Go into my vineyard!: as used here the quotation from Matt. 20: 4 is bitterly sarcastic in intention: the vineyard is the world of human souls, which are God's 'treasure', over which the clergy have a special responsibility. If, through greed for another kind of treasure, they have neglected their charge, they thereby imperil the 'treasure' of their *own* souls.

111   *Multi multa . . . nesciunt*: the opening of a work formerly ascribed to St Bernard, *Religious Reflections on our Knowledge of Man's Condition* (*PL*, clxxxiv, col. 485). The work belongs to a tradition of thought stemming from St Augustine (cf. Passus X, p. 98 above).

I became so upset . . . I fell asleep: there begins here an 'inner dream' or 'dream-within-a-dream', produced by the shock of strong emotion following Scripture's rebuke. Will is woken from it into the 'outer dream' by a similar experience at the hands of Reason (see end of Passus XI, p. 124).

Fortune: represents the life of vicissitudes subject to every desire and devoid of purpose and stability which results from his failure to pursue learning with self-knowledge and self-discipline. He now strays off the strict path recommended by Study in Passus X (p. 99) and succumbs to the temptations of sensuality and worldliness.

a mirror that was named Middle Earth: The idea of the earth as a mirror in which God's purposes could be studied (*speculum naturae*) was traditional (see Introduction, pp. xxxix–xl). But Langland also seems

to have in mind the notion expressed in Jas. 1: 23–4, that men who
hear the word of God but do not obey it are like those who look in a
mirror and then forget what they look like. The Mirror of the World
thus becomes a source of folly rather than wisdom. Langland's contrast
is between self-indulgence and worldliness on the one hand, pursuit of
the 'law of liberty' (Jas. 1: 25) and 'the will of God' (1 John 2: 17) on
the other. The latter is associated with a proper pursuit of learning.

111   *beautiful young women*: these three characters are personifications of the
vices so named in 1 John 2: 16. The third of them, who is perhaps to
be equated with the character Life in Passus XX (p. 246), is associated
both by Langland and John with Antichrist (see 1 John 2: 18).

Old Age: here gives Will a warning which is to be realized in Passus
XX (p. 247), the failure of sexual power being particularly mentioned.

112   *Recklessness*: a passing *ad hoc* personification of Will's impulse to care
nothing for the future; not bad in himself, he has an insouciance that
borders dangerously on presumption.

Plato the poet . . . God disposes: the word 'poet' here means 'literary
authority' (though Plato was in fact the author of some poems), as on
p. 99 above (cf. p. 250). The phrase was proverbial, and close in sense
to Prov. 16: 9.

Childishness: another passing personification, here the irresponsibility
into which Recklessness can degenerate.

Holiness: occurs nowhere else as a personified character but was
thought of as especially appropriate to mature and later life.

my inseparable companion for a good forty-five years: on the simplest
reading, the reference to forty-five years implies that Will went astray
in young adulthood (say at 21, at the end of a university course in arts
and on the brink of studying theology) and has now reached about 65,
an advanced old age in this period. The sense on p. 126 may be
different; in the present passage Will is dreaming of himself as having
grown old, a condition he actually reaches in Passus XX.

penance that's paid . . . sense: a maxim of Canon Law found in the
fifteenth-century canonist William of Lyndwood's *Constitutio*.

113   *I'd heard Conscience say . . . baptized*: not an allusion to an earlier
passage, but a mere parenthesis appealing to Conscience's authority for
support.

hearing confessions and conducting funerals: implying that both offered
hopes of monetary reward, for example, as an incentive to 'easy'
absolution or as a gift or legacy from the dead person's relatives.

Contrition by itself . . . For unless you are born again . . . Heaven: the first
quotation is a common theological maxim which hints that confession
may not be as necessary for salvation as baptism. The second, from
John 3: 5, states the unconditional necessity of baptism for salvation.

Honest Fidelity: ('Lewte' in the original) appears only here as a character (and, fleetingly, in the trial of Meed; see Passus IV, p. 40, where the name may be translated as 'Loyalty' in the context). The quality signified is highly esteemed by Langland, since Lewte is Holy Church's Lover (p. 15) and one of the Magi's gifts to Christ (gold) on p. 228, where its synonym is Righteousneess. Langland here seems to have in mind the personal integrity of a man, a moral rather than a legal concept.

114   *Harbour no voiceless rancour . . . day*: Lev. 19: 17, and no such sentiment is found in the Epistles of Peter (but cf. 1 Pet. 1: 22 on brotherly love). But there may be an allusion to 1 Tim. 5: 20, which gives as a reason for publicly rebuking sin 'that the rest also may have fear', whereas Leviticus says 'lest you incur sin through him' (that is, share his guilt by tacit complicity in wrongdoing). Possibly, too, Langland has in mind Gal. 2: 11, Paul's opposition to Peter at Jerusalem 'because he was to be blamed'.

Do not judge . . . judged: Matt. 7: 1, expressing one of the fundamental principles of Christian moral teaching as found in the Sermon on the Mount. The following verses were quoted earlier in Passus X (p. 103). Langland here enunciates the central dilemma of the moral satirist.

Don't harbour silent grievance . . . brother: the quotation from Lev. 19: 17 is repeated, Langland clearly regarding the sentiment (and so, presumably, the words) as Pauline.

You thought, . . . you: the psalm quotation (Ps. 49(50): 21) has appeared earlier in full in Passus X (see p. 103), where the rest of the verse provides authority for rebuke of others.

if the subject that's involved is somebody's sin: this alludes to the secrecy of the confessional or to confidential knowledge (for example, on the part of bishops) of some secret sin or scandal.

It's better to feel sorry . . . right: Fidelity's recommendation to put up with wrongs anticipates that of Reason a little later when he himself rebukes Will for his unwillingness to 'suffer' (that is, tolerate) faults (p. 123).

Praise little—and blame less!: this is a proverbial phrase attributed to Seneca by Vincent of Beauvais.

her theme . . . and her text: the text Scripture draws on is Matt. 22: 14, the conclusion of the parable of the wedding feast.

115   *My thoughts went back to Holy Church*: alludes to p. 10; but Holy Church had not told Will that baptism guaranteed salvation by itself.

All you who are thirsty . . . waters: Isa. 55: 1, echoed in Apoc. (Rev.) 21: 6, 22: 17. Langland may have in mind the idea of Christ's redeeming blood as 'feeding' all Christians (sacramentally in the Eucharist), as in Repentance's prayer after the confessions of the Deadly Sins in Passus V (see p. 59 and note). But the sacrament in mind *here* seems to be baptism, and he may be alluding to the traditional patristic interpretation of the water flowing from Christ's side together with blood (John 19: 34) as symbolizing respectively baptism and the Eucharist. This seems confirmed by what he says below.

115   *The man who believes ... saved!*: Mark 16: 16 promises rather than guarantees salvation, but Will takes baptism as a sufficient, not just a necessary, condition for this.

even if a Christian wanted to renounce his faith . . . : Will's comparison of a lapsed Christian to a runaway serf holds good in theory, but in point of fact is strained: although at this period it would have been difficult to renounce Christianity formally without severe social penalties it was all too possible to disregard its practical demands, and a runaway serf could obtain his freedom by remaining undetected in a free borough for a year and a day, as many did.

His tender mercies ... works: Ps. 144(145): 9 has a different meaning in context—(see p. 52 above and note).

116   *someone who had broken out from Hell*: the speech of Trajan extends from here to p. 122 without interruption, and includes digressive comments which are not especially appropriate to him but which are generally apt to a figure endowed with his supernatural authority. Trajan, here an exemplar of integrity and justice ('lewte' and 'truthe'), was emperor AD 98–117, and represents the possibility of salvation without baptism. Pope St Gregory is supposed to have been so moved by Trajan's just life that his prayers and tears for the emperor resulted in the latter's release from Hell. Trajan's outburst against 'books' (of which Scripture is aptly the custodian) is a dramatic way of asserting that it is not knowledge of the truth so much as a *life* of 'truth' (that is, good works and integrity) that counts in the end. In the dialectical argument of the poem it is meant to stand as a limiting case, not as a standard or norm.

the Legends of the Saints: the very popular *Golden Legend*, a collection of lives of the saints by the thirteenth-century archbishop of Genoa, Jacobus a Voragine, gives the details. It is a work Langland draws on again later (see p. 176).

117   *Without love ... law isn't worth a straw!*: Trajan's argument, which had earlier been about 'truthe' (a virtue he properly embodied) now becomes one about *love*, which for Langland is closely associated with 'truthe' (see esp. Holy Church's words on p. 12).

The man ... remains dead: John 3: 14, here echoes Holy Church's citation of Jas. 2: 26 at the end of Passus I (see p. 13). John has been speaking about loving the brethren, something not especially apt to Trajan, who, while not actively persecuting Christians, was certainly no friend to them. But Langland may be recalling earlier v. 10, which makes a pregnant link between 'truthe' and love: 'Whosoever is not *just* is not of God, nor he that loveth not his brother.' This will have enabled him to see justice as somehow 'one with' love or charity in practice, though conceptually to be distinguished from it, justice being a virtue of reason and charity a fruit of supernatural grace.

Jesus Christ . . . in the guise of poor people?: alludes to Christ's words in Matt. 25: 35 ff., that charity shown to the poor and humble is to be taken at the Last Judgement as an act of love shown towards Christ himself.

we should not invite our own relatives . . . my sake: the quotation is taken from and develops Luke 14: 12, and has especial force as an address to the rich and powerful from one who was himself both in life.

118 *nobles . . . by birth*: 1 Pet. 2: 2, from a passage on the 'royal' condition of those redeemed by Christ.

He who sins becomes . . . sin: John 8: 34, where Christ is answering the Jews' claim that they are *not* slaves and so do not need to be freed. Trajan's argument is that everyone has in a sense been made equal through being redeemed by Christ (that is, all were 'slaves' of sin, now all are 'free', with no further inequalities counting from henceforth). It is not a claim for social equality but for responsibility to be shown by the rich towards their poorer brethren.

Bear one another's burdens: Gal. 6: 2 refers in context to moral support rather than material (cf. the teaching of Jas. 2: 15–17, 5: 9).

her faith would save her: (Luke 7: 50), in Latin in the original, which emphasizes the special relevance of this lesson for the learned.

recorded in St John: in fact from Matt. 7: 2 (no parallel in John).

119 *Better to examine . . . things*: not from Gregory but attributed to Augustine by Peter Lombard, and also occurs in ch. 5 of the pseudo-Bernardine work quoted at the beginning of Passus XI (see note to p. 111, 'Multi multa . . . ').

when he was on the way to Emmaus: Luke 24: 13–33; no reason is given for the disciples' failure to recognize Jesus.

For we are all pilgrims: that is, 'wanderers (from our true home, Heaven)', as in Heb. 13: 14; the contrast with the professional pilgrim encountered in Passus V (see p. 59 ff.) could not be stronger. Trajan's description looks forward to that of the character Patience, who appears first in Passus XIII (see p. 138 below).

St John the Baptist . . . asked for alms: a conjectural inference; Matt. 3: 4 tells against the idea. The following reference to Mary's family is also an inference; both Matthew (ch. 1, esp. v. 16) and Luke (1: 27) make Joseph a descendant of David.

When Martha made that great complaint . . . Magdalen: the story comes from Luke 10: 38–42; Mary the sister of Lazarus was commonly identified with Mary of Magdala on the basis of John 11: 2 (alluding to Luke 7: 38 ‖ Matt. 26: 7). She became a type of the contemplative life, as in Anima's reference to her on p. 176, which draws on the account in the *Golden Legend*. Here, by inference, it is *poverty* that receives the praise owed strictly to contemplation, because it is the material condition necessary for the latter. The phrase 'the best part' is the reading of the Vulgate and the one familiar to Langland; the Greek original has 'good'.

119   *every wise man . . . praises poverty*: the theme which is to dominate Passus XIV and play an important part in the final section of the work.

120   *Poor, I can play . . . brood*: from the twelfth-century rhetorician Alexander of Villedieu.

    Give me neither poverty nor wealth: the text of Prov. 30: 8 actually reads 'beggary' for 'poverty', and goes on to warn against the moral dangers attendant on each of the two extremes—denial of God through pride and dishonesty resulting from dire need. Both views are to find illustration in Passus XX; but here Langland is concerned to set up a tense contrast between the classic Old Testament view of moderation as virtue and the eschatological Christian vision of radical perfection through renouncing all for God.

    As St Luke testifies: actually from Matt. 19: 21, Christ's reply to the rich young man. It concludes with a promise of treasure in Heaven and an invitation to become his follower; but the following verses warn against the extreme difficulty of winning Heaven if one is rich. When the disciples ask who *can* be saved, Christ replies with a variant of the second quotation, but for 'one who wills it' has 'God'. See also Matt. 17: 19.

    As David says . . . Nothing is impossible . . . Those who seek . . . thing: the first alludes to Ps. 36(37): 25 (the preceding verse of which is to be quoted later in the Tree of Charity scene in Passus XVI: see p. 189); the third quotes from Ps. 33(34): 11, contrasting the fate of the poor man who seeks God with that of the rich who do not. On the second, see previous note.

    Judge me . . . sinner's: Ps. 42(43): 1, especially apt in context as this was the psalm said by the priest at the beginning of mass.

    Trust in the Lord: Ps. 36(37): 3, a psalm given over to affirming that God will support the just and destroy the wicked, and warning against envying the apparent prosperity of the latter.

    The very claim . . . position: this point concerns not dependence on God but rather being content with one's lot and not seeking to exploit one's clerical state for financial gain. Langland affirms that a man would not have been ordained to the priesthood without a guarantee of his upkeep from a patron, spiritual or lay (this was his 'title' and should protect him from indigence).

121   *the resources befitting the status of a knight*: this passage doubtless reflects a decline in the calibre of priests following the ravages of the plague, which killed off nearly 60 per cent of the clergy. The analogy drawn

with knighthood has its dangers, but Langland presumably wishes to ensure that priests are not led into bad ways through lack of either financial or personal qualifications. The explanation for this comes later in Passus XV, where Anima traces the moral and spiritual decline of the community to the 'rottenness' of the clergy (see p. 170).

a legal document is open to challenge . . . left out: the second comparison of bad priests is to incompetent scriveners. Langland doubtless had personal experience of the copying of legal documents, a means of supplementing his income as himself a clerk without benefice. The application of the quotation from Jas. 2: 10, 'He who offends in one point . . .', to incompetence in saying the services is neatly done, as is that of Ps. 46(47): 7–8. Both texts have in mind, of course, a proper spiritual attitude in morality and worship respectively; but he characteristically refuses to dissociate this from precision and exactness in following liturgical rubrics, the 'letter of the law'.

knights of God: the notion of priests as 'knights of God' echoes Holy Church's earlier description in Passus I of the archangels as the 'knights of God' (see p. 11). Trajan's attack on clerical greed likewise echoes her similar onslaught at the end of Passus I (see p. 14).

ignorancia . . . ignoramus-priests!: that in question is bishops' ignorance of their ordinands' lack of learning as well as the latter ignorance itself.

122 *Kind*: God thought of as the creative principle immanent in the universe, the source of both life and death (as appears from Wit's description of his nature in Passus IX (p. 86) and that of his activities in Passus XX (see p. 244). Visions of the earth's plenitude owe much to the tradition of thought associated with the School of Chartres and with twelfth-century Latin poets such as Alan of Lille (*The Complaint of Nature*).

Reason followed all the animals . . . procreated: the aspect of Reason foremost here is that of the divine law or purpose (*ratio*) embodied in the disposition of the natural world.

123 *breath through their bills*: the billing of pigeons before mating.

you don't accompany man and his mate . . . misfortune: Will has in mind above all the human tendency to excess, that departure from 'mesure' (moderation) which leads to so many ills and was first denounced by Holy Church in Passus I.

Who has more to put up with than God?: Reason here argues for the virtue soon to be encountered embodied in the pilgrim Patience. The divine patience or 'sufferance' has a long-term, if sometimes obscure, *purpose* and is therefore in accord with 'reason'. Reason contrasts Providence with the short-sighted behaviour of men, who resort to revenge and other means of 'putting things right' that only cause more harm.

For the sake of God . . . creature: 1 Pet. 2: 13; the preceding and following verses are also relevant to the argument here.

124   *Patience is a pretty virtue ... well*: the proverbial verses (in French) express a thought close to that of the scriptural passage.

Do not strive ... concern: the quoted verse is Ecclus. 11: 9; the thought of the passage also draws on vv. 2 and 7.

And God saw all that he had made ... good: Gen. 1: 31.

for the benefit of man, ... temptation: Reason's reply is deliberately provocative in its paradoxical assertion of the goodness of creation and the flawed nature of man; he is assuming Will's familiarity with the notion that the Fall has predisposed human nature towards going wrong.

No one from fault lives free: *Distichs of Cato*, i. 5.

I immediately blushed, overcome with shame: the violent access of emotion wakes Will out of the 'inner dream' he had fallen into on p. 111 through a similar experience and returns him to the calmer, more discursive ambience of the outer dream that lies nearer to the everyday world of waking reality.

125   *and grasped yet more by means of Reason*: if Will had pursued his studies in the proper spirit of patient enquiry he would have grown in understanding of the principles and natures (*rationes*) of things.

Had you but held your tongue ... become: the quotation is adapted from Boethius' *Consolation of Philosophy*, II, prose 7, 74–6.

the accusation of being proud and presumptuous: the speaker's blunt and abrasive language exemplifies the verbal equivalent of the humiliation which the drunkard undergoes on rising from the ditch. Will comes to accept that his own impassioned outbursts have been the equivalent, in a clerk, of the sot's bouts of drunkenness.

126   *Imaginative*: the 'vertu imaginatif' (*vis imaginativa*), in medieval faculty-psychology the power of forming images of things past or to come, from which the intellect can draw more general ideas by a process of abstraction. It thus covers both memory and our 'imagination' (in both the creative and speculative/anticipatory senses).

for the last forty-five years: the reference here, occurring in the outer dream of the third vision, may be an accurate statement of Will's imagined age—at the peak of 'middle life', the time of crisis and final decision (cf. p. 112 and note, 'my inseparable companion').

If not in the first watch ... second: Luke 12: 38 alludes in context to the Second Coming of Christ or, in terms of the individual's destiny, the moment of his death, when he will meet God for judgement. The three watches of the night were customarily interpreted as the three ages of man—youth, middle age, and old age respectively.

Those whom I love, I chastise!: Apoc. (Rev.) 3: 19 (echoing Prov. 3: 12), a warning against religious lukewarmness and an exhortation to repent before it is too late (cf. previous note). The view of the plague and other disasters here is the same as that of Reason in his sermon to the people in Passus V. The interpretation of 'Although you beat me . . .' (from Ps. 22(23): 4) is somewhat unexpected, but is being adapted to fit in with the first.

busy saying your Psalter, . . . eat!: alludes to Will's occupation as a chantry clerk, saying psalms for the souls of the dead and receiving some payment from their relatives for doing so.

pairs of friars enough . . . to!: Imaginative, in accordance with his nature as defined in note above, both *recalls* the friars of Passus VIII and *looks forward* to those of Passus XIII; both sets give definitions of the three Do's.

find a place for pleasure . . . pursuits: *Distichs of Cato*, iii. 6.

127 *In one of his epistles*: 1 Cor. 13: 13. The trusty loyal faith below, shown in obedience to the commandments, is 'lewte' in the original.

Rocamadour: (in Lot, France), a famous pilgrimage shrine of our Lady.

Job, among the Jews: Job is out of place in this list of those who died in sin despite their great natural endowments. The pagan four represent respectively philosophy, medicine, literature, and earthly rule. Langland draws on medieval traditions that each died a violent and unholy death, and all are cited as examples of excessive self-esteem based on their outstanding gifts.

Felice's loveliness . . . her: Felice is the unhappy heroine of *Guy of Warwick*, a popular romance; Rosamund was Henry II's mistress, allegedly poisoned by Queen Eleanor, and buried at Godstow, near Oxford.

Though eloquent . . . laws!: a Latin epigram of Godfrey of Winchester.

Give, and you shall receive: the positive injunction from Luke 6: 38 comes after warnings against judging and condemning, and an exhortation to forgive.

128 *Those who know God's will . . . rods!*: adapted from Luke 12: 47, and here applies to the possession of learning or intellectual gifts; verse 48 is also relevant (on the need to give an account of the use to which we have put our natural gifts).

puffs up the soul: 1 Cor. 8: 1, which concludes 'but charity edifies'.

the Spirit . . . will: John 3: 8, from Christ's discussion with the learned Pharisee Nicodemus, implying (cf. v. 10) that the truth of the Gospel may be less easily apprehended by the learned than by the simple; for the rest, the general sense is that intended by such beatitudes as the first (Matt. 5: 3), the common interpretation of which was the humble whose hearts are not set on riches.

We speak what we know . . . seen: John 3: 11 is Christ's affirmation that his teaching comes from God directly.

128   *No one knows where the spirit . . . goes*: from John 3: 8, completing the earlier quotation. Langland however gives this text his own idiosyncratic twist, taking the references as distinguishing two types of knowledge, that derived from divine revelation (and embodied in Scripture, hence in the keeping of the learned or clergy) and that coming from direct observation or experience (natural knowledge of practical earthly matters). To contrast the first and not just the second of these with grace is firmly to restrict the pretensions of learning, but also to lay a basis for a defence of the latter if it is inspired and accompanied by charity.

  Moses bears witness . . . adultery: in Lev. 20: 10, which actually specifies stoning not just for the woman but for the adulterous man, too. The New Testament account of the woman taken in adultery is in John 8: 1–11, verse 5 directly citing the passage from Leviticus. St Jerome's interpretation (that Christ's wrote in the sand the sins of the woman's accusers) was widely accepted. It is an odd understanding of 'learning', since Christ's knowledge presumably is not of the kind others could have had; but Langland's use of 'clergie' covers the knowledge of how to write ('literacy') as well as knowledge of a higher sort. But he may also have had in mind Augustine's reference to Christ as the divine lawgiver, writing down the new law of mercy with his own finger as God had done on the stone tablets given to Moses (Homily 33 on St John's Gospel, vii. 6).

129   *how could bread become the body of Christ . . . learning?*: refers to the learning necessary for ordination as a priest. Langland goes on to allude to the warning in 1 Cor. 11: 27–30 against receiving Holy Communion unworthily (that is, while still unconfessed and in a state of sin). The comparison of learning to a mirror echoes Paul's advice to judge ourselves in order not to be judged by God (verse 31) and the image in Jas. 1: 22–4 alluded to at the opening of Passus XI (see p. 111 and note 'a mirror . . .').

  never disparage logic: Imaginative obliquely answers Trajan's point on p. 117, agreeing with him in substance, but recognizes that learning has its uses, whatever the defects of individuals who have it, and that properly pursued it is of great spiritual benefit.

  a blind man . . . armed into battle: alludes to the blind King John of Bohemia who was killed at the Battle of Crécy in 1346.

  There's no more chance . . . axe?: Imaginative's contention is not a contradiction of Trajan's: there *is* a chance, however, slight, that a blind man could hit an enemy in battle, and the case of Trajan is a unique, isolated instance of the spirit breathing wheresoever he will— that is, of divine grace being specially granted without direct acquaintance with Christian doctrine, possibly as a sign of the ultimate and absolute dependence of salvation on the free will (*potentia absoluta*) of an omnipotent God. But the *typical* case is of such knowledge being acquired by learning it from those who possess it—that is, the clergy.

130   *the Ark of the Covenant*: its care was entrusted to the Levites (Num. 1:
      50–1), and Saul was punished for daring to perform the sacrifice, a
      task preserved in early Old Testament times to the Levites (1 Kgs. (1
      Sam.) 13: 12). Oza, son of Abinadab, touched the ark in order to
      steady it but was struck dead by God (2 Kgs. (2 Sam.) 6: 6–7).
      Langland thinks of the Christian priesthood as the New Testament
      equivalent of the tribe of Levi: anyone who usurps their prerogatives
      will be punished by God. In this he differs sharply from Wyclif, who
      held that bad priests forfeited their sacramental powers.

      Do not lay hands . . . anointed!: Ps. 104(105): 15 refers to the immediate
      descendants of Abraham, but Langland here intends the priesthood,
      the sacrament of orders involving an act of anointing. Imaginative's
      warning is to be repeated to Will by Patience in Passus XIII (see p.
      140).

      Why, even knights . . . clergy: refers to the religious elements in the
      ceremony of knighting which had become an integral part of the
      conferring of this 'order'—the vigil at the altar, the ritual bath, the
      mass.

131   *For the wisdom . . . God*: 1 Cor. 3: 19 refers not to the natural
      knowledge of the pagans but to worldly wisdom or philosophy which
      gives an inadequate account of man's nature and end. But Langland
      was doubtless aware of a long tradition of hostility to Greek learning,
      especially Aristotelian science, which dated back to the early Fathers of
      the Church and was still not dead in his day.

      the Holy Spirit will come down: Imaginative's prophecy (of what has
      already been fulfilled in history but is yet to come in Will's vision)
      echoes Holy Church's account of the Incarnation (see p. 12).

      Shepherds there were speaking . . . there came wise men . . . East: The
      story of the shepherds is from Luke 2: 14–15, and 2: 7 (the inn), that
      of the Magi from Matt. 2. It may be these Langland intends by 'sages',
      where the original has 'poetes', although possibly he also had in mind
      the supposedly 'Messianic' Fourth Eclogue of Virgil (this seems
      unlikely given the critical view of the latter on p. 127 above) or the
      notion of shepherds as 'poets' deriving from recollection that David,
      the poet of the Psalms, had been a shepherd. The curious remark
      about the inn doubtless affirms that Jesus's family were not beggars:
      they were at least *seeking* a room at the inn, as beggars would not have.
      Post-scriptural tradition made the Magi kings as well, and this is the
      way he presents them in Passus XIX (p. 238), where they offer Christ
      the richest of earthly gifts. But here he suppresses this aspect in order
      to conjoin the wise with the humble ('poor in spirit') in contrast to the
      rich, powerful and worldly wise.

      This is what you said: Imaginative paraphrases and summarizes Will's
      argument at the end of Passus X (see esp. p. 110).

131–2 *Suppose you were to take . . . watery death?*: Imaginative's exemplum
      recalls that of the friar in Passus VIII (see pp. 82–3) in form but not in

spirit. He now urges the direct spiritual value of learning where there is a right disposition to use it.

132 *Blessed are those . . . over*: Ps. 31(32): 1, but v. 5 is also relevant, since it mentions acknowledgement of one's sinfulness to *oneself*, something Langland associates with contrition and distinguishes from the formal act of confession to a priest. His stress on the importance of sorrow for sin echoes that of the confessor Repentance to Envy in Passus V (p. 46) which the latter, a typically 'ignorant' sinner, comically misunderstands.

until Lent arrives: alludes to the obligation to make confession at least once a year, particularly during Lent, an obligation taken only in its minimal sense by Langland's ignorant sinner.

and when the . . . blind: Matt. 15: 14 (and parallel, Luke 6: 39).

Dominus . . . meae: Ps. 15(16): 5 which aptly begins 'Preserve me, O Lord'. Ability to read a psalm-verse enabled a man to claim benefit of clergy and so escape execution after a first conviction for certain offences. The gallows were at Tyburn, in the Edgware Road near Marble Arch.

Now, as for the thief . . . on Good Friday: the purpose of this passage is not to disparage the Good Thief's faith but to counter Will's tendency to an extremist position which can easily become a form of moral minimalism ('If last-minute repentance is sufficient, then why is any more necessary?'). Imaginative does not mean that the thief, once saved, is still in danger of losing Heaven; rather that the repentant sinner, once forgiven, should not rest content with the fact but actively strive after holiness. Langland's stress on hierarchy in Heaven is at one with the traditional view of such as Dante, and reflects the importance he attaches to good works (contrast the author of *Pearl*, who stresses the notion of the absolute sufficiency of grace).

133 *saints Simon and Jude*: apostles who share the same feast day, described in the *Golden Legend* as having undergone martyrdom together in Babylonia.

Never feel free . . . forgiven!: Ecclus. 5: 5. The whole chapter warns against presumption, and verse 8 specifically against putting off repentance.

God renders . . . works . . . why did it seem . . . should be!: Ps. 61(62): 13, and an adaptation of Ps. 134(135): 6 (cf. also Ps. 113b(115): 3). They are complementary in their doctrine: the one stresses God's justice, the other his mercy. Imaginative leaves open the question of why grace is given to some but not others; he rests on God's absolute power and right. An explanation is offered later by the Samaritan in Passus XVII, who argues that mercy is shown to the merciful (see p. 205), and by Christ in Passus XVIII, who claims the right to show mercy to those whose sin is in any way mitigated (p. 223). At this point, Imaginative is concerned to produce in Will a proper sense of wonder and awe before God in order to counteract his earlier presumption.

134   *has ever known the cause of all this*: Imaginative's outburst is not an attack on the desire for scientific knowledge as such but rather a reminder that the answer to the question 'Why?' is known to God (Kind) alone, because it is not a scientific question at all.

why didn't Adam . . . body?: an example of the kind of triviality into which even a legitimate scientific curiosity can degenerate if not governed by reverence and theological good sense.

the peacock's plumage . . . plucked: the pence and nobles seem apt images suggested by the medallion-like markings on the peacock's tail-feathers.

135   *Avienus*: a generic name for a collection of fables, after the fourth-century Latin fable-writer. The peacock as emblem of the rich is found in a fable in Robert's *Fables Inédits* (no. 39), but the detail of the feet has not been traced.

Aristotle: in the *History of Animals*, IX. 25, he notes that the lark is edible, but does not make this didactic comparison.

There's no written authority . . . Solomon: Imaginative implicitly contrasts our ignorance about their fate with our knowledge of the salvation of Trajan (recorded in the *Golden Legend* and elsewhere).

all the Christian authorities . . . faith: the prime authority is John 3: 3, which affirms the necessity of baptism for salvation.

Salvabitur vix . . . salvabitur!: the first part of the quotation is adapted from 1 Pet. 4: 17–18. Imaginative's conclusion is logically entailed in the scriptural text, and his subsequent distinction between three types of baptism follows scholastic practice, taking into account the context of the authority cited, which makes clear that 'just man' here means 'believing Christian' (see vv. 13–17). It was held that in addition to ordinary baptism there was a baptism of blood undergone by the martyr ('witness to Christ') who might not have had the chance of formal baptism, and a baptism of fire (through a direct infusion of grace into a soul, generating the faith, and thence the hope and love, necessary to ensure salvation). The relevance of this last notion to the case of Trajan has been doubted, given the varying accounts of the manner in which he was saved through Pope Gregory's prayers and tears, and Imaginative does not elaborate the point. Instead he seems to rely implicitly on the notion of God's absolute power as able to suspend the normal workings of his dispensation (his 'ordained power'). Precisely how this is to be understood is one of the 'whys and wherefores' he has earlier rebuked Will for pursuing (p. 133 above). Langland's theological position here has been described as 'semi-Pelagian', that is, allowing an important role to righteousness of life in achieving salvation, while at the same time relying on the *ultimate* working of divine grace to make such righteousness both possible and meritorious—the 'absolute power' referred to in such quotations as that on p. 133, 'Because his will was it should be!' (though in Trajan's case the quotation preceding this, 'God renders to everyone according

to his works', tells in his favour and not against him: Langland sees the
emperor as the converse of the Good Thief).

135   *There came a divine fire . . . illumination*: from a Pentecost antiphon,
referring to the descent of the Holy Spirit in the form of fire at
Pentecost (Acts 2: 3) which illuminated the minds of the apostles,
enabling them to preach the Gospel in foreign tongues. But the
connection of this notion with that of the spirit illuminating the mind
so as to *arouse* faith doubtless derives from Matt. 3: 11, where the
Baptist foretells that Christ will baptize 'in the Holy Spirit and fire'.

136   *Now, consider the righteousness . . . principles*:the difficult argument here
may be summarized as follows: if a man lives justly without knowledge
of Christ (and the case of Trajan shows this to be *possible*) his spiritual
condition must imply a readiness to believe in revealed truth should it
ever be made known to him, since the effect of such belief is the same
righteousness he already displays (by a mysterious operation of God's
grace, the 'spirit that breathes where it will' of John 3: 8 (see p. 128)).
'Justice' and 'faith' are not identical concepts, but there is a 'homology'
or inner congruence between them, as suggested by the key Pauline
text 'the just man lives by faith' (Rom. 1: 17, Gal. 3: 11), which draws
on Hab. 2: 4, and which Paul employs to contrast the faith of Abraham
(which 'justified' him) with the Law. Langland's reasoning seems to
be: if faith makes a man just, then mustn't a man who is just have a
kind of (implicit) faith that is making him just (otherwise how could he
be just)? In that case, there is a further virtue implied in a just man's
righteousness—the second 'theological' virtue, hope, even if he has no
direct knowledge of Christ on which to found that hope. He must,
therefore, have a tacit *will* to be saved and, as Conscience is to remark
in Passus XIII, 'good will is a treasure beyond price' (p. 144), a
thought anticipated by Imaginative at p. 136 below.

The word DEUS does . . . to the faithful: the ingenious *interpretatio* of
the four letters making up the name of God in Latin (DEUS) is found
in a gloss in a manuscript of the *Laborintus* by the thirteenth-century
rhetorical writer Everard the German; it was presumably fairly well
known.

Though I should walk . . . fear: Ps. 22(23): 4, but the preceding verse,
'He hath led me on the paths of justice' and also verse 6, 'And thy
mercy will follow me . . .' are crucial for the argument being developed
here. Though walking in the darkness or shadow of ignorance, the just
pagan Trajan has been *led* in righteousness by God and so will be
followed by his mercy (that is, saved).

Intellect and wisdom . . . human!: there is an element of paradox in
Imaginative's conclusion: although he has been arguing from Trajan's
case that *knowledge* of Christian truth ('clergie') is not unconditionally
necessary for salvation, it is precisely such knowledge that has made it
possible for him to argue the case at all—that is, to see in Trajan's

justice the lineaments of an implicit faith which can save him. The result is to leave Will no choice but to accept the value and importance of learning, while at the same time having acquired a deeper grasp of the complexity of its nature, its connection with humility and love, and the need to preserve it from corruption by desire for material advantage.

137   *I found myself brooding deeply about this dream* . . . : this passage summarizes much of the content of Passūs XI and XII. Interestingly, the vision of Kind's generosity at p. 122 is ascribed to the power of Imaginative, although strictly it is only Kind's role as instructor that he speaks of (in Passus XII, p. 134). Langland seems to have considered the ability to appreciate God's immanent presence and action in the natural world as a special preserve of what we would now call 'imagination'.

I accepted promptly: is Will's eagerness to come due to the fact that Conscience invites him or that he is to meet Clergy ('Learning')? Certainly, his new attitude to the latter must be the result of his instruction at the hands of Imaginative.

138   *Patience was standing*: Patience is presented as a wandering solitary or pilgrim hermit (*eremita peregrinus*), a person devoted to a life of prayer and drawing his meagre subsistence from alms given by lay-people and clergy. If Conscience is identical with the important character in the first vision, then he may be regarded as a representative of the pious members of the knightly class who were anxious to fulfil their social role properly and support the Church and those in need.

the most distinguished person present: the degree of doctor in the highest of the faculties was the pinnacle of academic distinction; the title was bound to call to mind the leading authorities of the day, who shared their name with that of the canonized Doctors of the Church, some of whom are to be named.

a variety of dishes: those served at this banquet are spiritual ones, texts from scripture and the Fathers which dramatically embody the precept of Christ to live by 'every word that proceeds from the mouth of God' (Matt. 4: 4).

they ate and drank . . . had: Luke 10: 7 forms in context part of Christ's mission-instructions to his disciples and refers to literal food. The rest of the verse constitutes a tacit rebuke to friars who *did* 'remove from house to house' (along with other ill-defined categories of mendicant).

no ordinary meat . . . fare: the allegory boldly mingles literal and metaphorical kinds of food and eating, on the basis that the friars' luxurious habits are paid for by wrongdoers in return for easy absolution. But all will have to be paid for on Judgement Day (*post mortem*): the food will leave 'a bitter after-taste' (Pearsall).

You who sup . . . agony!: the source of this quotation remains unidentified.

138   *Do Penance . . . perseverance*: penance and perseverance in prayer and
       virtuous acts are appropriate sustenance for a pilgrim-hermit; both
       spirit and tone here recall the resolve of Piers in Passus VII after
       receiving the pardon, and a link is forged between Piers and the
       character Patience (see p. 79).

139   *Blessed are those . . . Blessed the man . . . Those whose sins . . . ; I said, I
       will confess . . . Lord*: all from Ps. 31(32), the second penitential psalm
       (respectively vv. 1, 2, 1, 5) with the 'Have mercy . . .' (Ps. 50(51): 1),
       the fourth penitential psalm. These expressions of trust and
       reassurance are apt to one who has made his confession (the 'covered
       dish' alludes to the secrecy of the confessional).

       All who are holy . . . time: Ps. 31(32): 6.

       A contrite and humble heart . . . despise: from the *Miserere*, Ps. 50: 19(51:
       17), the best-known penitential psalm and one constantly 'in the
       mouth' of the devout man who seeks to do well.

       Woe to you mighty drinkers of wine!: Isa. 5: 22; the following verse is
       especially apt, as it can be read as an allusion to 'easy absolution' of sin
       in return for payment, and hence to the perpetuation of injustice.

       the dean of St Paul's: on St Paul's Cross, a great preaching-place, see
       note to p. 96.

       In hunger and thirst . . . fratribus: from 2 Cor. 24–7; the last verse is left
       in Latin, as is that below, which is not from St Paul but is an inference
       drawn from the Pauline text about the danger in false 'brothers'
       (punning on 'friars', the literal meaning of which was 'brothers'). Both
       texts are translated together at the foot of the page. Langland's point is
       that the friars find this text an uncomfortable one to preach on, since
       their opponents are all too ready to turn the scriptural reference to
       false 'brothers' against those who bear that name as an order.

140   *Master Jordan Jeroboam*: may allude to a contemporary Dominican
       friar named William Jordan; but Langland's satire on the whole does
       not work in this way, and more probably the reference to a 'jordan'
       (chamber-pot), like that to the 'bottle-belly' (here rendered
       'Jeroboam'), is a transparent description of obvious meaning.

       the Apocalypse of Golias . . . Life . . . of St Avereys: the *Apocalypse*,
       attributed to Walter Map, has a description of greedy abbots. Various
       explanations have been suggested for the name 'Avereys', including
       Aurea, Avoya, and the Moslem philosopher Averrhoes. Possibly
       Langland was inventing an imaginary 'St Avarice' (= Greed), like St
       Truth in Passus V (see p. 60).

       his companion: the Doctor presumably has another friar as his
       companion, like the one who speaks in Passus VIII (friars usually
       travelled in pairs). The 'trinity' or triad referred to is the three Do's
       (Do-well, Do-better and Do-best), and the implication is that the friars
       have a written source somewhere which claims that all three are to be
       found in their order. This is an expanded form of the criticism made in

Passus VIII, where the Franciscan claims that Do-well lives with them (see p. 82).

141 *'Do-well?'... what he preaches*: the Doctor's account drives a dangerous wedge between knowing what is right and doing it, of which he seems oblivious. The effect is once again to call in question the moral standing of the learned, since the theologian represents the pinnacle of this category.

The man who both acts and instructs... Heaven: Matt. 5: 19, taken in context, allows the interpretation put on it by the friar; but the spirit of the latter's approach is at variance with the Gospel passage and seems prone to the same charge of minimalism as that found in the earlier doctrine of the Friars Minor in Passus VIII.

I have seven sons: presumably the seven arts of the medieval university curriculum. They are meant to lay a basis for the learning of moral and spiritual truth; but Clergy himself is troubled by the evident discrepancy between clerks' learning and their goodness or piety. The allusion to 'someone called Piers Plowman' is the first mention of Piers since his tearing of the pardon and dispute with the priest. Clergy is much less hostile to Piers's attitude than was the latter, but he remains neutral rather than convinced about the supremacy of love.

Love the Lord your God... Lord, who shall dwell... tent?: Matt. 22: 37, Christ's formulation of 'the greatest and first commandment' (to love God), and Ps. 14(15): 1, a very important psalm that describes in both negative and positive terms what it is to 'do well'.

what Piers Plowman has to say: this account of Clergy's does not refer back to anything Piers has actually said earlier in the poem and must therefore be taken as a reflective summary of his long first speech in Passus V (see pp. 60–3). The meaning of 'infinites' is 'things without boundary or limit', but the precise reference is not certain; humility, obedience, suffering, and hope are among the notions most relevant, but the *separate* mention of faith seems to exclude any too-definite categorization of the three Do's as the theological virtues of faith, hope, and charity. Conscience's reply seems to confirm that a certain obscurity is indeed present.

142 *I do know Piers well*: Conscience's claim corresponds to Piers's own claim to have been instructed by Conscience, in his dispute with the priest at the end of Passus VII (see p. 79 above).

The patient are victorious: proverbial, but not a direct quotation from Scripture, though texts like Matt. 10: 22 have been adduced. Three key ideas are involved in Langland's use of the word 'patience'— suffering, perseverance, and calm acceptance of pain and wrong (patience in our ordinary modern sense).

Learn. Teach. And love your enemies: Patience's definition is not so very different from the Doctor's in content, but differs in tone and above all in its stress on love of one's enemies, the most distinctive of Christian

moral doctrines and the one most appropriate to the character of
Patience himself. The character Love is one of those personifications
who only appear 'offstage', but her role is an important one, and
Langland closely associates her with reconciliation and concord. Cf.
the later mention of Love's letter to Peace, one of the Four Daughters
of God who is, significantly, 'clothed in patience', in Passus XVIII (see
p. 215).

you must love your own soul . . . your enemy: to love one's own soul is to
love the image of God within oneself, an image also to be found in each
other human being. Love of God *leads* to love of one's neighbour; but
the starting-point is not a remote transcendent deity, rather a proper
self-understanding, to be achieved through exercising the moral virtue
of patience. The speaker thus echoes both Scripture's insistence on the
need for self-knowledge, at the opening of Passus XI (see p. 111), and
the earlier insight of Piers at the end of Passus V, where he locates
truth in the human heart, decked with a chain of charity and the
meekness of a child (see p. 62). The connection of patience with doing
well is strongly suggested by a text such as Rom. 2: 7, which shows
patience to be by no means a merely passive quality. Also important is
Rom. 12: 18–21, especially 20, which quotes the verses of Prov. 25:
21–2 alluded to in the 'coals' image. The violence of Patience's
metaphors ironically enhances the true power of the virtues of meekness
and love in face of *literal* violence.

It's firmly wrapped up in there: the mysterious remarks that follow bear
more than one interpretation according as we read the original as
meaning 'about' or 'in a box'. If the latter, there may be an oblique
allusion to the box for carrying the consecrated Host. But this is
unlikely since the speaker is not a priest, and more probably he is
alluding to the hidden meaning of his statement about the power of
suffering and love to overcome evil, and has in mind generally the
passion of Christ, or the 'Our Father', in which the submission to
God's will shown in the Passion finds verbal expression (it is this he
offers Haukin later in Passus XIV; see p. 154).

Ex vi transitionis: the power of transitivity by which a verb
grammatically 'rules' its direct object; but there may also be a punning
allusion to the *transitus* or exodus from Egypt recalled in the Jewish
Passover, of which the Passion of Christ is understood as the New
Testament figural fulfilment (or 'antitype'). The Saturday mentioned is
the vigil of Easter, from which the dates of the Church's movable
feasts were reckoned. The Wednesday is that of Easter week, but the
precise sense is unclear. The mass of that day has various themes, such
as feeding, but perhaps the most important is the victory of Christ
through suffering (the Epistle includes Acts 3: 18, a crucial text).

The full of the moon: the Paschal full moon stands as a symbol of
Easter, and the whole passage may be interpreted as a cryptic account
of the power of the Christian sacraments, which take their origin and

efficacy from the passion and death of Christ. The name of this, the suffering love which fears nothing, is disclosed below.

143 *Caritas . . . nothing*: from 1 John 4: 18; but the best commentary on it, from which the preceding account of love's power derives, is 1 Cor. 13: 4–7, especially 4: 'Charity is patient.' These are the two most important texts underlying Langland's thought about the meaning of Christianity in the part of the work that begins with the fourth vision.

minstrel-romance: the Doctor of Divinity dismisses Patience's claims for the power of Christian love as the sort of fantastic invention encountered in the wilder popular narratives of the day. His proof is the impotence of the leaders of the Church when it comes to settling disputes between themselves or the rulers of states. He alludes to the Great Schism of 1378, in which two popes contended for the see of Peter, Urban VI at Rome, supported by England, and Clement VII at Avignon, supported by France. The schism exacerbated relations between England and France after the uneasy truce of 1375–7, and in 1380 another English assault on France, under Thomas of Woodstock, was launched.

tall stories: the Doctor alludes to the common reputation of pilgrims and travellers for inventing tall tales about their experiences (cf. Prol. p. 2).

I intend to set off with Patience here: the union of Conscience, the pious knight-layman, with Patience, the pilgrim-hermit, marks an important stage in the poem. Their coming encounter with Haukin, the type of the common man, is therefore of great symbolic significance.

bits of largesse: Clergy's sarcastic reply envisages Conscience's decision as tantamount to becoming a wandering minstrel, going about the country with no fixed abode and looking for gifts and tips here and there. The Old Testament book he alludes to could be Job, the theme of which is patient submission to the will of God. But Conscience is rejecting not the Bible as such, only theoretical knowledge which does not touch the heart and alter one's life.

144 *certain people here*: Conscience clearly indicates that his evaluation of academic knowledge of religion (theology) has been adversely affected by the experience of the Doctor.

Mary Magdalen . . . treasury?: the allusion to Mary Magdalen follows the traditional identification of her with the woman who anointed the feet of Christ (Luke 7: 37 and Matt. 26: 7). Zacheus the tax-collector told Christ he would give half his goods to the poor (Luke 19:8) and the widow put her two brass mites, all she had to live on, into the Temple treasury (Luke 21: 1–4). The point of the contrast is not to attack the rich man (Zacheus is promised salvation at Luke 19: 9), but to distinguish between a qualified and a total commitment of the self to God. Mary Magdalen and the widow-woman are emblems of the passive dependence on God that Conscience has recognized in Patience

and is proposing to try. The edged quality of his response to Clergy
can be seen in the whispered words, 'Dear God . . .', which contrast
the ideas of 'full' and 'half ' in a way suggested by the three examples:
patience represents 'full' assent of the will to God, 'learning' perhaps
something only half-way or half-hearted.

144   *me to advise you*: 'the day' when Conscience needs Clergy in fact comes
late in Passus XX (see. p. 249); the only 'help' he gets comes from the
friars.

no trouble in the world . . . put right!: the suggestion seems to be that a
combination of pious laity, upright clergy, and holy contemplatives
would make an unbeatable Christian alliance, capable of solving the
world's political problems and its spiritual ones as well. The outcome
of the siege of Unity at the end of the poem shows such a combination
to be unrealizable in the contemporary world as it is.

a pair of pilgrims: this allegorical journey recalls that described by Piers
in Passus V; it represents an attempt to bring the faculty of Christian
conscience and the virtue of Christian patience into direct contact with
ordinary uneducated active humanity, 'l'homme moyen sensuel', the
type of all those depicted in the field of folk.

145   *a minstrel*: Haukin sells wafers (biscuits and fancy confectionery),
something 'real' minstrels often did along with their entertainments to
eke out a living. He himself is not a minstrel, however, in the sense of
either a skilled musical performer or a crude comic entertainer; his link
with Piers comes from his activity as a provider of food.

a lead seal: the *bulla* on a papal pardon was stamped with the heads of
the apostles saints Peter and Paul.

146   *In my name . . . recover*: Mark 16: 17–18, speaks of the powers Christ
left to his apostles. It is these that are referred to below.

the power St Peter possessed: Haukin objects that papal pardons have
not power to cure the real physical ailments of the people, and so he
implicitly questions the power of the pope which is implied in his
authority as successor of St Peter. The quotation from Acts 3: 6
contrasts the material poverty of St Peter with his spiritual riches,
including the power to heal the sick in the name of Christ.

He can't work miracles . . . favour: miracles require faith, and before
there can be a renewal of faith the pride of people must be purged by
drastic means, such as famine. This echoes the end of Passus VI (see p.
74), the prophecy of a great famine to come.

Stratford . . . Mayor of London: Haukin recalls (as a foretaste of the
famine to come) the great dearth of 1370, when John de Chichester
was mayor of London. Stratford-atte-Bowe (where Chaucer's Prioress
acquired her French) was a centre from which bakers supplied the
daily needs of London.

a coat of Christian faith: Haukin, having been baptized, has been
clothed in the white robe of innocence, but has dirtied it through his

sins. The devastating full-length portrait that follows shows him to sum up all the vices displayed earlier in the field of folk. What makes Haukin such a sobering figure to contemplate is not that he is exceptionally wicked but that he is typical or representative of the average member of the Church.

147 *his own order*: this may allude to the growing practice of affective piety outside the constraints of formal religious orders, something widely regarded with suspicion and hostility, as the career of Margery Kempe in the next generation illustrates. Langland is sceptical about any form of 'religious' life that dispenses with rules.

148 *If I set out . . . No man . . . masters!*: the first quotation from Gal. 1: 10 and the second from Matt. 6: 24 are both called into service here to criticize the hypocritical worldliness of Haukin, and are generally apt, though in context the first concerns the authority of Paul's calling and the second the antithesis between serving God and serving money.

Will . . . Wat: here simply type-names for Haukin's neighbours.

His mouth . . . These sons . . . swords: the first quotation, from Ps. 9b(10): 7 comes in the context of a description of an evil man, from which various details may have contributed to the portrait of Haukin. The second, from Ps. 56(57): 5, provides the basis of Langland's earlier image of the tailor's scissors.

not Christ himself: Haukin's resort to superstitious remedies results from his failure to turn to God in his need. The two characters alluded to may have been familiar figures in contemporary London, Emma perhaps the same who occurs in the song quoted at the end of the Prologue (p. 7).

149 *fast-days*: sexual intercourse even between the married was discouraged during these times (see p. 93 and note, 'only at the proper time').

ways of obtaining wealth: this passage, like others in the description of Haukin, echoes earlier ones in the account of the Seven Deadly Sins in Passus V (in this case Greed, at pp. 49–51).

150 *a foot . . . never planted!*: under the system of strip-farming, Haukin found it easy to steal land or corn from cultivated plots that lay directly adjacent to his.

my agents: Haukin seems to slip slightly out of character here, becoming a personification of collective avaricious traits rather than simply an underpaid wafer-seller. Bruges was a major centre for the Flemish cloth trade and Prussia the commercial centre for the distribution of English cloth in Poland and Western Russia. Haukin is to be imagined (or is imagining himself) here as one of the English wool-traders who were beginning to grow rich as the trade expanded.

Where . . . also: Matt. 6: 21, which comes from the Sermon on the Mount, underlines the contrast between Christian values and the materialism which is Haukin's sole concern. The preceding two verses are especially pertinent here, as their reference to the moth consuming earthly treasures has a bearing both on the immediate context (wealth from the wool-trade) and the larger situation (the care of Haukin's coat: see the beginning of Passus XIV (p. 153), where Conscience tells how penance will protect the coat against the moth of sin.

151 *woe to you . . . moment*: Luke 16: 25, from Luke's equivalent of Matthew's Sermon on the Mount, also contrasts earthly with heavenly conditions, and material with spiritual values.

Those who . . . punishment: a legal maxim, unenforceable in earthly law as regards the abuse in question, but one Langland holds will operate in the next life.

The man . . . sight: Ps. 100(101): 7–8 is a dire warning against pride, which ends in a threat of death. Langland is by implication making the support of scurrilous jesters a sin that will lead the nobility to Hell.

152 *The man . . . me*: from Luke 10: 16, but very close to John 12: 48. The poor as the minstrels of the King of Heaven is a very characteristic Langlandian 'transformation' of an earthly institution or practice into a spiritual or 'heavenly' one. Actual royal minstrels were a privileged class of highly paid professional musicians, and a visit from one of them was a great privilege to any household. Langland's point is that in treating *them* honourably, a noble is honouring the King, who is their patron; so also, by treating the poor as God's minstrels, men are honouring God.

Turpiloquium: Eph. 5: 4, echoes its initial appearance in the Prologue. The specific application to scurrilous jesters is Langland's own.

153 *one cloak*: his fleshly human nature, which is incapable of avoiding involvement in the affairs of daily life; it is also his soul, which has a heavenly destiny, and which must be kept pure through virtuous living and use of the sacraments.

I have . . . come: from Luke 14: 20, giving worldly concerns as an excuse for not following the Gospel.

one end of the day . . . next!: echoes the words of the Minorite friar in Passus VIII (p. 82) and is taken up despairingly by Haukin himself at the end of Passus XIV (p. 165).

sorrow for sin . . . satisfaction: Conscience expounds the doctrine of sacramental penance, relating its parts to the three Do's. The first part, contrition, is a preliminary to the first act of *doing* well, oral confession to a priest. This cleans the soul from sin. Doing better consists in making satisfaction for the sin, thereby imbuing the soul with a firm tincture of virtue. Do-best may be seen as the activation of the penitent's purpose to amend his life thereafter (that is, his resolve not to sin again). With this, the practical life of Haukin, morally neutral in itself, will become transformed into a continual opportunity to grow in virtue (keep the cloak in its pristine brightness) instead of sinking back into vice.

154 *I'll provide . . . win the day!*: Patience now assures Haukin that he will be given spiritual food to help him grow—the virtues that are obtained through prayer and the Eucharist. 'Do not be anxious . . .', from the Sermon on the Mount (Matt. 6: 25–6) provides the conditions for this growth—a proper degree of detachment from exclusively material concerns, together with sufficient trust that God will provide the spiritual strength to endure any physical deprivation that follows from putting the claims of the Kingdom first. The important preceding verses 9–13 contain the 'Our Father', and the version of the petition for bread ('Give us this day our supersubstantial bread', v. 11) was usually taken as alluding to God's spiritual nourishment through the Eucharist. Patience here specifies the virtue of humble and submissive trust in God ('patience').

Whatever . . . do . . . Man . . . God: the quotations from John 14: 13 (the Last Supper discourse) and Matt. 4: 4 (Christ's temptation in the desert) underline the 'trust' theme by affirming that prayer is answered, and that the 'Our Father' said with faith will really procure what it petitions. The second quotation is itself based on Deut. 8: 3, in which Moses reminds the Israelites that God fed them with manna when they were in want, and that this is a lesson to place one's trust in life in the word of God.

Thy will be done!: the petition singled out by Patience is the crucial third one used by Christ in his own prayer in the Garden of Gethsemane (Matt. 26: 42), the supreme example of the virtue of 'patience'.

155 *The man . . . straw!*: this verse (of unknown origin) expresses the medieval attitude of *contemptus mundi*—scorn for the things of this life in comparison with the world to come. But what Patience is actually trying to inculcate is not contempt for God's creation but a *proper* respect for it—one which sees material things in due proportion to their Creator.

He spoke . . . You open . . . blessing: the first psalm quotation is from Ps. 148: 5, which exalts the supremacy of God as Creator, the second from Ps. 144(145): 16 which, with its preceding verse, was commonly used as a grace before meals. The rhetorical question that links them makes the crucial point: our very existence is sustained at every moment by the will of God, so it makes no sense to act as if it depended upon our own will.

It's recorded . . . they awoke!: Patience's three examples of how men have survived by trusting in God are taken from the Old Testament (the Israelites in the wilderness, Num. 20: 11 for the rock; 3(1) Kgs. 17: 1 (also quoted in Jas. 5: 17) for Elias; the *Golden Legend* (ch. 100), the Seven in Sleepers of Ephesus who fled the Decian persecution and awoke after sleeping 200 years in a cave, in AD 448). The second of the two examples is rather oddly used by Langland, since the drought is a *punishment* on the people for evil, and the proper lesson to be drawn is from the survival of Elias, who was fed by ravens, rather than from that of the Israelites, who survive in *despite* of God rather than through their dependence on him. But Patience may be intending this as an example of the proper way to accept even adversity sent as punishment from God (the final result is that God sends rain in answer to Elias's prayer).

155   *But moderation....* : Patience's argument takes up that of Holy Church in Passus I (see p. 9). The cardinal virtue of temperance is opposed to gluttony, sloth, and, in a sense, all sins, to the extent that they can be seen as departures from the desired norm. Patience wittily points out that a virtue whose nature is to be moderate cannot be valued to excess, by definition.

156   *Too much ... brood!*: from Peter Cantor (*PL*, ccv, col. 331) is closely based on Ezek. 16: 49, which not only links pride, excess, and sloth but also ascribes to these vices a refusal to help the poor and needy. The basic story of the destruction of Sodom is in Gen. 18 and 19.

    faith ... shield: the image of faith as a protective armour is from Eph. 6: 11–17.

    contrition ... against mortal sins: in his exposition of the theory of penance, Patience affirms the importance and value of each phase or element; contrition is basic, and suffices, but sincere oral confession followed by satisfaction are increasingly perfect ways of achieving reconciliation with God. The first verse of the second penitential psalm, on our sins 'having been covered over', had earlier been served at the feast of Conscience in Passus XIII (see p. 139) in the context of making confession. Satisfaction is here understood as restoring the soul to a state of original justice in readiness for Heaven.

    Where does Charity live, though?: Haukin's bemused question about Charity's whereabouts echoes the tone of Will's earlier concerning Dowel (p. 82) and that of the folk of the field concerning Truth (p. 60). In each case, the only convincing proof that a value or virtue exists is to find it embodied in a real person.

    Is patient poverty ... of?: Haukin's second question returns to the matter in hand—patient poverty—and initiates an enormous discourse on this virtue, and on the dangers of wealth, which is not ended until Haukin's third question at p. 162.

157   *Can you find ... him!*: Patience quotes in the original from the Vulgate text of Ecclus. 31: 9. The biblical context is without his note of scepticism, however, as to whether such a person can be found.

    he's claiming ... right!: Patience is not arguing that man earns salvation by his own merit but that it would be against nature ('kynde') and so against God's nature ('Kynde') if any creature were made solely to suffer. His position perhaps implies that earthly suffering is some sort of purgatory or satisfaction for sin in itself.

Even the angels . . . favour: Patience reasons first that the rich have an unfair advantage, then that their advantage may in fact be illusory: they will have to pay for it.

The rich . . . nothing!: the quotation comes from two psalms, the first line from Ps. 75(76): 6, the second and third from Ps. 72(73): 20. The whole of the latter psalm has a bearing on this passage, as it deals with the effect of sinners' (apparent) prosperity on the faith of poor believers. The 'sleep' of both images is, of course, death.

158 *St Matthew*: the vague allusion may be to Matthew's story of the rich young man (quoted on p. 160 below), or perhaps to the parable of the labourers in the vineyard, which illustrates God's justice as the exact payment of what is due as promised.

To start and end . . . much!: the quotation from St Jerome's letter to Julian (*PL*, xxii, col. 965) has the word *difficile*, perhaps echoing Matt. 19: 23 (which has the same word in the Vulgate text).

rich people . . . pity: Patience takes up again the idea of *pity* that he had used in two different senses earlier (pp. 157, 158): if the rich show pity to the poor, their riches will not have proved a matter of regret nor will their fate be a sad one, like that of the proud in the psalm.

double payment: Patience's way of expressing belief that God's providence, though inscrutable, is just. It will be counterbalanced later by Anima's notion of 'double harm' (see p. 168): from those to whom much is given, much will be expected.

a rare occurrence: Patience now warns that though 'double payment' is a theoretical possibility, riches remain a real danger in most cases for most people.

159 *Midsummer Day*: between Midsummer (24 June) and Lammas (1 August), when the first loaves were made from the newly harvested corn, supplies of bread became scarcer, prices rose, and beggars found it harder to get left-over scraps.

You could . . . wished it!: Patience here expresses his nature as 'unquestioning acceptance of the will of God': if inequality exists, there must be a reason for it, even if man does not know why. His attitude is in contrast with that of Will in Passus XI, who was rebuked by Reason for asking why sin is allowed to exist and received the answer as another question, 'Who puts up with more than God?' (see p. 123, and cf. 117).

Turn back . . . saved: from Isa. 45: 22, the context being one of faith in the final justice of God, who creates peace as well as evil.

160 *Let . . . our Lord*: Patience compares the Passion of Christ, the merits of which are available to sinners in the sacrament of Penance, to a royal document of acquittal from some legal charge. He urges Haukin to have real faith that his sins will be released provided he has the will to

develop the virtue of humility (patient poverty) on which the 'words' of remission can be 'inscribed' as if on a parchment.

160   *names are engraved in . . . churches*: Patience's example of pride, the desire to have one's benefactions recorded for posterity, is a deliberate echo of Lady Meed's promise to the friar-confessor in Passus III (see esp. p. 24).

seven sins: they are here seen as manifestations of pride, but the most potent form that manifestation takes, in the given context and historical setting, is greed for material wealth.

impossible . . . kingdom: Matt. 19: 23–4; probably in the original 'it *is* possible for a rich man to enter Heaven (just possible—but very difficult!)'.

for their works . . . follow them: Apoc. (Rev.) 14: 13 concludes a verse promising the reward of Heaven ('rest from their labours') to those 'who die in the Lord'. Their good works go with them to judgment, and they are unimpeded by a heavy baggage of possessions.

Blessed . . . Heaven: verbally from Matt. 5: 3, but omitting the words 'in spirit' after 'poor' as in the parallel Luke 6: 20. The references to 'works' earlier and to patience later show that Langland does not see Heaven as an automatic reward for earthly poverty but as, at least in part, a recompense for the resigned acceptance of such a state.

162   *stews*: so called after the small heated rooms within the tenements where the prostitutes plied their trade. They were mostly south of the Thames in the district of Southwark.

that was the garb . . . race: Patience draws on the fact that Christ actually was poor rather than rich to make a special claim for the poor as a class, irrespective of their virtues: it is they to whom 'the gospel is preached' (Luke 7: 22) and who have been chosen as 'rich in faith and heirs of the kingdom' (Jas. 2: 5).

marriage with Poverty: like marrying into God's own family (the closeness of divine love to the condition of self-abandonment open to the poor is also stressed later by the character Need in Passus XX (see p. 243). Langland may have in mind St Francis, the most famous of all rich young men who willingly gave up his wealth to marry the Lady Poverty. Compare the rich young man of Matt. 19: 21.

Paupertas . . . bonum: from the *Gnomae* of an obscure writer known as Secundus Philosophus, quoted in the *Speculum Historiale* of the thirteenth-century encyclopaedist Vincent of Beauvais (x. 71). The phrase 'God's gift' is significantly not from a pagan source but from St Augustine's treatise *On Patience*.

163   *Poverty . . . is the basic virtue*: Patience now embarks on what is virtually a sermon, explaining to his unlearned hearer the full content of the Latin text he has quoted as his authority. This recalls Holy Church's instruction of Will in Passus I and contrasts with Piers's

confident intuitive understanding of the scriptures in Passus VII (Piers having been taught by the disciplines of abstinence and conscience).

Do not be a judge... man: Matt. 7: 1 (from the Sermon on the Mount) is, of course, forbidding the passing of *moral* judgement on others; it is not a prohibition on exercising *legal* duties as juryman or judge.

164   *donum Dei*: Poverty here not merely reduces the occasions of sin but is a positive aid to virtue, a 'blessing in disguise'.

sanitatis mater: poverty is conducive to physical health because it requires abstinence from excess, which for Langland was a major cause of illness as well as leading to other sins like lust and sloth.

Alton Pass: the Alton road on the forested Surrey–Hampshire border was a haunt of outlaws on the lookout for merchant-trains going to the markets and fairs at Winchester.

A poor man... singing: the verse is a quotation from Juvenal, *Satire* 20, 1. 22.

Paupertas... semita: not from Seneca, but expresses sentiments close to the Stoic philosopher's, for example, in his *Epistle* 8.

tune his tongue to truth alone: Patience means not that the poor feel able to speak out without fear so much as that they are not tempted to lie, and in fact tell the truth habitually because their custom is to speak hardly at all.

loss-free business: Patience's paradoxical point is that to incur a measure of loss by not seeking too much profit actually results in another form of gain—goodwill from men and God alike.

patience... bread, sobriety... drink: Patience here takes up the metaphor used by Piers in the pardon scene in Passus VII, where spiritual is contrasted with material food (see p. 79). He alludes to the treatise of Augustine mentioned in the note to p. 162, 'Paupertas...', above, which speaks of 'the patience of the poor of Christ who will be made rich in Heaven' (echoing Jas. 2: 5).

165   *tears... eyes*: Haukin's tears, though recalling those of Will and Robert in Passus V (see pp. 44 and 58), are less from fear of punishment than from sorrow at having offended a loving God. Deriving from a desire to repent and amend, they are what medieval spiritual writers called 'religious tears'.

166   *a state of idiocy*: Will's growing indifference to the ways of the world, the result of his learning the lessons of patience and poverty, leads to his being regarded as a 'fool'—a word that will assume great importance in the final passus (see p. 244).

fine-drawn substance: the ethereal being Will sees resembles a ghost, so he is understandably anxious to know whether it is a spirit blest or goblin damned.

in many places I am 'Christian': the speaker is at one level the personification of the universal spiritual substance, the soul to be found in all human beings. He is thus sometimes Christian, sometimes not, but in each case capable of receiving divine grace. But he is also meant to stand for the Dreamer's own deepest and innermost self, the site of vision and grace.

166   *door-keeper* . . . *there*: Peter was traditionally represented with keys in hand as the gatekeeper of Heaven (on the basis of Matt. 16: 19), while Paul's sword was the emblem of his martyrdom (he was beheaded).

166–7 *Anima . . . Soul*: the generic title under which man's spiritual nature is designated. According to medieval faculty-psychology in the neo-Augustinian tradition here drawn upon, the soul is also named according to each of the functions it exercises. The basic one is that of giving *life* to the physical body, and so the soul here has the same name as it was given in Passus IX in Wit's allegory of the Lady Anima (see p. 87). *Animus* represents the volitional side and is equal to 'will' as affective rather than rational (that is, the part of us that wants something rather than the part which can freely will even what it finds painful, *voluntas*, which is not in this list). *Mens* is the thinking part, equivalent to the earlier character Thought and the knowledge to which its exercise leads (Wit). *Memoria* has a special religious force in this context—thought about divine things during prayer. *Ratio* is not abstract, analytical or logical reason but the practical faculty which reasons about right action.

167   *Sensus . . . Spiritus*: *Sensus* is the power which learns and acquires practical knowledge through the physical senses (for example, ploughing, sewing) and is close to English 'Kind Wit'. Conscience is the *habitus* or disposition of the reason towards concrete moral judgements: it keeps a record or tally of the state of the soul. *Love*, more properly a virtue than faculty, here seems to stand for the appetitive power when properly directed. *Spiritus* refers to the spiritual substance in a state of separation from the body whose union with it constitutes the human composite nature.

You know them all!: there follows in the original the complete Latin definition of the soul as given in Isidore of Seville's *Etymologies* (XI. i. 13). St Augustine is the chief representative of this way of thinking about the soul in the medieval period, and Langland is working in this tradition.

I am going . . . henceforth!: Isa. 14: 13–14 refers in context to the king of Babylon, but was traditionally applied to Lucifer and, by allegorical extension here, to the overweening human will to know all. Cf. p. 11.

168   *Too much honey . . . man!*: the Latin quotation from Prov. 25: 27 warns against excessive theological curiosity if it is unaccompanied by holiness: the more one knows, the more severely one will be judged. This doctrine of 'double harm' may be compared with that of 'double reward' in Passus XIV (see p. 158 and notes).

Blessed . . . work!: the quotation from St Bernard's treatise *On the Order of Life (PL*, clxxxiv, col. 566) contrasts mere *verba* with *opera* (words, read or spoken with works actually performed).

Craving . . . heir: this quotation, also from St Bernard, is from his fourth homily on the Ascension (*PL*, clxxxiii, col. 311). Knowledge without piety and love is regarded by Bernard as worldly or 'carnal'.

Wisdom . . . be!: Rom. 12: 3, in a context where Paul is warning against the wrong kind of 'wisdom', that of the world, which seeks self-aggrandisement and material profit and success (see esp vv. 2 and 16 of this chapter).

Listen to me . . . damnation: Anima warns against the dangers of sermons that speculate on deep theological mysteries before unlearned congregations who cannot profit from them, but require simple and clear moral instruction and exhortation. Many of these were given by university-trained members of the great mendicant orders.

169   *the great ones . . . pleasing*: the friars show off their learning in order to attract benefactions and patronage from the wealthy nobility—an example of the 'carnal' attitude condemned by Bernard.

Let them wallow . . . Why adore . . . falsehood?: from, respectively, Ps. 96(97): 7 and Ps. 4: 3, and skilfully link idolatry with cupidity and deceit. The source of this idea is the *Glossa Ordinaria's* comment on Ps. 4: 3. Langland has in mind the morally corrupting effect on the preacher of misusing his God-given skills and abusing his religious responsibility.

Do not be . . . persons: actually this is a quotation from Jas. 2: 1 (a text drawn on extensively in Passus XIV) echoing Deut. 1: 17, part of the divine positive law of the Old Testament. Anima's attack quickly shifts from the friars, a dangerous but inessential part of the Church, to the establishment itself, the corruption of which can prove fatal.

170   *hypocrisy . . . snakes inside . . . interior*: the second similitude clearly echoes scriptural texts on hypocrisy such as Matt. 23: 27, Acts 23: 3; but the first is unknown. It is a fact of natural history, however, that snakes build nests in dunghills and compost-heaps, and Langland may also have been remembering the Baptist's denunciation of the (hypocritical) Sadducees and Pharisees as a 'brood of vipers' (Matt. 3: 7).

the wolf . . . the shepherd!: the image of the wolf in sheep's clothing comes from Christ's warning against false prophets in Matt. 7: 15. The image of the evil tree in the immediately following verses (16–20), echoing the Baptist's words in 3: 10 (see note above), may underlie the application of the figure to the priesthood in the quotation that follows.

All good comes forth . . . in the priests!: the long quotation (in Latin in the original) is from a homily wrongly attributed to the fourth-century Greek Father of the Church, St John Chrysostom (Homily 38 on St Matthew, Migne, *Patrologia Graeca*, lvi, col. 839).

171   *I will please the Lord . . .* : the *'Placebo'*, from Ps. 114(116): 9, a text
      familiar from its use in the Office of the Dead. As a (presumably
      unordained and so unbeneficed) psalter-clerk, Langland would have
      had a particular reason for objecting to the worldliness of the clergy,
      who used their income to buy fine clothes rather than the service-books
      which were the tools of their consecrated 'trade'.

      Ah, you poor . . . distress: Anima's reflections lead him into an impasse:
      the gift-offerings of corrupt men end up in the hands of corrupt
      clerics, a providential act of poetic justice; but still the poor suffer.

      But what . . . ourselves!: after the death of corrupt clergy, their money
      ends up in the hands of similar people, and the whole process starts all
      over again. Why the goods of this world do no good to the needy
      remains a mystery to be accepted patiently since it cannot be
      explained.

      You cannot . . . child: Matt. 18: 3 illustrates the humility needed for
      accepting the Gospel. Anima envisages the charitable man as simple,
      unpossessive, and detached from material things. His image echoes
      that of Piers in Passus V (see p. 62 above).

172   *Long Will*: the poet here fuses his own identity as a 'clerkly maker'
      with that of his dream-persona Will, indicating his own name (Will
      Langland) and the quality of perseverance (*longanimitas*) which
      characterizes the spiritual and poetic quest of the Dreamer-Poet.

      Charity . . . its own: from St Paul's famous paean on charity in 1 Cor.
      13: 4–5.

      a looking-glass . . . face to face: medieval mirrors, like those in St Paul's
      day, were of polished metal or stone and gave a much less distinct
      reflection than the modern kind (hence 'darkly', that is, indistinctly).
      The quotation is from 1 Cor. 13: 12.

      choice scarlet . . . Turkistan: the charitable man regards wealth and
      poverty with equanimity because he sees them as gifts of God and does
      not love possessions 'carnally' (for their own sake). Turkistan silk, a
      rare, costly stuff, like scarlet wool symbolizes worldly rank and status.

173   *Thy-Will-be-done*: Anima's instruction echoes that of Patience in Passus
      XIV: what sustains Charity is the same 'piece of the Paternoster', the
      third of the petitions (cf. p. 154 above), and the crucial one. If this is
      wholeheartedly accepted, all else follows. In the supper-image that
      follows, Anima recalls the allegorical feast at Conscience's house.

      Hope-in-the-Lord: from Ps. 41(42): 6 (*Sicut cervus*), the one quoted by
      Piers when he embarked on a life of prayer (cf. p. 79), and preceded
      by a reference of feasting (vs. 5) which could have suggested this
      metaphor to Langland.

      Our Father . . . Hail Marys: saying the rosary is one of the occupations
      of Charity. In a set of rosary beads, the beads for the 'Our Fathers'
      were often painted a different colour to those for the 'Hail Marys'.

a laundry... every night...: Anima's image of the laundry of penitence takes up the washing and cleansing metaphor of Passus XIII (Haukin's coat); even at a higher spiritual level, sorrow for sins is necessary. The image used here in the quotation from Ps. 6: 7 echoes that used by Piers in Passus VII (from Ps. 41(42): 4).

a contrite... O god: from Ps. 50: 19(51: 17), the fourth penitential psalm (the *Miserere*), sung on Ash-Wednesday and especially associated with Lent.

without... Piers Plowman: this important statement has two functions: it obliquely indicates that Piers is *the* means to the discovery of Charity (as, earlier, he had been the one who knew the way to Truth) and also that Piers is to return in a new and deeper role. Anima, as the Dreamer's spiritual nature, gives him access to profounder insight than was available to the surface levels of the mind.

And God saw their thoughts...: from Luke 11: 17 or Matt. 9: 4; but neither says 'God' (the subject is Jesus). Langland emphasizes the association between Piers and God as an arresting way that prepares for the profoundly mysterious allegorical action of the inner dream that is to follow.

174   *Peter, that is, Christ*: this second assertion of Charity's hidden location, in the secret recesses of the heart, adds a new equation—that of Piers with the apostle Peter, whom Jesus appointed head of the Church, and who in that sense 'is' or stands for Christ.

Don't be... hypocrites!: from Matt. 6: 16, from the Sermon on the Mount, refers to fasting rather than alms-giving, but the lesson is the same: love of God within will manifest itself in a happy and bountiful demeanour. In line with medieval thought on all the virtues generally, Langland holds that doing well should make man happy, not miserable.

Edmund and Edward: the two saint-kings referred to are Edmund, king of the East Angles (martyred 869) and Edward the Confessor (d. 1066).

more often... those days!: the meaning here is that a bishop or abbot is more likely to be found as an embodiment of charity than any friar. The founder of the Franciscans, Francis of Assisi (d. 1226), was hailed as such, but criticism of his and the other mendicant orders had been growing sharper as the fourteenth century wore on.

Blessed the rich man... blemish: from Ecclus. 31: 8, warning against worship of riches but praising those who use them rightly; this verse immediately precedes that quoted by Patience in Passus XIV in answer to Haukin (p. 157). Anima is not claiming that such people are not rare.

175   *marriages... for cash down*: Anima refers to the securing of divorces (forbidden by the Church) under the guise of canonical annulments, for which canon lawyers were supposedly open to taking bribes.

175 *In peace . . . rest*: the immediate context of the quotation (Ps. 4: 9) makes the source of the peace enjoyed by charity 'the light of God's countenance'—his favour of grace; but Anima goes on to stress the notion of sharing in God's suffering (as he shared in man's, through the Passion of Christ).

176 *The Golden Legend*: like Patience earlier (p. 155), Anima cites this work for examples of complete reliance on the love of God for 'sustenance' even in the bodily sense, though he goes on to interpret these narratives in a further, allegorical sense.

St Anthony . . . desert saints: in chs. 21 and 128 of the *Legend*. The early desert saints were the traditional founders of 'monasticism' (literally 'the solitary life'). Anthony died in 356, Giles in 700.

Paul . . . Friars: (of Thebes), by tradition the first hermit (died *c*.340). He was visited by Anthony and was said to have been fed by a raven on that occasion. The order of Augustinian Friars Hermits received a rule based on that of St Augustine in 1256, but claimed that their origins went back to the earliest hermits (that is, that they were the oldest of the mendicant orders).

Paul the apostle: was a tent-maker (Acts 18: 3), and his trade has been confused with that of Paul the Hermit, who made baskets.

Mary Magdalen: (*Golden Legend*, ch. 95) said to have lived in solitude in a cave in Provence for thirty years, where she was fed on angels' song (a symbol for the all-sufficing nourishment of pure contemplation).

177 *the humble should be supported by the gentle*: a kind of symbiotic relationship between Christian lay-people, active in the world, and hermit-contemplatives, given to prayer, and supported by the latter in their simple needs.

God's fools: the original reads *foweles* for 'fools', but this gives poor sense since it is the birds who bring the food, not receive it, and there may be a confusion between 'fowls' and 'fools', the latter giving a firm and clear meaning: those who trust in God are 'fools' in the eyes of the world (a title used of the Christian believers in Passus XX in the siege of Unity; see p. 244). On the other hand, Langland may have in mind Matt. 6: 26, with its implicit comparison of trusting believers with the birds of the air, and have run two metaphors together: Christians (*like* birds in their trustfulness) will receive food *from* (real) birds sent by God—that is, from some source known to Providence alone.

Will the wild ass bray . . . vices!: the first two lines are from Job 6: 5, the next three probably from a sermon or commentary upon this text, as yet untraced.

If only laymen . . . pray for others!: a warning against further enriching the monastic orders in a time when popular hostility was rising and was shortly to burst out in the Peasants' Revolt of 1381, when great monastic houses like Bury St Edmunds were destroyed.

178   *He has ... poor?*: from Ps. 111(112): 9 and the initial thrust is against the *monks*, for failing to use their accumulated wealth sufficiently to relieve the poor. But Langland cannot resist an ironic gibe against the friars who, in one sense, *do* fulfil the prophet's words.

    To deprive the poor ... what may suffice: mostly from the twelfth-century theologian Peter the Chanter (Petrus Cantor; see *PL*, ccv, cols. 147, 149, 152).

    Luxemburgs: coins of silver alloyed with base metal, imported from Luxemburg. Edward III forbade their importation.

179   *Every day now you can see it*: Anima now embarks on a generalized tirade against the decline in learning and culture, which he associates with the poor moral and spiritual calibre of the clergy.

    Grammar ... English: the attack on the decline of standards of grammar and in the study of a 'modern foreign language' (here obviously French) sound very topical today; but Langland is remembering a time when French was first learned early in a child's career and was used as the medium in which Latin was then taught. His generation (that of Chaucer and Gower) was the last one to be trilingually literate.

    every intellectual problem: Langland has in mind the *disputatio ad quodlibet*, the open discussion presided over by a skilled master in which virtually any topic could be handled. Such accomplishment he sees as dying out in the universities.

180   *Faith alone suffices*: from st. 4 of the *Pange lingua*, the great hymn of St Thomas Aquinas sung on the feast of Corpus Christi (held on the Thursday after Trinity Sunday). Langland means that simple lay-people who truly believe will not be blamed by God for the defective performance of the liturgy by their priests. They will be in the same position as Moslems and Jews who have never heard of Christ and do the best they can (cf. Trajan's remarks in Passus XI, esp. p. 121, and Imaginative's at the end of Passus XII (p. 136).

    Mahomet had been a Christian: the hostile portrait of Mahomet here given, that of a Christian heretic, derives from Hildebert of Lavardin's verse life (twelfth century) and from the *Speculum Historiale* of the thirteenth-century encyclopaedist Vincent of Beauvais (Bk. xxiii, ch. 40).

    the dove ... God's messenger: the allusion is to the descent of the Holy Spirit upon Christ at his baptism in the form of a dove (Matt. 3: 16).

    the truth about the English clergy!: the implication of what Anima does not 'dare' to say is clear: that the English will be led into heresy by their clergy as were the Syrians.

181   *Seek ... find ... salt of the earth*: the first quotation is from Matt. 7: 7, that after the proverb, from Matt. 5: 13 (both from the Sermon on the Mount). Langland plays on the meaning of the word 'preserve': the

clergy, the salt of the earth, must preserve or save the souls of the lay-people.

181   *Eleven men*: the twelve apostles minus Judas, though in fact Matthias was chosen to replace the latter before the beginning of their missionary work (Acts 1: 26).

England and Wales were entirely pagan: these lines summarize the account in Bede's *Ecclesiastical History* of how Pope St Gregory the Great sent Augustine to preach to the English in 597. Ethelbert, king of Kent, was converted in the same year. Anima's contrast between speech and action is a characteristic polemical point of Langland's about the modern clergy.

182   *cloth . . . from the weaver*: this comparison of christening to the process of preparing woollen cloth for manufacture hinges on a pun in the original (the word for baptism is 'fulling', the same word as that used for the cleansing of cloth). The cloth had its nap raised by means of the dried heads of the fuller's thistle arranged in a frame ('carded with teazles'). The 'tucking' process was one of thickening by moistening, heating, and pressing the cloth (the process now called 'fulling').

heathen . . . Heaven . . . land: the second analogy plays on the fact that 'heathen' and 'Heaven' are homophones in Langland's dialect, although the ideas they express are in contrast or opposition. The etymology of 'heathen' given is correct; as with the synonym 'pagan', it reflects the fact that remote country districts were the last to be converted to Christianity. Here the unbaptized ('heathen') soul is like wild uncultivated land ('heath').

St Matthew's account: Matt. 22: 4, the parable of the wedding feast. But no fowls are mentioned in the scriptural passage, and the image of calling birds by whistling is Langland's invention. He has superimposed his own view that the laity learn from the example of the clergy upon the framework of the parable (which has a quite different meaning and purpose).

183   *Lord, remember . . . Ephrata*: Ps. 131(132): 6; see the note on it earlier in Passus X (p. 96). The context of the psalm verse (David's resolution to find the Ark and build a resting-place for it) makes the sense clear: the clergy must put their essential vocation (the pursuit of charity and the spread of it) before all else, and at whatever cost.

Go out . . . creature: Mark 16: 15; the context describes the miracles and signs performed by the apostles in spreading the Gospel.

Nazareth . . . Damascus: all sees *in partibus infidelium* (non-existent bishoprics in lands held by the Moslems). Anima wants the holders of these titular sees to live up to them and preach Christianity there, even at the cost of their lives.

The Good Shepherd: John 10: 11 is the classical text on the duty of a priest to put the good of his people before all else.

Go into my vineyard!: Matt. 20: 4, from the parable of the labourers in the vineyard, was traditionally interpreted as a summons to priestly mission. Significantly, it is followed by the quarrel between the sons of Zebedee over precedence in the kingdom, which Christ settles by predicting his own coming death and the need for his disciples to be prepared to die in turn. This has a close bearing on Anima's argument on the bishop's calling as one to exemplary martyrdom.

Seek . . . find!: Matt. 7: 7, from the Sermon on the Mount, implies that the Moslems, who are already monotheists, are implicitly in quest of knowledge of Christ, something they can get only from missionaries prepared to risk death by preaching to them.

184   *metropolitan*: the striking notion of Christ as 'metropolitan' (the bishop of the chief city of a region) owes something to the theology of Christ as the high priest of the New Covenant developed in the Epistle to the Hebrews (see esp. Heb. 10: 19–21). Traditionally, the flow of water and blood from the side of Christ in John 19: 34 was interpreted as a symbol of baptism 'into the death of Christ'—that is, becoming a Christian implies readiness to die for Christ.

St Thomas: Thomas à Becket, martyred in 1170; his shrine at Canterbury was at this time one of the richest in Europe.

Do not put your sickle . . . corn: Deut. 23: 25 refers to literal reaping but has been skilfully adapted in the light of Matt. 9: 37–8 (Christ's metaphor of evangelization as the reaping of a field of corn) to become a warning against unestablished bishops' interference in the affairs of parish clergy.

the book of conscience: the vivid image originates in St Jerome's Commentary on Dan. 7: 10, and was much developed by later medieval homilists such as Alan of Lille.

185   *the red noble . . . the cross of Christ*: the cross and the crown were stamped on the reverse and obverse of the gold noble. Such values represent the 'corruptible crown' of 1 Cor. 9: 25 as opposed to the 'crown of justice' of 2 Tim. 4: 8.

Templars: the Order of Knights Templars was suppressed in 1312 by Pope Clement V, one of the chief charges against them being greed for wealth.

He hath put down . . . seat: from Luke 1: 52, Mary's answer to Elizabeth's salutation (the *Magnificat*).

By the first-fruits . . . tithes: Deut 12: 6 prescribes the rules for the Levites, the priestly order in the Old Covenant. Anima's position is that in a reformed Church the clergy will have to live on the gift-offerings of the laity, not on income derived from lands in their possession.

the emperor Constantine: (d. 337) endowed the Church with property and various privileges, though the document known as the 'Donation of Constantine', which enumerated these and various rights of the Pope, was an eighth-century forgery. The legend of the angel to which Anima alludes was cited by the followers of Wyclif, but its use here suggests no more than that Langland shared their dissatisfaction with clerical abuses arising from material wealth, not that he followed Wyclif's views on the nature of the sacraments, priestly authority, or doctrine generally. The insistence on disendowment does not amount to a cry for a 'poor' clergy, as the next note indicates.

186   *Every consecrated bishop . . . need*: these lines present a (somewhat idealistic) picture of the episcopacy exercising a purely spiritual leadership but with enough material wealth to be able to distribute charity. Langland's assumption is that a laity inspired by the unselfishness and holiness of the bishops would supply the latter with enough in the way of offerings to enable them to give it away to those in real need.

In my house . . . Carry the tithes . . . house: the two quotations, the first from Isa. 3: 7 (in context not at all about religious rulers), the second from Mal. 3: 10 (not Hosea), together underline the linked theme of sufficiency for charity and dependence on generosity in giving such a sufficiency to the Church. The context of the Malachi passage makes it clear that God will reward those who fulfil their obligation of giving tithes faithfully.

Love God and your neighbour: alluding to Matt. 22: 37–40 (a text drawing on Deut. 6: 5 and Lev. 19: 18), Christ's summary of the whole moral law of the Old Covenant.

miracles, wonderful works of power: the feeding of the five thousand described in Mark 6, was a 'Messianic' miracle, fulfilling Old Testament prophecies of how God would come to save his people at the appointed time.

Lazarus, come forth!: the raising of Lazarus, described in John 11, is instanced as the supreme miracle of Christ, denial of which illustrates the faithlessness of the Jews. The charge that Christ worked his miracles by diabolic power (and was therefore a false prophet, not the true Messiah) is made in Matt. 12: 24 ff., but not with reference to the raising of Lazarus.

187   *When the Holiest . . . end*: Dan. 9: 24–6, which deals with the rejection of the Messiah by the Jews, which will result in their punishment. Here Langland reads the prophecy as meaning that the special status of the Jews as the anointed holy people of God will come to an end with their rejection of the Lord's anointed (Christ).

they all of them worship God the Father: Anima concludes by arguing that, since Jews and Moslems alike agree in worshipping the one true God, it should be more than possible to convert them to Christian faith in its fullness. His implied understanding is that, since the missionaries to England converted the pagans (who did not believe in God at all), it can only be the want of faith and courage in the clergy which is now holding up the conversion of Moslems and Jews.

188 *Haukin the active man*: Will's reference to Haukin underlines the affinity between the two characters: Will represents the aspect of the ordinary man that is capable of instruction at a higher level (through vision), and it is significantly Haukin's master Piers who will disclose the new vision to Will.

The tree itself . . . 'Patience': most trees have the same name as their fruit; here, the distinction points to the symbolic nature of the image, patience being the trunk and branches (the substantial basis) on which eventually the fruit (the spiritual virtue to which all Christian life is directed) appears. Langland's main source for the idea of the tree of charity seems to be St Augustine's commentary on 1 John (*PL*, xxxv, cols. 1,993, 2,020, 2,033).

Heart: here symbolizes the affective and spiritual centre of human nature. Holy Church has already located Truth here in Passus I (see p. 12) and Piers in Passus V (p. 62) has repeated this, both linking Truth (God as object of knowledge) with Love or Charity (God as object of the will).

Liberum Arbitrium: translated henceforth as Free Choice, a rendering which is closer than Free Will to the union of affective and cognitive elements denoted by the technical term.

I fell . . . into a deep faint: here begins an inner dream or dream-within-a-dream provoked by the ecstatic shock of hearing a name long brooded-over (hence a 'love-dream', on the model of a dream about the beloved stimulated by the sound of the name).

189 *When the just man . . . him*: Ps. 36(37): 24. Compare Prov. 24: 16 and p. 82 above.

These winds: the traditional Three Temptations, the World (worldliness, love of material goods, to which the bounteous generosity of God the Creator is opposed), the Flesh (bodily pleasure, to which the suffering of Christ, the Wisdom of God (1 Cor. 1: 24) is opposed), and the Devil (positive malignity of will, to which the grace of the Spirit, operating through the power of Free Choice, is especially opposed).

190 *The ground . . . is called 'goodness'*: Piers now describes the tree from its other aspect, that of an emblem of the divine nature, the essence of which is goodness, shared in different ways by the three Persons of the Blessed Trinity. Piers's look of admonition is rightly interpreted by Will, who is now in a maturer state of spiritual receptiveness. There is a correspondence between the divine and human established through the Incarnation.

the marriage-fruit . . . turn out sour!: Piers now describes the tree once again under its human aspect—as emblematic of the different grades or levels at which mankind can achieve the virtue of charity. The ascending order is the common medieval one—marriage, widowhood, virginity. Cailloux in Burgundy supplied a highly esteemed pear. The maiden-fruit ripens first because it is nearest the sun (virginity is the state most receptive of divine grace) and becomes sweet without swelling with either desire or its consequence, pregnancy.

190 *Piers reached up to the top*: in this allegorical action, Will observes each of the estates or conditions of humanity up to the time of Christ falling into the hands of Satan. The special appropriateness of the figure is due to the fact that Adam's sin, which has consigned all men, including the just, to Hell, was to pluck forbidden fruit from a tree.

191 *Limbo*: the place of the just who died before Christ, meaning 'border region', a part, but the furthest part, of Hell.

Then Piers . . . stolen: Piers's act initiates the Incarnation: it shows redemption as a free act of God, for whose action in nature and in history Piers here stands as an emblem or figure.

Jesus, the son of Justice: (that is, of Truth, God the Father, the judge of all) and also the sun of justice, as in the prophecy of Malachi (4: 2).

the time of time's fulfilment should arrive: time is fulfilled with the birth of Christ, when the tree of human nature, growing through history, bears its ultimate fruit, God-made-man, in whom also Charity is to be fully embodied.

Behold the handmaid . . . word: Luke 1: 38.

he learned the skills of battle: in this metaphorical account, the growing-up of the human Jesus under the tutelage of Piers (here an emblem of God's power acting in time, or, alternatively, of the divine nature of the Second Person, the Wisdom of God, operating upon the human Jesus) is figured as the training of a young knight by a senior one, and also that of an apprentice physician by a doctor of medicine. Compare also Gal. 4: 1–5.

For it is not . . . ill: Matt. 9: 12; the close association between sickness and sinfulness, and the use of one as an emblem of the other, is taken by Langland from the New Testament.

192 *he healed Lazarus*: the story of the raising of Lazarus is told in John 11, but the accusation of possession by a devil occurs in John 10: 20, in response to Jesus's implied claim to power over death (the idea that doubtless suggested putting the provocative statement here).

I shall overthrow . . . the house of prayer: this account draws on both John 2: 14–19 (the claim about rebuilding the Temple) and Matt. 21, the quotation 'My house . . .' coming from Matt. 21: 13 (parallel Mark 11: 17), and itself being taken from Isa. 56: 7.

193 *It is you . . . 'Hail, Master!'*: directly quoted from Matt. 26: 25, 49 respectively.

It must be . . . comes!: Matt. 18: 7, not addressed to Judas directly in context, but obviously appropriate to his case; it may have been suggested by the reference to hanging in preceding verse 6.

battle against death and the Devil: the notion of Christ's crucifixion as a battle against death is formulated in the Easter Sequence *Victimae paschali laudes* (v. 3) and derives from scriptural texts such as 1 Cor. 15: 55–7.

on mid-Lent Sunday . . . Abraham: the vision resumes at an earlier stage in the liturgical cycle of the Church's year, mid-Lent or *Laetare* being the fourth Sunday in Lent, when the Epistle reading (Gal. 4: 22–31) deals with Abraham and his two sons. By making Faith-Abraham a herald-at-arms (whose task was to announce the names of knights at a joust), Langland continues the dominant chivalric metaphor of Christ's conflict with Satan as a duel to gain men's souls.

194 *three men in one body*: the blazon or device on the shield recalls the image of the Trinity in the inner dream from which Will has awoken (see p. 190 above).

Truth, 'the Son': the original has for 'Truth' 'Soothfastnesse', an allusion to John 14: 6, and not the same word ('Treuthe') as is used in the first vision to refer to God (the Father).

Christ, Christianity and all Christians: this comprehensive definition draws on the theological doctrine of the mystical body of Christ, which teaches that Christ and his Church are one, united in one faith, lord, and baptism.

the states of marriage: the analogy between the Trinity and the persons in a marriage depends on the notion that nature is something shared by, respectively, the divine persons and the human (divinity; humanity). It is ingenious in an almost 'Metaphysical' way, the failures in correspondence being as striking as the successes.

195 *My God, my God . . . me?*: Ps. 21: 1, spoken by Christ on the cross (Matt. 27: 46). The Son is a 'widow' as having been forsaken by God, not in virtue of her spouse having died.

Accursed the man . . . Israel!: the nearest source for these lines is the Hereford Breviary readings for the Feast of St Anne, but the sense of the maxim has many parallels.

the Spirit . . . and the Son: the quotation expresses the essential Western Christian view of the dogma of the Trinity (that the Holy Spirit proceeds from both Father and Son), in contrast to the Eastern (Orthodox) view that he proceeds only from the Father. Langland's calling the Spirit the Free Will of both links him with the human will and the power of *Liberum Arbitrium* or Free Choice.

I saw God one summer-time: Abraham's story is found in Gen. 18 ff. The notion that Abraham had knowledge of the Trinitarian nature of God is based on the appearance of the three angels to him at Mamre (Gen. 18); the traditional interpretation is found in the Sarum Breviary's Vespers antiphon for Quinquagesima Sunday. The circumcised 'son' may be either Ishmael (Gen. 17: 23) or Isaac (Gen. 21: 4), though both were circumcised before, not after, the command to sacrifice Isaac.

196   *As you promised . . . for ever*: from Luke 1: 55, part of the *Magnificat* sung at the service of Vespers.

by the offering of bread and wine: it was not Abraham but Melchizedech who offered bread and wine (Gen. 14: 18); both are mentioned together as offering sacrifice in the prayer *Supra quae* in the Canon of the mass.

from a man who has baptized him: Abraham speaks as having heard from John the Baptist (who had been put to death by Herod; see Matt. 14: 1–12) the very words with which the living John greeted Christ at the Jordan (John 1: 29). John, the last of the prophets, will have joined Abraham in Limbo after his death (see p. 191 above). Both are 'heralds' of the new faith in Christ.

a leper: the Lazarus of Christ's parable (Luke 16: 22); Langland has given a graphically literal rendering of the phrase 'Abraham's bosom' (traditionally interpreted as Limbo) in this scene. Along with Lazarus are the rest of the just who died before Christ.

197   *Can sin so long hold out . . . for us all?*: the importance of these lines is to point up the *gravity* of sin and the absolute need for the direct intervention of God to save man from its power.

I burst into tears: Will's tears and his preceding words recall those of Haukin at the end of Passus XIV in a deliberate verbal echo. Like Haukin, Will has had to be forcibly convinced of the seriousness of sin before he can undergo full conversion of heart.

198   *I am Spes . . . Mount Sinai*: Spes turns out to be evidently Moses, and it is appropriate enough that the Mosaic Law should be seen as being fulfilled in that of Christ (cf. Matt. 5: 17); but whereas Abraham was a traditional figure of Faith, the identification of Moses with Hope seems original, if unsurprising (cf. Deut. 34: 4). The Law was given to Moses on Mount Sinai (Exod. 19).

not sealed: the 'letter' is not sealed, it is *open* and *public* but lacks the royal seal of confirmation (actual seals often had the form of a cross). Letters-patent were sealed with the Great Seal.

Love God . . . neighbour: based on Matt 22: 37–9, a summary of the Ten Commandments given to Moses on tablets of stone, and the gloss or commentary is the following verse, Matt. 22: 40. The text itself runs together Deut. 6: 5 and Lev. 19: 18.

thanks to this charm: the term 'charm' is of course ironic (cf. Haukin's charm in Passus XIII (p. 149); the figures mentioned were all famed for outstanding moral virtue and adherence to the law of God. The term 'saved' has a conditional, not an absolute, sense, however; these just Old Testament figures are all in Limbo, waiting for the death of Christ to 'seal' their claim and set them free.

It's really astonishing . . . the truth?: Will's outburst is not meant to suggest either that faith is preferable to hope (because easier) or that the two are incompatible, but to prepare for the action that follows, which illustrates the impotence of both really to *save* man from sin (only Christ, Love incarnate, can do that).

199 *We caught sight of a Samaritan*: the enacted story of the Samaritan, in which Will is first spectator then participant, is drawn from the parable in Luke 10: 30–6, which illustrates what is meant by loving one's neighbour, and who one's neighbour is. The interpretation furnished is a traditional homiletic one; what Langland has done is to revitalize it in the telling, and to place it in the wider context of his 'chivalric' re-presentation of Christ's battle with Satan.

200 *the Law of Christ*: glossed in Gal. 6: 2 as love of one's neighbour ('bearing one another's burdens'); allegorically, after the rescue of man from the wounds of sin, he is to be healed and restored by living a life of charity.

201 *the blood of a child . . . virgin*: the startling imagery of child-cannibalism and witchcraft is meant to work as a means of renewing well-known ideas of the sacraments of penance and the Eucharist as needed for salvation. The chief sources include 1 John 1: 7 (washing in blood) and John 6: 54 (eating the flesh and blood of Christ).

Caro: the interpretation of the Samaritan's horse as the human nature that 'carried' the divine Second Person was also traditional.

Death . . . death of you!: (Hos. 13: 14) occurs also in the service of Lauds on Holy Saturday (first antiphon). See also p. 211 below.

202 *God . . . compared to a hand*: the extended comparison of the Trinity to a hand may be original, but the notion of God holding the universe within his hand was a familiar one found, for example, in the sixth-century hymn *Quem terra, pontus, aethera*, sung at matins in the Office of the Blessed Virgin Mary. The quotation 'he was conceived . . .' is from the fourth article of the Apostles' Creed.

For I will draw . . . myself: John 12: 32; the application to the Father may have been suggested by the immediate context (see v. 28).

203 *the whole wide universe in themselves*: see note on God 'compared to a hand' (p. 202) above.

Thou art creator of all things . . .: from the Compline hymn *Jesu salvator saeculi* (st. 2).

204 *He who sins . . . sin*: Mark 3: 29; the sin against the spirit is the wilful refusal to respond to the grace of repentance.

to extinguish God's grace: the image leads by a natural transition to the second extended analogy for the Trinity, that of the torch.

a torch or a taper: a torch was piece of twisted hemp enclosed in wax; a taper a wax candle.

grace devoid of mercy: not a quotation, but is so presented to highlight its paradoxical nature; lack of mercy in men has the effect of rendering even divine kindness inoperative.

205 *Now, for men . . . the lovelessness of humankind*: this passage explores the difficult doctrine of grace and free will: Langland is saying that for God's grace (which is always at hand) to be properly operative, it needs some antecedent good will in man. It is the lack of any trace of this prior disposition that constitutes the 'sin against the Holy Spirit'.

I say . . . I know you not!: Matt. 25: 12, from the parable of the ten virgins, especially apt in context since the oil which the foolish virgins lacked to fill their lamps was commonly interpreted as charity or love.

Pamplona: indulgences were issued to the abbot of Roncesvalles, near Pamplona in northern Spain, and distributed in England from the house of St Mary Rounceval at Charing Cross, to which Chaucer's Pardoner was attached.

206 *If I speak . . . nothing*: 1 Cor. 13: 1, which introduces a passage of St Paul which places charity above all virtues, including faith and hope; its evocation is partly ironic here, for the Samaritan is speaking not of those who have other virtues but lack charity, but of those who are positively uncharitable, even if they are outwardly religious.

worthless beacons . . . Not everyone . . . Heaven!: the image of the beacon that cannot be seen may have been suggested by Matt. 5: 14–16. The quotation that follows, from Matt. 7: 21, has a verse following which is very close to the argument of the passage from 1 Cor. 13 (especially v. 2).

Think of Dives: the parable of Dives ('the Rich Man') and Lazarus the beggar (in Luke 16: 19–31) is that already drawn on at the end of Passus XVI (see p. 196 and note).

this is the very worst: murder is not instanced as the unique sin against the Holy Spirit but as the clearest form of lack of charity or resistance to the power of grace.

207 *Vengeance . . . just men!*: the italicized part of the quotation is close to the wording of the prayer in the tract of the Mass of Holy Innocents (28 December), the probable context of Langland's outburst on the murder of the innocent. The idea of the blood of the innocent crying out for vengeance goes back to Gen. 4: 10 (Cain's murder of Abel).

Very rarely indeed do we see . . . mercy: the Samaritan's view is very like that taken in the Lady Meed section; unless evil is punished, justice will not be done, and justice is rooted in reason, which is an attribute of the divine nature itself.

Your sin . . . stolen: the same quotation which appeared earlier in the confession of Greed in Passus V (see p. 51). Langland's thought on the need for restitution is consistent in both the earlier and the later parts of the poem, as is his thought on retributive justice.

208 *His tender mercies . . . works*: Ps. 144(145): 9, which also appears at the end of Greed's confession (see p. 52 and note, 'Misericordia . . .').

There are three things: the exemplum is drawn from Pope Innocent III's *De Contemptu Mundi* (1, 18), which itself uses passages from Prov. 19:

13, 27: 15, and 10: 26. The three sources of sin are bodily frailty, outward affliction, and willed evil. It is the last of these that 'quenches' mercy, as smoke puts out the flame when the wood is wet.

My power . . . infirmity: 2 Cor. 12: 9. The strong indication that the virtue in question here is hope, and the clear evidence that in the third example charity is the virtue needed to combat unkindness, may justify us as seeing faith as the virtue needed to combat natural frailty.

unkindness is absolutely contrary . . . right: it at once quenches sight (a symbol of willingness to turn and repent) and extinguishes divine mercy (because the blinded will refuses to make the initial movement of sorrow).

210   *Palm Sunday*: when clergy and people processed around the church (as they still do) chanting the hymn *Glory, praise*. Up till now, Will has been dreaming of Lent and its events, and now his waking life and the content of his dream converge, the latter resuming from where Passus XVII left off.

barefoot . . . spurs of gold: the conflict in which Jesus will 'win his spurs' (prove his claim to be dubbed knight) is the coming battle with the powers of evil and death.

Blessed is he . . . Lord!: Matt. 21: 9;? occurs in the *Sanctus* (at every mass) and also in the processional antiphon for Palm Sunday.

Piers's coat of arms: that of simple human nature, not the blazon described by Faith in Passus XVI (see p. 194); Jesus is 'in disguise', and this means concealing his divinity.

211   *the Jews or the Scribes?*: Langland seems to think of the Scribes, the experts in the Jewish law, as a separate group from the Jews, unless he is simply contrasting them as a part with the people as a whole.

I, even I . . . O Death!: Hos. 13: 14; see note to p. 201, 'Death . . .', above.

Crucify him!: in the original many of these quotations are in Latin, and present a continuous sense of the immediacy of the Gospel Passion accounts read in Holy Week. They have all been translated in order to give a clear and uninterrupted narrative, but much of the poignancy and solemnity of the original is thereby forfeited, as well as the contrast with Langland's own colloquial expansions.

a poisoned drink: Langland believes that the vinegar on a sponge (Mark 15: 36 and parallels) is meant to hasten Christ's death, a view he abandons in the C-text revision of this passage.

212   *Truly, the Son of God*: Matt. 27: 54, spoken by the centurion and others.

Longinus: the name given in the apocryphal *Gospel of Nicodemus* (well-known in Middle English translations) to the Roman soldier who pierced the side of Jesus with a spear (*lancea*, Gk *longke*), in John 19: 34, to ensure that he was dead. His story is briefly told in the *Golden Legend*, ch. 47. Langland makes him a Jewish knight in order to represent emblematically the chivalric defeat of the Jews by Jesus, his restoration of sight contrasting with their continued refusal to believe in Christ (in medieval art Synagoga, a female figure symbolizing Judaism, was depicted blindfolded).

213   *Vengeance fall on your heads*: Faith's denunciation of the 'villainous' ('ignoble'/'evil') behaviour of the Jews has ironic edge from the fact that he is Abraham, father of the Jewish faith and founder of the Jewish nation. Their punishment for rejecting Christ is to lose both their civil rights (as historically they did) and their claim to be God's chosen people, along with independence as a nation. Unable to earn a living from the land, they will be forced into usury, a practice condemned by both Christian and Jewish law, but in practice permitted to the Jews by Christian rulers in Europe.

When God shall send . . . done!: from pseudo-Augustine, *Contra Judaeos* (*PL*, xlii, col. 1,123–4), loosely based on Dan. 9: 24, and read in a lesson for the fourth Sunday of Advent.

according to the Scriptures: the source is not so much Scripture as the *Gospel of Nicodemus*, but the latter was inspired here by the famous verse Ps. 84(85): 11. The phrase 'according . . .' is from the Nicene Creed (end of third clause), and the preceding 'descent . . .' from the Apostles' Creed (article 8). Langland's point is to stress these events as matters of essential Christian belief.

215   *there is no way . . . Hell!*: from a response in the third Nocturn of the Office of the Dead (*Sarum Breviary*, II, 278) and loosely based on Job 7: 9.

That God . . . guile!: from the hymn *Pange lingua* of Venantius Fortunatus, sung on Good Friday. The deception—which explains why Jesus did not bear the arms of the Trinity (see p. 210 above)— required concealing from the Devil that God had become man in order to redeem mankind from Adam's sin by dying on the cross, though innocent.

she existed before . . . did: the notion that Justice is the eldest of the Daughters of God, prior even to Truth, may be due to seeing the latter as connected with God's self-revelation to man, and the former as part of his unrevealed essence; but this remains uncertain.

Love: here a name for God which now takes over from the title 'Truth' given him in the first vision (see p. 8 and note). In the earlier allegory of Passus XIII, Patience had also received instructions from Love, there personified as a female character (see p. 142 and note, 'Learn . . .').

216   *Sundown . . . gladness*: Ps. 29(30): 6, applied here to Easter morning.

letters, open for all to see!: these letters-patent complement those of Spes in Passus XVII (see p. 198), and also fulfil their hope; it is not stated but implied that they have been 'sealed', since Christ has now died and so ratified their content.

I shall have ... rest: the psalm-verse, Ps. 4: 9, begins the office of matins on Holy Saturday. Love, it will be recalled, is 'the plant of peace' (see p. 12 above).

217   *too little ... enough really means*: Peace here rounds out and completes Holy Church's teaching in Passus I that 'enough' is the one true 'remedy' (p. 9), by showing the importance of experiencing not 'too much' (which is sin) but 'too little' (which is suffering). She now develops an argument which amounts to a 'theodicy', a justification of the ways of God, and especially of the existence of the various forms of evil—suffering, sin, want, and death.

Book: stands for the Bible; his two eyes signify the literal and figurative senses, or else the Old and the New Testaments.

218   *the physical elements ... this*: Book appeals to the 'witness of the elements'—the air, water, fire, and earth that constituted creation in the old physics—to the fact that Jesus, from birth to death on the cross, was divine.

Bid me to come ... the water!: Matt. 14: 28.

the sons of Simeon: the 'just and devout man' of Luke 2: 25; his sons are raised from the dead in the *Gospel of Nicodemus*, and tell the story of Christ's harrowing of Hell.

giant: the image of Christ as a giant who will soon break down Hell's gates recalls Samson (Judg. 16: 3), who carried off the gates of Gaza. There may also be an allusion to Ps. 18(19): 6, whose *gigas* was commonly interpreted as referring prophetically to Christ.

Lift up your gates, you princes!: Ps. 23(24): 7, 9 (sung at the second Nocturn of matins on Holy Saturday); in context the gates in question are those of Heaven, at God's triumphal return after defeating his enemies. Langland, following Christian liturgical tradition, makes them refer to the gates of Hell, of which the victorious Christ is also master.

Lazarus: Satan alludes to the raising of Lazarus from the dead (cf. p. 192 and note), though it was Christ's voice that summoned him, not his spirit in the form of a light. Satan is unaware that Lazarus was resuscitated, not resurrected from the dead.

219   *he who is Truth itself ... words*: Lucifer relies on the 'Truth' of God, using the same arguments as the Daughter of God, Truth, at pp. 214–15 above. His case is answered by Christ at p. 221 below.

seven thousand years: the figure is unusual and perhaps the result of metrical necessity in the original. The common estimate of the time elapsed from the Fall to the Harrowing was four thousand (as in the well-known carol 'Adam lay y-bounden').

220   *a short one!*: the 'short answer' alluded to is that given in the account of the first and second temptations in the desert in Matt. 4: 4, 7.

the wife of Pilate ... Jesus was: Langland follows the tradition developed on the basis of Matt. 27: 19 (the dream of Pilate's wife) that the Devil attempted to prevent the crucifixion of Christ. The somewhat obscure statement, '*I* wanted ... to prolong his life ...', seems to mean that even after death Jesus would continue to fight the power of sin, and that could only mean trouble for the devils (as it does).

220 *It was all your fault ... Heaven*: Satan here repeats the account first given in Passus I by Holy Church (see p. 11).

Now shall the Prince ... out!: John 13: 31; the speaker is Christ in the source. Possibly it is meant to be a free-standing 'authorial' comment on the situation; but there is a special ironic aptness in having this claim to victory placed in the mouth of Satan, where it becomes an admission of defeat.

Who is this? ... The king ... : from Ps. 23(24): 10.

the people in darkness: Isa. 9: 2, quoted in Matt. 4: 16, and appearing in the Latin *Gospel of Nicodemus*.

221 *Behold the Lamb of God!*: John's greeting to Christ in John 1: 36.

a reptile's form ... female: the traditional representation of the serpent in visual art—a standing, lizard-like creature with a woman's face.

An eye ... tooth: from Exod. 21: 24 (transposed); Jesus infers that *any* return of the same will be just, including deceit for deceit.

I did not come ... it: Matt. 5: 17, referring in context to the law of Moses specifically; here it has a wider sense of 'justice based on the law of reason'.

222 *He falls ... himself*: Ps. 7: 16, especially apt here in context.

the time of vintage ... Jehoshaphat: the image of the fruit of the Tree of Charity has here become transformed into the Biblical one of the vine—the dead as the grapes ripened for pressing to form the drink of love. The valley of Jehoshaphat (Joel 3: 2, 12) was traditionally the place of judgement and the expected site of the Last Judgement, the vintage-image expressing the anger of God. Langland has imposed upon it the more positive associations of harvesting images such as those of Matt. 13: 39 and the image of Christ drinking new wine in the kingdom (Mark 14: 25).

brothers by baptism: alludes to the common Pauline idea that through baptism all Christians are adopted children of God and co-heirs with Christ (cf. Rom. 8: 15–17, Gal. 4: 4–6), but also perhaps invokes such institutions as brotherhood in arms (among knights: an example would be that of Palamon and Arcite in Chaucer's *Knight's Tale*).

Against you ... sinned: Ps. 50: 6 (51: 4). Since sin is an offence against *God*, forgiveness of sin is a matter for God alone.

Even on earth they do not hang ... treason: refers to the actual custom of pardoning someone who had managed to survive hanging (something attested in the period). The main point is that God will hardly be *less* merciful than a human monarch: man having already been punished for sin by the penalty of *death*, there is no call for a second capital punishment (damnation), only for a spell in prison (Purgatory).

223 *No evil . . . unrewarded*: from Innocent III's *De Contemptu Mundi* (III, 15), already quoted in part in Passus IV (p. 39). It expresses the essential moral view of God characteristic of the Old Testament.

Hold, enough!: (*parce*) may allude to Neh. (2 Esd.) 13: 22, as well as to the *Dirige*, the matins office for the Dead.

he could never see his own blood . . . I heard . . . speak: the strongest claim anywhere in Langland for the literal truth and efficacy of the Incarnation. The quotation from 2 Cor. 12: 1 seems a floating parenthesis spoken by the poet and perhaps implies a value for his vision akin to that of the apostle Paul himself.

Enter not into judgement . . . Lord: Ps. 142(143): 2, the whole of which, especially perhaps verse 10, is relevant in this context of Christ's liberation of the souls from Hell.

Astaroth: the Babylonian Ishtar, here just a name for a devil.

those he wanted . . . not: Christ leads away the souls of the just and leaves behind the rest, but with the possibility that at the Last Judgement they too may be saved if there are 'mitigating circumstances' (see 'any circumstances' above).

224 *Flesh sins . . . God-flesh-within*: from st. 4 of the hymn 'O High Eternal King' sung at the vigil and matins of Ascension Day, emphasizing once again Langland's profound faith in the mystery of the Incarnation. Although it is Easter morning, the Ascension is anticipated as the culminating event of Paschal-tide, the Easter season.

Breaking through cloud . . . Love!: quoted from the *Book of Parables* of Alan of Lille (*PL*, ccx, col. 581–2), a passage echoing Tobit 3: 22.

for ever . . . end: the formula that ends the great prayers of the Church.

Mercy and Truth . . . kissed: Ps. 84(85): 11, the basis of the whole allegory of the Four Daughters of God.

Te Deum Laudamus: the great hymn of praise sung at matins every Sunday except during Lent, the penitential season; its reappearance here symbolizes the dawning of Easter, and brings together the inner world of the dream and the outer one of liturgical observance.

How sweet it is . . . unity!: Ps. 132(133): 1, expressing the vision of the Redemption as having brought about unity between man and God, and thence between man and man, and foreshadowing Langland's way of speaking of the Church in Passus XIX as 'Unity' (see p. 236).

225 *Kit . . . Calote*: both type-names for a (nagging) wife and a (disobedient) girl, and so may not have autobiographical reference; but Catherine and Colette were certainly known names of the time, and in

the C-text too Langland refers to his wife as Kit, the familiar form of the former (see C. v. 2).

225   *Creep on your knees . . . walk!*: the call to creep to the cross reflects the penitential practice of venerating the cross on Good Friday, but underlines the continuing need for penance and humility if the fruits of Christ's victory are to be assured. The power of the cross symbol to ward off evil was widespread in popular belief, the 'shadow' notion perhaps going back to such texts as Acts 5: 15.

226   *to receive Holy Communion*: Will is ready for Communion, so has presumably confessed his sins and made his peace with God; but instead of receiving it he has a vision of the crucified Christ that reminds him of the continuing human cost that underlies the sacramental forms of the eucharistic elements. This is the most explicit identification so far of Piers with Christ.

Christ? . . . Why do you call him that?: Will here shows the same doctrinal literal-mindedness earlier displayed in discussing with Spes the commandment to love (cf. p. 198). The instruction that follows enables Langland to clarify the relation between the earthly ministry of Jesus and his role as the glorified Saviour after his resurrection, using the model of aristocratic society as a means of illustrating the doctrine.

to kneel and bow the head . . . Jesus?: alludes to Phil. 2: 10, quoted below on p. 228.

227   *the status of franklins*: members of the gentry immediately below the nobility.

their honoured prophet . . . a crown of thorns: the conclusion of Conscience's account of how Jesus was received by his people is, of course, bitterly ironic; but its tone is less violent than that of Faith in Passus XVIII (see p. 213).

228   *what the name 'Christ' signifies*: the literal sense of 'Christ' (translating Hebrew *Messiah*) is 'the Anointed One', and Langland has probably associated the dogmatic title of Jesus given by believers with the anointing of kings still preserved in the English coronation service.

why he is now here like this: Conscience here expresses one of the central ideas in Langland's work, one which had already been articulated earlier by his travelling-companion Patience in Passus XIV (see p. 160). He takes it further in stressing the need actively to *imitate* Christ in his sufferings.

Glory to God in the highest!: from the Nativity account in Luke 2: 14.

Magi: 'sages', but the tradition that they were kings goes back to Tertullian (second century). This, along with an allegorization of the gifts, appears in the *Golden Legend*; but Langland has his own interpretation of the gifts which is appropriate to his vision of Christ as king and conqueror.

the gift ... mystically signified by the incense: the commonest interpretation of the gifts is 'divinity' (for incense), 'royalty' (for gold) and 'humanity suffering' (for myrrh).

229   *a wedding-feast in Judaea*: the miracle of Cana is recorded only in John 2: 1–11. Langland's allegorical interpretation sees it as a 'sign' of the New Testament transformation of the imperfect Mosaic law and the first step in the degrees of doing well. The pattern of thought here is to equate Christ's act of power with Do-well, his acts of compassion with Do-better, and his acts of pardon with Do-best.

230   *Jesus, son of David*: compare the account of the entry into Jerusalem in Matt. 21: 12.

    For every thousand ... again!: 1 Sam. 18: 7; Langland develops the idea that the 'son' of David should also have been acknowledged with the cry that greeted a military conqueror, and in doing so echoes the metaphor he gave to Holy Church in her instruction to Will in Passus I (see p. 11).

    Christ has risen from the dead!: based on one of the Synoptic accounts, for example, Matt. 28: 1–6.

231   *Was it not fitting ... bliss?*: Christ's words to the disciples on the way to Emmaus (Luke 24: 26).

    Thomas: an early tradition made Thomas the apostle of India. The account of Thomas and his confession of faith is based on John 20: 26–9.

232   *He gave power to Piers, ... a pardon*: the natural interpretation of 'Piers' here is the apostle Peter, although on p. 226 above he was Jesus and in the ploughing-allegory that follows his identity as the ploughman is to the fore. This implies Langland's belief in the spiritual oneness between Christ and his followers in faith, which has been slowly developed throughout the poem, principally through the figure of Piers, on the basis of John 14: 20–3.

    the Comforter and Advocate: these two terms translate 'Paraclete', the original form taken from John 14: 26. The account of the descent of the Holy Spirit draws on Acts 2: 3.

    Veni Creator Spiritus: sung especially at Pentecost; 'grace' as a gift of the Spirit is mentioned in line 3 of stanza 1. The Spirit has already been identified with Grace by the Samaritan (see esp. p. 204).

233   *Antichrist*: the classic source-text for the idea of Antichrist, round which an elaborate medieval tradition developed, is 1 John 2: 18–22 (cf. also 2 John 7). The mention of 'unction from the Holy One' in verse 20 may have suggested giving a warning against Antichrist to the Spirit at his descent.

    the forms of grace ... one: 1 Cor. 12: 4. St Paul mentions mainly spiritual graces, but Langland makes the Holy Ghost the source of all good qualities and talents, including those needed in natural and in everyday social life, showing thereby the oneness of religious and secular in the ideal order emblematized by 'Unity'. The world of the first two visions has returned, but is now seen in a deeper and more theologically comprehensive perspective.

234   *applying tough Folvillian methods*: in the original 'Folville's laws', after the behaviour of a notorious criminal gang active in Leicestershire in the earlier part of the century. The expression is ironical, since the knights who are to act thus (following the precepts of Piers in Passus VI: see esp. p. 64) will be enforcing, not breaking the law.

Piers is to be my . . . ploughman: these words recapitulate the ploughing-action of the second vision, but the ploughing in question is now clearly allegorical or spiritual, the 'cultivation of truth'. Piers is at once associated with the original ploughman, type of the honest lay Christian, and with the apostle Peter, to whom Christ gave the power to be his deputy on Earth (Matt. 16: 18 f.)

of finer quality than all the rest: the fourth Gospel contains lofty spiritual teaching, and a special stress on the mystery of Christ.

four working horses . . . ploughing: the basic work of preparing the ground for Christian faith is done by the Evangelists (ploughing), a fit image of the turning-over or conversion with which faith begins. The refinement of faith into formal belief and understanding (harrowing) is done by the four great Doctors of the (Western) Church, on whose teaching Langland has drawn extensively in the work till now. Their harrow is the Bible itself—signifying their method of interpreting one text by another, and especially the typological method favoured by Langland himself, that of seeing persons and events of the Old Testament as anticipating and being fulfilled in persons and events in the New.

235   *his seeds, the Cardinal Virtues*: those on which natural and social existence was thought to hang (*cardo*, 'hinge') were associated with some at least of the spiritual gifts enumerated in Isa. 11: 2–3 (esp. counsel with prudence, piety with justice, and fortitude with the cardinal virtue so named). The importance of temperance has already been stressed by Holy Church in Passus I, and the special importance of justice is noted by Conscience in his argument with the brewer (see p. 239 below). These virtues formed the basis on which the specifically spiritual ones, Faith, Hope, and Charity (the 'theological virtues') were built.

Spare me, O Lord! . . . Be of brave heart . . . blamed!: the prayer, from Job 7: 16 occurs in this form in the matins of the Office of the Dead. Its link here with one of Cato's *Distichs* (ii. 14) illustrates Langland's sense of the relatedness of 'secular' and 'religious' virtues in the Christian scheme of things.

236   *cultivate the cardinal virtues . . . their teaching*: an important passage stressing the need to study the Bible and the works of the moral

philosophers alike in the light of the Church's tradition of interpretation. It clearly illustrates the orthodoxy of Langland's religious position. He sees a properly educated mind and heart as the right location for the fruit of charity to grow in (cf. Anima in Passus XVI, esp. p. 188, which anticipates this passage in its reference to hoeing and weeding).

the cross . . . to save mankind: the essential point here is that the Church is built on the passion, death, and resurrection of its founder, and unified by the sacrament of the Eucharist, which calls these events to mind each time mass is said.

a cart called Christianity: the primary sense of 'Christianity' is 'baptism', the means by which humanity (the corn) is brought from the fields (the world) into the barn (the Church). The baptized Christian is advanced on his journey by the sacrament of penance, administered by a priest.

Piers is at his ploughing: now has a wider sense—not just St Peter the apostle but all the faithful pastors of Christ throughout history: the siege of Antichrist is both an early historical event (the Neronian persecution) and an ongoing ordeal for the Church facing a hostile and sinful world.

Pride . . . assembled a huge army: the events from here on recapitulate those of the second vision, with the Deadly Sins assaulting the Church in force and eventually prevailing.

237   *a smart new coat of paint—sophistry, it's called*: the key weapon in Antichrist's armoury is religious hypocrisy, the sin warned against by Anima in Passus XV (see esp. p. 170). The pretence of real contrition, and the correlative of absolution granted without sincere repentance, combine to corrupt the penitential process on which the preservation of a good conscience and, with it, the growth of holiness, depend.

238   *the waters of sorrow . . . eyes*: again important as a symbol (now part of an allegorical action) of true inward repentance (cf. the earlier tears of Will, Haukin, and then Will again at the end of Passus XVI). The tears fill the defensive moat around the inner fortification of the Christian community, representing the primary bulwark against pride and worldliness.

for the season of Lent, at least!: Conscience's words make clear the recurrent, cyclical character of Christian penitence, which must exist at all times, but is especially intensified during the liturgical season of Lent, at the end of which all may make their confession, render satisfaction, and receive their Easter communion with a clear conscience. The terms of the pardon are ' "make satisfaction", and then you are at one with God'.

And forgive us . . . against us: the fifth petition of the Lord's Prayer, which makes unity and peace with God conditional on unity and peace with one's neighbour.

238   *a brewer*: vulgar and mercenary, he represents the recalcitrant worldliness that makes religion into a mere formal show and spiritual values a mockery.

239   *an ignorant vicar*: his cynicism accompanies a genuine sense of grievance. The cardinals were much resented for their worldly extravagance and interest in collecting money for the pope. During the Avignon papacy (until 1377) many had to engage in raising money from the Jews and other financiers instead of looking after the relics of the martyrs in Rome at the churches for which they were given titular responsibility.

240   *Piers... emperor of the World*: the brunt of this remark is that Conscience (perhaps signifying the pious laity of the gentry and knightly classes) should be active in public affairs, while those of the Church are left in the hands of the ordinary people and the clergy who have their interests truly at heart (= Piers); but this may be too specific an interpretation.

   the Pope... to kill their bodies!: presumably alludes to the scandalous war between Urban VI and the antipope Clement VII which broke out in 1379 following the Great Schism of 1378. The palpable disunity in Christendom at the highest level doubtless lay behind Langland's choice of 'Unity' as his special name for the Christian Church ideally conceived.

   God will send his rain... just: Matt. 5: 45, and associating Piers's charitable generosity with that of God himself. Piers here symbolizes both the ideal ploughman and the ideal priest, each of whom works for the good of his fellow Christians.

   Thou shalt not kill... says the Lord: the first part of the quotation, from Exod. 20: 13, is quoted in Luke 18: 20, the second, from Deut. 32: 35, in Heb. 10: 30.

   Change that worldly acumen... soul!: the bad example of the cardinals has led to cynicism about the reality of the cardinal virtues, and the affectation of a mere simulacrum of each of them.

241   *the Spirit of Understanding... manorial rolls!*: the virtue of prudence having been corrupted into 'an eye for the main chance', the nobleman now illustrates the corruption of understanding (the spirit of understanding mentioned in Isa. 11: 2: see note to p. 235, 'his seeds...') into the quest for profit, and (proper) strength into unjustified coercion.

   I am head of the law!: the King's claim to act justly risks the confusion of true justice (rooted in reason and right) and mere power (deriving from his position as the ultimate legal authority in the land). His attitude opens the way to that exploitation of kingdom and people of which Richard II was to be accused in the next decade (by, among others, Langland: see C. III. 207–9).

But yet . . . lust!: the couplet quoted by Conscience is probably some familiar legal dictum of the time, and stands in sharp contrast to the one quoted by the ignorant commons in the Prologue (see p. 5), with which this king would doubtless be willing to agree.

242   *I encountered Need*: an allegorical presentation of an inner argument or debate: where does *he* stand in the world? Need has been variously regarded by interpreters, but at the simplest level he is just the fact of physical necessity which justifies itself and which avoids blame by observing the rule of moderation (temperance)—that is, by not letting strict necessity degenerate into an excuse for sloth or greed. The 'law of nature' mentioned below is the instinct for survival, not the natural moral law of reason.

none of the virtues . . . Temperance!: the critique of the other three cardinal virtues as capable of being twisted into vices is a shrewd one in the light of the previous Passus with its brewer, nobleman, and king, and the defence of temperance is one which echoes Holy Church's stress on its special value as early as Passus I.

243   *Man may propose . . . dispose!*: proverbial, close to Prov. 16: 9. Cf. p. 112.

Need is closer to God than anyone else: Need's argument for the *value* of the state of destitution is a powerful one, drawing on a Christian tradition of Franciscan spirituality with its roots in the Bernardine meditations on the humanity and vulnerability of Christ. The lines translated here as verse are not a direct quotation but stand out by their intensity and strangeness. The text drawn on is Matt. 8: 20, spoken after the Sermon on the Mount to a scribe who wants to become a disciple of Jesus, but the crucifixion is an obvious choice as Christ's moment of greatest destitution and need. The doctrine is an exaggerated version of Patience's lessons on poverty in Passus XIV: need forces humility on a man and so compels him to recognize his absolute dependence on God.

Antichrist: a diabolic power (he deceitfully 'imitates' God) who works through the World and the Flesh, including the carnal desires of religious such as friars, ostensibly vowed to poverty.

244   *The only exceptions were the fools*: the notion of spiritual people as 'fools' derives from 1 Cor. 3: 10, which contrasts the Christian attitude to wealth and honour with that of worldly people, who regard Christians as fools. Langland's irony is very Pauline in flavour. For his own attitude to such folly, see the opening of Passus XV (p. 166).

Let's shout out loud for Kind . . . minions: Conscience's appeal to Kind to teach the worldlings a lesson means allegorically that God's power will be felt by such only through the inexorable operation of natural laws—for example, illnesses and plague—which show up the fragility of earthly life and its pleasures; the last of these is death, the negative face of God the Creator of Nature. Cf. pp. 216–17 earlier on the value of death for appreciating the true nature of life.

245 *to see whether people . . . Christians again*: Langland's view here is more pessimistic than in the second vision, where natural portents frightened sinners into repentance; here, survival of disasters like the plague only makes people worse.

246 *Life burst out laughing*: Life here represents what contemporary moralists call the Pride of Life, the unreformed, 'natural' exuberance of mere physical existence and transient well-being, oblivious of dependence on God and contemptuous of anything that smacks of religion or the spirit.

247 *Life and his lover Fortune . . . tumble*: allegorically, the worldling gives himself over completely to the vicissitudes of life, instead of wedding his soul to eternity, like the foolish rich man of the parable in Luke 12: 16 ff., a passage of great relevance in this context (see esp. vv. 20–1).

Sloth: the essence of which for Langland is spiritual indifference; he is fittingly married to Despair, the spiritual condition 'common to all' who ignore the promptings of conscience.

ran off to Physic . . . might help: Life does not take the hint that with the coming of age he ought to think about death and the next life, and detach himself from the pleasures of the body. Medicine failing, he seeks refuge in a mindless whirl of pleasure-seeking.

managed to run over my head . . . mark: the abrupt return of Will to centre stage reminds us that the sins we have been witnessing are not those of 'other people' but (actually or potentially) those of all mankind, of whom Will is the representative in so far as he embodies the faculty of the will, just as in Passus V he wept at the pangs of repentance (see p. 44).

248 *Kind, give me my revenge*: that is, against Age for humiliating him physically—and what he wants is a quick death to relieve him from the miseries of further physical existence. But what Kind recommends is an inner spiritual detachment, which he can win by entering the house of Unity and not leaving it (that is, dying) till he has qualified himself to do so.

What is the best skill to learn?: this dialogue is the climax of the poem's instruction, or a summary of its whole message: life *is* a process of learning, and ignorance in itself is not a good; but what has to be learnt is not a body of abstract or even technical knowledge, but something to be got 'by heart' and then put into practice continuously.

a severe siege from seven mighty giants: the Seven Deadly Sins; the last time the term was used, it was applied to Christ breaking down the gates of Hell in Passus XVIII (see p. 218). The irony is unmistakable: Christ's victory, though once for all, does not have any effect unless ratified and substantiated by the free will of human beings throughout time.

249   *a scandalous Irish priest*: this attack on drunken and profane Irish clergy
      is presumably based on hearsay; there is no evidence that Langland
      had ever been in Ireland.

      Need approached . . . simply greed: the thrust of this intervention by
      Need seems unmistakable: it does not suggest an affinity between him
      and the friars as mendicants but an insistence that they take their
      calling literally and accept extreme poverty and deprivation, instead of
      expecting both the credit of living holy lives and the comfort of
      material satisfactions. 'What the angels feed on' is God alone.

250   *Never be envious . . . learn to love*: Conscience repeats the lesson of Kind
      (learn to love) by reminding the friars of their original vocation as
      understood by the great founders. The implication is that the laity and
      gentry will or ought to support religious mendicants with their bodily
      necessities so as to enable them to preach the Gospel to the poor, not to
      study philosophy in the universities and then preach sermons that
      unsettle the people's faith, and above all not to try and take over
      parishes from the secular clergy.

      He reckons the stars . . . names: Ps. 146(147): 4 underlines the common
      medieval belief that everything in the universe had been created
      according to a principle of mathematical order (cf. Wisd. 11: 21), that
      the number of the blessed was fixed, and would be an even number
      (cf. Apoc. (Rev.) 7: 4), and that the number of the damned would be
      uneven or uncertain. The analogy from contemporary military practice
      is apt in the context.

      The one and only exception is the friars!: because, being mendicants,
      their numbers are not limited by the need to accommodate them in
      religious houses.

      logic and law—and, of course, contemplation too: Langland's irony is
      stinging here, as his target is something he particularly hates—the
      neglect of prayer and charity for rationalism and fruitless debate. He is
      not strictly fair to either Plato or Seneca, but their names stand loosely
      for authorities who argued for the value of common ownership, and
      such ideas were taken up by revolutionary preachers of the time such
      as John Ball, a leader of the Peasants' Revolt a few years after the
      poem was completed.

251   *Thou shalt not covet thy neighbour's goods*: the tenth commandment is
      found in Exod. 20: 17. The passage here seems a direct attack from the
      author on the chief fault of the friars as he sees it—the giving of 'easy
      absolutions', with the resulting effect of weakening people's moral
      sense and hence the power of conscience to restrain sin and foster
      virtue. The term 'curates' here does not mean assistant vicars but
      parish priests with cure of souls (that is, full responsibility for the
      spiritual well-being of their people). Langland sees shame as playing an
      essential part in the penitential process, and fear of it as a major
      deterrent from sin. Confession to the friars runs the risk of becoming

insincere because of the absence of shame and the possibility of venality.

251   *for saying this*: the 'this' refers either to the last speech of Conscience or to the diatribe which apparently came from the author.

Conscience summoned a doctor: a strict confessor who insists on real punishment and real satisfaction for sin.

252   *only Piers Plowman*: the reference is to Piers as an emblem of the ideal Pope, who has the authority to send an indulgence in the appropriate circumstances.

Friar Flatterer: Conscience's apparent excessive tolerance of one whose name evidently gives him away as a danger perhaps indicates the limits Langland senses in the power of this otherwise admirable character: every man has to follow his *own* conscience in matters of morality and sin, and to impose a particular course of action on another is in fact to prevent his own conscience from functioning freely. Conscience's attitude as a power or authority within the Church is aptly illustrated by the way in which Peace (something clearly of importance within Unity) is circumvented by Good Manners (see p. 253 below). The problem of trying to reconcile principle with harmony was and remains a major one for the Church.

253   *Sir Piercer-of-your-private-places*: his allegorical name alludes to the text of 2 Tim. 3: 6, with a deliberate sexual innuendo brought out in Peace's recollection of a previous encounter with the man.

Good Manners: one of those ambiguous qualities which can lead to toleration of evil through unwillingness to risk unpleasantness. The implication is that Conscience is wrong to extend such indulgence to the friars.

254   *as honorary members of our fraternity*: the friar makes exactly the same promise to Contrition as his predecessor in Passus III was asked for by Meed (see p. 24), and had doubtless willingly agreed to. The implication of this whole scene is that the friars' interpretation of penance is corrupting the whole Church, and with it, to some degree, inevitably the collective conscience of Christians.

drowned in a daze: intellectual confusion about the real condition of his soul, brought about by 'bad' confessions which do not encourage either real sorrow or determination to do better in the future.

and hunt the whole earth for Piers the Plowman: Piers once again symbolizes the ideal religious authority, no longer to be found within the visible institutional framework.

some source of income to live on: Conscience sees the only solution to the friars' corruption to lie in their being formally endowed with enough to live on: need for the material things of life *forces* them to obtain money by giving easy absolutions. But his comment does not of itself constitute a condemnation of the character Need, whose earlier argument had offered another solution much more to Langland's usual way of thinking—that the friars should live as ascetically as hermits, not seek comfort and physical well-being. The conception of 'need' held by the *friars* does not coincide with that of the character Need (see p. 249 above and note).

Kind, avenge me now!: Conscience's departure to become a pilgrim does not necessarily constitute a formal rejection of the Church (Unity) as such, so much as a renewed quest for spiritual reality by detachment from the world and a turning to God for help in the darkest hour. A *literal rejection* of the Church would be incompatible with a continuing concern for the reform of the mendicants in the *interest* of the Church's well-being. His final prayer is addressed to God under three different aspects—to the Father as creator (and, as we have seen, destroyer too), to punish evil-doers through the powers of nature; to the Son as Piers Plowman, a concrete embodiment of charity, now more than ever needed again on Earth, whether as saint or pope or other example for people to see and imitate; and finally, to the Holy Spirit as grace—including the grace to persevere to the end. There is no epilogue or afterword to follow Conscience's cry, since at this juncture his attitude and the Dreamer's have coalesced into one and become indistinguishable. All that remains for the wakened Dreamer is to go on, like Conscience, 'walking the world'.

INDEX OF PROPER NAMES

The Oxford World's Classics Website

www.worldsclassics.co.uk

- Browse the full range of Oxford World's Classics online

- Sign up for our monthly e-alert to receive information on new titles

- Read extracts from the Introductions

- Listen to our editors and translators talk about the world's greatest literature with our Oxford World's Classics audio guides

- Join the conversation, follow us on Twitter at OWC_Oxford

- Teachers and lecturers can order inspection copies quickly and simply via our website

www.worldsclassics.co.uk

American Literature

British and Irish Literature

Children's Literature

Classics and Ancient Literature

Colonial Literature

Eastern Literature

European Literature

Gothic Literature

History

Medieval Literature

Oxford English Drama

Poetry

Philosophy

Politics

Religion

The Oxford Shakespeare

A complete list of Oxford World's Classics, including Authors in Context, Oxford English Drama, and the Oxford Shakespeare, is available in the UK from the Marketing Services Department, Oxford University Press, Great Clarendon Street, Oxford OX2 6DP, or visit the website at www.oup.com/uk/worldsclassics.

In the USA, visit www.oup.com/us/owc for a complete title list.

Oxford World's Classics are available from all good bookshops. In case of difficulty, customers in the UK should contact Oxford University Press Bookshop, 116 High Street, Oxford OX1 4BR.

Classical Literary Criticism

The First Philosophers: The Presocratics
and the Sophists

Greek Lyric Poetry

Myths from Mesopotamia

APOLLODORUS   The Library of Greek Mythology

APOLLONIUS OF RHODES   Jason and the Golden Fleece

APULEIUS   The Golden Ass

ARISTOPHANES   Birds and Other Plays

ARISTOTLE   The Nicomachean Ethics
                    Physics
                    Politics

BOETHIUS   The Consolation of Philosophy

CAESAR   The Civil War
                    The Gallic War

CATULLUS   The Poems of Catullus

CICERO   Defence Speeches
                    The Nature of the Gods
                    On Obligations
                    The Republic and The Laws

EURIPIDES   Bacchae and Other Plays
                    Medea and Other Plays
                    Orestes and Other Plays
                    The Trojan Women and Other Plays

GALEN   Selected Works

HERODOTUS   The Histories

HOMER   The Iliad
                    The Odyssey